AMERICAN EDUCATION

Its Men

Ideas

and

Institutions

The Support of Schools in Colonial New York by the Society for the Propagation of the Gospel in Foreign Parts

William Webb Kemp

ARNO PRESS & THE NEW YORK TIMES
*New York * 1969*

Reprint edition 1969 by Arno Press, Inc.

*

Library of Congress Catalog Card No. 72-89192

*

Reprinted from a copy in Teachers College Library

*

Manufactured in the United States of America

Editorial Note

AMERICAN EDUCATION: *Its Men, Institutions and Ideas* presents selected works of thought and scholarship that have long been out of print or otherwise unavailable. Inevitably, such works will include particular ideas and doctrines that have been outmoded or superseded by more recent research. Nevertheless, all retain their place in the literature, having influenced educational thought and practice in their own time and having provided the basis for subsequent scholarship.

Lawrence A. Cremin
Teachers College

The Support of Schools in Colonial New York by the Society for the Propagation of the Gospel in Foreign Parts

The Support of Schools in Colonial New York by the Society for the Propagation of the Gospel in Foreign Parts

By

WILLIAM WEBB KEMP, Ph.D.

PROFESSOR OF EDUCATION, UNIVERSITY OF MONTANA; SOMETIME FELLOW IN EDUCATION, TEACHERS COLLEGE, COLUMBIA UNIVERSITY

TEACHERS COLLEGE, COLUMBIA UNIVERSITY
CONTRIBUTIONS TO EDUCATION, No. 56

PUBLISHED BY
Teachers College, Columbia University
NEW YORK CITY
1913

THE SOCIETY'S SEAL

"The Society for Propagating the Gospel is the brightest light shining in the candlestick of the Reformation."

(Hon. Rufus King, quoted by Bolton.)

PREFACE

This monograph represents primarily an attempt to describe the work of the Society for the Propagation of the Gospel in Foreign Parts, in behalf of elementary instruction in the province of New York. The writer has included, however, such evidences of secondary instruction by the Society's agents as have been found among the available records; and the evidences of other schools in the province, as these were from time to time reported by the S. P. G. schoolmasters. The Negro school carried on by the Bray Associates in New York City has been included also because of the very close alliance between their activity and that of the Society.

The sources for the study have been found almost entirely in various London archives. This material, the writer feels, has been exhaustively reviewed. American sources, for the most part, refer back to the London records, but both these and other available local sources have been examined.

Attention should be called to certain peculiarities in the page references to some of the volumes of the S. P. G. manuscripts. This is because the paging is irregular. For instance, "S. P. G. Journal, I, p. (10)" indicates the second part of that volume. Again, "Letter-book A, 9, 7 fol. 97" is so written because the volume is divided into fifteen sections, the New York part beginning at fol. 97. The above reference would indicate the seventh letter in the New York section.

In the preparation of material the writer hereby acknowledges the generosity of the following: His Grace, the Archbishop of Canterbury, and His Lordship, the Bishop of London, for the privilege of research among the archives of Lambeth and Fulham Palaces; C. F. Pascoe, Esq., Keeper of the Records and Secretary of the S. P. G., for his many courtesies and cordial encouragement; the secretaries in charge of the records of the S. P. C. K.; the officials of Sion College Library; the Rev. Wm. T. Manning and Vestry of Trinity Church, New York City; and the Rev. R. T. Henshaw and Vestry of Christ's Church, Rye. To Dr. Paul Monroe and Dr. W. H. Kilpatrick there is due especial gratitude for their scholarly guidance; and to Dr. F. P. Graves, for his generous help in reviewing the manuscript.

Teachers College, New York,
August, 1913

CONTENTS

PART I

GENERAL INTRODUCTION

PART I

GENERAL INTRODUCTION

CHAPTER I

EVENTS PRECEDING THE FOUNDING OF THE S. P. G.*

The seventeenth century was a period of extraordinary mental activity throughout Europe, no less in religious lines than in the field of natural philosophy. Schools of religious thought led to the formation of numerous sects, various systems being drawn from the great Protestant revolt of the preceding century. In England the century opened with two opposing religious bodies, —the orthodox Church of England and that body of reformers known as Puritans, the English followers of the Geneva School. With the coming of the period of the Commonwealth antagonistic sects increased until there were as many as sixteen, varying with each other in extreme positions and showing no nearer agreement than the acceptance of Biblical authority for their respective doctrines. Of all these sects the Quakers seem to have taken the most extreme views and, accordingly, to have suffered the greatest persecution. Much of this was due, not to their religious opinions, but to their having associated with these tenets an attitude toward the State that was viewed as antagonistic to its preservation and safety. A state of affairs similar to this prevailed on the Continent where the repeated divisions arising from the ranks of the two earlier divisions of "Lutheran" and "Calvinist" or "Reformed" crowded the seventeenth century with religious contentions.

* For the details of much of this introduction I am indebted to Pascoe, Two Hundred Years of the S. P. G.; and Allen and McClure, The History of the Society for Promoting Christian Knowledge. Specific acknowledgment will not be generally made.

In close association with the religious discord were the political struggles of the century. Together they had a most disintegrating effect on the social life of the period, in consequence of which education and morals found themselves at a low ebb. This is particularly the case in England in the period following the Commonwealth and the Civil War, where, probably, the morality and intelligence of the masses had never been in worse condition. A view of the teachers of this period is illustrated in the following quotation: "Amongst those of the late *Reforming Age* all learning was utterly cried down, so that with them the best Preachers were such as could not *read*, and the ablest Divines such as could hardly *spell* the letter. None were thought fit for the *Ministry* but *Tradesmen* and *Mechanicks*, because none else were allowed to have the Spirit. Those only were accounted like *St. Paul*, who *could work with their hands*, and in a literal sense *drive the Nail home* and be able to *make a Pulpit* before they *Preached* in it. . . . Latin was with them a mortal crime, and Greek, instead of being owned for *the Language of the Holy Ghost* (as in the New Testament it is), was look'd upon as the Sin against it."[1] The early minutes and correspondence of the Society for Promoting Christian Knowledge show clearly the concern of the followers of the Church of England because of the prevailing ignorance and decadent morality of the time. "It is certain that Zeal for religion grows extremely cold. The infinite disputes about Opinions, and the Licenciousness of Innovators . . . have everywhere occasion'd a certain disgust for Piety, which upon that account is nowadays much decay'd and very scarce. This Loosness has passed from Doctrines to manners, and there is nothing more rare than the practice of Christian Virtues."[2] In a letter to the Governor of Jamaica the Society says: "That Inundation of Profaneness and Immorality which we find of late broke in upon us, puts all serious persons here into no small consternation at the prospect of those Judgements which according to the ordinary course of Divine Providence overtake an Apostatiz'd People."[3]

[1] Quoted from a sermon by Robert South preached at Westminster Abbey, 1692, by Overton, Life in the English Church, 1660–1714, p. 240.

[2] From "A Memorial for the Preservation and Furtherance of Religion," read at a meeting of the S. P. C. K., August 19, 1701—quoted by Allen and McClure, *op. cit.*, p. 10.

[3] From a letter drawn up by Dr. Bray and adopted at a meeting of the S. P. C. K. January 6, 1700–01—quoted by Allen and McClure, *op. cit.*, p. 10. (This dating is according to the "Old Style" year which began on March 25th. It was not until 1752 that the year began on January 1st.)

A great amount of evidence of this nature is adducible to show the apprehensiveness of the Church of England as well as the leaders of non-conforming sects over the unwholesome conditions of the latter half of the seventeenth and the earlier decades of the following century. England was flooded with pamphlets dealing with one phase or another of the growth of vice and debauchery and the ignorance of the true principles of Christianity.[4]

A reaction to the excesses of the time began to assert itself toward the end of the seventeenth century. The Pietistic movement in Germany under the influence of Spener and Francke was begun in Frankfort as a protest against impiety. At almost the same time a similar movement started within the Church of England led by Dr. Anthony Horneck (1641–1697). Horneck was a German who came to England after the Restoration, was put in Orders, and, in 1671, began preaching in London. Through his sermons, in large measure, there were founded, from 1678 on, many church societies which were devoted at first to religious conference and mutual edification only, but which soon started a Christian warfare for the winning of proselytes. These societies grew to the number of forty-two in London and Westminster alone and similar institutions were founded throughout the kingdom.

In 1691 societies for the reformation of manners began to be formed. Their membership was made up of both churchmen and non-conformists and their object was to secure and put into operation laws against profaneness and debauchery. In "The Two and Twentieth account of the Progress made in the cities of London and Westminster and Places adjacent by the Societies for Promoting a Reformation of Manners," it is claimed that, "By furthering the Execution of the Laws against Profaneness and Immorality, and other Christian Methods the said Societies have in Pursuance of their Design from the first of December 1715 to the first of December 1716, prosecuted divers sorts of offenders" such cases as drunkenness, breaking the Lord's Day, profane swearing and cursing, keeping of gaming houses, and lewd and disorderly practices to the number of nearly two thousand.[5] The Stage, too, came in for bitter antagonism

[4] Thousands of such pamphlets are to-day preserved in the Archives of Sion College Library, Victoria Embankment, London.

[5] From, "Sermon to and Account of the Societies for the Reformation of Manners," 1717—Sion College Archives, 43: F: 21, No. 15.

because of its tendency to use "lewd and profane expressions" and the clergy were urged "to lay open in their Sermons, the intollerable Liberties and Corruptions of the Stage, with the Great Dishonour that such abuses must necessarily bring upon Religion and the Nation."[6] But in spite of orders from Queen Anne, regulating the play-houses, the problem continued a serious one.[7]

The foregoing account has seemed material, to the writer, as explaining the great religious awakening of the Church of England in both the home and the foreign fields which began at the very close of the seventeenth century. The work of the Church societies and of the societies seeking the reformation of manners had prepared the way for the success of the Society for Promoting Christian Knowledge and the Society for the Propagation of the Gospel in Foreign Parts. They were the direct antecedents of them. The S. P. C. K. took up immediately the work of the earlier societies, broadening their scope, introducing and emphasizing the agency of schools for the inculcating of religious education, and directing attention to the reform of conditions in the English foreign possessions as well as at home. Fortunately, this work was inaugurated at a time when political events were unusually favorable and they must be noted as one of the causes making possible the successful activity of the two great missionary societies of the National Church.[8]

At about this time England was being aroused to the neglected state of religion and morality in the colonies and especially to the extremely precarious condition of the National Church there. The Church of England had lagged behind in the field of mission work in the nation's foreign possessions, to the extent, at least, of any organized system like that of the eighteenth century.[9] Colonization of America was at first carried on through private adventures, under grants from the Crown, and by means of small numbers of families. The different groups of colonists

6 S. P. C. K. Minute-book, 1698–1706, Feb. 7, 1705–06.

7 *Ibid.*

8 The Peace of Ryswick, 1697, brought to an end the costly struggles that had been carried on in Europe throughout the century. The question of Royal title was settled for England and all domestic strife was at an end. The Crown welcomed the opportunity now before it to reform the internal administration.

9 Priests of the Church of England had been sent out to minister on the American shores, with the attempted settlements of the sixteenth century. Such provision was included in the expeditions of Martin Frobisher, Sir Humphrey Gilbert and Sir Walter Raleigh.

were nearly all dissenters from the National Church. Moreover they disagreed radically with each other in religion and church government and this was intensified through settlements made by other nationalities of Europe. Such religious foundations as were made were dependent on the opinions of the local group and were fostered altogether by themselves or by agencies in their old homes. Officially, it is true, the Church had interested itself in the state of spiritual and ecclesiastical affairs in the colonies as early as 1634. A commission was formed to regulate them which was to be under the control of the Archbishops of Canterbury and York. In this same year the jurisdiction of the Bishop of London was extended to the English congregations and clergy abroad. The Bishop was one of the Council for Virginia. As a Member of the Company he was applied to for "help and assistance in procuring Ministers." This is probably "the first instance of the Bishop of London's concern in the Ecclesiastical affairs of the Plantations."[10] In 1638 a movement was started to send a Bishop to New England[11] and shortly after the Restoration a Bishop of Virginia was nominated,[12] but neither plan was carried out. In 1675 Henry Compton, then Bishop of London, instituted an inquiry into the status of the See of London's "pastoral charge of sending our Ministers into our British Foreign Plantations, and having the jurisdiction of them." He "found this title so defective that little or no good had come of it," there being "scarce four Ministers of the Church of England in all the vast tract of America and not above one or two of them, at most, regularly sent over."[13] It was not until ten years after this that Compton was able to procure from the Government definite measures extending the jurisdiction of the Bishopric of London over the Plantations. In 1685 he got permission from the King to present to the Committee for Trade and Plantations the following proposals: (1) "That he may have all ecclesiastical Jurisdiction of the West Indies, excepting the disposal of Parishes (that is, the right of presenting, instituting and inducting), Licenses for Marriage, and Probate of Wills;" (2) "That no Schoolmaster coming from England be received

10 Bishop of London to the King in Council 19 Feb. 1759, Documents relative to the Colonial Hist. of N. Y., VII, pp. 360–9.

11 Classified Digest of the Records of the S. P. G. 1701–1892, p. 743.

12 Dr. Bray to the Bishop of London, Oct. 28th, 1723, Fulham Archives.

13 Quoted in, Classified Digest of the Records of the S. P. G. 1701–1892, p. 2.

without License from his Lordship, or from other His Majesty's Plantations without they take the Governor's License."[14] From this time until the close of the Revolution the affairs of the English Church were under the care of the Bishop of London.[15] Acting on his vested authority the Bishop appointed Commissaries for the various colonies, beginning with the selection of Rev. James Blair for Virginia and Rev. Thomas Bray for Maryland, in 1790 and 1796 respectively. Appointments for other colonies followed as the work of the church developed.

It must be noted that the extension of the Bishop of London's jurisdiction was only in part. The intervening distance and the political character of the colonies precluded the possibility of an exercise of power such as that possessed by a Bishop in England. Without a resident Bishop in the colonies many things ordinarily under the care and authority of such a person had to be done by some other authority. "Such are the repairs of the Churches and the providing books and other necessities for the service, the Instituting, and Inducting Incumbents, the repair of the Glebe houses, the probate of the Wills, Licence for Marriage, examining and approving Clergymen, and schoolmasters, and the correction of vice and immorality by coercive power . . . therefore these powers are placed by several Acts of Assembly, partly in the Church Wardens, partly in the Justices of the Peace, and partly in the Governors of the Respective Provinces."[16] The Bishop's delegated power to license schoolmasters was probably exercised throughout, in the case of those who professed the doctrine of the Church of England. Of these, however, there were comparatively few,[17] schoolmasters being for the most part obtained in the colonies. As to non-conforming schoolmasters, or schoolmasters hired by the Society, *in the colonies*, the authority of the Bishop was not acknowledged in any apparent way, nor does he seem to have attempted to ex-

---

14 Extracts from the Journals of the Committee of Trade and Plantations relating to the Bishop of London's jurisdiction in the British colonies, Hawks Transcripts G. C.; Doc. re. Col. Hist. N. Y. *op. cit.*, VII, pp. 360–9.

15 Save a short period when this jurisdiction was transferred to the Archbishop of Canterbury. See the Royal instructions to Gov. Dongan of N. Y. in N. Y. Col. Docs., *op. cit.*, III, p. 372; also Clews, Colonial Educational Legislation, p. 227.

16 Doc. re. Col. Hist. N. Y., *op. cit.*, VII, p. 369.

17 Fothergill has listed more than 30 such who between 1695 and 1748 qualified for the Royal bounty of £20 passage money. Fothergill, Gerald, A List of Emigrant Ministers to America 1690–1811.

ercise authority therein.[18]

The activity of Bishop Compton in behalf of the spiritual welfare of the colonies was soon supplemented by "several eminent Persons who observing this great Calamity, became zealous to redress it."[19] Among the first of these was Sir Leolyne Jenkins who, declaring that there were too few "Persons in Holy Orders, employed in his Majesty's Fleets at Sea, and Foreign Plantations," provided in his will, Nov. 9, 1685, two fellowships at Jesus College, Oxford. The bequest was on condition that the said two Fellows "may be under an indispensable obligation, to take upon them Holy Orders of Priesthood and afterwards they go to Sea, in any of his Majesty's Fleets, when they or any of them are thereto Summoned . . . and in case there be no Use of their Service at Sea, to be called by the Lord Bishop of London to go out into any of his Majesty's Foreign Plantations, there to take upon them the Cure of Souls, and exercise their ministerial Function, reserving to them their full Salaries, with the farther Encouragement of twenty Pounds a Year apiece, while they are actually in either of the Services aforesaid."[20] Another bequest from the Honorable Robert Boyle, Esq., settled an annual salary on "some learned Divine or Preaching Minister forever," requiring him, among other things, to encourage undertakings for promoting the Christian religion in foreign parts.[21] He also bequeathed money to the College of Virginia for supporting nine or ten Indian children there, and providing them with a Christian education.[22]

As has been stated above no organized mission work in the colonies had been undertaken up to this time by the English Church. The work was too vast to be made permamently suc-

---

18 As a proof of this the S. P. G. in 1731 resolved "to desire the Lord Bishop of London to direct his Commissaries abroad to receive and examine any complaints which may be made against Schoolmasters employed by the Society, and transmit to them the state of such matters." S. P. G. Journal, V, 320. To this the Bishop replied, that his Commission from the Crown did not include such power and he "could not comply with the request." *Ibid.*, p. 328.

19 Humphreys, Historical Account of the S. P. G., p. 4.

20 Quoted by, Humphreys, *op. cit.*, pp. 4–5; Annual Reports S. P. G., 1706, p. 7–8. One of these Fellows, Rev. Henry Nichols, was appointed first S. P. G. Missionary in Pennsylvania, at Chester 1703—S. P. G. Letter-book, A, 2, p. 170; Pascoe, *op. cit.*, p. 840, 852. Nichols' fellowship was worth £40 per annum—Jonathan Edwards to Sec., S. P. G., Letter-book, A, 3, p. 97.

21 Humphreys, *op. cit.*, p. 6.

22 "Instructions from Gov. Nicholson to Robert Hicks and John Evans in treating with the Indians, as to trade 1700, in Virginia."—Fulham Archives. Boyle was one of the Promoters and first Governor of the "S. P. G. amongst the Heathen Natives, of New England, and the Parts adjacent in America," incorporated by Charles II.—Humphreys, *op. cit.*, p. 6.

cessful through the isolated efforts of the heads of the Church, or through a dependence on individual initiative. What was needed was the coöperation of religious societies and this the Church came to realize with the opening of the eighteenth century. Before this, however, the non-conformists had inaugurated a religious society movement for work in New England. The instigator of it was John Eliot, who devoted more than forty years of his life to the evangelization of the Indians about New England. Through correspondence and tracts his work became known in England. Parliament, in 1649, was induced to pass an ordinance establishing "A Corporation for the Promoting and Propagating the Gospel of Jesus Christ in New England." The said corporation consisted of a president, treasurer, and fourteen assistants and was to be called "the President and Society for the Propagation of the Gospel in New England."[23] After the Restoration the Corporation naturally required a new charter and letters patent were issued by Charles II for the same in 1661. The renewed organization was chartered as the "Company for the Propagation of the Gospel in New England, and parts adjacent in America."[24] Churchmen and dissenters constituted its membership.[25] Meetings were to be held in London "as occasion shall require," and the powers were as follows:

"The Governour, or any 13 of the said Company, may under their seal appoint Commiss^rs^ resideing in the said Colonyes, or parts adjacent in America, for them to treat and agree with Ministers, Schoole Masters, etc^a^, to reside in the parts aforesaid, for such Salaries and allowances to bee paid them for their paines, etc^a^, in the Civilizeing teaching, and instructing the Natives in the true Religion & Morality, in the English toung, and in the liberall Arts & Sciences, as also in educating & placeing, their children in some trade or Lawfull calling, and also to buy Books, Tooles, and other Implements necessary for the same, and for payments of such sallarys, allowances, and expences aforesaid. And to do any other acts according to the Orders or Instructions of their said Commissions or orders, from time to time sent from the Govern^r^ or any nine of the said Company, which said Commiss^rs^ shall from time to time give an account of their proceedings, as they shall be required from the said Gov^nr^ or any nine of the said Company."[26]

With such collections as were made a fund was established, the income of which made it possible to maintain missionaries for

[23] Classified Digest, *op. cit.*, p. 2.

[24] *Ibid.*, p. 3; Abstract of patent, Perry, Historical Collections relating to the Colonial Church in America, pp. 646–7; Acts of Privy Council, 1613–1680, p. 332; Lambeth Mss. 1123, a copy of which is in Hawks Transcripts, G. C.

[25] Classified Digest, *op. cit.*, p. 2.

[26] Abstract of the Patent, Perry, *op. cit.*, p. 648. The first Governor of this society under Charles II was Robert Boyle, Esq., founder in 1660 of the Royal Society and benefactor to the College of Virginia.

instructing and converting the Indians, and chief among them was Eliot.[27] The society carried on its operations in New England and parts of New York until the Revolution, there after transferring to the British possessions in America.

Organized effort wholly under the auspices of the followers of the Church began with the founding of the Society for the Promoting of Christian Knowledge. This was a movement that undertook to incorporate in the one association all of the underlying purposes of the religious society movements which had preceded. It had for its aim the counteracting of schisms, the opposing of profaneness and immorality by coercive force, the care of the spiritual welfare of transmaritime possessions, the spread of religious education there and at home, among the poorer classes especially, and the effecting of the above by means of missionaries, schoolmasters, the disseminating of literature, and the establishing of libraries.

The originating spirit in the founding of the S. P. C. K. was Rev. Thomas Bray, D. D., who had been named the first Commissary of Maryland.[28] His services therein, as also in the formation of other affiliated societies of the Church, were remarkable. Dr. Bray was born in 1656 at Marton, Shropshire, and was educated at Oswestry Grammar School, and Hartford College, Oxford. Following preferments as curate and chaplain, he was, in 1690, made Rector of Sheldon in Warwickshire. His activities were numerous in connection with the various "Religious Societies," the "Societies for the Reformation of Manners,"[29] the revival of Church discipline among the Clergy,[30]

---

27 The difficulties of the work are brought out in correspondence between Eliot and Richard Baxter of London. See the Baxter Mss. in the Archives of Dr. William's Library, Gordon Square, London, especially III, pp. 94 and 264; and V, p. 83.

28 See p. 6.

29 Archives of Sion College Library, Bray Mss., p. 46. These Mss. were bequeathed to Sion College by Dr. Bray, most of them having been assembled by him about 1705. *Ibid.*, p. 59–60.

30 "He cannot imagine what can be better pushed in order to keep the Rural clergy to their rule, & close to their Duty, and thereby to advance their character & reputation and to create a due veneration towards ym ye Resolutions there formed being these, That they will meet in their Library Monthly or oftener, to Consider or confer as upon ways & means of Augmenting ye same .... to consult upon ye best methods of ffurnishing ye common People wth small practical Devotional Peices, & Principling ye children & Youth wth Catechetical Instruction, of Erecting Schooles for ye Education of Poor Children, of getting ye Laws Put in Execution agt Profaneness &c. Imorality &c. by what other means they can best discharge their Pastoral Care & Duty & Promote Publick Good."—From, "Part 1., A Narrative containing what passed from Dr. Bray's first acceptance of the Commissary's office of Maryland in the Yeare 1696, to his arrival there 1699"—Bray Mss., p. 50, in Sion College Library. The same Ms., p. 72 ff., being part of the appendix of this narrative, gives an account of a series of such monthly meetings.

and the improvement of prison conditions in London.[31]

His success as pastor and as author of a series of "Catechetical Lectures" designed for the religious instruction of poor children brought him to the notice of the Bishop of London. He was selected in April, 1696, to go out to Maryland as the latter's Commissary in response to a petition from that province for the help of a "Superintendent, Commissary, or Suffragan."[32] This office he was "content to accept," "if their Lordships the Bishops thought fit to assist him in providing Parochial Libraries for the ministers that should be sent." For, said Bray, "since none but the poorer sort of clergy, who could not sufficiently supply themselves with books, could be persuaded to leave their friends, and change their country for one so remote," it would be impossible for them to answer the ends of their mission "without a competent provision of books."[33] Whereupon his proposal being well approved "and due Encouragement being promised in the Prosecution of the design both by their Ldps and others, he did thereupon with all possible Application set himself wholly to provide Missionaries, and to furnish them out with Libraries, with an Intent, so soon as he should have sent both, to follow after them himself."[34]

As early as 1692 Maryland had been divided into parishes and a legal maintenance provided for ministers in each.[35] The Act was neglected until the arrival of Governor Francis Nicholson August, 1694, who revived it by an additional one "for the increase and maintenance of Religion."[36] But Royal confirmation of the laws was delayed by certain objectionable features, so that the maintenance of the clergy was too uncertain[37] and it was three years before Bray was able "to follow after." On "Decr 16, 1699 he took his voyage, and arrived in Maryland, after an extreme tedious, and dangerous Passage, the 18th of March following."[38]

---

31 *Ibid.*, p. 46. Also see, "A General Plan of a Penitential Hospital" for reforming the method of detaining women prisoners, *ibid.*, pp. 65, 107, 331.

32 *Ibid.*, p. 32.

33 From a "Memoir of Dr. Bray" in a *Report* of Dr. Bray's Associates, 1906, p. 32.

34 Bray Mss., *op. cit.*, p. 35.

35 *Ibid.*, p. 32.

36 *Ibid.*, p. 101, being a printed pamphlet on "The present State of the Protestant Religion in Maryland."

37 *Ibid.*, p. 41.

38 *Ibid.*, pp. 55–56.

In the interval between his appointment and his setting out for Maryland Dr. Bray was "fully employed under my L^{d} of London in Enquiring out, and providing Missionaries to be sent" into that and other colonies. But above all it was his care "to furnish out all whom he had an hand in sending with good Libraries of necessary and useful Books."[39] In order "better to promote both this main Design of Libraries, and to give the Missionaries direction in the use of them in the prosecution of their Theological Studies, he published two Books one Intituled, Bibliotheca Parochialis, or a Scheme of Theological Heads, both general and particular as are more peculiarly requisite to be well Studied by every Pastor of a Parish: Together with a Catalogue of Books which may be Read on each of these Points.'"[40] The second book bore the title, "Apostolick Charity its Nature and Excellence considered in a Discourse upon Dan. 12. 3. Preached at St. Paul's at the Ordination of some Protestant Missionaries to be sent into the Plantations. To which is Prefixt: A General View of the English Colonies in America, with respect to Re-"gion, in order to shew what Provision is wanted for the Propagation of Christianity in those parts."[41] As a result of his zeal for libraries we are told that "by the exactest account that has been procured upwards of fifty Libraries, it appears, were founded by Dr. Bray in America and other countries abroad, and sixty-one Parochial Libraries in England and Wales;" and that "he sent into America upwards of 34,000 religious Books and Tracts."[42]

With the first thirty libraries sent over an expense of £2,000 had been incurred towards which there was collected only £1,500. The deficit Bray had to meet personally. "Besides y^{t}," he writes, "I have spent Three full Years and upw^{ds} in ye carrying on of this Design solely at my own Charge & have undergone an unspeakable Labour & Fatigue in ye prosecution thereof."[43] The question of funds, therefore, became all-important

39 *Ibid.*, p. 37.

40 *Ibid.*, p. 40. Observe the burdensome title which was customary at that time.

41 Published in London 1698. One copy of this is in the New York Public Library; another is in the Library of the General Theological Seminary.

42 Appendix to a second edition (1808) of "Publick Spirit Illustrated in the Life and Designs of the Reverend Thomas Bray D.D.," published in 1746. The Bray Mss. in Sion College Library contain about 26 catalogues of these libraries and two or more volumes of such catalogues are among the manuscript records of the "Associates of Dr. Bray."

43 "A Memorial of Thomas Bray, D.D., relating to ye Libraries sent into America," Lambeth Archives, 941, fol. 71.

for the furthering of his elaborate plans. "Upon these Accts, I say, it will be scarcely Possible for me to go into Maryland till I am Reimbursed ye charge I have been at,"[44] he continues.

It was this exigency that seems to have impressed upon him the impossibility of succeeding without the assistance of a specially chartered society. He had struggled hard over the problem of public funds. Queen Mary had generously granted a Royal bounty of £200 a year during her life[45] and the Princess of Denmark, afterwards Queen Anne, had encouraged him with a "Noble Benefaction."[46] Later an attempt was made to get the aid of the House of Commons. A bill being brought up in 1697, "to alienate Lands given to Superstitious Uses and Vest them in Greenwich Hospital," Bray petitioned for a portion of this, but the bill was never reported.[47] The following year he tried and failed to obtain the grant of a debt of £1,500 due to the Crown since the reign of Charles II.[48] "All designs failing," the narrative declares, "of getting a publick ffund for the Propagation of the Gospel in fforeign Parts, he therefore formed a design, whereof he even then drew the Plan, and layd it before the proper person, with others of Consideration, of having a Protestant Congregation pro Propaganda Fide by charter from the King. But things did not seem then so ripe as to Encourage him to proceed at that time in the attempt."[49] "However, to prepare the way for such Charter Society, he soon after endeavored to form a Voluntary Society both to carry on the Service already begun for the Plantations, and to Propagate Christian Knowledge as well at Home as Abroad, hoping withal in time to get such Society Incorporated as afterwards he did. And it was not long till he found some worthy Persons willing to engage in it, who have since encreased to a Considerable Body and a vast deal of Good has been done by them, not only in assisting him in sending Libraries Abroad but by their dispersing a Vast Number of Good Books at Home, among our ffleets and Armies and in raising Charity Schools in, and about the City, and by their

---

44 *Ibid.*

45 Humphreys, *op. cit.*, p. 11.

46 Bray Mss., *op. cit.*, p. 39.

47 *Ibid.*, pp. 42–43.

48 *Ibid.*, p. 43; Lambeth Archives, 941, fol. 71.

49 Bray Mss., *op. cit.*, p. 43. Other papers bear out this evidence and go far to show that Bray conceived both the names and the purposes of the S. P. C. K. and G.

Correspondencies in promoting the same in several parts of the Kingdom besides."[50]

The quotation just given refers, of course, to the S. P. C. K. the original plan of which Dr. Bray had formulated in 1697 and laid before the Bishop of London.[51] This plan comprised the germ of both the S. P. C. K. and the S. P. G. It was presented to the former society in response to a resolution calling for Bray's scheme which was passed at the first meeting.[52] The following draft is taken from the Bray Mss. of Sion College Library:

"A General Plan.

"Of the Constitution of a Protestant Congregation, or Society, for the Propagation of Christian Knowledge as layd before the Ld Bp of London, and some others in the Yeare 1697, upon the unsuccessfulness of the Bill for Vesting of Lands Given to Superstitious Uses in Greenwich Hospital, and to provide for Protestant Missions.

"First that it consist of (   ) Members two thirds, some of the London Clergy of the Chiefest Note, and one third of such others as are Eminent for their Worth and Affection to Religion and the Church of England; And among these that the Senior Chaplains to the Ld Abp of Canterbury and Bp of London be always standing Members, and that the Ld Bp of London have always a negative in the Election of any other Member Elected.

"Secondly that these persons be Incorporated by Charter, as the R. Society, or the Sons of the Clergy are, And be thereby Impowrd to Meet, and Consult as often as there shall be occasion, upon the best means and Methods of promoting Religion and Learning in Any part of his Majesties Plantations, abroad.

"Thirdly that it be under their care 1st to Enquire out fit and proper persons, to present to the Ld Bp of London for the time being, for his Ldps Licence to go Chaplains into the fforeign Plantations, and that they be answerable for such men as shall appear to have been Ill qualifyed for such a Mission.
2ly That they proceed to perfect the Design of fixing Parochial Libraries throughout the Plantations, in order to render both these Missionaries usefull and serviceable in the Propagation of the Christian ffaith and Manners (3ly) That it be in their power to Alott such Gratuities or Pensions as they shall think fit, as rewards to those Ministers concerning whom the Ld Bp of London's Respective Commissaries shall Certifie that they merit more than ordinarie by their Learning, Labour and Success in their Ministry and Mission; as also that it be in their power to propose and alot what Pensions they shall think fit to such Ministers as shall most hazard their Persons in attempting the Conversion of the Native Indians: 4ly That it be their Care to make some provision for such of our Missionaries, Widows and Children, as are left unprovided, especially for the Widows, and Orphan Children of such, who by their Zeal and Industry in Converting of Souls may have Occasion'd the Loss of Life or Goods.

"Lastly to Enable the Congregation pro propaganda fide to discharge these forementioned Trusts that they be Impowerd by their Charter to receive Gifts, Grants, Legacies &c. not exceeding (   ) per. An. as by the Charter shall be limited."

"Secondly, As to the Propagating Christian Knowledge at home."

---

50 *Ibid.*, p. 44.

51 *Ibid.*, p. 62.

52 S. P. C. K. Minute-book, 1698-1706, March 8, 1698–99.

"1st. That they proceed to provide Catechetical Libraries, in the Smaller Parishes of this Kingdom to enable the poor Clergy to perform their duty of Catechising according to the 39 Canon:

"And the Market Towns wth Lending Libraries for any of the Clergy to have Recourse to, or to Borrow Books out of, as there shall be occasion.

"2ly. That they proceed also to set up Catechetical Schools for the Education of Poor Children in Reading, Writing, and more especially in the Principles of the X^an^ Religion."[53]

Bray returned from Maryland after one year of service. Prejudices had been raised against the establishment of the Church there, and he came back in the hope of securing Royal assent to a bill for its proper constitution. Meantime the S. P. C. K. had grown to such an extent that a division of its work became necessary. Bray, accordingly, led the movement to organize, by charter, a separate Society for the Propagation of the Gospel in Foreign Parts, and thus leave to the older society the work in the home field. On March 15, 1701, he petitioned the King for Letters Patent for such a charter.[54] The petition being favorably received a charter was drawn up by Bray and the S. P. C. K. and received the Royal sanction June 16, 1701.[55] In a letter dated "July 15th 1701" and addressed "May it please Yor Excellency," Dr. Bray says:

"I bless God I have obtained a Charter Incorporating a Society for ye propagacon of the Gospel in foreign parts which I hope will be able many Wayes to assist all good Endeavors wth you & to ptect the Churches abroad from such Usage as it lately met with in Maryland."[56]

Yet another society remains to be credited to the achievement of Dr. Bray, which, like the previous ones, was devoted to the betterment of religion and education at home and in America. The condition of the Negroes and Indians in the colonies had ever excited a feeling of pity in Dr. Bray. In the Archives of Fulham Palace there is a manuscript endorsed, "Dr. Bray's Plan of a congregation Pro propaganda ffide" in which he lays down the plan of a society for carrying on work "amongst yt Poorer sort of people, as also amongst ye Blacks & Native In-

[53] Bray Mss., *op. cit.*, p. 342. There are two other copies of this scheme; on p. 62, the copy does not include work "at home"; on p. 321 is a rough draught probably the original one.

[54] Classified Digest, *op. cit.*, p. 5.

[55] The charter is printed in full in Pascoe, *op. cit.*, p. 932, being a copy of the first printed edition, that of 1706.

[56] Bray Mss., *op. cit.*, p. 257. The letter is undoubtedly intended for the Governor of Maryland.

dians."[57] Through his interest and concern, work similar to that represented by the Catechetical Schools of England was included in the aims of the Society of 1701. Later, "on a visit which he paid to Holland to seek the King's patronage of his designs, he made acquaintance with a gentleman at the Hague, M. Abel Tassin, more commonly known as Sieur D'Allone, secretary to the King, whose mind was also turned towards the subject, and who gave the sum of nine hundred pounds in his life[58] to be applied to the instruction of Negroes. Dr. Bray, at his request,[59] undertook the disposal of it, and being attacked by a dangerous illness[60] about Christmas 1723, nominated certain trustees, his Associates, whose authority was ratified by a decree in Chancery"[61] obtained on June 24th, 1730.[62] In addition to the instruction of Negroes, which continued until long after Independence had been won, the Associates were also devoted to the work of distributing books in England and in the Plantations, thus perpetuating the library work of the founder.

Dr. Bray died Feb. 15, 1729–30, at the age of seventy-three years, bequeathing his estate to the promotion of his designs in different parts of the world. His power to create and organize the great extension work of the Church was extraordinary. In view of his services to the colonies he deserves to be known as one of the greatest contributors to that period of American history.

---

57 This is undated but was probably prepared in the interval between Bray's being commissioned to Maryland and the founding of the S. P. G. Very likely it was suggested to him by the work of the "S. P. G. for the Natives of New England" which has been already alluded to.

58 See Extracts of D'Alloune's letters, S. P. G. Letter-book, A, 19, pp. 21-23. The actual sum received from D'Alloune is difficult to determine. Not only did he make gifts during his life, probably to the amount stated in the quotation above, but in his Will, dated the 1st of July 1721, he bequeathed one-tenth of his English Estate, and the arrears of his pension due from the Crown "at ye time of my death." The income from it was to be used by Dr. Bray and his Associates for "Ye erecting a school or Schools for ye thorough Instructing in ye Xtian Religion ye Young Children of Negro Slaves & such of their Parents as show themselves inclineable . . . . ." S. P. G. Letter-book, A, 19, p. 17. (This is a copy of an extract from his Will.)

59 S. P. G. Letter-book, A, 19, p. 18.

60 *Ibid.*

61 From, "Memoir of Dr. Bray," in the Report of Dr. Bray's Associates, 1906, pp. 34–35.

62 Archives of the Bray Associates, Minute-book, 1729–1735, p. 1; S. P. G. Journal V., p. 257.

CHAPTER II

THE WORK OF THE S. P. C. K. AT HOME AND ABROAD.

The Society for the Promoting Christian Knowledge formally began its work on March 8, 1698–9,[1] with five members, viz: Dr. Bray, Lord Guilford, Sir Humphrey Mackworth and Mr. Justice Hook, members of the English bar, and Col. Maynard Colchester, a country gentleman of Gloucestershire, who had already established on his own account a charity school in that shire. On April 19th Mr. John Chamberlayne was elected and became the Society's secretary, later being selected for the same office in the S. P. G. In the next few months many of the prominent clergy of the Church had become members, and corresponding members were enrolled from centres in England, Wales and Ireland, and from the English territory beyond the sea. Moreover the Society invited and received the coöperation of men on the continent who were engaged in similar work of reformation.[2] Unusual success seemed to attend the venture from the beginning. The four resolutions of the first meeting indicate the range of the Society's interest and the guiding hand of Dr. Bray. They are recorded in the Minutes as follows:

"1. Resolv'd that Col. Colchester and Dr. Bray go and discourse *George Keith* in order to be satisfyed what progress he has hitherto *made towards the instruction and conversion of Quakers*, and to know what he designs to attempt further, under the conduct of God's Providence and assistance, in order to redeem that misguided people to the knowledge and belief of Christ, and that they report the same to the Society to-morrow morning.

"2. Resolv'd that we consider to-morrow morning how to further and promote that good Design of erecting Catecheticall Schools in each parish in and about London, and that Col. Colchester and Dr. Bray give their thoughts how it may be done.

"3. Resolv'd that the Right Honble the Lord Guilford be desired to speak to the Archbishop that care may be taken that a Clause be provided in the Bill for imploying the poor, to have the Children taught to read and be instructed in the Church Catechism.

---

1 S. P. C. K. Minute-book.

2 Professor Francke of Halle, and later his son; Osterwald of Neuchatel; Mr. De Beringhen of the Hague; and Dr. Brincke, a Danish Minister of Copenhagen, were some of these associated members.

"4. Resolv'd that Dr. Bray be desired, as soon as conveniently he can, to lay before this Society his Scheme for Promoting Religion in the Plantations, and his accompts of Benefactions and Disbursements towards the same."[3]

Here are proposals to enter upon the work of combating the growth of sectaries particularly "that misguided people," the Quakers, of supporting Charity Schools, of espousing the welfare of children apprenticed by ensuring them some religious education, and of supporting Bray's plans for the American colonies. The Society, shortly thereafter, added other aims that had been undertaken by the earlier organizations mentioned in preceding pages. It prosecuted cases of profaneness. It observed and brought to public notice the infractions of the Stage. Following Bray's ideas, it took up the task of circulating books and founding libraries, at home as well as in the colonies. Later it engaged in translating books into foreign language to further increase their dissemination. In order to improve the moral and spiritual condition of the mariners of England it began the distribution of books and tracts to them, and the records of the Society contain numerous acknowledgments thereof by famous sea-fighters of the past, from Sir George Rooke hero of Gibraltar to Admiral Lord Nelson hero of Trafalgar. The Society early took up the problem of the reforming of Newgate and the other prisons in and about London,[4] and through its efforts the conscience of the nation was awakened out of its indifference to such matters. The Society became a friend to the Reformed Communities on the Continent in their struggles for life. When the Crown of England secured a part of the Salzburg emigrants for its domain in Georgia, the S. P. C. K. collected, between 1731 and 1734, nearly £5,000 for them.[5] This was the beginning of an interest in the settlement in Georgia that continued until the separation of the colonies from the mother-country by means of which salaries for missionaries and schoolmasters were secured to the emigrants. As early as 1710 the Society began work in the East Indies, by assisting the Danish missions there

[3] S. P. C. K. Minute-book, 1698–1706, March 8, 1698–9.

[4] A report containing vigorous proposals was presented at the meeting of February 22, 1699–1700. It is printed in Allen and McClure, *op. cit.*, p. 54 ff.

[5] Attached to a "circular letter" of the S. P. C. K., Oct. 4, 1734, in behalf of the Salzburg emigrants, there is an "account of the Money Received and Disbursed by the Trustees for receiving Benefactions etc." From this it appears that £314 were already advanced to a "*Conductor, Two Ministers,* and the *Schoolmaster,*" and that £2237 had been invested "to secure the Payment of 90 l. per ann. Salaries to the *Two Ministers* and *Schoolmaster,*" sent out to Ebenezer in Georgia. From, the Sloane Mss., British Museum, 4053, fol. 278.

with funds, and then by taking over these missions entirely about 1728. It continued such support till the S. P. G. undertook the charge in 1825.

The educational work of the Society, however, made up the most important part of its operations for the first century. It was, indeed, the first society in Great Britain which came forward to advocate and support the general education of the people. In accordance with the resolution of the first meeting it was ordered on the 10th of March, that a form of subscription be prepared for circulating in the parishes and, therewith, a form to insure a more dependable and permanent fund. Four days later the following "forms" were reported and approved of:

"The *Form of Subscription to ye Charity Schools* Erected or Promoted by the Honble. Society, &c.:—

"*Whereas* it is evident to common observation, That the growth of vice and debauchery is greatly owing to the gross ignorance of the principles of the Christian Religion, especially among the poorer sort. And also whereas Christian vertue can grow from no other root than Christian Principles, we whose names are underwritten, inhabitants of the Parish of [   ] in the County of [   ], being touched with zeal for the honour of God, the salvation of the souls of our poor brethren, and the Promoting of Christian Knowledge among the poor of this Parish, do hereby promise to pay yearly during pleasure, by four equal quarterly payments, viz., at Michaelmas, Christmas, Lady-day, and Mid-summer, such respective sums as we have hereunto subscribed for and towards the setting up a School within this Parish for teaching poor Children (whose parents are not able to afford them any education) to read and write, and to repeat and understand the Church Catechism according to the Rules and Orders lately printed and published by the direction of the Honble. Society for Propagating Christian Knowledge.

"As witness our hands this [   ] day of [   ] Anno Domini."

"The *Form of Insurance of Charity Schools.*

"We whose names are underwritten having agreed to promote the setting up of Schools for Instructing Poor Children in the Principles of Christianity in the several Parishes where they are most wanted in and about the City of London, and having also to that purpose agreed to provide a sum of money to be imployed by way of insurance for ye encouragement of such well-disposed persons as shall undertake to set up the same in such methods as we shall from time to time direct. Now we do hereby further agree that we will severally pay the respective sums which we have hereunto subscribed (to be disposed of according to the discretion of this Society) to the Treasurer for the time being, who shall or may receive the same (or such part thereof as the Society shall think necessary to be raised) on demand, and shall and may dispose of and lay out ye same accordingly."[6]

Even before this Col. Colchester had been "desired to find out three persons to begin an endeavour of setting up Schools in

[6] S. P. C. K. Minute-book, 1698-1706, March 16, 1698–9. Printed in Allen and McClure, *op. cit.*, p. 27. The term "Charity Schools" is used here for the first time in the Society's Minutes.

three Parishes,"[7] and nearly every succeeding meeting devoted a large proportion of its time to the work of religious education of the poor. By the end of November, 1699, more than two thousand children[8] were being cared for in the charity schools. The Society thereupon appealed for a nation-wide movement on the part of the Clergy, doing this by means of the following document:

"The First Circular Letter from the Honourable Society for Promoting Christian Knowledge to their Clergy Correspondents in the several Counties of England and Wales.[9]

"The visible decay of Religion in this Kingdom, with the monstrous increase of Deism, Prophaneness, and Vice, has excited the zeal of several persons of the best character, in the Cities of London and Westminister, and other parts of the nation, to associate themselves in order to consult together how to put a stop to so fatal an inundation.

"The cause thereof they believe in great measure to arise from the barbarous ignorance observable among the common people, especially those of the poorer sort, and this to proceed from want of due care in the education of the Youth, who, if early instructed in the Principles of true Religion, seasoned with the knowledge of God, and a just concern for their everlasting welfare, cou'd not possibly (with the ordinary Assistance of God's good Spirit) degenerate into such vile and unChristian practices as they now generally do.

"To remedy these Evils, which cry aloud to Heaven for vengeance, they have agreed to use their best endeavours to incline the hearts of generous and well-dispos'd persons to contribute toward the erecting of Schools in these Cities, and the parts adjacent, for the instruction of such poor Children in Reading, Writing, and in the Catechism, whose Parents or Relations are not able to afford them the ordinary means of Education; and as they look upon this to be the most effectual method to train up the poorer sort in sobriety and ye knowledge of Christian Principles, so they assure themselves that the good effects which may be wrought thereby will prove a powerfull argument to engage others in better circumstances to make so necessary a provision for their children.

"The success of this undertaking (whereby the education of above two thousand poor Children is already taken care for) encourages them to hope that, if the like industry and application were observ'd in the other parts of this Kingdom, the Children and Youth might be universally well principled, and the growing generation make a conscience of fearing God; and these hopes have induced them to use their utmost endeavours to prevail with all pious and well-inclined Christians in ye several parts of ye nation to joyn their hearts and purses in advancing to perfection so excellent and glorious a work."[9]

Through this and succeeding appeals the Church was gradually impressed with its own responsibility for a system of national education on a religious basis. It assumed the responsibility and, under the leadership of the S. P. C. K., developed a system

---

7 S. P. C. K. Minute-book, *op. cit.*, March 12, 1698-9.

8 See the following "Circular Letter."

9 Adopted by the Society Nov. 16, 1699. Printed in Allen and McClure, *op. cit.*, p. 43.

of Church schools that were thus maintained through the seventeenth century and until the work was taken over, in 1811, by "The National Society for the Education of the Poor in the Principles of the Established Church throughout England and Wales," known by the shorter name of "National Society."

By 1704 there had been established 54 charity schools in London and Westminister, and within ten miles thereof. In them, 1386 boys and 745 girls were enrolled[10] of whom 306 boys and 75 girls were put out apprentices. In 1708 there were 74 schools and 5706 boys and girls.[11] In the next decade the schools had increased to 1358 (in London 127, in other parts of Great Britain and Ireland 1231) with 28,610 children (in London 5109, in other parts, etc., 23,501).[12] In 1728, the statistics showed 132 schools for London, 1279 for South Britain, 78 for North Britain, and 161 for Ireland. This made a total of 1650 schools with 34,051 children of whom 7079 were girls.[13] And in 1742 the movement had grown to 133 schools for London, 1329 for South Britain, 131 for North Britain, 128 for Wales, and 186 for Ireland. Thus the total for this year was 1907 schools, with 43,847 children of whom 6664 were girls.[14] Doubtless the educational work of the Society had within fifty years grown to be the most significant movement of its kind in any country. The report of 1711 shows how far-reaching the Society's influence had become, the movement having been taken up in various parts of Northern Europe, as well as in America. The report adds: "Some of our preceding Anniversary Charity-Sermons, and Accounts of Charity-Schools, have been translated, by a very eminent Hand, into High-Dutch, and two Charity-Schools have already been set up at Copenhagen on the Model of ours, and Endeavours are using to do the like in several Parts of Ger-

10 An Account of Charity Schools 1704,—Sion College Archives, 42: F: 2, No. 1. This list of 54 contains some schools that were set up before the Society organized, probably by private initiative as the same account shows: "All the Schools abovementioned have been set up within the space of Eight Years last past except that in Norton-Folgate, and 1 of the 3 in St. Margaret, Westminister which were set up about 3 or 4 years before." In the Account of Charity Schools, 1718, it is stated that Blue-Coat School in St. Margaret was set up Lady Day (March 25th) 1688 for 50 boys, and Norton-Folgate School in 1691 for 60 boys.—Sion College Archives, 43: F: 3, No. 6.

11 Account of Charity Schools 1708, Sion College Archives, 43: F: 2, No. 3.

12 *Ibid.*, 1718—43: F: 3, No. 6.

13 *Ibid.*, 1728—43: F: 23, No. 11.

14 *Ibid.*, 1742—43: E: 10, No. 5. Eighteen of the Irish schools are herein reported as being "encouraged by Royal bounty of £1000 per Ann." It was impossible for the writer to make a complete search through the enormous masses of bound pamphlets of Sion College Library. However, he succeeded in finding 20 reports for years between 1704 and 1742.

many and Switzerland. It is inexpressible, with what Zeal and Application, the Religious Education and Catechizing of Children has been of late promoted in other Protestant Countries beyond the Seas."[15] Work similar to that of the S. P. C. K. was set on foot in Scotland about 1709,[16] and there is no doubt that school support in America by the S. P. G. received great stimulus from its sister organization.

The initial expense of the schools was met by the members of the Society but subscriptions soon came in which by the end of the first year amounted to £450. By 1704 annual subscriptions had grown to £2164 and individual schools had received benefactions from private donors in the sum of £3202. Additional revenue came from special collections made in the churches annually on a day set aside for the preaching of "Charity Sermons." In 1704 this amounted to £1042. The funds had doubled by 1708 and were gathered from the same sources. We learn that in 1717 the workmen in county Durham "allow one farthing and an half per shilling, per week, which together with their master's contribution, maintains their poor, and affords about £17 per annum for teaching their children to read."[17] But this type of contribution could not have been frequent. The great body of the fund represents the philanthropic activity of the upper classes in behalf of the poor. From the 1704 report we learn that, "The ordinary Charge of a School for 50 Boys Cloath'd comes to about 75 l p. ann. for which a School-Room, Books, and Firing are provided, a Master paid, and to each Boy is given yearly, 3 Bands, 1 Cap, 1 Coat, 1 pair of Stockings, and 1 pair of Shoes"; and "For 50 Girls, 60 l p. ann. etc. . . . and to each is given yearly, 2 coyfs, 2 Bands, 1 Gown and Petticoat, 1 pair of Knit-Gloves, 1 pair of Stockings, and 2 pair of Shoes."[18] Details of the cost of clothing the children are given in various reports; that for 1710 is as follows:

"The Charge of Cloathing a Poor Boy of a Charity School in London.[19]

	£	s	d
I Yard and half quarter of Grey Yorkshire Broad Cloth 6 quarters wide, makes a coat	00	03	00

15 From report of Society for 1711, printed in Allen and McClure, *op. cit.*, pp. 122–3.

16 *Ibid.*; also, Sloane Mss., British Museum, 4051, fol. 313; also, Lambeth Mss., 1123, a copy of which is in Hawk's Transcripts, G. C.

17 Account of Charity Schools, 1717.

18 Account of Charity Schools, 1704—Sion College Archives, 43: F: 2, No. 1.

19 Quoted by Allen and McClure, *op. cit.*, p. 141.

Making the Coat with Pewter Buttons and all other materials	00	01	00
A Waistcoat of the same Cloth lined	00	03	06
A pair of Breeches of Cloth or Leather lined	00	02	06
1 Knit Cap, with Tuft and String, of any Colour	00	00	10
1 Band	00	00	02
1 Shirt	00	01	06
1 Pair of Woollen Stockings	00	00	08
1 Pair of Shoes	00	01	10
1 Pair of Buckles	00	00	01
	00	15	01

"The Charge of Cloathing a Poor Girl of a Charity School in London.

	£	s	d
3 Yards and half of blue long Ells, about Yard wide at 16d. p. Yard makes a Gown and Petticoat	00	04	08
Making thereof, Strings, Body-lining, and other Materials	00	01	00
A Coif and Band of Scotch Cloth plain with a Border	00	00	09
A Shift	00	01	06
A pair of Leather Bodice and Stomacher	00	02	06
1 Pair of Woollen Stockings	00	00	08
1 Pair of Shoes	00	01	08
1 Pair of Buckles	00	00	01
	00	12	10

School inspection began by the appointment of agents whose primary duties were to assist in the setting up of the schools. They made reports weekly.[20] Then the Society sought the assistance of the Bishop of London for directing Parochial ministers "frequently to catechise" the children.[21] In 1700 Rev. Mr. Coghan was elected "Inspector of all the Charity Schools in and about London and Westminister" at a salary of £20 a year.[22] Thus the inspection was to be done by the parish clergy and, in large centres, by a minister specially designated, a work which seems to have been conscientiously looked after throughout all sections. Rules and orders for Charity Schools are found in the accounts of 1704.[23] The qualifications required a master to be "a Member of the Church of England, of a sober Life and Conversation, not under the Age of 25 Years; one that frequents Holy Communion, one that hath a good government of himself and his Passions; one who understands well the Grounds and Principles of the Christian Religion, and is able to give a good account thereof to the Minister of the Parish, or Ordinary, on

---

[20] The first report occurs May 18, 1699. See S. P. C. K. Minute-book, 1698–1706, under this date.

[21] *Ibid.*, Nov. 30, 1699.

[22] *Ibid.*, Jan. 13, 1700–1.

[23] Sion College Archives, 43: F: 2, No. 1. Dr. Bray was requested to formulate and bring in the first orders March 16, 1698–9, S. P. C. K. Minute-book, 1698–1706.

Examination; of a good Genius for Teaching; one who can write a good Hand, and who understands the Grounds of Arithmetick." He must keep school "from 7 to 11 in the Morning, and from 1 to 5 in the Evening, in the *Summer* half-Year; from 8 to 11 in the Morning, and from 1 to 4 in the Evening, the *Winter* half-year." Three holidays a year were allowed "at the usual Festivals and by no means during *Bartholomew Fair* for fear of any harm by ill examples," and the regulations held that "a Register of Attendance is to be kept and the *Tardy* as well as the *Absent* is to be noted." Orders were also given concerning the curriculum. The Master must "teach them the true Spelling of Words and distinction of Syllables, with Points and Stops." "As soon as the boys can read competently well, the Master shall teach them to write a fair legible hand, with the grounds of Arithmetick, to fit them for Service or Apprentices." The girls were "to learn to read etc., and generally to knit their stockings and gloves, to mark, sew, make and mend their Cloathes, several to learn to write, and some to spin their Cloathes." Instruction in Church Catechism came twice a week, when it was required that the Master "shall first teach them to pronounce distinctly and plainly; and then, in order to practice, shall explain it to the Meanest Capacity, by the help of *The Whole Duty of Man*, or some good Exposition approved by the Minister." To guard their manners and behaviour he was "to correct the beginnings of Lying, Swearing, Cursing, Taking God's name in Vain, and the Prophanation of the Lord's Day." The children were to be "brought to Church by the Master twice every Lord's Day and Holy Day." It was further maintained that "they are always to have ready their Bibles, bound up with the Common Prayer. When a sufficient number know the Catechism, he is to give notice to the Minister, so that they may be catechized in the Church." Finally, "Prayers are to be said in School, Morning and Evening, and the children are to be taught to pray at home, when they rise and when they go to Bed, and to use Graces before and after Meat."

In the beginning the Society took up the work of publishing Christian literature,[24] circulating the same through gifts outright and through the setting up of libraries in the parishes.[25]

---

[24] S. P. C. K. Minute-book, 1698–1706, March 10, 1698–9.

[25] S. P. C. K. Minute-book, 1698–1706, Dec. 3, 1699.

Books for the Charity Schools were included among the rest. Distribution was gratis at first and continued to be so where means of purchasing were wanting. Large quantities of Bibles, New Testaments, Prayer-books, elementary books of instruction and tracts were thus provided for the schools. After 1703 effort was made to get a partial return for the books, and small rates, less than cost price, were charged to places that were in a position to contribute something. Catalogues of the Society's publications were issued as early as 1706 and prices ranged from a few pence to four and five shillings. There were two marked exceptions, viz.: "A Quarto Bible with a Chronological Table" was worth 18 shillings and "Philips's English Dictionary" was worth 16 shillings. In the Accounts for the Years 1713 and 1715,[26] as well as for succeeding years, there appear two interesting lists that show the range of the Society's publications, and the large number of books made available for the use of the schools. The first is, "A Catalogue of Books fit to be put into the Hands of Masters of Charity Schools." Following a considerable list of doctrinal works, there are a number of treatises directly applicable to the instruction of youth in Christian principles and secular knowledge, for example:—

"The Christian Monitor. Price 3d.
Professor *Franck's* account of the Hospital at *Halle*, intituled *Pietas Hallensis.* Price 3d.
Munro's Just Measures of the pious Institution of Youth, 2 Vol. Pr. 9s.
Mr. *Talbot's* Christian School-Master. Price 2s.
The Christian Education of Children. Price 1s.
A Method for Instruction of Children and Youth. Price 4d.
Sermons at the Anniversary Meeting of the Charity-Schools in London.
Disney's First and Second Essay concerning the Execution of the Laws against Immorality and Profaneness. Price 5s. 6d.
Philip's English Dictionary. Price 16s. Or, The Abridgment of it. Price 5s. 6d.
Mr. *Turner's* Spelling-Book, and *English* Grammar. Price 1s. 6d.
Mr. *Snell's* New Copy-Book. Price 5s.
John Johnson's Arithmetick.
Hatton's Arithmetick. Price 4s.
Vernon's Compleat Counting-House. Price 9d.
Ayre's Youth's Introduction to Trade."

The second list contains books prescribed for the use of the scholars, as follows:—

"Books *Proper to be Used* in Charity Schools.[27]
"A Bible, Testament and Common-Prayer Book.

---

[26] Sion College Archives, 43: F: 1.
[27] These lists are printed in Allen and McClure, *op. cit.*, pp. 186–7.

The Church-Catechism.
The Church-Catechism broke into short Questions.
Lewis's Exposition of the Church-Catechism.
Worthington's Scripture-Catechism.
The first Principles of practical Christianity.
Dr. *Woodward's* Short Catechism, with an Explanation of divers hard Words.
New Method of Catechizing.
Prayers for the Charity-Schools.
The Christian Scholar.
An Exercise for Charity-Schools upon Confirmation.
Pastoral advice before, and after Confirmation.
The Whole Duty of Man by Way of Question and Answer.
Abridgement of the History of the Bible, which may be well bound up at the Beginning of the Bible, or at the end.
The Anatomy of Orthography: Or, a practical Introduction to the Art of Spelling and Reading English.
The Duty of Public Worship proved, &c.
Lessons for Children, Historical and Practical &c.
Hymns for the Charity-Schools."

Later reports show a number of additions to these lists, those of a secular nature being:

"Archbishop *Wake's* Commentary on the Church-Catechism.
Monro's Essay on Christ and Education.
Dr. *Talbot's* Christian Schoolmaster.
An Exercise against Lying.
An Exercise against Taking God's Name in Vain.
The Way of Living in a Method and by Rule; Or a Regular Way of Employing our Time.
The Devout Psalmodist."[28]

Throughout the period of S. P. C. K. support and long after the National Society took charge of the schools, they were supplied with books by the former society, either at an exceedingly low rate or else by free grant.

The interest of the S. P. C. K. in the Plantations was awakened at the outset, as is shown by one of the Society's first resolves.[29] Shortly thereafter Dr. Bray had submitted, "A General View of what has appeared to me to be wanting for the Propagating Christian Knowledge in the Plantations, so far as hitherto and at this distance I can give an estimate." The things "wanting," in Bray's estimation were: (1) To fix Parochial Libraries as an encouragement to Clergymen, the same to be stocked almost wholly with religious treatises. (2) "To give further means of Instruction and Edification to the people in the Plantations, it is requisite there should be considerable quan-

28 From an Account of Charity Schools, 1727—Archives of Sion College Library, 43: E: 9, No. 11.
29 See p. 17.

tities sent of practical Books to be distributed gratis amongst ym." (3) "To train up their youth in the knowledge of Christ, Catechetical Free Schools for ye Education of the Children of the Poorest Planters appears highly expedient." (4) To make suitable provision for the wives and Children of Missionaries who die in the service. (5) "To reduce the Quakers, who are so numerous in those parts, to the Christian Faith, from which they are totally Apostatiz'd" by means of special missionaries to them. (6) "And lastly, in order to convert the Indian Nations, it seems a likely method, could there be provision for the Education of some of their Youth in Schools for that purpose, who, after a thorough Instruction in the Christian Faith, might be sent back amongst their own natives, as ye properest persons to convert them and to deale with them for their soul's good."

The Minutes of the first two years and more show a constant desire to support Dr. Bray in his colonial schemes. The personal debt incurred by him was assumed by the Society. This amounted to £631.[30] Additional money was collected and packets of books were dispatched across the sea.[31] Writing to the Governor of Virginia, Mr. Chamberlayne, the secretary, says, "The main part of their Design, with relation to America, is to assist Dr. Bray in Raising of Libraries for the Clergy, and in Distributing practicall Books amongst the Laity."[32] But more than this, a start was made in sending missionaries. On March 17, 1700–1 "Dr. Bray reported that 9 Missionaries to the Plantations are in a very fair way of being completed, £400 per annum being already subscribed, besides £50 extraordinary."[33]

Support of schools in the colonies was not taken up, however, the Society having its resources fully taxed with such work as it did undertake. Yet it is evident that schools were to be encouraged in time. In an attempt to secure the coöperation of American Merchants and Planters in the Society's work, the secretary solicited, among others, Mr. Elias Neau, merchant of New York, for assistance. He said, in part,

"The success of this undertaking (that is, the work of the S. P. C. K. in England), whereby the Education of so many Thousands of poor Children

30 S. P. C. K. Minute-book, 1698–1706, June 8, 1699 and Nov. 9, 1699.

31 *Ibid.* Aug. 17; Sep. 1, 21; Oct. 5, 12; and Nov. 30, 1699. Sep. 12, 19; Oct. 10; and Dec. 16, 23, 1700. March 17, 24, 1700–1; Apr. 21, Aug. 5, 1701.

32 By order of the Society, Oct. 3, 1700.

33 S. P. C. K. Minute-book, 1698–1706, under date given.

is already taken care for, encourages them to hope that, if the like Industry and application were but observed in our Plantations, the Children and Servants of our Merchants and Planters in those parts might be universally better principled and Instructed, and the growing generation make a conscience of fearing God, with not only their Children, but likewise with all their servants, too many of which at present are designedly kept in profound Ignorance by their unchristian Masters and Governours, to the great scandall of the Reformed Religion. Little do such prophane persons think what a dreadful account they have to give when inquisition shall be made for the blood of those poor creatures' souls at the great day of Retribution.

The Progress which this Society has made for Propagating Christian Knowledge in our Plantations appears by the noble Provision of Books for ye Clergy in those parts (whereof the World has had already an accot in Print), and that so blessed a Worke may not fail of success they are soliciting further benefactions for supplying from time to time what shall be wanting to accomplish it, and they do not in ye least doubt of your best Endeavours to procure what Assistance you can from ye Merchants and Planters in yor neighbourhood and acquaintance, and to send us the names of such persons as you apprehend may be willing to Joyne with you and us in so noble and Christian an undertaking."[34]

Before any definite action on schools could be taken plans were set on foot for the incorporation of the S. P. G. On October 28, 1701 the Society's activity in America practically came to an end, it having been "Resolved that from henceforwards the usuall Subscriptions to the Plantations shall cease."[35] Packets of books continued to be sent over or were put into the hands of the S. P. G. missionaries before their departure. They were usually of the value of one or two pounds. This and the assistance rendered the emigrants to Georgia,[36] between 1732 and the Revolution, complete the record of the work of the S. P. C. K. in what is now the United States.

---

34 Letter written October, 1700. Quoted by Allen and McClure, *op. cit.*, p. 227.

35 S. P. C. K. Minute-book 1698–1706, under date given. This, of course, was owing to the chartering of the S. P. G.

36 See p. 17.

CHAPTER III

THE FOUNDING AND GENERAL WORK OF THE S. P. G.

"The Society for the Propagation of the Gospell in Forreigne Parts" was incorporated by Royal charter granted by William the Third, June 16, 1701. The preamble of the instrument recites the reasons for incorporating and the purposes of the corporation in general rather than specific terms:

"Whereas Wee are credibly informed that in many of our Plantacons, Colonies, and *Factories* beyond the seas, belonging to Our Kingdome of England, the Provision for Ministers is very mean. And many others of our said Plantacons, Colonies, and Factories are wholy destitute, and unprovided of a Mainteynance for Ministers, and the Public Worship of God; and for Lack of Support and Mainteynance for such, many of our Loving Subjects doe want the Administration of God's Word and Sacraments, and seem to be abandoned to Atheism and Infidelity and alsoe for Want of Learned and Orthodox Ministers to instruct Our said Loving Subjects in the Principles of true Religion, divers Romish Priests and Jesuits are the more encouraged to pervert and draw over Our said Loving Subjects to Popish Superstition and Idolatry.

"And Whereas Wee think it Our Duty as much as in Us lyes, to promote the Glory of God, by the Instruccon of Our People in the Christian Religion And that it will be highly conducive for accomplishing those Ends, *that a sufficient Mainteynance be provided for an Orthodox Clergy to live amongst them*, and *that such other Provision be made, as may be necessary for the Propagation of the Gospell in those Parts:*

"And Whereas Wee have been well assured, That if Wee would be gratiously pleased to erect and settle a Corporacon for the *receiving, manageing, and disposeing of the Charity of Our Loving Subjects*, divers Persons would be induced to extend their Charity to the Uses and Purposes aforesaid."[1]

The fact is to be noted, that such other provision as might be necessary, in addition to the maintenance of clergy, was made a fundamental object of the organization. It seems to have been an elastic clause that had in view the extension to the colonies of much of the work of the S. P. C. K. in England, and the furthering of the work of Dr. Bray in the Plantations. The charter incorporated 94 members, more than half of whom represented the leading dignitaries of the Church. All of the

[1] The charter in full is printed in, Pascoe, *op. cit.*, p. 932. Italics not in original

original founders of the S. P. C. K. were in the list of charter members as, indeed, were practically all of the active members of the latter society and many of its corresponding members.[2] In the first hundred years the membership rose to 300 and was for some time limited to that number. During the nineteenth century it grew to 6000. Broad powers were conferred on the Society, as is shown by the section of the charter relating thereto:

"And Wee further Will, and by these Presents for Us, Our Heires and Successors doe Ordaine and Grant unto the said Society for the Propagation of the Gospell in Forreigne Parts, and their Successors That they, and their Successors, or the major Part of them who shall be present at the first and second Meeting of the said Society, or at any Meeting on the Third Friday in the Months of November, February, May, and August, yearely for ever, and at noe other Meetings of the said Society, shall and may Consult, Determine, Constitute, Ordaine, and Make any Constitutions, Laws, Ordinances and Statutes whatsoever; as alsoe to execute Leases for Yeares, as aforesaid, which to them, or the major Part of them then present shall seem reasonable, profitable, or requisite, for, touching or concerning the Good Estate, Rule, Order and Government of the said Corporation and the more efectuall promoteing the said Charitable Designes: All which Lawes, Ordinances, and Constitucons, soe to be made ordained and established, as aforesaid, Wee Will, Command, and Ordaine, by these Presents, for Us, Our Heires, and Successors, to be from Time to Time and at all Times hereafter kept and performed in all Things as the same ought to be, on the Penalties and Amercements in the same to be imposed and limited, soe as the same Lawes, Constitucons, Ordinances, Penalties, and Amercements, be reasonable, and not repugnant or contrary to the Laws and Statutes of this Our Realme of England."

The business of the Society was to be transacted at monthly meetings but it soon became necessary to facilitate work by the appointment of a committee whose duties should be, "to receive proposals that may be offered to them for the Promoting the designs of this Society, and to prepare matters for the consideration of the Society."[3] This body became known as the "Standing Committee"[4] and became the quasi-executive head of the Society. The monthly meetings on the other hand represented a council for adopting or rejecting the committee's proposals.[5]

The funds of the Society began with a donation of £56 plus, subscribed by 12 members. It was used to cover the expense of getting the charter passed. On Oct. 17, 1701 a form of sub-

[2] S. P. C. K. Minute-book 1698–1706, Nov. 4 and 18, 1701; compare also with S. P. G. Charter.

[3] S. P. G. Journal, I, p. 39, March 6, 1702–3.

[4] June 18, 1703,—S. P. G. Journal, I, p. 109.

[5] Essentially every measure adopted for the American colonies was initiated by the Standing Committee and then submitted for final action. Very few recommendations were ever rejected by the Society.

scription was drawn up which soon netted over £184.[6] Immediately following, subscription rolls were circulated throughout England and, by the end of 1701, £204[7] had been subscribed. This form of fund-gathering was carried on yearly and brought in sums ranging from £500 to £950. Besides this private benefactors (members of Royalty and outsiders, as well as members of the Society) made frequent donations which far exceeded the subscriptions. In 1701, for instance, £1332 were acquired in this manner. For a decade thereafter the "donations" were comparatively small. In 1713, there was recorded £1610, and from 1717 on to the end of the century the median for this particular source of revenue was £2000. The general fund was considerably augmented by public house to house collections for which Royal Letters were issued on six different occasions in the eighteenth century. By such means the Society collected in the reign of Queen Anne, £3060 (1711) and £3887 (1714); in the reign of George I, £3727 (1718); in that of George II, £15,278 (1741) and £19,786 (1751); and in that of George III, £19,372 (1779). Special funds began to be received from 1713 on and came in steadily. The median for these was about £1500 annually. They were different from the general fund in that they were fixed by their donors for specific benefactions and had to be so administered. Yet one other source of revenue remains to be mentioned,—the interest from the funds themselves. The expenditures for the first half century taxed the income to the utmost, but after that, through timely investments, funds began to be dividend-producing. In this way over £21,000 had been added to the general fund by 1780. During the same period (1701–1780), when interest was centred for the most part in the colonies that formed the American union, the entire collections reached the sum of £392,804. The entire expenditures, on the other hand, were £349,433, two-thirds of which represented the Society's benefactions in the said colonies.

For over two hundred years the S. P. G. has been engaged in a work of evangelization that ranks as the greatest in point of accomplishment and as the most extensive in all history. Not

---

[6] S. P. G. Journal, Sept. 19, & Oct. 17, 1701—printed in Classified Digest, *op. cit.*, p. 822.

[7] For this and the following statistics, I am indebted to the Table of Income and Expenditure 1701–1893, given in Classified Digest, *op. cit.*, pp. 830–32; also in Pascoe *op. cit.*, pp. 830–32; see also Humphreys, *op. cit.*, pp. V–VI.

only has it been active in every province where the British flag has gone, but its succor has been vouchsafed to nearly every country in Europe where it has been sought. Its work and influence have been tremendous and far-reaching. The primary object has been, from the start, the spread of the Church of England and its doctrines. In English territory the goal has been more extreme,—that of making the Church the dominating influence religiously, thus carrying out and securing, as far as possible, the fundamental belief in Church establishment. Various lines of activity have been adopted to effect this purpose in the two and more centuries. Chiefly they have been: (1) the providing of Missionaries under Church Orders; (2) the establishment of Church organizations; (3) the inculcating and keeping alive the doctrines of the Church, and the feeding of the Missions by means of (a) distribution of Church literature, and (b) the support of schools; (4) the distribution of libraries to the missionaries for their better equipment; and (5) the assisting and founding of colleges to insure the supplying of a trained clergy.

Throughout its existence the Society has been devoted to the welfare of colonial settlers and "heathen natives" alike. This twofold aim was stated in the first anniversary sermon preached before the Society by the Dean of Lincoln. He therein said:

> "The design is, in the first place to settle the State of Religion as well as may be among our *own People* there, which by all accounts we have, very much wants their Pious care: and then to proceed in the best Methods they can towards the *Conversion* of the *Natives.*"[8]

In 1710 there was a temporary departure from the design thus laid down. Resolutions were passed purporting that the work of propagating the Gospel "does chiefly and principally relate to the conversion of heathens and infidels" and declaring a stop to the sending of missionaries to new fields among the Christians.[9] An exclusive policy such as this would have been was not pursued, though increased efforts were made for some time in behalf of the Indians and Negroes. The resolution, however, gave a basis for some of the opposition which the

---

[8] S. P. G. Anniversary Sermon, 1702, p. 17. Italics not in original.

[9] April 28, 1710, printed in Classified Digest, *op. cit.*, p. 69. The action thus taken was the result of a wave of interest in the Indians, created at London, by the visit of four Indian Sachems, their object being to solicit the aid of Queen Anne in furthering religious instruction among them.

Society met with in New England and elsewhere a few decades later.[10]

The first missionaries were sent over in 1702, going to the Carolinas, Pennsylvania, New York, New Jersey, and New England. From then until 1785 the Missionary Roll shows a list of 309 men employed in that field of the Society's service. New York received the largest number for any single colony, namely, 58, Pennsylvania including Delaware 47, and New Jersey 44. Thus nearly half of them labored in the middle colonies. The southern colonies were assisted to the number of 107, of which South Carolina got 54, North Carolina 33, and Georgia 13.[11] The New England colonies received 84.[12] Throughout the century the provisions made for the support and equipment of these 309 disciples of the Church occupied by far the greatest portion of the Society's time, and required the major part of its funds.

In addition to the salaries vouchsafed,[13] there were frequent packets of books and tracts sent them both for their own use and for distribution among the people. Further, they were granted at the outset £10 in books and £5 in tracts.[14] And as an encouragement for their undertaking the voyage, they were allowed £20 from the Crown. Such a bounty was settled in the reign of Charles II[15] upon every minister and schoolmaster going to the colonies, and it was renewed by succeeding sovereigns.[16]

Provision for the religious instruction of the colonists was started about two years after sending out the first ministers. In 1703 a catechist for New York was appointed.[17] Early in

---

10 To be referred to in the following pages.

11 The Society supported only 2 missionaries in Virginia and 5 in Maryland. This, with occasional grants of books, constituted all of their work in these two colonies. This was because they were so much better provided for in comparison with the distressing Church conditions in the other colonies. For all of the figures quoted here, see the Missionary Roll of the Society, in Classified Digest, *op. cit.*, pp. 849–56.

12 Adding the numbers for the individual colonies gives a total of 340 and not 309. This is due to transfers from one colony to another, causing some names to be counted more than once.

13 £40 or £50 sterling per annum, were usually allowed; sometimes less amounts.

14 S. P. G. Journal, I, p. 109. S. P. G. Letter-book, A, 9, p. 47; *ibid.*, A, 7, p. 82, showing a long list of the above sent to ministers and schoolmasters between 1704 and 1712; *ibid.*, A, 13, p. 34. So many instances of these gifts are found throughout the S. P. G. records that there can be no doubt of its being a general rule during the entire period.

15 Humphrey, *op. cit.*, p. 8.

16 Fothergill, A list of Emigrant Ministers to America, 1690–1811, p. 10; Lansdowne Mss., British Museum, 8851, fol. 150 ff; Lambeth Mss., 1123, III, fol. 255 (dated 1762).

17 S. P. G. Journal, I, p. 98. The date is Jan. 15, 1702–03. The appointment was made for the province of New York, but more than a year elapsed before the catechist began his labors, which were confined to New York City rather than to the province as a whole. See S. P. G. Letter-book, A, 2, p. 20.

1705, "A motion being made about an endeavour of erecting Charity Schools in the Plantations, Agreed that this motion be referred to the Committee & that it be an Instruction to consider of employing the widows of Clergymen in such Schools."[18] But no immediate action was taken on the motion and the Society's activity in this field remained much in abeyance for the first decade. The fact is attributable, not to indifference to the need of such work, but to the more urgent demands for setting upon a substantial footing the Church itself. In Bray's reports on colonial conditions, and in reports sent back by George Keith and the other pioneer missionaries, emphasis had been laid over and over again on the general neglect of worship according to the Church of England.[19] The same appeal for churches was stressed in the early petitions[20] which the Society received from settlements in various parts of the colonies and the income was inadequate to meet all of these petitions.[21]

During the entire period of its work in the American colonies the Society became involved in various forms of controversy. After 1750 opposition increased in bitterness and became more general. In the Revolutionary years and for a few years preceding, it grew to hatred of an intense degree, as both Church and Society naturally ranged themselves on the side of the Crown. Some of the controversies that arose were provoked by the Society's representatives or else by the Church party. It seems definitely clear that there were always representatives of the militant type[22] who gave strong color to suspicions of the

18 March 16, 1704–5, S. P. G. Journal, I, p. 189.

19 "Memorial Humbly Layd before his Grace the Lord ABp of Canterbury the Lord Bishop of London and the other Bishops of this Kingdom representing the present State of Religion in the Several Provinces on the Contint of North America in order to the Providing a sufficient Number of Proper Missionaries so absolutely Necessary to be Sent at this juncture into those Parts."—Hawks Transcripts, G. C. This report is without signature or date but the context is convincing proof that it is by Dr. Bray. See also, extract from Keith's Journal, in Classified Digest, *op. cit.*, pp. 10–11; letters of Keith Dec. 11, 1702, Hawks Transcripts, New York, I, p. 9; and Feb. 24, 1702–03 S. P. G. Letter-book, A, 5, I, p. 87; also letter of John Bartow, Aug. 14, 1706, Hawks Transcripts, New York, I, p. 125; also letter of John Talbot, Sept. 1, 1703, S. P. G. Letter-book, A, I, p. 125; also letter from Gov. of New York, Apr. 27, 1699, in New York Colonial Documents, IV, p. 520.

20 See for example the Salem, New Jersey, petition quoted in Classified Digest *op. cit.*, pp. 53–54, and the letter from the Vestry of Philadelphia, 1704, *ibid.*, p. 34; also Perry, Hist. Col., *op. cit.*, II, p. 5.

21 "Whereas it appears by the List of Missionaries & Schoolmasters that the annual charge of the Society to such Missionaries & Schoolmasters amounts to £1065 & whereas the yearly subscriptions of the Society amounts to no more than £759. Committee agreed to move the Society to consider of some method to advance the income of the Society." July 18, 1707, S. P. G. Journal, I, p. (86).

22 "It must not be a blind, outrageous Zeal That will make Proselytes here ... Nothing of what the Dissenters . . . imagine proceeds from a Spirit of Bitterness against 'em will ever do any good to the church . . . . Mr. Commissary Price shows too much of this spirit in Preaching and Conversation." Extracts from a letter of Gov. Belcher of Mass. to the Bishop of London, July 24, 1731, Fulham Archives.

non-conformists that the Church government in the colonies was bent on an establishment like that which the mother-church enjoyed in England. The Society at no time proclaimed such an aim, or any positive militancy, save probably towards the Quakers. Yet it is blameworthy to the extent that it did not sufficiently attempt to prevent over-zealousness and over-aggression,[23] and to the extent, also, that it was apt to espouse quietly the cause of such of its militant representatives as appealed to England for assistance. On the other hand, the Dissenters, the Quakers, and most of the non-conforming sects, showed an open hostility to the success of the Society and the growth of the Church interest. They viewed each step taken by the Church party as a most objectionable attempt, either open or veiled, to advance Church establishment.[24] So that, through this means, frequent injustice was done the Society and the Church.

Only a few of the incidents of these controversies can be noted here. When Keith, leading the first band of missionaries which the S. P. G. sent out, began his labor in Boston, June 1702, he fortunately introduced a subtle invitation to controversy. He succeeded in stirring up Increase Mather, an Independent preacher. A short pamphlet war ensued,[25] which from this time on recurred intermittently between the opposing forces in all the colonies, particularly in New England and the middle colonies.[26] The most conspicuous pamphlet war in New England was that of 1763–64 between Rev. Johnathan Mayhew, and East Apthorp, the Society's missionary at Cambridge. The former charged the S. P. G. with a departure from the original purpose of work on

---

23 However it can be said that the Society did give definite instruction that the missionaries must give no offence "by intermeddling in affairs not relating to their own Calling and Function." See, Instruction for the Clergy, part 1, No. XI. Again in part 2, No. X, of the same, they are instructed to visit those Parishioners "that oppose us, or dissent from us, to convince and reclaim them, with a Spirit of Meekness and Gentleness." These instructions are printed in Pascoe, *op. cit.*, pp. 837-9.

24 This hatred of Episcopacy is well illustrated by a cartoon reproduced in Perry, History of the Colonial Episcopal Church, I, p. 426.

25 Keith's Journal, p. 2; quoted in Classified Digest, *op. cit.*, pp. 41–42.

26 Pamphlet controversies to judge from their frequency and the numerous issues from the press, evidently occupied much of the time and thought of New England in the eighteenth century. For a bibliography of these, reference may be made to "Archælogia Americana," VI, 307–661, which contains a catalogue of publications in what is now the United States, prior to 1775. The flood of tracts against the Church and the Society was the source of great annoyance to the missionaries. Their appeals for literature to offset the pernicious charges were almost constant between 1710 and 1775. See for example S. P. G. Letter-book, A, 19, pp. 243 and 448. On the other hand the Society maintained a constant supply of writings in defense of the Church and its doctrine, and against the unorthodox sects. See S. P. G. Journals, I, p. (293); III, pp. 55, 71; IV, p. 179; VI, p. 49; VII, pp. 40, 262; VIII, pp. 112, 281; IX, p. 251. See also S. P. G. Letter-books, A, 10, p. 95; A, 19, p. 457; A, 25, p. 159; B, 11, p. 21; B, 12, p. 149; B, 13, pp. 26, 47, 62.

the frontier among the Indians.[27] Apthorp successfully answered this. Mayhew further charged misrepresentation of colonial conditions on the part of the Society's missionaries regarding their work and influence, and there was occasional basis for this, in spite of constant efforts by the Society to prevent it.[28]

Other animosities were engendered in New England the study of which shows that bigotry and sectarianism prevailed with both parties. New England printers refused to print the Church Catechism or other tracts,[29] making dependence on England a necessity in this respect. The schools of the Dissenters looked well to the preparing of children against the danger of conversion to Episcopacy. An observer of this jealous care on the part of the schools, writing to the Society, spoke of it as "The great veneration for the dissenting Religion and its Ministers, Ceremonies and Peculiarities, which is with Surprising and indefatigable Industry instill'd into their Children with every Part of their Education."[30] A strong sectarian spirit prevailed at Harvard and Yale. Episcopal students at Harvard were "much discouraged from coming to our worship on Sundays" and were threatened with being entirely restrained on the "only pretence, That they are hindered in their Studies by it."[31] This is less prejudiced in spirit, however, than the suggestion of the missionary, George Keith, that "a President and two or three fel-

---

27 The only possible basis for this has been referred to; see p. 31. The history and proceedings of the S. P. G. substantiate the denial made by Apthorp.

28 A series of these controversial pamphlets by Mayhew and Apthorp are in the New York Historical Society Library bound in a volume entitled: Mayhew, "Select Tracts." Another list of them may be found in Perry, Hist. Col., *op. cit.*, III, pp. 688–90. A cargo of books for the spread of infidelity, the freight of which was £45, was imported from London about Dec. 1743,—S. P. G. Journal, IX, p. 254. See also a letter of the Archbishop of Canterbury to Samuel Johnson against over-sanguine accounts by young missionaries,—Lambeth Mss. 1123, March 30, 1763; and a letter from this dignitary to Mr. Caner of Boston,—*Ibid.* A copy of each of these letters is in Hawks Transcripts, G. C. From the latter the following is quoted: "Nothing should be said against the Dissenters in general, but all endeavours used to satisfy them, that we desire only to make due provisions for the Members of our own Church and have no design to invade the rights or disturb the peace of theirs. Dr. Mayhew's enormities should be set forth, not with bitterness but with mild expostulation, the Dissenters themselves should be begged to consider how much he wrongs us, the proper Questions should be put home in a serious yet gentle manner to his own Conscience. Allowances should be craved for the misinformation which the Society may have received, and the mistakes which it may have made, and the dissenters should be reminded that in one thing or another perhaps in some like things, they may have need of allowance also that mutual moderation always a christian duty is more especially needful when we are surrounded by unbelievers eager to take advantage against us all."

29 S. P. G. Letter-book, B, 13, p. 140.

30 Roger Viets to the Sec., Simsbury, June 25, 1766, S. P. G. Letter-book B, 23, p. 376.

31 Timothy Cutler to Bishop of London, July 6, 1739, Fulham Archives. See also Perry, Hist. Col., *op. cit.*, III, pp. 225–6, for a complaint of Harvard's ecclesiastical exclusiveness towards the Church of England.

low members of the Church of England be sent out from Oxford or Cambridge in England to instruct the youth att Cambridge in New England, by her *Maties Authority*, wch if it could be done" might in a few years "induce the people of N. England to conforme;"[32] or than the accusation of John Talbot that the college had "gone a great way to Poison this country with Damnable Doctrines . . . worse than Heathenism or Atheism" and recommending that some grave, wise tutor and philosopher be sent there "to teach them humanity in the first place, that in time they might be brought to Christian Principles & Practices, for at Present they are not much better than the Quakers, & in the Latter much Worse."[33] In 1727 the Society's missionaries at Boston started a controversy with the Harvard overseers which continued for four years or more and which greatly increased the bitterness towards the Episcopal party. These missionaries laid a claim to the right to sit with the overseers in their deliberations.[34] It was based (1) on their interpretation of the charter of establishment, (2) on the fact that the Church party paid its proportion of rates for Harvard's support, and (3) on the precedent that earlier Church of England clergy had been invited to sit and vote in that body, enjoying such privilege for some twenty years, although for two or three years last past the courtesy had not been extended.[35] The claim was denied by the overseers and later by the General Court of Massachusetts. Appeals were made to England but they were ineffectual. Memorials were then renewed before the overseers and the latter promptly dismissed them again, thus excluding the Church representatives from the management of Harvard College.[36] Since there were no clergy of the Church in Massachusetts at the founding of Harvard, the original charter could not have meant to include such persons in the governing board. The teaching elders of the six next adjoining towns, who were

[32] Keith to Dr. Bray, Feb. 26, 1702–03, S. P. G. Letter-book, A, 1, p. 88.

[33] Talbot to the Sec., April 7, 1704, S. P. G. Letter-book, A; 1, p. 181.

[34] Clergy of New England to the Sec., July 20, 1727, Perry, Hist. Col., *op. cit.*, III. pp. 224–26; Cutler to General Nicholson, Aug. 10, 1727, *ibid.* p. 228.

[35] Memorial of the Ministers and others of the Church of England to the Lieut. Governor and General Court July 24, 1727, S. P. G. Letter-book, B, 1, p. 205; same to Bishop of London, July 20, 1727, Fulham Archives; Cutler and Myles to the Lieut. Gov. and House of Representatives, Feb. 3, 1727–28, S. P. G. Letter-book, B, 1, p. 204; Cutler to Bishop of London, June 25, 1730, Fulham Archives.

[36] For the several steps here given see Cutler's letters to the Bishop of London, Sept. 11, and Oct. 10, 1728, and June 25, 1730, Fulham Archives; also Cutler's second Memorial to Harvard Overseers June 11, 1730, and the latter's resolution of June 17, 1730, Fulham Archives; also Cutler's letter of May 13, 1731, *ibid.*

named as members, were intended to be Independents, the orthodox ministers of that colony. But aside from this, the action of the overseers was one based on prejudice and a fear of the increase of the Church's influence. Their earlier toleration and the public tax long shared by all parties established an equity in favor of the protesting clergy. If the Bishop of London took any action on behalf of his ministers, there is no indication of it in the many papers in Fulham Archives relating to the controversy. One can feel reasonably certain that he sounded the advocates of political expediency and found inaction the safest. The S. P. G., however, in responding to appeals from Boston, concluded that "the Society cannot properly concern themselves in this affair."[37]

Opposition to the Church was also experienced at Yale, in spite of the fact that Elihu Yale and Bishop Berkeley, who were the chief benefactors of the college in the early period, were both "Gentlemen of the Church."[38] It must have given profound concern to the Independents of New England when at the Yale Commencement of 1722, Timothy Cutler, Yale's president, Daniel Brown, tutor in the college, and Samuel Johnson, the Independent pastor of Westhaven, besides three other pastors, declared themselves for the Church of England "in ye face of ye whole country."[39] The Church party appreciated the significance of the declaration and encouraged it by holding out promises of support from England.[40] From this time on Yale graduated a considerable number of professors of the Church of England, sometimes five, sometimes ten in a class.[41] All of this time the opponents of the Church, who were predominant in the Government, held control of the College and enforced a thoroughgoing sectarian attitude. Students were fined for attending the Church of England services. A fine of £11 was imposed against two sons of Mr. Punderson, an S. P. G. missionary,

---

[37] S. P. G. Journal, Nov. 15, 1728, V, p. 178.

[38] Samuel Johnson to the Society, 1754, S. P. G. Journal, XXI, pp. 376–9.

[39] S. P. G. Letter-book, A, 16, pp. 302, 298; S. P. G. Journal, IV, p. 242. Cutler became an S. P. G. missionary at Boston; see above. Johnson became missionary at Stratford and afterwards first President of Kings (Columbia) College. Brown was appointed a missionary, but died after entering on his new duties.

[40] Geo. Pigot to the Sec. Oct. 3, 1722, S. P. G. Letter-book A, 16, p. 298; Churchwardens and Vestry of Newport, R. I., to the Sec. Oct. 29, 1722, *ibid.*, p. 309; Gov. Nicholson to the Sec. Jan. 11, 1722–3, *ibid.*, p. 95. It is worth noting here that very soon after *this*, invitations to Episcopal ministers to sit with the Harvard Overseers were stopped.

[41] S. P. G. Letter-book, B, 13, p. 266; *ibid.*, 16, p. 24. By 1754 about 1-10 of the 100 students were Episcopalian, S. P. G. Journal, XII, p. 376–79.

"for non-attendance in the Hall or attending the Ch. of Eng. services the ⅜ths of the Sundays it is performed at New-haven."[42] Dereliction in the matter of religious worship was a serious offence then. It could be punished by fines or public whippings.[43] "It seems to us," said Dr. Johnson, "an insolent treatment to deny our children a publick Education unless they constantly attend their meetings when we have a Church within a few Rods of the College, especially since . . . the parents of these children do annually bear their proportion in the support of the college."[44]

The payment of rates for the support of the ministers of the Dissenters was exacted of the partisans of the Church generally in New England.[45] It was an ever-present source of irritation to them. At times resistance was attempted, but such cases were decided on partisan lines.[46] In 1748 it was said that the Church party in Boston were paying "a fifth of the poor's rates, notwithstanding the Town contains ten Presbyterian Meeting Houses, one Irish, one French, one Anabaptist, one Separatists, and one Quakers."[47] Unpopular as this must have been to the struggling Episcopal churches, it was merely the carrying out of a policy long maintained for the benefit of the Church of England at home. Moreover, the Church was taking advantage of the same privileges in colonies where the national religion was established.

One other phase of controversy in New England is to be noted. In 1761 the government of Massachusetts passed an act to incorporate certain persons by the name of the Society for propagating Christian Knowledge among the Indians of North America.[48] Representatives of the Society in Boston became suspicious that the intent of the act was "to frustrate the pious Designs of the S. P. G."[49] and sent the alarm to England. Charges were immediately prepared against this new scheme and

---

42 S. P. G. Journal, XIII, pp. 57–9.

43 A case is reported of an old man of eighty-five being whipped at the Town sign-post for leaving the Meetings of the Independents and attending the Church of England. S. P. G. Journal, XII, pp. 376–79.

44 *Ibid.*

45 Perry, Hist. Col. Epis. Ch., *op. cit.*, I, pp. 296–7, 299, 300f.

46 See the letter of Churchwardens and Vestry of New Cambridge to the Society, Perry, Hist. Col., *op. cit.*, III, p. 432.

47 A letter from Sir Harry Frankland to his Uncle, about the State of Religion at Boston, Dec. 13, 1748. *Ibid.*, p. 423.

48 Lambeth Archives, 1123, III, p. 271.

49 *Ibid.*, p. 269.

apparently presented to the Board of Trade, where the act was to be reviewed before final presentation for the action of His Majesty in Council.[50] The Committee of the Board of Trade advised the repeal of the act. "And on the 20th of May 1763 His Majesty in Council was pleased to repeal the said Act."[51] The dangerous features brought out in the objections to the new society are not warrantable in such papers as are to be found in either Lambeth or Fulham archives. It appears upon the face of the Church of England antagonism that it was prompted by a jealousy of the work of its S. P. G., and that the Church was suspicious of any and all measures that were enacted in New England.

At the beginning of their labors in New York the Church and the Society encountered some prejudice on the part of the Dutch. Albany is reported to have opposed so strongly the building of the first English church in 1716 that the workmen were committed to jail to prevent work being carried on.[52] As late as 1762, too, objection was raised to the election of a brother of the Society's missionary as an elesor on the ground of his faith, and the point was carried.[53] On the other hand, the Dutch in southern New York were tolerant and the relations between them and the English Churchmen were amicable to an unusual extent.[54] An exception to this occurred in the rule of Governor (Lord) Cornbury (1702–1709). The Governor came to New York with the usual orders from the Crown,[55] regarding the licensing of ministers and schoolmasters, and he proceeded to carry out the same to the letter. He applied his orders to the ministers and schoolmasters of the Dutch Reformed Church, although they claimed exemption on the ground of the charter

50 A draught of the objections to the act is in Fulham Archives, endorsed: "Recd from the ABp of Canterbury, 1763." It was based on a series of objections prepared by Wm. Smith of Pennsylvania, then in London, and sent to the Archbishop, Nov. 22, 1762. Lambeth Archives, 1123, III, p. 282.

51 *Ibid.*, p. 308. This interesting note is added: "No Bishop was present either at the Committee or the Council." But it is safe to say that the formal charges reached the Committee and Council in ample time, as well as personal objections from the Bishops concerned.

52 Col. John Bradstreet to the Sec. July 2, 1762, Hawks Transcripts, New York, II, p. 305. Bradstreet was in charge of the King's forces at Albany.

53 *Ibid.*

54 S. P. G. Letter-book, B, 1, p. 112.

55 "Royal Instructions given to Gov. Cornbury in 1703," copy of same in S. P. G. Journal, II, July 11, 1712; sections 60 to 65 of the same quoted in Pascoe, *op. cit.*, p. 60.

previously granted their church by William III.[56] He has been charged also with breaking up some of the Dutch schools on Long Island through his misguided zeal.[57] Ill-feeling was caused between the Dutch and the Church party for the time being as a result of Cornbury's policy. Fortunately this did not survive him, for his successors adopted a pacific attitude. But in Lord Cornbury's defense it must be said that he had the statesman's vision in respect of the need of universalizing the English language, in order to successfully unify the colonies under the British flag.[58]

Antagonism was started between the English non-conformists and the adherents of the Church of England with the enactment of Church establishment in the colony at a much earlier date.[59] But the Cornbury administration brought it into the open as it had not been before. First he was as vigorous in the matter of licenses for their representatives as he was with the Dutch. Then he encouraged the missionaries appointed to the established churches, to occupy and make use of the churches, parsonages and glebes which had heretofore been provided and occupied by the Dissenters. In Jamaica, on Long Island, a controversy of this kind arose[60] though for the first seven years the Dissenters bore their grievance with "a most laudable silence and wonderful patience."[61] During the interval between the death of the S. P. G. missionary and the arrival of his successor the Dissenters seized the parsonage and glebe and held it against all arguments and trials at Court. The controversy lasted for more than twenty years,[62] and was a source of prolonged and bitter irritation.

---

56 Provisions in the incorporation act of the Reformed Protestant Dutch Church, quoted in Dunshee, (ed. 1853) p. 57. In the same change from Dutch to English control, moreover, the Dutch had wisely preserved for themselves their full ecclesiastical and educational rights.

57 Smith, Wm., History of New York, p. 114.

58 See Cornbury's letter to this effect, Hawks Transcripts, N. Y., I, pp. 83–86; also similar suggestions from Thos. Moore in a letter to the Sec., New York, Nov. 13, 1705, S. P. G. Letter-book, A, 2, p. 122.

59 Sept. 22, 1693. Trot's Laws of the British Plantations relating to the church and clergy, religion and learning, p. 263; Col. Laws of N. Y., I, pp. 328–31.

60 In 1710. See letter of Thomas Poyer to S. P. G., Dec. 3, 1710, Hawks Transcripts, New York, I, p. 234; S. P. G. Journal, II, Jan. 19, 1710–11.

61 See quotation from a letter of Cotton Mather Oct. 14, 1706, sent to the Sec., S. P. G. Letter-book, A, 6, p. 82. One suspects that the "wonderful patience" was due somewhat to the presence of Cornbury as Governor.

62 S. P. G. Journal, V, p. 314; S. P. G. Letter-book, A, 23, p. 328; also A, 12, pp. 264, 266, 259, and A, 13, pp. 363, 439, 451. For the Society's appeal to the Queen and the resulting orders in Council, see Hawks Transcripts, New York, I, p. 296.

In April 1752, Mr. Wetmore, the S. P. G. missionary at Rye, reported: "The party disputes which have run high among us for several years, to my great grief obstruct the success . . . in my endeavours to promote a becoming zeal for piety and reformation of manners among the looser sort of my Parishoners which are too numerous."[63] Shortly afterwards he wrote again, "Factions and parties keep up but are more quiet than for some years. . . . Licentiousness and wickedness abound more than ever, occasioned by factions fanned by those sorts of teachers."[64] Writing about this time from New York city a group of the Society's clergy expressed the fear that without good governors "the Church must sink in these countries (and indeed the State too) notwithstanding our utmost efforts amid such active and indefatigable Enemies as we are surrounded with."[65] The tone of these quotations immediately preceding needs probably to be discounted in part, yet it indicates thus early the ushering in of the spirit of revolution. In a more practical way the opposition to the Church of England in New York province was shown in the active antagonism to the founding of King's College on a semi-Episcopalian basis.[66] At the first suspicion of such a possibility the enemies of the Church began a violent campaign of writing to defeat the design. Dr. Johnson, the first president, described the situation to the Archbishop of Canterbury in these words:

"Among the pernicious Books the *Independent Whigg* grows much in vogue, & a notable sett of Young Gentlemen of Figure in New York have of late sett up for writers in that way in a weekly paper called the *Independent Reflector*. Several worthy Gentlemen of the Church in that Province have of late been embarked in a Design of Erecting a College as a Seminary of the Church, tho' with a free & generous Toleration for other Denominations. Upon which these Reflectors have been indefatigable in their paper & by all possible means both private & public endeavoring to spirit up the people against us & to wrest it out of the Church's Hands & make it a sort of free thinking or latitudinarian Seminary, as your Grace will see by several of these papers Mr. Smith will lay before you.

We have several of us been writing in the Churche's Defence against them,

---

63 Hawks Transcripts, New York, II, p. 242.

64 *Ibid.*, Oct. 2, 1752.

65 Letter signed by Samuel Johnson and four other missionaries, Jan. 29, 1755, Hawks Transcripts, New York, II, p. 252.

66 The president was to be of the Church of England and the Episcopal prayers were to be used in its services.

& endeavoring not without some success to defeat their pernicious Schemes."[67]

Even after the Charter had been granted in 1754 the "clamor raised against it by their inveterate enemies" so far prevailed that it was impossible to procure from the Assembly more than half of the funds raised by lotteries for building the College.[68] Available documents bearing on this struggle indicate that a spirit of toleration prevailed on the part of the Church that was admirable under the circumstances, and furthermore that the opposing of the charter was quite as political in its nature as it was religious.[69] The Vestry of Trinity Church in a letter to the Society claimed that the Episcopal party "never insisted on any condition, till we found some Persons labouring to exclude all systems of Religion out of the Constitution of the College."[70] When the Church did interpose for a religious foundation, it "had the countenance of many good men of all Denominations, and in particular the Ministers of the Foreign Protestant Churches" in the city, who acquiesced, too, in serving as Governors of the College.[71] "We can with a good Conscience Declare" continued the Vestry, "that we are so far from the Bigotry & Narrowness of Spirit, they have of late been pleased to charge us with, that we would not were it in our Power lay the least Restraint on any Man's Conscience, and should heartily rejoyce to continue in Brotherly Love & Charity with all our Protestant Brethren."[72]

---

67 Letter of June 25, 1753, Lambeth Archives, 1123, I, p. 64. See also the following from the missionary of Rye (Mr. Wetmore) Oct. 9, 1753:
"The affair of erecting a College in that province has given occasion to a set of young lawyers to publish the doctrines of the Independent Whig, & Tindal's Rights &c. with the design to promote Republican Principles of Govmt & a Contempt of the National Constitution of the Ch., to prevent if possible, the establishment of the College, upon a Foundation, that may give a Prospect of promoting religion in the way of the National Ch. but it is hoped the Endeavours used to antidote the malignity of their writings will have a good effect." S. P. G. Journal, XII, pp. 320–21. The Church party was strong enough to get the charter passed in Council by a majority of two-thirds, and to secure its approval by the Assembly. *Ibid.*, XII, pp. 387–88.

68 S. P. G. Journal, XII, pp. 105–6; *Ibid.*, XIV, pp. 68, 71; S. P. G. Letter-book, B, 3, p. 315.

69 The opponents on religious grounds were the two chief dissenting sects, Presbyterians and Independents. And closely associated with them were a group of political opponents. The leader of these was one William Smith, a lawyer, who with others of his profession, especially Livingstone and Scott, showed bitter hatred for the Church and College and were believed to be the chief writers of the hostile papers mentioned above. In his History of New York, which appeared in the midst of the controversy, Smith included all the newspaper complaints against the Society and missionaries. These were the occasion of distrust and enmity for long years, and may have suggested the line of attack which Mayhew took up in Massachusetts shortly thereafter. See letter from President Johnson to Archbishop, King's College, March 20, 1759, Lambeth Archives, 1123, II, p. 130; also Samuel Auchmuty to the Sec., Hawks Transcripts, New York, II, p. 463.

70 S. P. G. Letter-book, B, 3, p. 315.

71 *Ibid.*

72 *Ibid.*

The effect of this warfare began to show itself in England as enemies of the colonies established the connections with the Church's foes at home. Such an object was doubtless studiously planned, in order that the Government might realize to what extent the dominance of the Episcopal cause would prove politically unwise. Charges made on the one side were assiduously made known on the other, and defences of the Church and Society were frequently made necessary. The following extracts are taken from one of these defences written by one of the most reliable pens of that period:

"It is indeed my Lord, a thing of most melancholy consideration that by such unaccountable methods our Adversaries should have procured such a *formidable* multitude at home to be disaffected to the Society, and that any should treat it with such insolence as to use even *threatening intimations* when at the same time there never was the least ground for that which it seems is their grand complaint viz., that the Society have *unwarrantably changed their object from the propagating of Christianity and Protestantism to the propagation of one form of it in opposition to other Protestants.* This my Lord I believe never was designed nor attempted by the Society to this day. There have been indeed a multitude of Proselytes to the Church especially in New England, but this has not been an originally designed but an accidental effect. No my Lord the Fact has been plainly this, of the course of which I have been a Witness almost 40 years.

"There have been considerable numbers of honest conscientious English People of the Church who have settled in many of the principal Country Towns in New England as well as other parts of America. Some of these have been sensible men, &, as is natural to suppose they have pleaded the cause of their Church with their Dissenting Neighbours, till they have prevailed to proselyte some Dissenters to joyn with them, & being uneasy with the dissenting way, which was then generally very poor, & to them very uncouth, they at length being impatient for the Service of the Church, have joyned in petitioning the Society for Ministers, which after long solicitation they obtained. The consequence of which hath been that some Dissenters from curiousity, & others invited by their Neighbors have been led to frequent the service of the Church which upon experience they have admired, & by degrees endeavoured to propagate. Thus it was at Stratford, & at length it propagated to several Neighboring Towns: 'till from about 80 Families with whom I began, it propagated in 10 or 12 years to several Congregations; for whom, as the burthen grew too great for me I procured them Ministers, till at length when I left that Province there were 25 small Churches & 10 or 11 Ministers. In all which time, I never once tryed to proselyte Dissenters, nor do I believe any of the other Ministers did. We never concerned ourselves with them 'till they came to us, and when they did we could do no less than give them the best instructions and assistance we could in making a right judgement for themselves. And so far were we from promoting or taking advantage of any quarrels that happened among themselves that in many instances we obliged them to accommodate matters amicably with their former Brethren, or at least to do all they could towards an accommodation before we could receive them to our communion.

"Such my Lord hath been the method of our procedure when at the same time I all along maintained a very friendly correspondence with the chief men among them & endeavoured to do them all the good Office I could, & in particular, I procured a noble donation from Bp. Berkeley for their College in Land and Books to the value of much more than £1000 Sterling. But behold my Lord the gratitude of these men! At the same time that I was doing them these good offices, they were contriving & did send along a letter to the Bp. of London of complaint against us, full of gross untruths and misrepresentations, with a view to get all the Church people in N. England deprived of their Ministers, & then of their subsistence. This Letter his Ldship referred to the Society & I believe your Grace may find it among the Society's Papers of 1735. In reply to which the Society were so candid as to give them free liberty and to direct them to produce Evidence to make good their complaints against us which they endeavoured to do, but could make nothing of it, & I believe never replied at least we never heard any more of it.

"Amazing my Lord it is, that these people both at home & abroad cannot be content not only with the most indulgent Toleration by Law, but in many instances with the most kind treatment from the Church; but by how much the better they are treated, by so much the more indefatigably they are bent & engaged perfas & nefas, joyning and making interest with even the enemies of Christianity itself to undermine her, & if possible to raze her even to the foundation! And truly by their *threatening insinuations* it should seem as tho' they apprehended they are going near to effect it. *How much better our temper here towards them is than theirs towards us, may be obviously seen from this, that our College provides that their Children belonging to it have free liberty to go to their own Meetings where as in Connecticut their College will not admit that the Children of the Church belonging to it go to their own Church but punish them if they presume to do it.*"[73]

For years after attacks continued against the Society and its representatives some of which had foundation,[74] but much of which was based on prejudices and a growing tendency to place the Church with the Crown and the Government as allied enemies. Between 1765 and 1775 the conditions were extremely distressing to the S. P. G. ministers in New York,[75] and the British Government added to the aggravation by appointing to provincial offices some of their most avowed enemies.[76]

The Presbyterians had long been trying to procure a Charter of Incorporation for their Church. In 1766 they took up the matter with renewed activity. Having failed to effect anything through the governors,[77] they carried their petition to the King[78]

---

[73] Dr. Johnson to Archbishop of Canterbury, Kings College, March 20, 1759, Lambeth Archives, 1123, II, p. 130 ff. Italics not in original.

[74] For instance, not a few among the S. P. G. missionaries and schoolmasters were unworthy and subject to severe criticism. The Society attempted constantly to avoid employing such persons. It was sincerely earnest in this and cannot be justly held responsible for the cases of failure. Among so many servants of the Society at such remote distances, some might naturally be expected to fail. See for example, letter of John Bartow, West Chester, Oct. 15, 1765, Fulham Archives; also in Hawks Transcripts, N. Y. II, p. 335.

[75] Hawks Transcripts, New York, II, pp. 467, 471, 489, 476, 483, 481, 505. One of these (471) complains of an attack traducing the whole Bench of Bishops, execrating the Church and clergy and inflaming the people against Episcopacy, and adds: "It is not only the Church that they want to have demolished."

[76] Smith was made one of His Majesty's Council in New York. His appointment was vigorously protested by the President of Kings College, and by the Rector of Trinity Church. See Hawks Transcripts, New York, II, pp. 461, 435, 463.

[77] Samuel Auchmuty to Sec. Mar. 29, 1766, Hawks Transcripts, New York, II, p. 362.

[78] *Ibid.*, p. 372.

and sought to bring pressure on both King and Parliament through the Church of Scotland.[79] Undismayed by the intense opposition against themselves, the Church of England leaders took prompt steps to defeat the plan.[80] Charging the petitioners with being enemies to monarchy, only seeking favorable opportunity to show themselves such, they unfortunately evinced a retaliatory and sectarian spirit as strong as that of their opponents,[81]—a spirit, in fact, that was hardly in keeping with the defense of Dr. Johnson seven years before.

The work of the S. P. G. in New Jersey and Pennsylvania was continually opposed by the Quakers and the Society, in turn, kept up an uncompromising attitude toward them. Open hostility and contention were little resorted to, but the more favored position and power of the Quakers, especially in Pennsylvania,[82] proved a factor against which it was difficult to make headway. A large proportion of the tracts sent from London were against Quakerism, and this fact may serve to explain why the Quakers opposed the Church adherents more bitterly than any other sect. The Quakers defended themselves in kind and with a vigor, too, that was an evident annoyance to the missionaries of the S. P. G.[83]

With the influx of emigrants from various countries of Europe these colonies became peopled with a swarm of sectaries.[84]

---

79 *Ibid.* p. 362.

80 See Auchmuty's protest against the Charter in a letter to the Bishop of London, March 28, 1766, Fulham Archives; also copied in Hawks Transcripts, New York, II, p. 070 1. That the Church had opposed earlier attempts is shown by the following: "Ordered the Church Wardens pay to the Clerk of the Council the Sum of two pounds one Shilling being for fees accrued in opposing the Incorporation of the Presbyterian Meeting House in this City." Trinity Vestry Minutes, I, p. 125.

81 Samuel Auchmuty to the Sec., March 29, 1766, Hawks Transcripts, New York, II, pp. 362–3; same to Bishop of London, March 28, 1766, Fulham Archives; also in Hawks Transcripts, *op. cit.*, pp. 370–1. Auchmuty objected to a move that would put the Presbyterians on a par with the Church of England, or that would put the Church in danger in the province. Nor could he acquiesce in it while a Bishop was denied his own people.

82 This may have been due, in part, to the earlier lack of other forms of worship. See letter of Col. Quarry and others to Gov. Nicholson, Jan. 18, 1696–7, Perry, Hist. Col., *op. cit.*, II, p. 5.

83 "The most impious & atheistical books & Tenets are cunningly & privately as well as impudently & publicly spread abroad to countenance the Quakers." S. P. G. missionary at Burlington to Gov. Nicholson, May 11, 1714, S. P. G. Letter-book, A, 9, p. 203. Note also the following:

"I also herewith presume to send you a Philadelphia Almanac which if you please to peruse the same you will see what is doing here to ridicule what the noble Society are propagating. And in order to do such things the Quakers out of their public Stock have purchased a printing press and a Dutchman out of Holland to print such things, as their Monthly Meetings at Philadelphia shall allow; and they being the greatest body of people they are encouraged such like Alamanacks, and ours are thereby discouraged." Wm. Bradford to the Sec. Dec. 12, 1706, *ibid.*, p. 57.

84 Pennsylvania so indulged and favored all sectaries that it was probably more attractive than any other colony to the foreigner of the 18th century. Interesting evidences of this are to be found in Weber, The Charity School Movement in Colonial Pennsylvania, pp. 7–8.

Churchmen, German Lutherans, Calvinists, Mennonites, Moravians, New Born, Dunkards, Presbyterians, Anabaptists, Seceeders, New Lights, Covenanters, Mountain Men, Brownists, Independents, Papists, Quakers, Jews, all vied with each other.[85] It is no wonder that the relatively small number belonging to the national Church had to maintain their establishments under heavy odds.[86] The Church, upon the whole, gradually gained ground throughout the provinces. While literature was assiduously distributed against Quakerism and other sectarian doctrines, an attempt was made to deal with the sectaries themselves in moderation and charity. As a result, both German Lutherans and Dutch Calvinists were made friends to the point of close coöperation.[87] The English speaking sects were also less intolerant, and, in the absence of their own churches, frequented the services of the Church of England.[88]

When at about the middle of the century the dissenting movement in New Jersey and Pennsylvania began to show marked growth, open opposition was engendered between them and the friends of the Church. The latter actively opposed the founding of the College of New Jersey. The contention began at the first proposal for a charter. Appeals were sent to the Society and the Bishop of London in the hope of defeating the scheme.[89] Later the missionaries charged that the chief reason for fixing the College at Princeton was "that their conduct might be unobserved and their pupils uninfluenced by persons of other persuasions"[90]; and it was felt, they reported, that a missionary was needed, near by, to "gain over some of the pupils."[91] Through such an attitude it was impossible for the Society to avoid the suspicion of sectarian prejudice, and, in

---

85 This diversity of sects prevailed in the individual counties as well as in the province as a whole. See Perry, Hist. Col., *op. cit.*, pp. 366–7.

86 The following shows the disproportionate influence of the Episcopalians in a political way:

"At the last Election for the county to choose Assemblymen, Sheriff, Coroner, Commissioners, Assessors, &c., 5000 Freeholders voted, and yet not a single member of the Church was elected into any of these offices." From a missionary to the Sec., *Ibid.*

87 Proposals, in fact, for a union with the Church of England were made by both. *Ibid.*, p. 367.

88 Classified Digest, *op. cit.*, pp. 54–5; S. P. G. Journal, VI, p. 53, and VII., p. 296.

89 James Wetmore to Bishop of London, March 26, 1747, S. P. G. Letter-book, B, 15, p. 78; Samuel Johnson to same, Apr. 28, 1747, *Ibid.*, p. 51; Wm. Skinner to Society, Apr. 21, 1747, *Ibid.*, 16, p. 91.

90 Memorial of missionaries to Society, Feb. 6, 1758–59, S. P. G. Journal, XIV., pp. 190–2.

91 *Ibid.*

view of the efforts in behalf of Kings College, so soon thereafter, it is hard for the Church partisans to justify their position.

Yet, as a partial offset, the opposition to the Episcopalian influence at the College and Academy of Philadelphia may be cited. This was shared by both Quakers and Dissenters.[92] An attack was made on the means of support of these institutions. A large part of the support was obtained through lotteries, "uprightly managed by people of the best credit."[93] Lotteries had heretofore been resorted to for the purposes of fortifying the city and finishing the Episcopal Church, but they came to be used, almost solely, for acquiring funds for the College and Academy.[94] In 1759, during the absence of Provost Smith in London, measures were taken to suppress "Lotteries and Plays" by act of the Assembly.[95] The interpretation of the move as one intended to overthrow Smith and the Church interest was without doubt correct. The Presbyterian faction was fast increasing its hold on the College.[96] The Quakers had a peculiar dislike of Smith for pamphlets written, supposedly by him, and for his activity in helping to set up schools among the Germans to the detriment of Quaker influence.[97] They also opposed his open avowal of vigorous measures against the depredations of French and Indians on the frontier.[98] The Provost met this opposition in a militant spirit[99] and his enemies watched for an opportunity to humble him. This came when Smith caused the publication of an address criticising the Assembly.[100] He was committed to jail until he should make satisfaction.[101] The pro-

92 Lambeth Archives, 1123, II, p. 175, *ibid.*, III, p. 320.

93 *Ibid.*, II, p. 136.

94 *Ibid.*

95 *Ibid.*

96 *Ibid.*, III, p. 320.

97 *Ibid.*, II, p. 112. Smith was instrumental in having established a society in London for work among the Germans in Pennsylvania. It was organized in London about 1754, and was known as the Society for the Propagation of Christian Knowledge among the Germans in Pennsylvania. Smith and Benjamin Franklin were among the trustees appointed in the colony. One of the chief objects was to set up English schools among the Germans. The movement lasted about ten years. *Ibid.*, I, pp. 73, 76, 79, 80; II, pp. 90–93, 105, 125. For an excellent account of this work see Weber, *op. cit.*

98 Lambeth Archives, 1123, II, p. 112 f.

99 Reports from missionaries charged Smith with being too contentious, with "mixing politics with their real business and reviling those of their brethren who do not approve of this—especially Mr. Wm. Smith." Letter of Rev. Jenney to the Archbishop of Canterbury, *ibid.*, p. 124; see also letters of Archbishop, *ibid.*, fol. 128 and fol. 143; also fol. 149.

100 No action was taken against two other papers which had printed the same. *Ibid.*, p. 112 f.

101 *Ibid.*, pp. 112 and 113, the latter being "A brief Narrative of the case of Rev. Mr. Smith."

ceeding appeared so partial that he preferred to go to jail rather than make acknowledgment. Subsequently he carried an appeal to England,[102] and was acquitted of any offence.[103] It was while Smith was in London that the act against lotteries was introduced.

In the South the Society had almost a clear field, and the Church had more adherents in proportion to population than any other religious body. Sect rivalry caused the spread of books and tracts as elsewhere and there were occasional personal grudges against the Society.[104] But rivalry seldom developed contentious factions.

The great religious awakening that was at its height about the middle of the eighteenth century spread all over the colonies and was a "disturbing agitation" to the Church and missionaries everywhere. It originated in Great Britain and resulted in the organization of the Methodist societies which laid the foundation of the Methodist Episcopal Church. The fervor of the followers of the new religion was carried to America by some of its leading exponents.[105] Among them George Whitefield was the most active and a peculiar source of annoyance to the Episcopalians. Whitefield was himself a Church of England communicant but had grown impatient of much that his church held dear. He was a powerful preacher and went up and down the colonies on several occasions, creating the greatest religious enthusiasm wherever he went, from Boston to Georgia. He soon broke with the ministers of the Church who looked upon him as a dangerous fanatic, and was obliged to resort to the churches of the Dissenters or to private houses.[106] Ere long he began attacks on the Church, more especially on some of its primates at home.[107] He was further charged with printing libels in the newspapers against such Church publications as "The Whole Duty of Man" and advising people to burn them.[108] The Society was attacked by Whitefield who also announced, in his letters to the Archbishop of Canterbury and Bishop of London,

102 *Ibid.*, fols. 125, 140, 139.

103 *Ibid.*, fol. 137.

104 S. P. G. Letter-book, A, 10, p. 94; B, 5, p. 236.

105 Between 1735 and 1770.

106 Commissary Garden to Bp. of London, Charleston, Apr. 24, 1740—Fulham Archives.

107 *Ibid.*

108 S. P. G. Letter-book, B, 7 p. 195: B, 9, p. 111.

that the work of the S. P. G. was much overdrawn in the reports which were periodically sent over. The records in the Archives of the S. P. G. and Fulham Palace indicate very clearly the extent of the irritation which the progress and success of the Whitefield movement caused the Church party. To them it was a "terrible State of affairs."[109] From every quarter discouraging accounts were sent to England concerning the "unnatural condition caused by Whitefield." "A distant person," said one letter, "can hardly conceive the confusions that have attended this visit, the Discord among the People & among the Teachers (ministers) of this Town, & the sad intermission of business." "The longer he tarries, the more he seems to gain ground upon inconsiderate People, & to what condition he will bring us at last times only will shew."[110] The above serves to illustrate the feeling that was general among the Episcopalians. The usual pamphlet opposition was prepared in England and sent over by the S. P. G. in response to the frequent request for "proper antidotes."[111] The Commissary of South Carolina, in 1742, instituted proceedings against Whitefield and "suspended him according to the 38th Cannon of the Church."[112] But for years thereafter the movement started by this man continued and was looked upon by the missionaries as a great drawback to the progress of the Church of England.[113]

Another and one of the most serious obstacles the Society had to contend with is yet to be mentioned. The work of the Church was carried on at a very great disadvantage during the entire colonial period. This was because of the failure to get a resident American bishop appointed. The laws of the Church required that every minister must be regularly ordained by the bishop of the diocese who, in the case of America, was the Bishop of London. Therefore no colonial could become a minister of the Church without going to England for the ceremony of ordina-

109 S. P. G. Journal, IX, p. 29.

110 Quoted from a New England letter in a report to the Archbishop of Canterbury by the Sec., Jan. 18, 1754–5. Lambeth Archives, 1123, II, p. 89. See also Perry, Hist. Col. *op. cit.*, III, p. 394; Rev. A. Cummings, to Bishop of London, Aug 29, 1740, Fulham Archives; Rev. A. Garden to the same, Apr. 24, 1740, *ibid.;* S. P. G. Journal, VIII, p. 314, IX, p. 32. The extreme to which religious enthusiasm went is described in a letter to the Sec. from Lancaster, Pa., Dec. 17, 1770, Perry, *op. cit.*, II., pp. 448-9.

111 S. P. G. Journal, VIII, pp. 113, 232, 288; IX, pp. 32, 48, 141, 128, 107, 203; S. P. G. Letter-book, B, 9, pp. 6, 62; B, 7, pt. II, p. 113; B, 10, pp. 4, 15, 138; B, 11, p. 134; B, 13, pp. 61, 92.

112 S. P. G. Journal, IX, p. 48; also S. P. G. Letter-book, B, 10, p. 138.

113 Perry, Hist. Col., *op. cit.*, II, pp. 448–9.

tion. To do this involved a burdensome expense,[114] besides the many dangers consequent on sea voyages at that time.[115] When, after a few years, missionaries were recruited from conforming Dissenters and other candidates in the colonies, the need of a colonial bishop became all the more urgent. Aside from these difficulties the whole organization of the Church was such as to call for a resident primate of this kind. With the bishop on the other side of the Atlantic, the very soul of Episcopalianism was lacking. Of all the appeals sent from America to the Mother-Church, none was more emphasized or more frequently made than this. Lay members as well as the ecclesiastics urged it on every occasion.[116] That the heads of the Church and the Society were not responsible for the delay and failure is manifest from the fact that they seized every opportunity of pressing the matter, either formally or through individuals, as circumstances rendered advisable. In 1704 the Society reported that "earnest addresses" had been received "from divers parts of the Continent, and Islands adjacent, for a Suffragen to visit the several Churches."[117] Steps were taken to put the matter before the proper officers of the Crown[118] and the Queen herself.[119] The matter was entrusted to Archbishop Tenison as President of the S. P. G. He submitted to the Queen a plan for the maintaining a suffragan bishop, rather than an absolute bishop, in the colonies.[120] The Society became so hopeful of success in this project that it purchased a house for a bishop's residence at Burlington, New Jersey.[121] The object seemed about to be attained, when the death of Queen Anne put an end to it. With the successive Georges the scheme could never gain the same

---

114 The expense averaged £100 or more in colonial days. Classified Digest, *op. cit.*, p. 84.

115 Several of the Society's representatives were shipwrecked and others were made prisoners by the French vessels. See Lambeth Archives, 1123, II, Oct. 25, 1754; also Hawks Transcripts, New York, II, p. 339.

116 Hawks Transcripts, G. C., Nov. 2, 1705, and Apr. 28, 1709; S. P. G. Letter-book, A, 11, p. 335, 12, pp. 178–9: Hawks Transcripts, N. Y., I., p. 59; II, pp. 224, 254, 399, 400, 409, 445–6, 480, 456–7, 567; Lambeth Archives, 1123, II, Oct. 25, 1754, Sept. 27, 1750; S. P. G. Journal, II, p. 38; Perry, Hist. Col., *op. cit.*, II, pp. 405–6.

117 Annual Report, 1704, p. 2.

118 S. P. G. Journal, I, Nov. 17, and Dec. 15, 1704.

119 *Ibid.*, Aug. 15 and Sept. 19, 1707.

120 Such a proposal was probably outlined by the Bishop of London and tendered the Archbishop. See, "Bishop of London's Paper abt a Suffragan for the Plantations in America, Dec. 1707," Lambeth Archives, 711, fol. 18; also in Hawk's Transcripts, G. C.

121 S. P. G. Journal, I, Feb. 10, 1710; June 22, 1711; May 23, 1712; Feb. 6, and Apr. 10, 1713.

momentum. Plans were continued with much vigor, however, and a fund for the support of four bishops throughout the Plantations was inaugurated.[122]

The thought of an Episcopal bishop of any kind was most distasteful to non-conforming sectaries in America. To them it could mean nothing less than Episcopacy as powerful as in England, and such power, it was declared, "would be inconsistent with the Privileges of the People in those Parts."[123] Much of the opposition already noted in the Plantations was due more to this ever-present suspicion than to any thing else. Dreading the possibility, opponents were organized in England to watch and effectually block all steps taken in that direction.[124] With the hope of removing apprehensions that the existence of other religious communities would be imperilled, the following plan was drawn up by Bishop Butler in 1750 setting forth the proposals of the New England Clergy:—

"1. That no coercive power is desired over the laity in any case, but only a power to regulate the behaviour of the clergy who are in Episcopal Orders, and to correct and punish them according to the laws of the Church of England, in case of misbehaviour or neglect of duty, with such power as the commissaries abroad have exercised.

"2. That nothing is desired for such bishops that may in the least interfere with the dignity, or authority, or interest of the Governor, or any other officer of State. Probates of wills, licenses for marriages, etc. to be left in the hands where they are; and no share in the temporal government is desired for bishops.

"3. The maintenance of such bishops not to be at the charge of the colonies.

"4. No bishops are intended to be settled in places where the government is left in the hands of Dissenters, as in New England, etc., but authority to be given only to ordain clergy for such Church of England congregations as are among them, and to inspect into the manners and behaviour of the said clergy, and to confirm the members thereof."[125]

---

122 Two for the continent and two for the Islands. See Hawks Transcripts, G. C., June 3, 1715. See also, "Preamble to the subscription roll for the maintenance of Bishops in America." *Ibid.*

123 Letter to Bp. of London, June 12, 1749, Fulham Archives; see also Lambeth Archives, 1123, II, fol. 121.

124 Note the following illustration of this: "It was reported & Generally believed, that there was a design on foot to erect 2 New Bishopricks in the West Indies, this the Deputies thought & have since been well assured would be very disagreeable to many of our friends in those parts & highly prejudicial to the interest of Several of the Colonies, they therefore appointed 2 of their body to wait on some of his Majesties principle Servants & to acquaint them with their sentiments on this subject which was accordingly done & the Persons deputed, were very civilly received, & whatever the event may be, the part that the deputation has acted, has been so kindly taken abroad, that the house of representatives of the Province of Massachusetts Bay, have returned them their thanks in a Message signed by their Speaker." (1749) Extract from a "Short account of some Proceedings of the Deputies & Committee, appointed to take Care of the Civil affairs of the Dissenters," printed in 1767. Hawks Transcripts, G. C.

125 From Perry, Hist. Col. Epis. Ch., *op. cit.*, I, p. 408. The following, too, from Samuel Johnson to the Archbishop of Canterbury, March 20, 1759, is representative of the attitude of the Church in the middle colonies on this question:

"And now my Lord as to the business of Episcopacy in these Plantations. We never pretended to desire any in these Plantations. We never pretended to desire

Proposals of this kind, however, as well as the reasonings that accompany them were powerless to stem the tide of prejudice.[126] As early as 1750 the hopelessness of the cause was apparent to the S. P. G. The Secretary sent to America the following discouraging admission: "I write with freedom & in Confidence to you. The Bishop of London doth his best, & has not yet quite given over his Endeavours to obtain a Bishop for America, but some of the great men are so much against it and have given the Dissenters such assurances, that it will not be obtain'd, that I have little or no Hopes of seeing one."[127] Fruitless attempts were again made under George III. Earnest and continual endeavors were used with his successive ministers and ministries, "but without obtaining more than promises to consider and confer about the matter; which promises have never been fulfilled."[128] After the Stamp Act of 1765, in truth, there was altogether too much at stake for the English Government to jeopardize the hope of reconciliation by espousing a religious issue of whatever nature.

The controversies indicated in the preceding pages make up a record of trials and hindrances that proved to be a heavy handicap. The S. P. G. was carrying on the work of the National Church which was so thoroughly established and so powerfully dominant in England. Yet it had, nevertheless, to proceed in the face of obstacles that were doubtless greater than those encountered by any other colonial religious body in that century. In spite of it there is no doubt that the Society made commendable progress. There is no doubt, either, that the National

any Episcopate that should have any jurisdiction over them, or indeed any concern with them: so that they never, had any reason to have the least apprehension, much less such *terrible* apprehensions from it. All that ever we aimed at was no more than just what your Grace intimates—and when they enjoy without molestation their Presbytery in the full vigour of its Discipline, is it not a cruel thing that they should be so bitterly against the Churches enjoying her own form of Government and Discipline for want of which she suffers extremely, & many valuable Lives have been thrown away? And is she not reduced to a miserable pass indeed, that she cannot provide for her children abroad here, without their consent for it? We should be entirely contented if we were only upon an equal foot with them; but for that which is the established Church of our Nation, to be in these Colonies in a state that is so much inferiour to them is very hard indeed & what as your Grace justly observes they would think utterly intolerable, were it their own case; were they for instance obliged to send their Candidates 1,000d Leagues for Ordination!" Lambeth Archives, 1123, II, fol. 130 ff.

126 A General Congress of Presbyterian, Independent and Congregational ministers was reported to have been held at New Haven in 1767, having for its purpose the opposing an American Episcopacy and the preventing the growth of the Church of England. Hawks Transcripts, N. Y., II, p. 435.

127 Sec. to Dr. Miller of Braintree, Mar. 2, 1752, S. P. G. Letter-book, B, 18, p. 201; also the same to Mr. Garden, Charleston, July 21, 1750, *ibid*, p. 226.

128 Hawkins, Hist. of the S. P. G., p. 393, quoted in Classified Digest, *op. cit.*, p 748.

Church could not have maintained itself without the help of the Society. That a narrow sectarian spirit stood out in the acts of its members, the writer is convinced. He believes, however, that a like spirit was no more unusual in the various sects with whom difficulties arose. The S. P. G. entered the colonial field to minister to the communicants of the Church and to welcome into the Church any non-conforming person who might be brought to a different viewpoint by the reasonings of religious literature.[129] It did not stand at all for any militant form of proselyting. Such a policy had never been favored by the Church. At times, though, it did persist in acts of intolerance which were aroused by its own prejudices towards the spread of dissenting movements. Further, the S. P. G. came to America to minister to the needs of the natives and slaves and persistently labored in this field against great discouragements. And finally it came designing, in all feasible ways, to offer religious education according to National Church doctrine and custom.

---

129 The thousands of books and tracts were only *indirectly* of a controversial nature. They were aimed largely to establish a chain of logical reasons for defending the doctrines of their faith and for convincing Dissenters of the errors of doctrines in disagreement. In 1726, the Society resolved that they "do not send books of controversy abroad." S. P. G. Journal, V, p. 104.

CHAPTER IV

THE SOCIETY'S REGULATIONS CONCERNING SCHOOLMASTERS

The first steps taken by the S. P. G. for the beginning of formal instruction in the colonies have been already indicated.[1] Though the members recorded themselves as favoring the employment of the widows of clergymen in such "Charity Schools" as they purposed establishing in the Plantations, according to all available records, no further action was ever taken on that proposition. In May 1704 Mr. John Club, being ready to go as "poor Schoolmaster" for America,[2] was voted £5 assistance. Few of the Society's schoolmasters, however, were recruited directly in England. Between 1704 and 1731 only nineteen applications for such positions were filed with the Society by residents of England, and of these there are no records to show that more than nine of them were ever sent over.[3] If similar applications were made after 1731 there are no evidences of the same now in the S. P. G. Archives.[4] There were a good many men in the colonies willing to undertake the work of instruction for the assurance of the Society's assistance. The requests sent by the different communities for some form of instruction frequently, indeed usually, included a specific schoolmaster for whom a bounty was desired. The S. P. G. took formal action in this matter very soon after the receipt of some of the earliest peti-

---

[1] See p. 32. The first step of appointing a catechist will be taken up under Catechetical schools for Negro and Indian slaves.

[2] S. P. G. Journal, I, pp. 152, 163.

[3] For applications of those sent over see S. P. G. Journal I, pp. 152, (31), (285); II, pp. 94, 356; III, p. 364; IV, p. 154; V, pp. 20, 144; S. P. G. Letter-book, A, 14, p. 41. For applications of those not recorded as being employed, see, S. P. G. Journal, I, pp. (21), (26), (30), (304); II, p. 61; V, p. 299; S. P. G. Letter-book, A, 4, pp. 83, 95, 104; A,7,p. 76; A, 15, p. 14.

[4] This is possibly explained in part by the rule of the Society, adopted in 1712, that no schoolmaster should be sent out unless ordained deacon, when he was to have a salary not under £30. See Journal, II, p. 166; also, Regulation VIII, of the Collection of Papers appended to the Report of 1715. But as a matter of fact schoolmasters in deacon's orders were not sent out, save in very few cases.

tions.[5] In 1707, the Standing Committee reported, "that they had further agreed to move the Society to consider whether the Schoolmasters that are already settled in the chief Towns or Seats in the English Governments or the Continent of N. America may not be employed & retained by the Society . . . with some small salary to encourage the instruction of youth in the principles of the Christian Religion according to the Church of England; agreed that it be referred to the Committee to enquire into the number of Schoolmasters their names, Conditions, & Places of abode and report the same."[6] The policy thus suggested became a regular one. Either by means of gratuities on specific occasions or by means of annual salaries, the Society recruited most of its scholastic agents from the Plantations. But in doing so they were scrupulous to put no schoolmaster on an annual salary who did not conform to the Church of England and they extended very few gratuities to those who did not.[7] When the missionaries began to be recruited in considerable numbers from the colonies, as they did from about 1740, proposals were sent to England to employ the prospective candidates for orders in the service of the Society.[8] This was to be an encouragement to them, during the interval between graduation from college and final ordination as missionaries. The plan was adopted, it being, "Agreed that in appointing Catechists & Schoolmasters, a principal regard ought to be had to such persons as are already in Holy Orders, or intend to offer themselves for it."[9] Thereafter such candidates were assured of finding a temporary place till some vacant mission offered. Usually they were made catechists rather than schoolmasters where that was possible. The former position was more in line with the ecclesiastical functions of a missionary. It is unfortunate that the plan did not furnish enough teachers to equip the Society's schools generally from that time on. Where it could be carried out, it insured a higher type of schoolmaster

5 See petition of Col. Caleb Heathcote to Bishop of London, N. Y. Oct. 23, 1704, S. P. G. Letter-book, A, 2, p. 37; ditto from Wm. Huddleston to Rev. J. Postelthwaite, Master of St. Paul's Free School, N. Y. Oct. 9 & Dec. 2, 1706, *ibid.*, A, 3, pp. 8, 18.

6 S. P. G. Journal, I, (69).

7 For the Society's objection to maintaining any but their own orthodox ministers and schoolmasters, see S. P. G. Journal, VI, p. 232; Lambeth Archives, 1123, II, fol. 95.

8 Samuel Johnson to Sec. Nov. 10, 1740, S. P. G. Letter-book, B, 7, part 2, p. 31.

9 S. P. G. Journal, IX, p. 146, Apr. 15, 1743; see also S. P. G. Letter-book, B, 10, pp. 188, 191, 197.

than most of the other colonial schools were able to secure,—that is, one possessing college training.

The salaries of the schoolmasters varied. Usually they were £10 or £15 or £20 sterling. These allowances were worth from about one and one-half to two and one-half times as much in colonial currency in times of peace, and, in war time, frequently four times as much.[10] In 1707 Col. Caleb Heathcote, one of the Society's correspondents in New York and a leading figure in that colony,[11] proposed that the salary be henceforth fixed at £3 or £4 sterling in order to "enable an abundance of Places to have Schoolmasters" with the assistance of the Society's funds. Four pounds, at least, he felt to be sufficient encouragement, "*besides what the People in the respective places are able to give.*"[12] The Standing Committee favored the proposal to such an extent that it, "Agreed to report that it should be referred to the Governor of New York and all the other Gentlemen in these parts that are Members of the Society taking the advice of the Society's Missionaries, *to provide Schoolmasters in such places where they think them necessary* with a Yearly Allowance not exceeding £5 or £6 according to Col. Heathcote's Proposal." And, in turn, the Society "Agreed that the matter of Schools be left to the Gentlemen proposed by the Committee."[13] Experience soon showed that the people were either indifferent to or unable to meet their share of the responsibility, and the letters of the schoolmasters and their sponsors were urgent enough to prevent the threatened reduction. But the Society continued true to the record in following the advice of the governors and other gentlemen of the provinces, and of the missionaries as well, in the setting up or the assisting of schools wherever they seemed necessary. It did not cease, however, to express the expectation that the people of the colonies should coöperate in the work, and it wished in time to be relieved of financial burden in centres like the city of New York. This would enable its activity to be extended to the newer and more necessitous settlements.

---

10 S. P. G. Letter-book, A, 3, p. 161. This estimate is based on New York currency. It is typical, though there were variations from relative values in other colonies.

11 See his letter of Dec. 18, 1707, S. P. G. Letter-book, A, 3, p. 161.

12 *Ibid.* Later proposals from him fixed the salary at £5 or £6 sterling. S. P. G. Journal, II, p. 235.

13 S. P. G. Journal, I, p. 249, March 3, 1709–10.

In 1731 the Committee was desired to consider the former and present state of the places where the Society sent schoolmasters and to "represent to the Board in what places, the people are so improved in their circumstances that the Society may abate or withdraw the allowances hitherto made."[14] They reported at the next meeting[15] that they "have not yet received sufficient information to ground their report" in this matter. Subsequently the Board resolved on several occasions to consider the state of schools with this end in view, but no definite plan was carried through. Occasional withdrawals of support were decided on, the following being one instance: "Also that whereas Mr. Ellis himself represents in his letter, that there are four Schools in that town besides his—the Committee submit to Soc. whether there is any occasion to continue a School there."[16] Upon further consideration the Committee recommended the discontinuance of Ellis' support, which was agreed to.[17] The same action was taken in 1743 with regard to the charity school at New York[18] but representations from that city had sufficient weight with the Society to cause a renewal of its support.[19]

At the very beginning the S. P. G. established rules and regulations to govern the conduct of its missionaries and schoolmasters. These "Instructions" embraced every particular which seemed necessary for the guidance of the Society's agents and they described each with a faithful simplicity. With respect to their parishes, missionaries were told that, amongst the many functions pertaining to them, they shall "encourage the setting up of Schools for the teaching of Children;"[20] and that they must attend to the proper religious instruction of those persons under their care, by encouraging the catechizing of such, "whether children or other ignorant Persons."[21]

---

14 S. P. G. Journal, V, p. 328, Jan. 21, 1731.

15 Feb. 18, 1731, *ibid.*, VI, p. 4.

16 Feb. 17, 1737, *ibid.*, VII, p. 210. Ellis was schoolmaster at Burlington, New Jersey.

17 March 17, 1737, *ibid.*, VII, p. 219.

18 "There doth not appear any Reason to the Committee to support longer a School at New York, there being 9 English, one Dutch, one Latin and one French School in that City. * * * * Agreed to." Apr. 15, 1743, *ibid.*, IX, p. 140; see also S. P. G. Letter-book, B, 10, p. 193a.

19 March 16, 1743–4, S. P. G. Journal, IX, p. 246. For representations requesting further assistance, see letters of Commissary Vesey and Joseph Hildreth, the Schoolmaster, S. P. G. Letter-book, B, 11, pp. 117, 120–2.

20 Instructions for the Clergy printed in the Collection of Papers appended to th Annual Report of 1706; also in the reports of 1711 and 1715, and subsequent ones.

21 *Ibid.*

The first instructions for schoolmasters employed by the Society were also drawn up in 1706, and were the following:

"I. That they well consider the End for which they are employed by the Society, viz. The instructing and disposing Children to believe and live as Christians.

"II. In order to this End, that they teach them to read truly and distinctly, that they may be capable of reading the Holy Scriptures, and other pious and useful Books, for informing their Understandings, and regulating their Manners.

"III. That they instruct them thoroughly in the Church-Catechism; teach them first to read it distinctly and exactly, then to learn it perfectly by Heart; endeavouring to make them understand the Sense and Meaning of it, by the help of such Expositions as the Society shall send over.

"IV. That they teach them to write a plain and legible Hand, in order to the fitting them for useful Employments; With as much Arithmetick as shall be necessary to the same Purpose.

"V. That they be industrious, and give constant Attendance at proper School-Hours.

"VI. That they daily use, Morning and Evening, the Prayers composed for their Use in this Collection, with their Scholars in the School, and teach them the Prayers and Graces composed for their use at home.

"VII. That they oblige their Scholars to be constant at Church on the Lord's Day, Morning and Afternoon, and at all other Times of Publick Worship; that they cause them to carry their Bibles and Prayer Books with them, instructing them how to use them there, and how to demean themselves in the several Parts of Worship; that they be there present with them, taking Care of their reverent and decent Behaviour, and examine them afterwards as to what they have heard and learned.

"VIII. That when any of their Scholars are fit for it, they recommend them to the Minister of the Parish, to be publickly Catechized in the Church.

"IX. That they take special Care of their Manners, both in their Schools and out of them; warning them seriously of those Vices to which Children are most liable; teaching them to abhor Lying and Falshood, and to avoid all sorts of Evil-speaking; to love Truth and Honesty; to be modest, gentle, well-behaved, just and affable, and courteous to all their Companions; respectful to their Superiors, particularly towards all that minister in holy Things, and especially to the Minister of their Parish; and all this from a Sense and Fear of Almighty God; endeavouring to bring them in their tender Years to that Sense of Religion, which may render it the constant Principle of their Lives and Actions.

"X. That they use all kind and gentle Methods in the Government of their Scholars, that they may be loved as well as feared by them; and that when Correction is necessary, they make the Children to understand, that it is given them out of kindness, for their Good, bringing them to a Sense of their Fault, as well as of their Punishment.

"XI. That they frequently consult with the Minister of the Parish, in which they dwell, about the Methods of managing their Schools, and be ready to be advised by him.

"XII. That they do in their whole Conversation shew themselves Examples of Piety and Virtue to their Scholars, and to all with whom they sahll converse.

"XIII. That they be ready, as they have Opportunity, to teach and instruct the *Indians* and *Negroes* and their Children.

"XIV. That they send to the Secretary of the Society, once in every six Months, an Account of the State of their respective Schools, the Number of their Scholars, with the Methods and Success of their Teaching."[22]

[22] Printed in Collections of Papers as cited just above. The different provisions were proposed and adopted at separate meetings, on May 17, June 21, and July 19, 1706. S. P. G. Journal, I, pp. 21, 28, 30.

NOTITIA SCHOLASTICA; *or an Account to be sent every Six Months to the* SOCIETY *by each* Schoolmaster, *concerning the State of their respective Schools.*

1. Attendance daily given.	without Intermission, except Holydays
2. Number of Children taught in the School. about	30 generally often more
3. Number of Children baptized in the Church of *England*.	about 20 or 25
4. Number of *Indian* and Negroe Children.	4
5. Number of Children born of Dissenting Parents.	about 10 or 12 when no other School
6. Other Schools in or near the Place. 2 within a mile	but vacant a great part of the year
7. Of what Denomination. of the Congreational	persuasion
8. Other Employments of the Schoolmaster. bred a Sadler	but does little at his Trade

The Account to be attested by the Missionary (if any upon the Spot) and by some of the Principal Inhabitants,

Sa. Johnson, Missionary

John. Keys Clerk

COPY OF NOTITIA SCHOLASTICA

The reports called for by Section XIV of the instructions were not enforced with sufficient emphasis at first and they were much neglected. To put a stop to this there was drawn up in 1738 a special form on which reports were to be sent. Not only were they to be sent on this form, but it was required that they be attested by the missionary and by some of the principal inhabitants. The form, known as the Notitia Scholastica, is shown herewith.[23]

The new plan brought undoubted improvement in the method of reporting to the Society, and it increased the amount of attention usually given to this rule. Apparently, however, it was not many years until the use of the actual Notitiae fell into disuse, though it is possible that a large part of them has not been preserved in the regular archives. The information suggested by this form continued to be sent to the Secretary with fair regularity by most of the Schoolmasters. Severe reprimands were sent to those who were habitually negligent. To judge from these, it is probably safe to infer that reports were frequently overlooked or disregarded. So, too, part of the questions of the Notitia came to be ignored.

The Society's concern for the personnel of its lay agents is indicated by the following orders relating to Schoolmasters:[24]

"1. That no person be admitted as Schoolmasters till he bring certificate of the following particulars.

1. his age. 2. his conditions of life, whether single or mary'd. 3. his temper. 4. his prudence. 5. his learning. 6. his sober & pious conversation. 7. his zeal for the Xtian Religion & diligence in his calling. 8. his affection to the present government. 9. his conformity to the doctrine & discipline of the Ch. of England.

"2. That no person shall be sent as a Schoolmaster by Soc. till he has been tryed & approved by three members appointed by the Soc. or Comee who shall testify by word or writing his ability to teach reading, writing, & the Catechism of the Ch. of England & such exposition thereof as the Soc. shall order.

"3. That they observe the Instructions given to the Schoolmasters by the Soc. set down on page 33, 34, 35, of the said Collection of Papers.

"4. That no Testimonial shall be allowed of but such as are signed by the respective Minister of the parish where he last lived, & where this is not practicable, by some other persons of credit, & note, 3 at least of the Communion of the Ch. of England, whereof one shall be a Clergyman, & such as shall be known to some of the members of the Soc.

"5. That all Schoolmasters, in matters which they desire should be laid before Soc. do correspond only with the President or Secretary of this Soc.

"6. That if any Schoolmaster in the service of the Soc., shall return from the Plantations, without leave first had from the Soc., such Schoolmaster

---

23 Adopted, Nov. 17, 1738. S. P. G. Journal, VII, p. 293. "Agreed that 250 of the same be printed and sent to the respective schoolmasters." *Ibid.*

24 Proposed Feb. 8, 1711–12, S. P. G. Journal II, p. 165; adopted Feb. 15, 1711–12, *ibid.*, p. 166; printed in Collection of Papers, Report of 1715.

shall receive no farther allowance from the time he shall leave his service there.

"7. That all Schoolmasters sent over by the Soc. to the plantations being marryed men be obliged to take their wives with them, unless they can offer such reasons as shall induce ye Soc. to dispense therewith.

"8. That the salary of every Schoolmaster who is not dismis'd the Service for some misdemeanour shall continue one year, & no longer, after the Soc. have resolved at their bord to dismiss Such Persons from their Service."

Schoolmasters who were sent out from England were carefully examined on points specified above. It was also desired to show a similar care in the selection of men in the Plantations, but in reality the testimonials sent in behalf of applicants never reached this degree of explicitness. It was impossible, in view of the great distance and the consequent delay between letter and answer, and also in view of the men available, to exercise the close care in this respect that the Society so earnestly desired. The same difficulty was experienced as regards the standing rules in general. It required positive admonition and action at various times to maintain a moderate degree of faithfulness to them.[25] The Society, it appears, was not able to accomplish more than this during the first century of its labors.

That the Society sought the fullest light on the progress of its colonial agents is shown by the fact that it availed itself of every opportunity outside of the regular channels. Correspondence with leading men in the colonies was made use of. In the same spirit the colonial governors were again and again consulted. In 1712 Col. Francis Nicholson was sent out to the Plantations as Queen Anne's special commissioner for several purposes, including those ecclesiastical.[26] Already a member of the S. P. G., he was given a special deputation to "enquire into and concerning the Soc's Missionaries, Schoolmasters, & Catechists, as also the state of the Churches, Glebes, Libraries sent by the Soc. into the Plantations."[27] His reports were carefully drawn up and included, besides observations on the work then in progress, recommendations for further activity. Nicholson became Governor of Carolina in 1720 and was again deputized by the Society continuing throughout his colonial career its valued friend and counselor.

---

25 For example, "Also agreed that all Missionaries, Catechists, & Schoolmasters, who have neglected their duty as ordered by the Standing rules, be discharged. Com^ee ordered to enquire as to which Missionaries &c., had broken their Rules." March 6, 1715–16, S. P. G. Journal, III, p. 127. For special admonitions to schoolmasters from the Sec., see S. P. G. Letter-book, A, 11, pp. 367–371.

26 S. P. G. Letter-book B, 1, p. 181; *ibid.*, A, 7, p. 271.

27 Oct. 17, 1712. *Ibid.*, A, 7, p. 91. Members of the Society in the colonies were directed to coöperate with and assist Nicholson to the fullest extent. *Ibid.*, pp. 275–86, 476–85, 530–67.

About a decade after this the Society attempted to get the Bishop of London to enlist the commissaries as regular guardians or overseers of the schoolmasters. Indeed, all along there had been coöperation in this field on the part of the commissaries, but it had been irregular and entirely voluntary. Now it was proposed that they should be empowered hereafter to receive regularly and examine any complaints that might be made against the schoolmasters and transmit the state of such matters to the Secretary.[28] Unfortunately the plan was not approved by the Bishop, on the ground that it was not within his authority to do so.[29] Consequently interest in the schools on the part of the Bishop's special representatives continued on a voluntary basis. But their assistance in the endeavors for promoting education was valuable at all times. So was that of the missionaries with very few exceptions. The letters of the commissaries were as a rule fuller and freer than those of the latter. The information afforded by both these sources together with the accounts from the schoolmasters furnished a commendable amount of data in view of all the conditioning circumstances. In 1742 the state of the schools was deemed sufficiently important to be assigned to the consideration of a special committee. This was to be made up of "any 3 or more of the foll., with any other members who chose to be present: Dean of Winchester, Dr. Pelling, Dean of the Arches, Dean of Peterborough, Mr. Johnson, Dr. Roper, Dr. Best, Dr. Thomas, Mr. Spateman & Dr. Wilson."[30] What its exact status was is not clear from available records. It may have been merely temporary for the purpose of dealing with special complaints of neglect of duty which were then being lodged with the Secretary. Action was taken on these complaints, and a report was made at the meeting of the following month.[31] Yet this committee was further directed to consider "the State of the Society's Schools in America,"[32] which implies a task that could not have been even initiated with any degree of thoroughness in so short an existence. If, however, it continued to act there is nothing to enable its work to be distinguished from that of the Standing Committee. The probability is, then, that there was no change in the administrative machinery.

---

28 S. P. G. Journal, V, p. 320, Dec. 17, 1731.
29 *Ibid.*, p. 328, Jan. 21. 1731–2; this has been already referred to, see p. 6.
30 March 18, 1742–3, *ibid.*, IX, p. 132.
31 Apr. 15, 1743, *ibid.*, p. 140.
32 *Ibid.*, p. 132.

PART II

THE SUPPORT OF SCHOOLS IN NEW YORK BY THE S. P. G.

CHAPTER V

INTRODUCTORY

When the S. P. G. began its labors in New York Province the followers of the Church of England were in a decided minority. Sects had been many even from the beginning of English occupation, but ministers had been very scarce.[1] The Duke of York had maintained a chaplain in the Fort at New York City[2] and this was the only Church of England influence for more than twenty years. Besides the Dutch churches, some twenty Meeting places were soon established by either Presbyterians or Independents but above half of them remained vacant.[3] Governor Dongan in 1687 reported the following conditions:

> "Every town ought to have a Minister. New York has first a Chaplain belonging to the Fort, of the Church of England; Secondly, a Dutch Calvinist, Thirdly, a French Calvinist, Fourthly, a Dutch Lutheran . . . Here bee not many of the Church of England; few Roman Catholicks; abundance of quakers preachers men & Women especially; Singing Quakers, Ranting Quakers; Sabbatarians; Antisabbatarians; Some Anabaptists some Independents; some Jews; in short of all sorts of opinions there are some. . . . . The great church which serves both the English & the Dutch is within the Fort which is found to bee very inconvenient. The most prevailing opinion is that of the Dutch Calvinist."[4]

No attempt towards a settlement of the Church was made, it appears, until 1693, when, through the power of the Crown in

---

[1] "Ministers have been soe scarce & Religion many that noe acct. cann be given of Children's births or christenings." From a report of Gov. Andros 1678, Documentary History of New York, I, p. 61.

[2] *Ibid.*

[3] *Ibid.* Fully half of these Meeting places were on Long Island. Report of Dr. Bray about 1700 to the Archbishop of Canterbury, Hawks Transcripts, G. C.

[4] Feb. 22, 1687, *ibid.*, pp. 116–7.

the government of the colony, an Act of Assembly ordained that six Protestant Ministers (that is, Episcopal) should be appointed for the Province.[5] Trinity Church in New York City was founded a few years after this[6] but it was not until 1702 and by means of the Society's aid that the other churches were set up.[7]

In 1701 the population of the Province numbered 25,000. They were distributed "in Twenty Five towns; about Ten of them Dutch, the rest English."[8] In 1714 the population had grown to 45,000.[9] The strength of the Church of England in this interval (1701–1714) is indicated by the Vestry of Trinity Church in an address to the Archbishop of Canterbury. It says, "the greatest part of the Inhabitants of this Province are of the Dutch & French reformed Religion or Dissenters & Quakers & but 3 Countys within the Province would receive a Church of England minister, to wit, Queens County, West Chester, & Richmond & of these countys but the smallest number goe to the worship."[10] Statistics of the period show the same. Frequenters of the Church were not above 1200 and actual communicants not above 450 in the entire Province.[11] So preponderant were the Dutch and French languages that one of the earliest petitions to the Bishop of London from the assembled missionaries of the middle colonies carried a proposal as follows: "that their be no preachers permitted to preach among them (Dutch & French in the Province of N. Y. N. J. & Penn) but in the English Tongue or at least of Episcopal ordination that can preach both in English and in their own Tongues, Nor any Schoolmasters to teach any Vulgar Languages but the English, without a particular license from the Governor. . . . This expedient is thought by the Governor to be a likely means

5 "In the City of New Yorke One in the County of Richmond one in the County of Westchester two, one to have the care of Westchester, Eastchester, Yeanches and the Manner of Pellham the other to have the care of Rye, Mamaranock and Bedford, in Queens County two, one to have the care of Jamaica and the adjacent Towns and farms the other to have the care of Hempstead and the next adjacent towns and farms." Colonial Laws of New York, I, p. 328 ff.

6 1697.

7 Col. Morris to Sec., Hawks Transcripts, N. Y. I, 92f.

8 Quoted from a report in Classified Digest, *op. cit.*, p. 57.

9 Caleb Heathcote to Sec., Aug. 24, 1714, Hawks Transcripts, G. C.

10 Trinity Vestry Minutes, I, p. 70, June 24, 1709.

11 Reported by Heathcote, supra. He further says, "if an exact view was taken of all the people from the Western bounds of Pennsylvania, to the Easternmost parts of the English settlements, it would be found that to every professed member of the Church, there are 40 Dissenters."

of uniting the country both in their religious and civil interests."[12]

The religious and intellectual state of the colonists at the close of the seventeenth century occasioned many discouraging reports from officials both of the Crown and of the Society. "I am sorry to say it," wrote Governor Bellamont, "but 'tis an undoubted truth, the English here are soe profligate that I cannot find a man to be trusted, that's capable of business."[13] He cites specific cases and then adds, "those that are honest of the Dutch, being formerly kept out of imployment and business are very ignorant, and can neither speak nor write proper English."[14] Somewhat later one of the leading men of the Province referred to the people of New York, as the scum of New England,[15] having in mind, of course, the English colonists. Another addressed to the Society the following view regarding the County of West Chester:[16] "I found it the most rude and Heathenish Country, I ever saw in my whole Life, which called themselves Christians, there being not so much as the least marks or Footsteps of Religion of any Sort. *Sundays* being the only Time sett apart by them for all manner of vain Sports and lewd Diversions, and they were grown to such a Degree of Rudeness that it was intollerable, and having then the command of the Militia, I sent an order to all the Captains, requiring them to call their Men under Arms, and to acquaint them, that in Case they would not in every Town agree amongst themselves to appoint Readers and pass the Sabbath in the best Manner they could, till such Times as they could be better provided, that they should every Sunday call their Companies under arms, and spend the Day in Exercise; whereupon it was unanimously agreed on thro' the county, to make choice of Readers; which they accordingly did, and continued in those Methods for some Time." These preceding characterizations are colored no doubt by the almost unavoidable prejudices of men of strict orthodox tendencies. But they do give an insight into some of the conditions that must have been present in New York following the overthrow of the Dutch regíme.

---

12 Petition of Clergy to Bishop of London, Nov. 2, 1705, Hawks Transcripts, G. C.

13 Apr. 29, 1699, N. Y. Col. Docs., IV, p. 520.

14 *Ibid.*

15 Col. Morris to Sec., Feb. 20, 1711/12, Ecclesiastical Records, III, p. 1910; N. Y. Col. Docs., V, p. 318f.

16 Col. Caleb Heathcote, 1704, quoted in Classified Digest, p. 57.

There was a condition of illiteracy at this time certainly greater than it could have been in colonies like Massachusetts or Virginia. Probably ten per cent of the settlers could not write their names. At least, such a proportion of illiterates is shown in a petition of Protestants of New York to William III.[17] Lord Cornbury reported that most of the Sheriffs were of the same stamp, "most of them so ignorant that they can neither reade or write."[18] Regarding the education of children he said: "It is a melancholy thing to see how the youth are bred up in most of these parts."[19] Reports from other sources expressed the same concern. Said one: "the Children have no Education but what they have from their Parents, which binds them up both to their Parents Languages & Principles."[20] Another deplored the fact that "the children are running about for want of education as wild, uncultivated and unimproved as the soil was when their forefathers first trod it."[21] After the second decade of the eighteenth century there are not many complaints about the state of general intelligence. The missionary at Brookhaven on Long Island, for instance, found that the prejudices of education were not easy to overcome. This was in 1726.[22] Twenty years thereafter his successor informed the Society that the people of his parish were "generally dull and illiterate & too little disposed to receive instruction either by reading or otherwise."[23] In 1747, also, the Churchwardens and Vestry of Staten Island deplored the "undisciplined, rude and unpolished" youth of that place.[24] Such reports as these, however, stand out as the exception rather than the rule in the abundant correspondence which the Society received from New York between 1750 and 1780.[25]

---

17 Dec. 30, 1701. 687 persons signed of whom 61 made their marks. Ecclesiastical Records, III, p. 1486.

18 Cornbury to the Lords Commissioners for Trade and Plantations, Sept. 27, 1702. Documents relating to the Colonial History of N. Y., IV, p. 972.

19 Letter to Sec., Nov. 29, 1707. S. P. G. Letter-book, A, 3, p. 155.

20 Letter of Mr. Mackenzie, missionary on Staten Island, to Sec., Nov. 8, 1705. *Ibid.*, 2, p. 116.

21 Mr. Thomas, missionary at Hempstead, to Sec., Feb. 20, 1711/12, *ibid.*, 7, p. 141.

22 Thos. Standard to Sec., Oct. 1726, *ibid.*, 19, p. 404.

23 Isaac Browne to Sec., March 25, 1746, *ibid.*, B, 13, p. 283.

24 Address to the S. P. G., Feb. 24, 1746/7, *ibid.*, 15, p. 124.

25 As late as 1762 Myles Cooper, who afterwards succeeded Samuel Johnson as President of King's College, wrote back to England the following: "By the little that I have had an opportunity of seeing I am afraid that ye State of Learning is not very high among us." Lambeth Archives, 1123, III, fol. 284. But it is very probable that Cooper was too recently from the atmosphere and traditions of Oxford to be able to avoid using for comparison the standards of that great seat of learning.

Religious and intellectual conditions were made more discouraging by the people's manifest dislike of being taxed in any way for their improvement. Governor Dongan found that congregations, especially on Long Island, did not like to tax themselves to pay their ministers[26] and the missionaries had the greatest difficulty in getting any aid for themselves or for building churches. "The people are more apt to receive than to give," and they "think it a hardship to pay their dues," wrote Mr. Bartow, missionary at West Chester.[27] So in the matter of schools. There was a decided lack of enthusiasm for them in various places, caused by the objection to paying anything for their support. The following sent from Hempstead is to the point: "You desire an Account of the State of our Schools; Wee had a Schoolmaster settled among us for two years & a half, now we are destitute the people being utterly weary of the Subscription I had engaged them in; I hope in God's due time to induce them to settle another; I shall not be wanting to contribute towards it both by purse & persuasion as heretofore."[28] The complaint illustrates a general disinclination that had to be contended with throughout the century.[29] In other places sectarian prejudices caused not only an indifference to schools under the support of any other denomination but at times an active opposition to them. Rye had difficulty in getting a school erected for the S. P. G. master on account of a Presbyterian "love of distinction."[30] Rival schools were sometimes set up rather than have dissenters' children in the Society's schools.[31] Finally the poor condition of the majority of the colonists made it sometimes hard to assume any burdens that could be avoided or, indeed, to spare their children from the fields though free schooling were offered. Because of such conditions in West Chester County, Col. Heathcote advised the Society that "there are very few who are able to spare their children's time more than to learn to read & write & those who

26 Report on the Province of New York, Feb. 22, 1687, Documentary Hist. New York, I, pp. 116–7.

27 Letter to the Sec., Aug. 14, 1706, Hawks Transcripts, New York, I, p. 125.

28 Mr. Thomas to Sec., June 12, 1709, S. P. G. Letter-book, A, 5, p. 4.

29 See, for example, S. P. G. Journal, III, pp. 189, 401. S. P. G. Letter-book, A, 12, p. 364; 18, p. 193.

30 Flint Dwight, schoolmaster, to Sec., Nov. 12, 1735, S. P. G. Letter-book, A, 26, p. 75.

31 Thomas Temple, schoolmaster to Sec., Hempstead, June 20, 1744, *ibid.*, B, 13, p. 245. Samuel Purdy, schoolmaster, to Sec., Rye, Dec. 6. 1744, *ibid.*, p. 268; also Dec. 30, 1747, *ibid.*, 15, p. 116.

can afford to do more, of wch there are not 6 in the whole County, have ye benefit of the New York Schools wch is but 20 or 30 miles from them."[32] In 1709 it was reported that the poor on Staten Island could not be benefited by the schools there through their inability to pay any stated fee,[33] and a similar condition was reported of places on Long Island shortly thereafter.[34]

In 1713, one of the most interesting educational documents of eighteenth century New York, written by John Sharpe, Chaplain of the King's forces, thus summed up the status of education in the Province: "There is hardly any thing which is more wanted in this Country than learning there being no place I know of in America where it is either less encouraged or regarded."[35] With reference to conditions in the City itself, this document described the educational interest in the following terms:

> "The City is so conveniently Situated for Trade and the Genius of the people are so inclined to merchandise, that they generally seek no other Education for their children than writing and Arithmetick. So that letters must be in a manner forced upon them not only without their seeking, but against their consent, and there is no doubt but as the youth are very Ingenious, Subtile and of quick Capacities, it would in a short time gain upon their inclinations. The Improvement of a few would stir up Emulation not only in the Children but in their parents, and the happy influence would reach the most distant parts of the province."

The first provision made for education, following the English occupation of the Province, was the extension of the educational requirements of the apprenticeship system which was then in force in England. The Duke of York's laws laid down the following specification for the welfare of apprenticed children and servants:

> "The Constable and Overseers are strictly required frequently to admonish the Inhabitants of Instructing their Children and Servants in matters of religion, and the Laws of the Country, And that the Parents and Masters do bring up their Children and Apprentices in Some Honest Lawful Calling, Labour or Employment. And if Any Children become Rude Stubborn or Unruly, refusing to hearken to the voice of their parents or Masters the Constable and Overseers, (where no Justice of the Peace shall happen to dwell within Ten Miles of said Town or Parish) have power upon the complaint of their Parents or Masters to Call before them such an Offender, and to Inflict such Corporal punishment as the merit of the fact in their Judgement shall deserve, not exceeding Ten Stripes, provided that such Children and Servants be of Sixteen years of age."[36]

---

32 Oct. 13, 1704, *ibid.*, A, 2, p. 38. Similarly, Samuel Purdy to Sec., Rye, July 16, 1738, *ibid.*, B, 7, p. 145.

33 Mr. McKenzie to Sec., June 13. 1709, *ibid.*, A, 5, p. 18.

34 S. P. G. Journal, II, p. 353.

35 Proposals for Erecting a School, Library and Chapel at New York, March 11, 1712/13, Lambeth Archives, 841, fol. 18.

36 Colonial Laws of New York, I, p. 26.

In addition to the safeguarding of apprentices, schoolmasters who desired to set up schools were required to have the license of the governor. From 1686 to 1709 definite instructions were given the successive governors, beginning with Governor Dongan, as follows:

"38. And wee doe further direct that noe schoolmaster bee henceforth permitted to come from England & to keep school within our province of New York, without the license of the said Archbishop of Canterbury; And that noe other person now there or that shall come from other parts, bee admitted to keep school without your license first had."[37]

Just what the license required of the applicant is not clear. There is nothing to show that examinations preceded the license. Probably, then, it depended on the caprice of the governors, backed up by such testimonials as they might specify. Lord Cornbury was undoubtedly the most rigorous of them all in adhering to these orders from the Crown, applying it even to the Dutch schools, though they claimed exemption under their early grants of privileges.[38] Clews[39] and Pratt[40] have collected from the manuscripts of deeds in the archives of the Secretary of State, about thirteen of these licenses issued by Cornbury between 1704 and 1706. But this number does not represent the schoolmasters in active service during Cornbury's administration by at least eight.[41] Two licenses issued in 1712 by Governor Hunter are to be found in Clews. It is safe to say that fewer licenses were required by schoolmasters in his governorship, but two is hardly a correct representation. Following governors did not continue to exercise the function. The extent of the power of the Bishop of London to license has been already mentioned.[42] In so far as schoolmasters or men in deacon's orders were sent

37 "Instructions to our trusty and welbeloved Thomas Dongan Esqr, Our Captain General and Govr in chief in and over our Province of New York and the Territorys depending thereon in America. Given at our Court at Windsor this 29th day of May in ye second year of our Reigne," (1686). Docs. rel. Col. Hist. N. Y., *op. cit.*, III, p. 372; Clews, *op. cit.*, p. 227. All other instructions named the Bishop of London instead of the Archbishop as above in accordance with the extension of the Bishop of London's jurisdiction to America. For other Instructions, see: Governor Sloughter, Jan 31 1689, Docs. rel. Col. Hist. N. Y., *op. cit.*, III, p. 688; Governor Fletcher, March 7, 1691/2, *ibid.*, p. 821; Governor Richard, Earl of Bellamont, Aug. 31, 1697, *ibid.*, p. 288; Governor Hunter, Dec. 27, 1709, *ibid.* V, p. 135. Governor Lord Cornbury 1702, see previous citation; also Ecclesiastical Records, III, pp. 1487–8.

38 See Articles of Capitulation 1664, granting liberty of Church discipline, Ec. Rec. *op. cit.*, p. 557; and its reaffirmation 1674, *ibid.*, p. 662. See also, rights and privileges in the Charter of the Dutch Reformed Church, 1696, *ibid.*, p. 1153.

39 Colonial Educational Legislation, p. 235f.

40 Annals of Public Education in N. Y., p. 87f.

41 Wm. Huddleston to Sec., S. P. G. Letter-book, A, 4, pp. 57–8.

42 See p. 6.

out to New York, they were subjected to a series of qualifications much higher than any which were imposed in the colonies. They had to meet the regulations for schoolmasters prescribed by the S. P. G.[43] To this extent, therefore, it can be held that the Society's schoolmasters, in part at least, represented higher certification than did those of any other English schools.[44]

The first proposal for education by means of legislative enactment was made in 1691. A bill was proposed in the Assembly "to appoint a schoolmaster for the educating and instructing of Children and youth, *to read and write English,* in every town in the Province."[45] This did not become law. No further action was taken until the coming of Lord Cornbury as governor. In his first address to the Assembly, Oct. 20 1702, he urged "the erecting of Public Schools in proper places."[46] A movement was at once set on foot which resulted in the enactment of "An Act for Encouragement of a Grammar Free School in the city of New York," Nov. 27, 1702.[47] The interest of the Church in this measure is shown by the final clause which declared: "Provided alwayes, that such Schoolmaster shall, from time to time as vacancy happens, be chosen and recommended to the Comon Council of the said city for the time being, in order to be lycensed and approved by the Right Hon'able the Bishop of London or the Governour or Commander in Chief of this Province, for the time being, anything herein contained to the contrary thereof in any ways notwithstanding."[48] When the small percentage of the friends of the Church in the total population is taken into consideration, it may be questioned how the Episcopalian influence could have shown such strength. Whatever other reasons might be given, it seems evident that the directing hand of Cornbury in the government at this time was a fortunate thing for the Church and the Society.

Complying with the spirit and the letter of the Act, the Common Council of the city of New York petitioned Governor Corn-

---

43 See pp. 58 and 60.

44 This certainly would hold true when applied to the Plantations as a whole. It may also hold true of the Dutch schools in New York.

45 Journal of the General Assembly of the Colony of New York, I, p. 7, quoted by Clews, *op. cit.*, p. 277.

46 Ecclesiastical Records, III, p. 1502.

47 Colonial Laws of New York, I, pp. 516–7. The act provided a salary of £50 per annum "for the space or term of Seven Yeares."

48 *Ibid.* This provision did not go through unopposed. For the attempt to change it, see Ecclesiastical Records, III, pp. 1509–10.

bury to use his influence with the Bishop of London and the S. P. G. for the procurement of a schoolmaster, the Council being of the opinion that there was no available person in the city "proper and duly qualified to take upon him the office of schoolmaster of said city."[49] Governor Cornbury responded to the Council's request by the following interesting letter in which he made so apparent his desire to advance the Church's efforts for religious education:

> "Since mine to your Lp of the 15th Instant the mayor & Common Council of this City have been wth me to desire me to recomend a fit Person to be Schoolmaster of a Free School which is to be Settled here att the charges of the City, they will allow him 50l p. An. besides his Lodging. I therefore Intreat your Lp will send a good Sober Man fit for that purpose. I could wish he were in holy Orders, then he may be assisting to Mr. Vesey. Besides it will be one good Step towards bringing up the youth in ye Service of the Church of England, to begin wth the Prayers of the Church every Morning. I think if yr Lp pleases it ought to be a sober & grave man at the first beginning, & not too young a man, lest by the heat of his youth he may prejudice too good a design, which if well settled att first can't fail of good success. But this I submit to your Ldps better Judgement."[50]

The grammar school was opened early in 1704 by Mr. George Muirson,[51] who had been sent over to be schoolmaster at Albany.[52] In detaining him at New York, Cornbury explained that "there being no allowance yet settled for a Schoolmaster there & there being Fifty pounds a year settled here by Act of Assembly for a Schoolmaster in this City, I stopped him here for some time and ye rather because when he arrived here there were several youths going to be sent to Boston, wch I thought would be better to prevent, by stoping Mr. Muirson here."[53] But Muirson served only a few months. About November 1704 he returned to England to secure Holy Orders which he had come without.[54] Thus he hoped to qualify himself to be assistant to the Rector of Trinity Church.[55] Though his behaviour

---

49 Minutes of the Common Council of New York, II, pp. 517, 519, 520; also quoted in Pratt, *op. cit.*, pp. 85–6, and Clews, *op. cit.*, p. 235.

50 Cornbury to the Bishop of London, Dec. 21, 1702, S. P. G. Letter-book, I, p.90. Mr. Vesey was the Rector of Trinity Church and the Bishop of London's Commissary for the Province.

51 Cornbury issued a license to him Apr. 25, 1704, and he seems to have taken up his duties forthwith. For license, see Clews, *op. cit.*, p. 235.

52 Cornbury to Sec., Nov. 6, 1704, S. P. G. Letter-book, A, 2, p. 28.

53 *Ibid.*

54 This honor, it appears, had not been given before on the ground that Muirson was not University trained. Archbishop of York to Sec., June 30, 1703, *ibid.*, I, p. 94. But the requests from Cornbury and others overcame this prejudice, *Ibid.*, 2, p. 44.

55 *Ibid.*, p. 76.

as schoolmaster "was exceeding well"[56] his suddenly leaving the school stirred up such opposition to him and Mr. Vesey,[57] that his retention of the schoolmaster's position seemed "likely to be of very ill Consequence to the Church."[58] The Society therefore appointed him missionary at Rye[59] upon his return in 1705. After a lapse of over a half a year, Muirson was succeeded by Andrew Clarke who was sent over with the certificate of the Bishop of London in May 1705.[60] A license to teach was granted him by Lord Cornbury on August 14, 1705, which date probably marks the beginning of his teaching.[61] In 1708 Clarke was still in charge of the school, having "33 scholars" under his instruction.[62] In addition to the £50 per annum from the government he was receiving from each scholar the usual quarterly fee.[63] Just how long Clarke continued in this work or when the grammar school came to an end, the writer has not been able to definitely determine. By 1712 Clarke had gone into the employ of the Receiver General of the Province, as is indicated by the following extract from the minutes of the Common Council:

> "Mr. Andrew Clarke who was lately Elected Constable of the South Ward personally Appeared before this Court and Acquainted them that he could not serve in that Office by reason he was Imployed by the Receiver General of this Colony in Collecting her Majesties quitt Rents, it is therefore Order'd that the said Andrew Clarke do pay the fine for his said Refusal and that the Mayor Issue his Warrant to the Alderman of the said Ward to Elect another fitt person on Tuesday Next to serve in the said office for the year Ensueing."[64]

Sometime between 1708 and 1712, accordingly, Clarke's work in the school came to an end. At least it is possible that the "Grammar Free School" had an existence which lasted until 1712. There is reason to believe that he continued beyond 1708. His condition was certainly not an unhappy one. Indeed he had been, apparently, the best paid schoolmaster then in New York City, having, in addition to his fixed salary, the

---

56 *Ibid.*, also p. 27.

57 *Ibid.*, p. 76; also pp. 75, 77.

58 *Ibid.*

59 *Ibid.*, p. 126; also S. P. G. Journal, I, pp. 186, 190.

60 On May 2, 1705 he was granted the usual Royal bounty of £20 towards defraying the charge of his passage to New York whither he was going as schoolmaster. Fothergill, *op. cit.*, p. 20.

61 Pratt, *op. cit.*, p. 88.

62 Wm. Huddleston to Sec., July 15, 1708, S. P. G. Letter-book, A, 4, p. 58.

63 *Ibid.* That is, the same fee which private schoolmasters were then receiving.

64 Oct. 25, 1712. Quoted by Pratt, *op. cit.*, p. 89.

fees from his thirty-three pupils.[65] If the salary of £50 ceased in 1709, as the act would indicate, there was still reason for his continuing in the school. Huddleston, moreover, referred to Clarke's salary as having been allowed "for some years yet to come."[66] This was in 1708. There is no record of any such allowance by the government, so Huddleston may have been in error; or he may have intended to imply that the salary had been allowed for some years following the date of the enactment. On the other hand it is not impossible that the schoolmaster had reference to facts of which there are no available records at present. When, after many years, educational legislation was next adopted, the Assembly referred to this first experiment in the following indefinite words: "the not rightly applying of a temporary Salary heretofore allowed for a free school, has been the Chief Cause that an Encouragement for the like purpose has ever since been neglected."[67]

It was not until 1732 that the government renewed any direct interest in education. In October of that year an act was passed "to encourage a Public School in the city of New York for teaching Latin, Greek and Mathematicks."[68] The school was established for a period of five years and provision was made for free tuition to twenty youths in the proportion of ten for the city and county of New York, two for the city and county of Albany, and one for each of the counties of King, Queen, Suffolk, Westchester, Richmond, Orange, Ulster, and Dutchess.[69] The act itself appointed as master Mr. Alexander Malcolm[70] who, since 1731,[71] had been keeping "a private school within the said city," and who had "given a Satisfactory proof of his Abilities to teach Latin Greek and the Mathematicks."[72] In 1737 the school was continued for one year longer by another act,[73] and then abandoned by the government and by Malcolm, who went to London, was ordained, and became a missionary of the Society.[74] The

65 According to Huddleston, no private teacher had that number of pupils in 1708, among the English schools of the city. See letter above.

66 *Ibid.*

67 See Preamble to Act of 1732, Col. Laws, N. Y., *op. cit.*, II, p. 813.

68 *Ibid.*

69 *Ibid.*

70 *Ibid.*

71 Petition of Malcolm to Society, Dec. 21, 1739, S. P. G. Letter-book, B, 7, p. 267.

72 From preamble of the act, Col. Laws, N. Y. *op. cit.*, II, p. 813.

73 Passed Dec. 16, 1737, *ibid.*, p. 973 f.

74 S. P. G. Journal, VIII, p. 107.

funds vouchsafed by the two laws were not realized and Malcolm left with about half of his promised salary unpaid.[75] To the S. P. G., he reported the following: "That your Petitioner has lived these last eight years in the City of New York, Province of New York, in America, teaching the Latin and Greek languages, & the Mathematicks. But finding this kind of Education less valued and encouraged in that Young Colony than it ought to be, and than he had reason to expect from the Invitations and promises that drew him thither, he is desirous to go into Holy Orders."[76]

This attempt ended all official interest in the field of secondary education. There are evidences that such schools were privately conducted in various parts of the colony and, as a rule, for short intermittent periods. A few of these were undertaken in different places by the agents of the S. P. G. to improve their inadequate incomes.[77] Between 1716 and 1722, a Grammar school was persumably conducted in the city of New York by Rev. Robert Jenney. The records are definite as to half of the time at least. It was closely allied to the Society, through its master, though it was an entirely private venture. Jenney had been a chaplain in the Royal navy[78] and had been enrolled in the work of the S. P. G. as a schoolmaster in Philadelphia.[79] In 1716 he was dismissed from the service of the Society and served as chaplain to the King's forces in New York until 1722.[80] Then he was made the Society's missionary at Rye and Hempstead respectively. He wrote the Society in 1717 that he began first to teach "Latin Greek &c. for the service of a particular Friend only," but "his design had now become more universal" and had "in great measure removed that aversion to Literature beyond writing and Arithmetick, which did generally possess the Minds of the people." Though he had few pupils these were "the chief of the English Dutch & French."[81] On Sept. 15, 1718, Mr. Jenney's scholars were assigned regular seats in

---

75 See an act passed Nov. 3, 1740, to reimburse Mr. Malcolm for £111-7s-6d, back pay. Col. Laws. N. Y., *op. cit.*, III, pp. 86–7.

76 S. P. G. Letter-book, B, 7, p. 267.

77 See following pages.

78 Classified Digest, *op. cit.*, p. 852.

79 S. P. G. Letter-book, A, 4, p. 10. From here he went to New York as the S. P. G. assistant to Vesey, 1715–1716. Trinity Vestry Minutes, I, p. 108.

80 *Ibid.*, 14, p. 129; Classified Digest, *op. cit.*, p. 855; Trinity Vestry Minutes, I, p. 112. His dismissal was due to temporary economy on the part of the Society. *Ibid.*

81 Jenney to Sec., Nov. 4, 1717, S. P. G. Letter-book, A, 12, p. 350.

Trinity Church,[82] and a year later the school is still referred to in the Society's correspondence.[83] Another Grammar school somewhat affiliated with the work of the Society was founded in 1763. It was established by the College authorities to serve as a special preparatory centre for the higher institution. The lack of an efficient one was a drawback to the College. Referring to the large entering class of 1763, President Myles Cooper wrote: "I wish their learning were equal to their numbers, but in both we must expect to be deficient, 'till such Times as Schools in this Country are better conducted than they are at present. Indeed, the Governors of this College have come to a Resolution for establishing one under their own immediate Inspection."[84] And soon after Samuel Johnson, the retired president, wrote: "They have now at last established a good Grammar School, for want of which the College has much suffered."[85] It was deemed necessary to go to Boston in order to secure a worthy master for the school.[86] His arrival was thus announced to the Archbishop of Canterbury, by President Cooper: "The Schoolmaster whom we expected, is arrived, and has begun with very good Success. The Number of his Scholars already amounts to upwards of twenty and several more are engaged so that I am in great Hopes of soon having an Augmentation to the College; and not only so, but likewise of seeing the pupils much better qualified for admission, than ever we have yet found them."[87]

The writer has here assumed that there was at least one Grammar school in the city at this time and that the action of the Governors of the College was not because of the reverse condition. Reports of the Society's schoolmasters show that one or more Latin schools were conducted between 1741 and 1762. These of course, were of a private nature.[88] While no report could be found later than 1762, the supposition is strong

---

[82] Trinity Vestry Minutes, I, pp. 115–116.

[83] Thos. Barclay to Sec., May 25, 1710. S. P. G. Letter-book, A, 13, p. 452.

[84] Letter to the Archbishop of Canterbury, June 23, 1763, Lambeth Archives, 1123, III, p. 311.

[85] Aug. 10, 1763, *ibid.*, p. 316.

[86] *Ibid.*, p. 311.

[87] Sept. 23, 1763, *ibid.*, p. 324.

[88] These reports show for 1741, one Latin school; for 1742, one; for 1745, one; for 1747, one; for 1748, one; for 1749, two; for 1750, one; for 1751, one on March 28; for 1751, two on Dec. 9; for 1752, two; for 1761, two; for 1762, two. See reports of Thomas Noxon and of Joseph Hildreth, schoolmasters to Society, S. P. G. Letter-book, B, 9, p. 64; B, 10, p. 69; B. 13, p. 221; B, 15, pp. 88, 120; B, 16, pp. 44, 54; B, 17, p. 98; B, 18, p. 100; B, 19, pp. 68, 70; B, 20, pp. 58, 59; B, 3, pp. 153, 155. Reports covering other years are not to be found in the Society's archives.

that secondary education did not then abruptly cease. Doubtless it was represented among the schools of the city up to the Revolutionary period.

In legislative provisions for elementary education, New York was a poor contrast to Massachusetts, where every village had its school supported, in whole or in part, by the public. No effective governmental action in behalf of these was carried out during the entire period of English occupation. In the early decades of the eighteenth century private elementary schools were gradually set up in the towns and villages generally, but they were not continuously maintained by any means. The S. P. G. found at the outset of its work a great lack of English schools, and frequent mention was made of this in the letters to the Secretary.[89] Bray in 1700 emphasized this drawback to the contemplated activity of the Church in the Province and said in his report: "It will be further requisite to have free Schools erected at least one in every county, for the Education of their Children."[90] Keith's report to the Society, made two years thereafter following a survey of the field, declared there was "no *School house* yet erected in this Province" which "though it hath a great number of inhabitants, could never yet obtain a public legally Established School." This report further stated: "There is yet no provision for Schoolmasters made by law . . . and till then the Church of England Schoolmaster in the county of New York as heretofore, will be supported by the voluntary contributions of those whose children are instructed by him; notwithstanding it is humbly conceived that an annual Pension for the support and further encouragement of some Ministers and Schoolmasters in poor Towns will be of great use and service to the Church."[91] The unstable conditions of schoolkeeping prevalent in 1707 were set forth by Col. Caleb Heathcote, in a manner that seems fairly representative. He said: "As for my giving an account of the number of Schools I can assure you 'tis very difficult being so uncertain, some places having a Schoolmaster for a year at a time, and then perhaps

89 For example: "The greatest Disadvantage of ye Church in this Island is ye want of an English School for the Children." Mr. Mackenzie to Sec., Nov. 8, 1705, S. P. G. Letter-book, A, 2, p. 116.

90 "A General View of the English Colonies in America, with respect to Religion; in order to show what Provision is wanting for the Propagation of Christianity in those Parts," prefixed to "Apostolick Charity etc., *op. cit.*

91 "Account of the State of the Church in North America, by Mr. George Keith and others," Nov. 1702. Quoted in Pratt, *op. cit.*, pp. 96–97.

none in 7 years after, and many towns and places have never had any since their Settlement, that no regular Scheme can be found on that account, all that I am able to tell you is in General, that nothing is more wanting in America than helps of that Nature and that I may not fall short in any Information I can give you, I will endeavour ag^st my next to get a List of all the Schoolmasters in the province."[92] If such a list was ever sent by Heathcote, there is no present record of it. However, an account of schools was furnished subsequently by Mr. Huddleston, a schoolmaster in the city of New York. It refers only to English schools and is probably incomplete even for them, but it is doubtless one of the fullest accounts that is available for the period. After giving the data concerning Andrew Clarke's Grammar school, cited just above, the report continues:

"Mr. Cornelius Lodge hath about 20 Scholars; Mr. John Stevens 28 Scholars; Mr. John Bashford 8 Scholars and I have about 30 and no more since these new Masters taught, People here being fond of Novelties, so that by this Acco^t you may see that there are but 119 Boys taught by all the five Masters whereas I have heretofore for several years (as may appear by Testimonials heretofore presented to the Venerable Society) taught sixty Boys myself, and I am certain with as much satisfaction to their Parents as is now given, and as many Boys appeared in the Church as now generally do; I have nothing to charge any of the Gentlemen with but that they are all ingenious diligent and good men, but I am humbly of opinion that only two Masters betwixt whom if there were a right understanding might live well of their business, and wou'd be sufficient to discharge all that duty which now the five masters spend their time upon; and can but live very poorly thereon. On Long Island in King's County being generally Dutch there is no School Master. In Queens County at Jamaica at present I think there is one; At Flushing in the said County there is one Thomas Meeken a Quaker, teaches the people of that Town being mostly Quakers; I understand they allow him thirty pounds per Ann.[93] At Hempstead in the said County one Mr. Alexander Beard teaches, and hath about 20 Scholars as he told me and hath £34 per ann. by Subscriptions besides a House and some Lands while he teaches. In Suffolk County at Southhold Thomas Huddleston[94] who is my Brother is lately settled and hath by Subscription £30 per Ann, he hath 20 Scholars. At Southampton in the said County there is a Gentleman teaches but being a great distance from where I live have not as yet informed myself of his Name and Condition of his school; At West Chester I am informed is a School Master but know not his name at present. And in the said County at Rye teaches my Cozen Mr. Joseph Cleator whose incouragement your Hono^rs is acquainted with. At Staten Island in Richmond County is no English School Master that I know of having enquired therein. At Kingston in Ulster County no English Schoolmaster at present the people being mostly Dutch. At the City of Albany in said Colony there is a Soldier belonging to the Garrison teaches but what quantity of scholars he hath I know not."[95]

---

92 Letter to the Sec., Dec. 18, 1707, *ibid.*, 3, p. 161.

93 Onderdonk, Hist. Grace Church, Jamaica L. I., has Thomas Makin, teaching there in 1709. Quoted by Pratt, *op. cit.*, p. 94.

94 Licensed for Jamaica, Aug. 29, 1705. Pratt, *op. cit.*, p. 92.

95 Letter to the Sec., July 15, 1708, *ibid.*, 4, p. 58. The number 119 above includes the 33 under Clarke.

Subsequent letters from the Society's missionaries and schoolmasters made occasional reference to other neighboring schools.[96] When the Notitia Scholastica came to be used, schools were reported in a more regular manner, but enough negligence was shown in this respect to make the Notitiae untrustworthy as a complete record for most places. A marked exception to this, fortunately, is the information furnished by Mr. Noxon and Mr. Hildreth in their reports of schools in New York City. Sixteen of these Notitiae are preserved, covering the years given on a preceding page.[97] Besides the grammar schools and their own charity school, Noxon and Hildreth report the following:[98]

+	Dec. 17 1741	May 22 1742	Nov. 29 1742	Nov. 21 1745	July 16 1747	Jan. 8 1747/8
Dutch Schools	1	1	1	3	2	2
English do	6	7	9	6	6	7
French do	0	1	1	2	2	1
Hebrew do	0	0	0	0	0	0

	March 26 1748	Nov. 6 1748	Apr. 1 1749	Apr. 6 1750	March 28 1751
Dutch Schools...............	1	1	1	1	1
English do..................	8	7	9	9	10
French do..................	1	1	1	1	1
Hebrew do..................	0	0	0	0	1

	Dec. 9 1751	Apr. 10 1752	Oct. 28 1752	Dec. 22 1761	May 11 1762
Dutch Schools	2	2	2	2	2
English do..................	10	10	10	12	10
French do..................	1	1	1	2	1
Hebrew do..................	1	1	1	0	1

From the accounts of Hildreth and other agents of the S. P. G. there is a basis for believing that between 1740 and 1775 both the city and the province enjoyed school facilities probably comparable with the other provinces, except those of New Eng-

[96] At least one other English schoolmaster was teaching in the city of New York by 1708, as the following shows: "The purport of this letter is to recommend the bearer Mr. John Humphreys, a Graduate of Trinity College near Dublin, to the Honorable Society, as a sober & discreet person and one that has approved himself very industrious and diligent in the management of a School in the City of New York where he has lived these two years last past and discharged himself so well that I thought fit in conjunction with several of the Clergy in these parts to recommend him to my Lord Bishop of London for Holy Orders which I do without favour or affection or the last partiality." Rev. Mr. Evans to Sec., Philadelphia, July 12, 1710. *Ibid.*, A, 5, p. 146.

[97] 1741 to 1762, see p. 75.

[98] For references see footnote p. 75.

land.[99] But, being private ventures, the schools were most irregular and were almost constantly being interrupted, except in the city itself. This resulted in a serious handicap to any sequence of instruction for the children, as they changed from one master to another after the lapse of altogether too long intervals.

---

99 Valentine, History of the City of New York, p. 398, gives a list of schoolmasters in the city between 1695 and the Revolutionary War. There are 34 names in the list one of which, Hildreth, was employed by the S. P. G. Of the others four seem to be Dutch. The files of the newspapers of the period and much of the other data in the archives of the New York Historical Society point to the same conclusion.

CHAPTER VI

THE SOCIETY'S CHARITY SCHOOL IN THE CITY OF NEW YORK

With the exception of the employment of a Catechist in 1704, the S. P. G. began its support of schools in the city of New York early in 1706. This was done through a gratuity of "£10 in money and £5 in tracts" voted to William Huddleston, schoolmaster of that place.[1] Mr. Huddleston had been a private schoolmaster for many years before this,[2] although the exact date of the starting of his school is not known. He was in New York from the founding of Trinity Church and was an active worker in its affairs, holding the office of clerk at least from Jan. 27, 1697/8, if not from the very beginning.[3] From June 30, 1697 until 1714 he was almost continuously a vestryman of the church.[4] His name occurs frequently on the committees for inspecting the work of the church building[5] and for collecting funds.[6] As clerk he received a salary of £20 "currant money of New York"[7] at first, which in 1704 was increased to £30,[8] the same to be paid quarterly "during the time he officiated as the Clerk of the Church."[9] Lord Cornbury found Mr. Huddleston engaged in keeping a school upon his arrival in 1702,[10] and the Rector of Trinity on June 9, 1702 wrote of him: "*the Schoolmaster*, Mr. Huddlestone brings all his scholars to Church in order, &

[1] S. P. G. Journal, I, p. (11).

[2] Vesey to Sec., Nov. 21, 1705, S. P. G. Letter-book, A, 2, p. 130; also Heathcote to do., Nov. 14, 1705, *ibid.*, p. 118.

[3] Trinity Vestry Minutes, I, p. 14.

[4] *Ibid.*, p. 2. Between these dates his name appears in the list of members present on an average of at least two meetings in three.

[5] *Ibid.*, p. 2 ff.

[6] *Ibid.*, p. 18 ff.

[7] *Ibid.*, p. 14.

[8] *Ibid.*, p. 48. Berrian (History of Trinity Church p. 49) states the £20 was his compensation as Clerk of the Vestry and £10 as clerk of the Church.

[9] *Ibid.*

[10] S. P. G. Letter-book, A, 2, p. 132. Berrian, *op. cit.*, p. 34 is very misleading in his reference to Huddleston. Evidently he did not consult the Vestry Minutes with care.

these I have formed, with many others, into 3 distinct classes, according to Dr. Bray's proposal, by which means I hope, out of different nations, to compose the most glorious church in America."[11] On Dec. 28, 1702 the Vestry "Ordered that John Welsh, Wm. Welsh the Sexton's third Son be kept at School on the Churches Account and thirty six shillings be paid by the Church Wardens to Mr. Wm. Huddleston for his Schooling the last year, the Boy attending the churches service on the Lords Day and other Holydays."[12] Two months later it was again "Ordered that Wm. Huddleston's Accot of £2: 19: 3 for teaching Wm. Welsh to read and write be allowed and paid by the Church Wardens."[13] From these various citations, therefore, it is evident that Trinity School rests on a private school origin that dates many years prior to the usually accepted date of its founding in 1709.[14] Indeed it is presumable that when Mr. Vesey in his letter of 1705,[15] spoke of Huddleston's having been schoolmaster "many years," he referred to this early origin. Any doubt in the matter, however, is entirely swept away by the declaration of Huddleston himself, in a petition to the Society July 9, 1709, setting forth his service for twenty years in teaching school without any settled salary.[16] We have, therefore, positive evidence that the origin of the school, on or before 1689, antedates the origin of Trinity Church itself. Again there is an indication in the citations that, as "*the Schoolmaster,*" Mr. Huddleston enjoyed the particular favor of the Church's official recognition.[17]

The school met with marked success, for it reached an enrolment of sixty boys.[18] In time competing schools reduced the number of Huddleston's pupils to thirty.[19] It was in view of this, perhaps, that the aid of the S. P. G. was sought. In 1705

11 S. P. G. Letter-book, B, 1, p. 112.

12 Trinity Vestry Minutes, I, p. 43.

13 *Ibid.*, p. 44.

14 Berrian, History of Trinity Church, p. 89.

15 Previously cited, see p. 80.

16 S. P. G. Letter-book, A, 5, p. 21; S. P. G. Journal, I, p. (208).

17 In "An Account of the State of the Church in North America by Mr. George Keith and others" (Nov. 1702) mention is made of "the Church of England Schoolmaster in the County of New York." This undoubtedly referred to Huddleston. Quoted by Pratt, *op. cit.*, p. 96.

18 See quotation from Huddleston letter, p. 77.

19 *Ibid.* Several years after this in a memorial to General Nicholson he wrote as follows: "That your Excellency's Petitioner at the time he received these poor Boys into his School had at least £100 p. annum for teaching other children of the City." S. P. G. Letter-book A, 9, p. 212. That amount of salary is dubious but, if true, it was received only when his enrolment was as high as sixty.

Mr. Huddleston presented his request for an annual pension to the Society through Rev. John Postelthwaite, Master of St. Paul's Free School in London.[20] At the same time testimonials in his behalf were forwarded to the Society by Governor Cornbury, Rev. Mr. Vesey, Col. Heathcote, and others.[21] The matter was referred to the Committee and they reported March 15, 1705/6, that, "It was their opinion that it was not proper to allow an annual Pension to any Schoolmaster who is not appointed by the Society, but in regard to the ample testimonials that have been given of the said Mr. Huddleston in several letters . . . they are of opinion that some gratuity or present in money & books might be made the said Mr. Huddleston."[22] Whereupon the gratuity already mentioned was agreed upon.[23] The Society's favor was duly acknowledged, but Huddleston renewed his request to become the regular schoolmaster on a salary.[24] Writing to the secretary July 30, 1707, he said: "I beg the favour of you to remind the Honble Bord in my behalf that they wou'd be pleased to appoint me their Schoolmaster in New York, to teach such a number of poor children there, as they shall think fit and that they wou'd be pleased to allow me an annual pension for so doing. I have made bold by my humble petition to my Lord Bp. of London to pray him to move the Honorable Bord on my behalf on that head."[25] Two years later than this he was still reciting "the great want of a public school and praying he . . . be appointed Master of such a school with a yearly Pension, the better to enable him to maintain himself and large family."[26] Early in 1709 the Society made Mr. Huddleston a second gift, it being "4 dozen Copies of Brady

---

20 S. P. G. Journal, I, p. (8).

21 S. P. G. Letter-book, A, 2, pp. 130, 132, 118; S. P. G. Journal I, p. (11). The following is an interesting indication that Huddleston's school was looked upon as a Church school, and helps to explain the references to Mr. Huddleston as "the schoolmaster": "I have been desired to give you my Thoughts concerning one Mr. Huddleston, who is & has been a Schoolm^r^ in N. York for many years, & if I am not misinformed is recommended to ye Society for some Consideration in relation to his past & present Services, he has been known to me this many years & has undoubtedly taken a great Deal of Pains to train up all ye youth under his Care in ye Discipline of ye Church, obliging all that sent their children of what nation soever to buy them comon Prayer Books & that they should attend ye Divine Service refusing otherwise to receive them into his School, by wch means he has grafted ye Church not only amongst ye English but many of ye French & Dutch youth, that I make bold to recommend him as worthy of yor Consideration." From the testimonial of Col. Heathcote, S. P. G. Letter-book, A, 7, p. 118.

22 S. P. G. Journal, I, p. (11).

23 See p. 80.

24 S. P. G. Letter-book, A, 3, pp. 8, 18; 4, p. 4; 5, p. 21.

25 *Ibid.*, 4, p. 4.

26 S. P. G. Journal, I, (208); based on his letter of July 9, 1709.

& Tate's Psalms and 50 Copies of the Translation of the Common Prayer in Dutch,"[27] the former for his school, the latter for distribution.[28] At the meeting of December 2, 1709, he was formally made the Society's schoolmaster. It was then "Ordered that £10 for 1 year from this time be allowed to the said Mr. Huddleston in consideration of his being well recommended to the society & upon condition that he shall teach 40 poor children gratis and transmit certificate thereof to this board."[29]

The Charity School was set on foot, as it appears, sometime between February and July of 1710.[30] On July 24, 1710 Mr. Huddleston wrote accepting with pleasure the Society's offer and announcing that Vesey had published this in his Church,[31] and that he (Huddleston) had applied to the Mayor and Overseers of the poor, asking for their recommendation of worthy children, which was furnished in less than a month. These children he promised to teach to the utmost of his ability. He also asked the Society to consider that forty boys would take up the greater part of his time, and to allow him suitable yearly encouragement to discharge his duty with cheerfulness, as he had only eight paying boys left.[32] The reference to the "8 paying boys" throws some interesting light on the prevailing English attitude towards free schools. Parents who could afford it doubtless had their prejudices in favor of the "more select," private schools, though the following explanation was first made of Huddleston's loss of paying scholars: "He is an honest & capable man for that Service as any I know, but I am afraid what you mean a favour to him will not prove such without his Salary's increas't;

---

27 Feb. 18, 1708/9, *ibid.*, I, p. (154).

28 These were probably lost in transit, see S. P. G. Letter-book, A, 5, p. 21; Journal, II, p. 42.

29 *Ibid.*, I, p. (209).

30 In the Memorial to General Nicholson, May 11, 1714, Huddleston stated that he collected in 1709 a "school of 40 poor boys." In those days of slow ocean travel he could hardly have learned of his appointment before two months, which would be in February 1709 (old series). For quotation see S. P. G. Letter-book, A, 9, p. 212.

31 Publication was made "in the English, Dutch & French Churches of this place." *Ibid.*, 7, p. 231. The Society's bounty was not offered in a spirit of sectarianism, as is definitely shown by this fact.

32 S. P. G. Letter-book, A, 5, p. 163, Note also the following extracts: "The City of N. York is much obliged to the Society for appointing good Mr. Huddleston their schoolmaster with an allowance for teaching 40 poor children. He has already that Complement, and I doubt not but his care & diligence in the Society's business will in due time encourage you to augment his Salary which will be an Act of great charity both to the Master & Scholars." (Vesey to Sec., July 26, 1710, *ibid.*, p. 154.); "Mr. Huddleston who is the Clerk of our Church and Master of the School has begun to receive poor children and to instruct them gratis, he will have Customers enow upon that foot for we don't want poor." (Elias Neau to Sec., July 5, 1710, *ibid.*, p. 134.)

for he taught about that Number of Scholars before, which did support him; but since the addition of these the parents have call'd the other children all but eight, saying he will not be able to teach the 40 poor children and theirs too."[33] Afterwards the real reason appeared in one of the reports which said: "He has not above 7 Scholars, except those he teachers on Soc's bounty for the townspeople have taken away their children, being unwilling to send them to a charity school."[34]

At the end of the year the Society determined to continue the charity school voting an annual pension of £10 "during his (Huddleston's) teaching 40 poor children gratis."[35] At the same meeting £40 in books were voted him for the school.[36] Thus, through the joint assistance of Trinity Church and the S. P. G., the charity schoolmaster was assured of an annual income of £30 New York currency and £10 sterling respectively. In addition to this, there were perquisites belonging to the office of Clerk; that is, fixed fees for the performance of certain customary Church services. These were as follows: (1) "For attending at a Funeral, Five shillings and six pence"; (2) "For his attendance at a Marriage, six Shillings and Six pence"; (3) "For the Registering a Christening, Nine pence."[37] Besides, the Vestry in 1707 ordered that, "6sh be paid to the Church & to the Clerk three shillings" for the use of a "black Clothe Pall" presented by Gov. Cornbury, "on condition that no Person dying & belonging to Forte Anne shall be deny'd the use thereof Gratis";[38] and that, when pew assignments were made, "the Clerk to the Vestry receive six shillings for making out every such Assignment."[39] What addition to his two salaries the perquisites made it is impossible to say, but the sum total was inadequate for the proper support of himself and his large family. This was attested by him and vouched for by those who testified to his certificates.[40] Attempts to interest the Assembly in his behalf were unavailing and his salary from Trinity was

33 Col. Morris to Sec., July 25, 1710, *ibid.*, p. 143.

34 "Certificate of Gov. Hunter, Col. Heathcote, & Col. Morris re. the charity School in N. York," Feb. 23. 1711/12, *ibid.*, 7, p. 231.

35 Dec. 19, 1710. S. P. G. Journal, I, p. (329).

36 *Ibid.*

37 Trinity Vestry Minutes, I, p. 49.

38 *Ibid.*, p. 57.

39 *Ibid.*, p. 62.

40 S. P. G. Journal, II, p. 233; Letter-book, A. 7, pp. 146, 231, 233.

at times not forthcoming or else he misrepresented his plight. In 1712 he wrote the Society that he hoped his salary would be increased for he "had not had a farthing these 3 years, but the Soc's £10 P. A" which would scarce buy his family bread;[41] that most of his time was occupied in the school which had contributed largely to the growth of the Church; and that Col. Hunter had twice directed him to petition the Assembly, but it had had no result.[42] Finally, in view of his urgent appeals, as well of those of his friends, the Society in 1713 ordered an addition of £5 to be made to his salary.[43] For the remainder of his term of service and during part of the term of the succeeding schoolmaster the salary allowance was £15 per annum.

That Mr. Huddleston's school was to follow the plan of charity schools in England is shown by an entry in the Society's journal of proceedings, to the effect that, "he has received the book of printed orders with regard to the government of his school according to the method of Charity Schools in England, which he will continue to observe."[44] The reference was to the method and conduct of the school rather than to that more complete care of poor children which the S. P. C. K. schools represented. In one of Huddleston's letters he said: "The charitable subscriptions spoken of in it (the book of printed orders), are wanting here, both towards my personal support and the poor children under my care. . . . The occasion of the deficiency proceeds not *altogether* from want of good inclination in the people here, as from the infancy of the country, and the number of poor in it."[45] To this he adds: "the children need apparel, books, & necessaries, as charity schools in England."[46] While free tuition and free books were guaranteed from the beginning for the forty pupils, it was not until many years later that the expense of clothing the children was provided for. It was then assumed, not by the S. P. G., but by Trinity Church.

---

[41] Even this sometimes failed to reach him. In 1714 he complained that in almost 5 years only £30 were paid. *Ibid.*, 9, p. 212. And the Mayor certified to this, saying two bills for £10 each had been returned protested. *Ibid.*, p. 179.

[42] *Ibid.*, 8, p. 122. It might be held that in 1712 he was not acting as clerk. This cannot be proved for that year, but at his death he was succeeded in that office by his son. See Trinity Vestry Minutes, I, p, 130. The son engaged to undertake the office for the fees only and this suggested the possibility that the earlier salary may have been withdrawn by 1712. But the fact would have been of sufficient importance to be noted in the Vestry Minutes, it would seem.

[43] Sec., to Huddleston, Dec. 18, 1713. *Ibid.*, p. 327.

[44] S. P. G. Journal, II, p. 233.

[45] S. P. G. Letter-book, A, 7, p. 146.

[46] *Ibid.*

Mr. Huddleston was most painstaking in sending the Society testimonials of his work. His diligence and faithfulness was yearly attested by the mayor and by leading men of the city, as well as by the clergy. One of these sent in 1711, being about one year after instruction of the poor boys had begun, certified that seven of those first recommended to him were able to "read write & cast accounts" and had been put out to trades.[47] The following certificate sent in 1713 is typical of the testimonials furnished by the mayors and is quoted in full:

"Certificate of Mr. Huddlestone's teaching School at N. York.

"City of New York, [seal], ss.

"I Caleb Heathcote Esqr Mayor of the City of New York in America do Certify and make known to all whom these presents shall or may concern, That in ye year of our Lord one thousand seven hundred and nine by the direction of the venerable Society for the propagation of the Gospel in fforeign Parts, Mr. W^m^. Huddlestone Schoolmaster of said City received into his school forty poor Boyes of this City being recomended by the Mayor for the time being as fitt objects of their Charity as hath heretofore been certified which poor boyes he hath diligently and faithfully instructed in reading the English tongue, the Church Catechism the English Liturgy and singing of Psalms with writing and arithmetick of which several are already put out to trades and I having frequently visited the said School found the said number of boyes actually under his care, as by a List of their names hereto affixed may appear, and I do further certifie that he hath not as yet rec^d^ any reward or Incouragem^t^ for his Labour and Paines save the yearly allowance of ten pounds sterling from the said venerable Society and that two of his bills which he drew for the same for Ten pounds each are returned protested. In testimony of the truth whereof I have hereto subscribed my name and caused the seal of the said City to be affixed this twentieth day of September Anno Domini 1713. Annoq. Regni Reginae Annae nunca Magnae Britaniae &c., Duodecimo.

(Signed) CALEB HEATHCOTE."[48]

It is interesting to note that the statement has been based on visits made to the school. Subsequent testimonials were regularly of this nature, with few exceptions, though Col. Heathcote, whose interest in the Society and particularly in the Society's schools was so great, was probably a more frequent visitor than any of the succeeding mayors. Yet the fact remains that during all the century this charity school was usually inspected by one or more visitors in official capacity. It came to be performed regularly on the first Monday of each month by a committee of Trinity Vestry.[49] Accompanying Heathcote's certificate was a list of boys then in the school. Many of these were the original pupils of the 1710 enrolment. What proportion cannot be stated.

---

[47] *Ibid.*, A, 7, p. 231. Feb. 23. 1710/11.

[48] *Ibid.*, A, 9, p. 179. Inclosed in Huddleston's letter of Sept. 26, 1713.

[49] *Ibid.*, B, 3, p. 156, Apr. 27, 1763.

Several had been put out to trades according to Heathcote. On May 11, 1714 Huddleston stated the exact number of such boys to be 20. In the list that follows, then, perhaps two-thirds represents the original class:

"John Lowerere Senr	John Blackhead
Richard Sackett	Thom^s^ Kilmaster
John Sackett	John Baptist
Henry Stanton	John Deffore
John Hitchcock	Francis Warne
William Golding	John Wood
Francis Revoa	John Kilmaster
Peter Germine	John Rogers
Elisha Thebond	Robert Provoast
Job Thebond	John Martin
Stantley Holmes	Henry Lowerere
Thomas Cox	John Lowerere
John Cox	Wm. Lowerere
Jacob Cox	Edward Barnes
Israel Chadock	Benjamin Moore
James Joy	Edward Tudor
Daniel Dunscomb	James Jamison
John Dunscomb	George Fielding
John Bant	Wm. Fielding
John Boroughs	Saml Dunscomb
	(Signed) CALEB HEATHCOTE."[50]

As has been seen, the specified number of forty had been enrolled immediately. It had remained so until 1713, sometime after which there was an increase of pupils amounting to about twenty-five per cent. The certificate of 1717 stated that Huddleston refused no poor child sent to him.[51] The school lists bear out the statement. In 1716 the mayor found in the school "40 poor children on the Soc's bounty & 9 more whom he teaches gratis,"[52] but the list which accompanied the report contained fifty names.[53] The next year fifty names were given[54] in the February report and "more poor were daily pressing,"[55] but in August following forty-eight pupils made up the certified list.[56]

Three later lists in 1719, 1721, and 1722 showed fifty-one, forty-eight, and forty-six respectively,[57] so that the average

---

50 *Ibid.*, A, 9, p. 179. Inclosed in Huddleston's letter of Sept. 26, 1713. This is the first list the writer was able to find. Earlier ones were probably sent and have not been preserved.

51 S. P. G. Letter-book, A, 12, p. 408.

52 *Ibid.*, A, 12, p. 402. In a letter of July 22, 1715 he says that in looking over his list, he sees he has taught and is teaching 650 of the Dutch and French to read and write English since he began—meaning of course, the entire period of his teaching in New York. See S. P. G. Journal, III, p. 113.

53 *Ibid.* Of these, fourteen boys were holdovers from the first list.

54 *Ibid.*, A, 12, p. 260; S. P. G. Journal, III, p. 304.

55 *Ibid.*

56 *Ibid.*, A, 12, p. 408.

57 *Ibid.*, A, 13, p. 485; A, 15, p. 111; A, 16, p. 239.

attendance from 1716 to the end of his service was about forty-eight. An innovation, moreover, occurred about this time. In 1716, six girls were enrolled and three in the next year. As near as can be ascertained, therefore, girls were first admitted in 1716. From that time on they were regularly admitted, although they always remained in the minority.[58]

It was about this time that Mrs. Huddleston was associated with her husband in the care of the school. She undoubtedly had particular care of the girls, although in reporting her service Huddleston mentions her teaching the youngest children. He said: "I cannot but humbly acquaint you that the fifty Children, under my care now, must of course take up the most of my time, which it hath done for severall Years: and not only mine but my wife's time for four years past, hath likewise been spent in that Service in teaching those the Younger sort, poor and taken of the Streets, not knowing a Letter."[59] Other reports of Mrs. Huddleston were sent to the Society,[60] indicating that she regularly assisted in the school and devoted her time chiefly to that work. But for her service, or for the enlarged roll of charity pupils, the Huddlestons received very little additional reward. The mayor of the city in his certificate of 1721 in behalf of the schoolmaster said of him: "He hath no other Encouragement . . . save what the honble Society hath been pleased to allow him & a present lately made him from this Corporation of ten pounds (New York money) for almost Twelve Years service.[61]" This gratuity from the city was augmented by a gift of £10 sterling from the Society in 1722.[62] Upon the death of the Catechist of New York in 1722,[63] Mr. Huddleston was requested by Rector Vesey to take upon himself that office. This he continued to do until his death, a period of nearly two years.[64] Though the salary of catechist was £50 per annum no addition was made to Huddleston's regular allowance,[65] but

---

58 In 1719, there were 9 girls and 42 boys; in 1721, 15 girls and 33 boys; in 1722, 14 girls and 32 boys. *Ibid.*

59 Report to Sec., Aug. 29, 1719, *ibid.*, A, 13, p. 472.

60 July 29, 1721, *ibid.*, A, 15, p. 111; Oct. 3, 1722, *ibid*, A, 16, p. 207; June 15, 1722, S. P. G. Journal IV, p. 220.

61 *Ibid.*, A, 15, p. 111.

62 Voted June 15, 1722, S. P. G. Journal, IV, p. 220.

63 Sept. 1722, *ibid.*, V, p. 85.

64 Vesey to Sec., Nov. 8. 1725, S. P. G. Letter-book, B, 1, p. 85; also B, 1, p. 86; also A, 19, p. 411.

65 *Ibid.*, p. 86.

after his demise the Society voted the following order: "That the sum of £50 be given to Mrs. Huddleston as a reward for her late husbands Service in Catechising the Negroes and Indians."[66]

Early grants of books to the school have been mentioned.[67] Very soon after Huddleston's appointment as the regular Schoolmaster he informed the Secretary that most of the forty boys' parents were so miserably poor that they could not provide necessary books.[68] Throughout his work he frequently petitioned for these. The Society responded generously. Scarcely a single request, it appears, failed to be granted. Books lost en route were allowed the second time.[69] In the matter of all books of a religious nature, such as Psalm books, Psalters, prayer books, Church Catechisms, and explanations thereof, the Society sent out supplies for the school and for distribution.[70] The importance which the above books occupied in the school is shown by a comparison with the number of primers sent out. Of the latter a packet of fifty each was sent with the other books on two occasions between 1710 and 1723,[71] as far as the records show. There is no evidence of other non-doctrinal books having been sent. On the other hand it is possible that primers were included in the two or three money grants for books.[72] The following bill indicates the cost of the books at that time:

"A Bill for Books for Mr. Huddlestone. May 8th 1716."

	£	s	d
50 primers		8	6
25 psalters		12	6
A Quarto Common Prayer		7	0
	1	8	0[73]

[66] Apr. 15, 1726, S. P. G. Journal, V, p. 85. The S. P. G. had previously elected Huddleston to be Catechist on March 7, 1717/8. This was on account of the discharge of Mr. Neau from that office. It had been effected through baseless charges against the latter, which had been lodged with the Society. Huddleston was to have an increase of £10 per annum in consideration of the added functions. But Neau immediately cleared himself and was reinstated, so that nothing came of it.

[67] See p. 82–3.

[68] S. P. G. Letter-book, A, 5, p. 163, July 24, 1710.

[69] S. P. G. Journal I, p. (329).

[70] *Ibid.*, I, p. (329); III, pp. 113, 71, 219; IV, pp. 137, 220; S. P. G. Letter-book, A, 16, pp. 212, 228, 261; A, 17, p. 233; A, 10, p. 367.

[71] Feb. 3, 1715/16, S. P. G. Journal III, p. 113; S. P. G. Letter-book, A, 10, pp. 203, 367. June 15, 1722, Journal IV, p. 220; Letter-book A, 16, p. 261.

[72] S. P. G. Journal, I, pp. (11), (151), (329). It is also possible that such books were provided, in part, by the parents.

[73] S. P. G. Letter-book, A, 11, p. 356.

For a schoolhouse, Mr. Huddleston made his own provision, following the custom of the period. This was usually in his home, it would seem, though the point is not made very clear. One of his appeals for augmentation of salary complained that he was obliged to use it "upon Rent."[74] The Catechetical class he taught "in the Steeple every Sunday in the afternoon before Sermon, and after Sermon at his own house."[75] The probable reason for this is not difficult to suggest. Candle light could not be permitted in the steeple of Trinity and his own house offered the only alternative, having as it did school facilities. Upon two different occasions the Common Council, in appreciation of his valuable work and moved by his serious straits, came to his assistance in this respect. On Nov. 27, 1714 Huddleston wrote the Society that "the Mayor & Common Council having taken his condition in their serious consideration have allowed him the room where they meet for his School & the Sheriff, Mr. Harrison, has allowed him the whole City Hall for his comfort."[76] The school was being kept in the City Hall again in 1717, and the mayor for that year certified as follows: "He is diligent in teaching & catechising on week days & Sabbath afternoon in his school, which by leave of the Corporation he keeps in the City Hall."[77] The quotations probably indicate a temporary rather than a permanent or long continued accommodation. It is quite unlikely that he enjoyed the use of the City Hall all of the time from 1714 to 1717, for his complaint about rent was sent in the interval.[78] On the other hand, his school was looked upon as a semi-public institution about this time. The use of the City Hall is at once an indication of it, but, aside from this, the Common Council of the City in 1714 had under consideration the making of special provision for teaching the poor. The following item is from the Council proceedings: "Order'd that this Corporation do Petition the General Assembly for Leave to bring in a Bill to Enable this Corporation to Raise Money for Repairing the public Gaols, Keeping a sufficient Bellmans Watch in the Room and Stead of A

---

[74] July 22, 1715, S. P. G. Journal, III, p. 113.

[75] June 27, 1723, S. P. G. Letter-book, A, 17, p. 233.

[76] S. P. G. Journal, III, p. 71.

[77] Certificatei nclosed in Huddleston's letter of Aug. 15, 1717, S. P. G. Letter-book, A, 12, p. 408.

[78] See above letter of July 22, 1715.

Constable Watch providing fire and Candle for them *Maintaining a publick schoolmaster for teaching the poor* to *read & write* Defraying the Expense of Executing of felons, Maintainance of A Publick Whipper and Other publick & Necessary Charge not Exceeding one hundred and fifty pounds in one year and that the Mayor sign the Petition by Order of this Court and deliver it Accordingly."[79] Although no legislation followed to make a reality of this intention regarding a "publick schoolmaster," as herein expressed, it was only a few months later that Mr. Huddleston was enjoying the privilege of the City Hall. Some years thereafter the following record is found in the Council minutes: "Order'd the Mayor Issue his Warrt to the Treasurer to pay to Mr. William Huddleston the sum of Ten pounds Currt Money of this Province as a present of this Corporation for his Teaching severall poor Children to Read within this City. And Order'd that this be not brought into President."[80]

In 1718 the pupils of the Charity School were assigned seats in Trinity Church. It is recorded that their schoolmaster, on September 18, requested that his scholars might be allowed seats in the West Gallery. They were thereupon assigned, "the two hindermost pews over the North door in the West Gallery until a new Gallery shall be built."[81] Doubtless they had occupied other pews before this and from the beginning regularly attended the services, in charge of Huddleston. They seem to have been given pews over the North door because the location was not conspicuous.[82] Such an intention seems to be shown in the following, which was adopted at the same meeting: "Ordered that a New Gallery be built over the West Gallery if the charge thereof can be defrayed by Subscriptions and when built the front pews to be appropriated to Housekeepers & their wives, Masters of Vessels and their wives and Schoolmasters & their wives, and the range of pews at each end of the said Gallery for Mr. Jenneys & Mr. Huddlestons Schollars, Mr. Jenney to have the first Choice, the two ranges of pews in the middle to be in Common."[83]

---

79 Quoted by Pratt, *op. cit.*, p. 147. Dated June 12, 1714.

80 April 9, 1720. Quoted by Pratt, *op. cit.*, p. 148.

81 Trinity Vestry Minutes, I, pp. 115, 116.

82 In that day, and with the representative of the King of England in the congregation, the matter of rank and precedent were punctiliously observed, and pew assignment was very carefully looked after.

83 Sept. 15, 1718, Trinity Vestry Minutes, I, p. 116.

Mr. Huddleston died in August 1724[84] while in active service. More than half of his life had been spent as a schoolmaster in New York City. Beginning at about the age of twenty-seven he had taught continuously there for thirty-five years,[85] fifteen of which had been under the encouragement of the S. P. G. That this educational service to the city involved hardships and sacrifices, both for his family and himself, his testimonials clearly prove. In spite of financial burdens, his activity in the Church and in the school must have made him an important figure in the community.

Huddleston's death did not interrupt the school. For some years before he had placed his son, Thomas Huddleston, in the school as an Usher or Assistant,[86] having in view the training of a successor to himself. Thomas, therefore, continued to convene the scholars of his late father and in this had the support of the Church and the Mayor. Memorials were at once forwarded to the Society recommending Thomas Huddleston "for his Sobriety diligence and learning . . . as a person fit to be made Schoolmaster."[87] The recommendation was agreed to by the Society and his salary was made equivalent to that of his father.[88] At the same time he was made Clerk of the Church being allowed therefor the "fees Incident and belonging to the same" but no salary or other reward.[89] The record states that he appeared "before this Board and proposed to Execute the office" upon these terms,[90] which may be an indication that the Clerk's office had become fairly renumerative from the fees alone. But he received, besides fees, occasional gratuities from the Vestry,[91] until in 1727 he was put upon the annual

84 S. P. G. Journal, V, p. 85; Letter-book, B, 1, p. 85. There is, however, an uncertainty about this date. Aug. 1724 has been given by Mrs. Huddleston and Mr. Vesey. But another journal entry, a school report, and letters from Huddleston's son, as well as entries in Trinity Vestry Minutes indicate that the son conducted the school, succeeding his deceased father, as early as November 1723. Vesey's letter, B, 1, p. 85. above is an original copy.

85 In a letter, Nov. 24, 1722, he gives his age as "now 60 Years." S. P. G. Letter-book, A, 16, p. 212. From this the figures above are easily determinable with the help of the other data.

86 S. P. G. Journal, IV, p. 295.

87 *Ibid.*; also, S. P. G. Letter-book, A, 17, pp. 247, 312.

88 *Ibid.*, IV, p. 295; also Trinity Vestry Minutes, I, p. 134. The appointment is dated Feb. 21, 1723/4. If Wm. Huddleston's death occurred Aug. 1724, this date should be 1724/5.

89 Trinity Vestry Minutes, I, p. 130.

90 *Ibid.*

91 In 1724, £6; in 1725, £10; in 1726, £15. Trinity Vestry Minutes, I, pp. 130-136, 143.

salary of £15.[92] In 1726 the Society's allowance was advanced to £20 per annum.[93] This seems to have been a voluntary act on the part of the S. P. G., for there are not to be found the usual and frequent requests for assistance that characterized his father's term of office. Apparently the combined sources of Thomas Huddleston's income netted him a fairer sum than had been the case before. But he did urge the Society, in 1727, that, "It might be a great encouragemt to me and the School under my care if the Honble Society wou'd vouchsafe to recommend my case to his Excellcy our Govr and the Mayor & Corporation of this City to give me some Annual Allowce for teaching so many poor Children wch wth the Societys anual Bounty may be a Subsistence & comfort to me in that Service."[94]

Mr. Huddleston's first certificate vouched for forty poor children under his care, though the accompanying list showed but thirty-nine names. Girls were in the majority this year, for there were twenty-three, as compared with sixteen boys.[95] His next list sent shortly thereafter gave forty names, of which seventeen were girls.[96] Others were attending his school "for a small consideration," but neither the names nor the numbers of these were given.[97] In 1725, however, the names of two paying scholars are doubtlessly written separately from those of his other pupils. Of the forty-two, thirteen were girls, while five boys and three girls had been put out to trades. The curiously devised report of this year is herewith given:

"A List of the Childrens names taught on the Bounty of the Venerable Society by Thomas Huddleston their Schoolmaster.[98]

Thomas Bant	John Lea
Edward Osser	Joseph Paulding
Ebenezer Osser	Peter Carstang
John Sanders	James Warner
John Alton	James Bess
Taburill Johnson	Mary Golding
John Poole	Mary Burger
Charles Dobbs	Mary Mecarte
William Lea	Anne Warner
Chalenger Williams	Kathrine Lea.

92 *Ibid.*, pp. 149–50, 154, 159.
93 S. P. G. Journal, V, p. 86, Apr. 15, 1726, but beginning "from Xmas last."
94 July 3, 1727, *ibid.*, V., p. 136; also S. P. G. Letter-book, A, 20, p. 190.
95 S. P. G. Letter-book, A, 17, p. 312.
96 *Ibid.*, A, 18, p. 232.
97 *Ibid.*, A, 18, p. 200.
98 May 12, 1725, *ibid.*, B, 1, p. 101a.

Thomas Grinells Thomas Warner John Bartlate Abraham Blinck Isaac Blinck Gilbert Ash Matthew Bell Thomas Merchell Abraham Poole Gerret Cousyne	Frances Smith Mary Chrissel Mary Thomas Henter Blinck Johanna Cornelisa Hanna Bulson Judea Carstang Richard Harris William Cooker Jane Simpson
Cornelia New Chirck	Jane New Chirck

A List of the Names of those put to trades.

David Farkland John Thomas Thomas Welsh Phillip Lewis	Isaac Bedlow. Susanna Bedlow Kathrine Dobbs Sarah Harpman

In a second list sent in November of the same year Huddleston gave forty names and added: "John Sanders and Mathew Bell are gone to trades."[99] This report was followed within a week by a letter from which it may be inferred that additional pupils were again being received gratis, after the custom of the elder Huddleston. The letter in full, follows:

"I desire you to acquaint ye Honble Society that these were sent in after yt the Certificate was Signed; I could not turn them away by reason that they made such heavy complaints that they are forc'd to put them out for their daily bread and here is abundance of such fitt objects in this City; and have Signified ye names of these poor Creaters.

Wm. Welsh
Cornelius Bulsiny
Edward Nicholls
Charles Nicholls
John Nicholls
Anne Nicholls
Wm. Dewait
Eliz. Welsh.

I am
Sr
Yr Obedient Servt
THOMAS HUDDLESTON.

(Attest) JOH. JANSEN. Mayor."[100]

For the years 1726–31 there are five school lists available. Of these the lowest number of children was 50 and the highest 68,

[99] Nov. 3, 1725, *ibid.*, B, 1, p. 86b.

[100] Nov. 10, 1725, *ibid.*, B, 1, p. 83. From this it appears that some amount of schooling was deemed necessary for apprenticeship.

and the girls numbered from 15 to 20.[101] No tuition was charged by Huddleston during this period. He declared to the Secretary: "Neither their Parents nor the Corporation of this City allow me one farths in consideration of that service and my School may be most properly called the Honble Societys Charity School in the city of New York in America."[102] Six of the poor boys were put to trade in 1726[103] and in 1729 it was reported that a great many of them were then fit for trade.[104] This "fitting for trade" was popular among poor parents. "Poor people are daily coming," wrote Huddleston, "to see if there be a vacancy for their children, for they are not able to pay for their learning."[105]

The Society's manuscripts record only occasional requests for books.[106] These were dispatched in keeping with his requests, but at least one lot of them was seized by "the Salleymen & carried into their country."[107] His modesty in this respect must have been due to the careful preservation of such books as the school already had. Parents were not supplying them "being that," as he once said, "they are so poor that they are not able to purchase them."[108] No mention of any kind is made regarding the school house. This was apparently provided out of his own income.

It is evident that Mrs. Huddleston continued her gratuitous services. "I humbly Acquaint you that the teaching of these Children Occupyes not my time but allso my Mothers."[109] Upon the death of the schoolmaster in 1731,[110] Mrs. Huddleston remained in entire charge of the school until the appointment of a successor. This was from October 8, 1731 until April 22,

---

101 For example: June 17, 1726, 50 with 18 girls; June 8, 1727, 54 with 18 girls; July 10, 1729, 55 with 15 girls; May 23, 1730, 68 with 20 girls; and July 8, 1731, 57 with 17 girls. See S. P. G. Letter-book, A, 19, p. 428; A, 20, p. 221; A, 22, p. 40; A, 23, pp. 96, 364. Only one list of names of pupils was ever sent the Society after 1731. This was sent by Joseph Hildreth in 1743.

102 *Ibid.*, A, 20, p. 190, July 3, 1727. It may be noted, too, that this statement was made with regard, not to 40, but to "the 55 poor children of this place that are now under my Care at School." *Ibid.*

103 *Ibid.*, A, 19, p. 392.

104 *Ibid.*, B, 1, p. 61.

105 *Ibid.*

106 *Ibid.*, B, 1, pp. 106, 61; A, 19, p. 206; A, 20, p. 190. A grant of 12 primers was the only one found.

107 *Ibid.*, A, 19, p. 414.

108 *Ibid.*, A, 19, p. 392.

109 *Ibid.*, June 1726.

110 About October, Trinity Vestry Minutes, I, p. 161; S. P. G. Letter-book, A, 23, p. 343; Journal, V, p. 324.

1732, as attested by the Mayor of the City.[111] In appreciation of her work, the Mayor's certificate said: "She has had the same scholars as her son had at the time of his death, & the Mayor has sent her several poor children during the time that she taught. She discharged her duty with diligence & fidelity."[112] Indeed a material acknowledgment of her services to the city was made by the Common Council, as follows: "Order'd the Mayor Issue his warrant to the Treasurer to pay to Mrs. Sarah Huddleston widow or Order the sum of Eight pounds Current Money of New York as a Gratification for the trouble and Care she and her late Son Thomas Huddleston deceased have taken in teaching several poor children of this Corporation to Read and Write and Instructing them in the Principles of Religion, over and above the number allowed by the Venerable society for the propagation of the Gospel in foreign parts."[113] Earnest efforts were made to induce the S. P. G. to make Mrs. Huddleston her son's successor. A petition to this effect was dispatched to the Secretary, which bore the signatures of 68 leading men, including the President of the Council, Mayor, Aldermen, Justices, Lawyers and Merchants.[114] Recommendations from many of these officials and men of affairs accompanied the petition.[115] Her appointment was objected to by the officials of Trinity Church. Because of her advanced years they could not think her "Capable to discharge a Trust of duty of such great importance both to the City and Church."[116] In lieu of

111 Trinity Vestry Minutes I, p. 165; S. P. G. Letter-book, A, 24, pp. 265, 170; Journal, V, p. 140. She was allowed for this a half year's salary, £10. *Ibid.*

112 *Ibid.*

113 Oct. 14, 1731. Quoted by Pratt, *op. cit.*, p. 148.

114 *Ibid.*, A, 23, p. 375.

115 *Ibid.*, A, 23, p. 379.

116 Trinity Vestry Minutes, I, p. 161; S. P. G. Journal, V, p. 325. In one of the printed documents of Fulham Archives the responsibility for the opposition was charged to Rev. Mr. Vesey. The document is a partisan one, entitled, "A Supplement to the Vindication of Mr. Alex. Campbell—Wherein all the objections made to the said Vindication are answered particularly those in a late Paper, called, Mr. Noxon's Observations," dated Aug. 15, 1732. Referring to Vesey's attitude towards Mrs. Huddleston, this paper says, in a spirit of bitterness: "How basely Mr. Vesey has behaved towards Mrs. Huddleston, is very well known, for he obliged her to take out the Society's Bounty in Goods, from Hucksters and Shop-keepers with whom Mr. Vesey dealt, to the Prejudice and Loss of the said Mrs. Huddleston, at least a third of the Money. He has employed her Son Huddleston to write out his Merchants Accompts for several years, and sometimes till the Ringing of the last Bell on Sundays, neither has he paid her, or her Son, for his Pains and Troubles to this Day; On the Contrary, it was by his Interest, that she was disappointed of the School, which she was Ten Times more qualified to teach than Mr. Noxon. But Mr. Vesey had no regard to this, nor yet to the Desolation of a numerous virtuous Family, which was to ensue, in all Probability on this Disappointment." A similar complaint is found in a printed pamphlet among the Society's papers, (B, 1, p. 43.). It says: "It is a matter of wonder to the Privy Council, the Magistrates of the City, the Judges of the Province & to all sensible & disinterested people of this place, who have recommended Mrs. Huddleston (wh. recommendation the writer begs his Lordship once more to read), how Mr. Vesey could so impose upon his Lordship & Soc. against plain reason & matter of fact, or how the recommendation could prevail against that of so many worthy gentlemen & the united voice of the people."

this, the Churchwardens and Vestry recommended "her and her poor family to the Society as objects worthy of their Charity, both her husband and son having faithfully discharged their duties in their respective stations."[117] Acting on the advice of the Church, the S. P. G. denied Mrs. Huddleston's petition, but at once voted her a gratuity of £20 being the equivalent of one year's salary. Thus came to a close the service of the Huddleston family in New York City. Theirs was a record of personal sacrifice and earnest devotion to educational uplift, which covered a period little short of half a century.

Thomas Noxon was appointed the succeeding schoolmaster on January 21, 1731/2.[118] The action of the Society was based on the memorial of Trinity Church setting forth that Mr. Noxon was "a person of exemplary piety and virtue" having been for many years past and then being a vestryman of the Church.[119] The previous allowance of £20 per annum was voted.[120] In October of the previous year he had been made Clerk of the Church with £15 per annum and the perquisites of the office.[121] After two years he resigned the position of clerk.[122] Why he should voluntarily have given up this needful addition to his income as schoolmaster is hard to understand. There is a suggestion that his accepting the school over Mrs. Huddleston was unpopular and the cause of bitter feeling towards him, both as schoolmaster and as clerk.[123] Thereafter he made the "Soc's School his whole business,"[124] having "no allowance from their parents, or the City for his pains," and teaching them "only in consideration of the Soc's Salary."[125]

---

117 *Ibid.;* also, S. P. G. Letter-book, A, 23, p. 343.

118 S. P. G. Journal, V, p. 325.

119 Trinity Vestry Minutes, I, p. 161.

120 Jan. 21, 1731/2. S. P. G. Journal, V, p. 325.

121 Trinity Vestry Minutes, I, pp. 161, 164.

122 *Ibid.*, pp. 168, 177.

123 In the Fulham document noted on page 96. Noxon is thus objected to: "He is a strange-out-of-the-way Clerk who cannot sing by Note, and a most unaccountable Schoolmaster who can neither read nor write." "Mr. Noxon is very unfit for his present office and blunders almost every Day, in the face of the Whole Congregation. Some of the Congregation have expressed their sorrow and concern at this. Does not Mr. Noxon himself acknowledge his own insufficiency by making use of a Deputy when he himself is present? He does not attack him because he is a Member of the Church of England, nor because he does not sing by Note, but because he has accepted, and Mr. Vesey has recommended him to an Employment for which he is altogether unqualified." There is further suggestion of public ill-feeling in the fact that none of Noxon's reports were attested by the Mayor or other public officials.

124 S. P. G. Journal, VII, p. 305, Aug. 6, 1738.

125 *Ibid.*, p. 306.

Mr. Noxon began his service as Schoolmaster April 22, 1732 and continued for eleven years in this work. At the very outset a most significant step was taken by the Vestry of Trinity Church. Heretofore, as has been shown, there had been a cordial coöperation between the S. P. G. and the Church, as far as that had gone. The Church had assumed no official responsibility but the Rector and others had constantly watched over the school in their individual capacities. The Rector as well as the Mayor had regularly visited the school. On April 21, 1732 the Church, for the first time, took formal official recognition of the school by appointing a committee of inspection for it, in these words:

"Ordered that the Rector & Church Wardens or one of them with Mr. John Roade, Mr. Duane, Mr. McEvers, Mr. Augustus Jay & Mr. Moore or any three of them be a Committee to visit the Society's School in this City and to give proper Certificates and Directions relating thereto and to take Care that the pious Design of the Society be complyed with."[126]

That the action was at the Society's solicitation for a closer interest on the part of the Church, is fairly well indicated in the Vestry's address to the S. P. G. immediately following their appointment of the committee. The address said in part: "We . . . beg leave to assure them We Shall not only be very cautious in our recommendations but likewise upon all occasions in our power endeavour to Encourage and further their pious Intentions and pursuant to their Comands Signifyed in your said Letter We hereby Certify that the Said Mr. Noxon began to teach School on the twenty Second day of April last and we have appointed the Rector Church Wardens and some of the Vestry a Committee to visit the said School from time to time as occasion shall require to Certify the Number of Scholars Management and progress thereof who have this day visited his School and found in it upwards of forty poor children under his Instruction."[127] From this time all reports of Noxon's school were certified to by the gentlemen of the committee, whose visits seem to have been made with regularity.[128] Presumably it became a standing committee and was usually renewed yearly

126 Trinity Vestry Minutes, I, p. 164. This is the first mention of the Charity School in the Church Minutes.

127 *Ibid.*, p. 165. May 10, 1732; S. P. G. Letter-book, A, 24, p. 165. Ecclesiastical Records, *op. cit.*, p. 2591.

128 This is shown by the available reports of Noxon, which have the committee's attestation, but the reports are not completely preserved.

by the Vestry along with other standing committees, in a general resolution to that effect. On the other hand, the minutes of the Vestry contain a few specific resolutions relating thereto. On July 7, 1736, the committee was renewed, it being "Resolved that the Rector Churchwardens, and Mr. Ellerton be a Comittee to visit the Society's Scholl in this City under the Care of Mr. Thomas Noxon their Schollmaster and to report their opinion thereof to this Board with all convenient Speed."[129] A similar order was made in 1749,[130] and again in 1761. On this last occasion visits of inspection were definitely fixed, as may be seen in the following from the Minutes:

"Ordered that the Rector Two Churchwardens Mr. Nicholls Mr. Horsmanden Mr. Gabriel Ludlow Mr. Williams Mr. Mann Mr. Clarkson And Mr. Stuyvesant and as many more of this Corporation as please to attend or any three or more of them be a Committee to Visit and regulate the Charity School and to meet on the first Monday in every Month at Three o'Clock in the afternoon in the Vestry Room for that purpose also that they have Power to agree with & employ a School Mistress to teach the Girls to Reade and Sow upon such Terms as they shall think fitt."[131]

A few years after "the Committee for Inspecting the Charity School" was empowered to enlarge the school "if they think proper."[132] Finally in 1772 the Committee is again mentioned specifically on two different occasions.[133] Besides this evidence nearly all of the Notitiae and other reports of Mr. Noxon's successor were attested by these officials of the Church and thus indicate a permanent overseeing committee.[134] It seems reasonable to suppose, therefore, that a system of school inspection was carried on under the auspices of the Church from 1732 to the end of the century, and that it was practically a continuous system.

Mr. Noxon's enrolment in the first year was 44 scholars.[135] In 1740 it reached 66 scholars, the highest during his teaching.[136]

---

[129] Trinity Vestry Minutes, I, p. 184.

[130] *Ibid.*, p. 256.

[131] May 20, 1761, *ibid.*, p. 298–9.

[132] Apr. 21, 1764, *ibid.*, p. 312.

[133] "Ordered that Doctor Charlton, Mr. Van Dam, Mr. Kissam, and Mr. Duane be added to the Committee for visiting the Charity School." *Ibid.*, p. 369, Nov. 11, 1772. Also, "Mr. Laight added to School Committee." *Ibid.*, p. 370, Dec. 29, 1772.

[134] Hildreth, the schoolmaster, in 1761, 1764, 1765, 1769 and 1773 distinctly refers to the activity of the committee of 1761 and the regularity of its visits. S. P. G. Letter-book, B, 3, pp. 157, 158, 169, 164.

[135] S. P. G. Journal, VI, p. 40.

[136] *Ibid.*, VIII, p. 231. In 1733 he had "between 40 and 50," S. P. G. Letter-book, A, 24, p. 58. In 1738 the number was 49, Journal, VII, p. 306.

The following year he reported upwards of 60,[137] and in the last year of his service there were 56 enrolled.[138] In these two years, for the first time, a religious grouping of the children is given. Of the 60 pupils and more, 38 were baptized in the Church, and all others were "of dissenting Parents."[139] Of the 56 pupils in 1741, 30 belonged to parents of the Church of England, 10 to parents of the Dutch congregation, and the remaining 16 were children of the Calvinists and other dissenters.[140]

Twice, at least, Noxon desired books, Psalters and Catechisms for his poor children.[141] The Society sent him 50 of the former and 100 of the latter.[142] Not once was a primer asked for among the papers that are now preserved. No mention is made of a schoolhouse. The inference is that it was provided by himself. He probably employed an assistant or usher in the school, though he nowhere mentioned such help in his letters to England. The "Deputy" referred to in a previous footnote,[143] wherein Noxon was attacked for inefficiency, may mean his deputy in the school or in the Church. He was advanced in years, and the charge of inability must have had some foundation, in spite of the fact that the representations of the Church continuously vouched for his diligence and for his "behaving well" as a schoolmaster;[144] and in spite of Vesey's assertion that "he adorns his profession with a virtuous life."[145] Elsewhere it was asserted that Mr. Noxon could "neither read nor write English" and that he possessed no merit to support his pretensions to the school.[146] On December 8, 1742 Noxon wrote the Society requesting that his resignation might be accepted on Lady Day (March 25) 1743. He assigned as a reason for this that he was "now old & unequal to the fatigue."[147]

Mr. Noxon's resignation was accompanied by "a recommendation from Vesey, Charlton, & Churchwardens & Vestry of Mr.

---

137 *Ibid.*, IX, p. 7.

138 *Ibid.*, pp. 133, 58.

139 S. P. G. Letter-book, B, 9, p. 64.

140 S. P. G. Journal, IX, p. 58; Letter-book, B, 10 pp. 69–70.

141 S. P. G. Journal, VI., p. 40; VII, p. 305.

142 *Ibid;* also Journal, VIII, p. 306.

143 See p.97.

144 S. P. G. Letter-book, B, 1, p. 35.

145 S. P. G. Journal, VII, p. 306.

146 From a printed pamphlet, undated, among the S. P. G. papers, Letter-book, B, 1, p. 43. This is clearly overstated and is written in opposition to the Church and Society.

147 S. P. G. Journal, IX, p. 133.

Joseph Hildreth of N. York"[148] to succeed him. In view of this, Hildreth took charge of the school until the pleasure of the Society should be made known. But the Society did not favor the appointment, having determined at about this time upon other methods of recruiting and placing schoolmasters. The Secretary thus wrote to Mr. Vesey: "As to the appointment of a schoolmaster at New York, they cannot accept of Mr. Hildreth in the Room of Mr. Noxon whose Resignation they have received, because after mature consideration they are lately come to a Resolution that, in all future appointments of Schoolmasters and Catechists, they will have a principal Regard to such persons as are already in, or are qualifying themselves for Holy Orders, and that several young men educated in the Universities of New England, who are desirous of being employed in the Service of the Society, and are very well recommended both as to Learning and Morals, shall first be employed, and that they do not see sufficient Reason for their Support of a school in your City, where, according to Information, there are 9 English, one Dutch, one French, and one Latin School at this time."[149] The last point was certainly well taken, and the Church was in a position by this time to assume full responsibility for the charity school, as following events will indicate. The Rector and other church officials, however, did not share this view. They became greatly concerned about it and so expressed themselves to the Society. Upon the best information, Mr. Vesey gave assurance that there was "but one English School taught by the Schoolmaster of the Episcopal Church,"[150] and, he continued: "If the Honble Society will not be pleased to Support this School any longer, it will be a vast obstruction to the growth of our Infant Church, to wch it has been a constant Nursery for above forty years, and to the Children of the Poor who's Parents can hardly give them bread, may be deprived of the opportunity of Learning to Read &c., of being instructed in those principles of Christianity wch are necessary to save their Souls."[151] On March 16, 1743/4 the Society receded from its former position and voted Hildreth a salary from the time of his taking charge

148 *Ibid.*

149 S. P. G. Letter-book, B, 10, p. 193a, June 14, 1743.

150 S. P. G. Journal, IX, p. 244.

151 S. P. G. Letter-book, B, 11, p. 117, Dec. 9, 1743. A similarly urgent letter was sent by Hildreth, Nov. 1, 1743. Journal IX, p. 246.

of the school.[152] But it was cut down to £10, and was given on condition that he should teach 56 poor children gratis.[153] In 1746 his salary was advanced to £15 and remained at that figure for about twenty-five years.[154] He was appointed Catechist to the Negroes in 1770 at an additional allowance of £10,[155] and the two positions he continued to hold throughout the remaining years of his service. Hildreth also became Clerk of the Church in 1744 on a salary of £15 per annum.[156] From the year 1754 on he was also the recipient of frequent liberal "gratuities" from the Vestry, ranging from £20 to £60.[157] These were in fact the Vestry's salary allowance to him, being "An Encouragement to him for his Extraordinary Services and Care of the said School."[158] In 1770, £40 became the fixed salary allowed by the Vestry for this work,[159] to which an additional £20 per annum were added in 1772.[160] Mr. Hildreth therefore enjoyed an income far in excess of the incomes of his predecessors, as far as the figures indicate.[161] The actual purchasing power of the salary paid in New York currency was relatively less in the later years of his teaching. For this reason his condition was not as greatly improved over that of the previous schoolmasters as might appear. Before Trinity Church began an allowance he wrote the Society: "By reason of ye smallness of my Salary the dearness of all necessities, as well as House Rent, I was greatly discourag'd in the discharge of my duty to the poor Children, comītted to my care."[162] In 1767 he still maintained that he could not subsist in New York, but for the small additional allowance for

152 This being March 25, 1743. *Ibid.*

153 *Ibid.*

154 S. P. G. Journal X, p. 170.

155 *Ibid.*, XVIII, p. 431–2. Oct. 19, 1770.

156 Nov. 6, 1744. Trinity Vestry Minutes, I, p. 230.

157 Trinity Vestry Minutes. May 8, 1754, £20, I, p. 275; March 11, 1756/7, £20, *ibid.*, p. 283; May 25, 1758, £20 *ibid.*, p. 289; Sept. 13, 1759, £20, *ibid.*, p. 292; Oct. 30, 1760, *ibid.*, p. 296; Nov. 12, 1762, £60; *ibid.*, p. 306; March 20, 1764/5, £30, *ibid.*, p. 319; Dec. 23, 1766, £30, *ibid.*, p. 328; Dec. 15, 1767, £30, *ibid.*, p. 332; Dec. 19, 1768, £30, *ibid.*, p. 338; Jan. 11, 1769/70, £40, *ibid.*, p. 347; Nov. 15, 1770, £40, *ibid.*, p. 351.

158 *Ibid.* A joint gratuity of £20 sterling was granted Hildreth in 1767 by the Vestry & the S. P. G., *ibid.*, p. 329; S. P. G. Journal XVI, p. 388. Another gratuity of £10 sterling was given him by the Society in 1750, he having sustained a great loss by fire, *ibid.*, XI, p. 244.

159 Trinity Vestry Minutes, I, p. 351.

160 *Ibid.*, p. 365.

161 The Clerk's fees were also increased in 1766, making them much in excess of the fees which the Huddlestons enjoyed. *Ibid.*, p. 325.

162 S. P. G. Letter-book, B, 16, p. 54.

officiating as Parish Clerk,[163] because his combined salary was less than that of any other schoolmaster in the city.[164]

The increasing active interest of Trinity Church in the affairs of the Charity School has been already shown in two ways, namely, looking after the regulation of the school through inspecting committees, and fixing an additional salary on the schoolmaster. In the years before 1740 the Charity School was above all else the "Society's Charity School." All correspondence is to this effect. But during the administration of Hildreth New York takes a new attitude towards the institution. Gradually it comes to be generally referred to as Trinity Church School and after 1763 Mr. Hildreth addresses his communications from "Trinity School, New York."[165] The reason for this change was due to the fact that the Church gradually came to take the initiative in the school's affairs, which it had hesitated to do before. Not only was this true in the support of the schoolmaster, but also in providing for the material needs of the poor children, on a scale like that of the S. P. C. K. in England. Funds for the added responsibilities now assumed were necessary and these the Church took steps to acquire. In the second half of the eighteenth century the Church was able to maintain a Charity School Fund sufficient to permit a most praiseworthy fostering of the institution. The two chief sources of the fund were bequests, and the collections in the Episcopal churches on Sundays especially devoted to Charity School sermons. The Church received between 1727 and 1789 probably more than £5000 in gifts and bequests either for the poor or specifically for the Charity School.[166] Almost four-fifths of this amount was given while Hildreth was schoolmaster. Much of it was put out at interest, which at the current rate, 5 per cent,[167]

163 S. P. G. Letter-book, B, 3, p. 161. Hildreth was married and had four children. *Ibid.*, p. 158.

164 *Ibid.*, p. 158.

165 *Ibid.*, B, 3, p. 156 ff. The name was first used by Hildreth on Apr. 27, 1763, and is apparently the earliest on record.

166 Unfortunately some bequests are entered in the Vestry Minutes with no specific sum given. Most of the bequests were to the school directly. About £4000 was bequeathed in Hildreth's term. For these see Trinity Vestry Minutes, I, pp. 154, 214, 268, 272, 287, 285–6, 291, 295, 310, 297, 337, 345, 384, 446, 455, 520. See also for several of these, New York Historical Society Publications, 1896, pp. 188–9, 445, 369–70, 421–2; 1897, p. 317; and Berrian, *op. cit.*, p. 134.

167 Trinity Vestry Minutes, I, pp. 291, 295, 520.

netted a fair amount for the School.[168] Charity School sermons similar to those in vogue in England were begun for the first time in 1755.[169] They were ordered annually thereafter by the Vestry until 1775, when they were given up during the outbreak of the war and renewed in 1778.[170] These sermons were regularly advertised to the public through the medium of the newspapers.[171] They were the means of securing generous responses from the congregations of the two churches and from the public.[172] Funds thus collected were disposed of by a committee of the Vestry appointed annually for that purpose.[173] With gifts, bequests, and regular collections the Church was able to maintain a generous support for the school. Personal necessities of the children were provided, and additions were made to the schoolmaster's salary as heretofore shown. The school was supplied with wood and other necessities of equipment;[174] and an excellent charity schoolhouse was built and maintained.[175]

Mr. Hildreth served thirty-four years as the Society's schoolmaster and during this period there are available thirty-one

---

168 All but one bequest gave no specific direction other than for the benefit of the poor or the Charity School. The curious exception is the bequest of Mrs. Anne Chambers in 1774, from which the following provision is taken: "That the Same be kept and put out at Interest by them and the Yearly Interest or Income thereof be applied towards the Support of the Girls only belonging and to belong to the Charity School in the City of New York that is under their Care and Inspection and in rewarding such of the said Girls upon leaving the said School as they shall judge deserving thereof and in such Proportions as they shall think proper in Cash or otherwise which I intend as an Encouragement for their diligence and decent and orderly behaviour during their Continuance in the said School." *Ibid.*, p. 384. Note the following entry in the minutes of Sept. 17, 1781: "It is remembered that six additional Girls were admitted soon after her Decease in Consequence thereof & it is now Ordered—That the Committee appointed for visiting the Charity School do grant an order on the Treasurer thereof for such a Premium, to those Girls at their leaving the School, as they shall judge most deserving thereof, either in Money, Cloaths, Apprentice—Fee or in any other manner that shall in their opinion come within the meaning of the Will." *Ibid.*, p. 420.

169 *Ibid.*, p. 279; N. Y. Hist. Soc. Pub. 1870, p. 171.

170 Trinity Vestry Minutes, I, pp. 279, 282, 287, 292, 296, 300, 306, 317, 321, 327, 337, 345, 351, 361, 369, 410, 415, 420, 467, 480, 488, 511, 520. Also, N. Y. Hist. Soc. Pub., 1870, pp. 171–269.

171 The following from the New York *Mercury* of Jan. 3, 1757 is a typical illustration:

"On Sunday next in the Forenoon, a Charity Sermon will be preached at Trinity Church, by the Reverend Mr. Barclay; and on the Sunday following, in the Afternoon, a Charity Sermon will also be preached at St. George's Chappel, at both which a Collection will be made towards cloathing the Charity-Scholars."

172 Trinity Vestry Minutes, citations above; N. Y. Hist. Soc. Pub., 1870, pp. 185, 190, 173, 198, 199, 254.

173 "Ordered That Coll° Robinson, Mr. Reall & Mr. Gabriel Ludlow or any two of them be a Committee to examine which of the Charity Children are in want of Cloathing, and to lay out the Moneys Collected in the Church & Chappell for that purpose, as they shall think most proper." Trinity Vestry Minutes, I, p. 279. Other citations similar to those for Charity Sermons.

174 "Ordered that the Rector and Church Wardens furnish Mr· Eldrith the Society School Master with such a Number of Spelling Books and so much Wood for the use of the Charity Children there as they shall think Convenient." Aug. 10, 1747, *ibid.*, p. 245, also pp. 260, 267, 290, 293 (Iron Stove provided). The above grant of books is the only one recorded in the Vestry Minutes.

175 See following pages.

reports for twenty-six different years. Between 1753 and 1757 inclusive no reports are given and presumably they have been lost.[176] Though the Society, on appointing Hildreth, stipulated that 56 pupils should be taught by him, that number was not given in the reports until about 1759. But since he voluntarily gave catechetical instruction during this term to some 15 Negroes who came to him in the evenings, he more than met the stipulation. The Charity School averaged an attendance of 46 for the first five years and of 50 for the next five. Between 1758 and 1763 the usual attendance was 60, 48 boys and 12 girls; between 1764 and 1768 it was 72, with one-third girls;[177] and from 1769 to 1777 the average was 85, 55 boys and 30 girls.[178] Hildreth's school was doubtless the largest in the Province during the greater part of his teaching. He inferred as much in a report of 1765, wherein he said: "The number of charity children I teach is so great, 'tis not in my power to take in any private Scholars, and do justice to them all. . . . My duty in this School greatly exceeds that of any other School in this place."[179]

Up to 1764 half of the charity children were baptized in the Church of England; the others were reported as children of dissenting parents. After this date, however, no children of nonconformists are mentioned in the reports. The reason seems to be found in a policy adopted by Trinity Vestry in this year, whereby the children of the Episcopal congregation were to have the preference in the Charity School.[180] Between 1763 and 1775 about 20 girls and boys were yearly "discharged and put out apprentices to trades,"[181] and just once, in 1768, was it reported that three were discharged for not giving regular attendance.[182] The table shown herewith gives a much clearer

---

176 However the Society in 1761 decided to remind Hildreth "that he had not corresponded according to rule, & must do so in the future." S. P. G. Journal, XV, p. 170.

177 In 1764, the number of girls admitted was increased from 12 to 24 by the Committee of the Vestry. S. P. G. Letter-book, B, 3, p. 157.

178 In a report of 1770, Hildreth stated that the Vestry had "added 10 to the number who regularly attend." His statistics showed the addition to be 5 girls and 5 boys. S. P. G. Letter-book, B, 3, p. 165. But the vestry's decision is thus recorded: "Ordered that there be admitted Ten Boys more than are at present in the Charity School." Trinity Vestry Minutes, I, p. 351, May 30, 1770.

179 S. P. G. Letter-book, B, 3, p. 158.

180 "Ordered that for the future that whenever a Vacancy happens in the Charity School that the Poor Children belonging to the Congregation of Trinity Church have the Preference to those belonging to other Congregations." Trinity Vestry Minutes, I, p. 318. Nov. 23, 1764.

181 A few reports between 1759 and 1763 speak of "several boys" and "several scholars" thus put out.

182 S. P. G. Letter-book, B, 3, p. 163.

idea of the preceding features of the Charity School, as received by the Society from Hildreth:

STATISTICS FROM MR. HILDRETH'S SCHOOL[183]

Date	Number Enrolled		Baptized in church	Dissenting Children	Put Out to Trades	
	Boys	Girls			Boys	Girls
Nov. 1, 1743	40	16				
Nov. 1, 1745	40		20	20		
Sept. 19, 1746	50					
Oct. 16, 1747	48		20	28		
Jan. 8, 1747/8	40		20	20		
Mar. 26, 1748	46		20	26		
Nov. 26, 1748	40		20	20		
Apr. 1, 1749	50		30	20		
Apr. 6, 1750	50		30	20		
Mar. 28, 1751	50		30	20		
Dec. 9, 1751	50		30	20		
Apr. 10, 1752	50		30	20		
Oct. 28, 1752	50		30	20		
May 31, 1758	47		30	17		
May 20, 1759	61		36	25	6	
Dec. 22, 1761	48	12	40	20	"Several Scholars"	
May 11, 1762	48	12	30	30	"Several boys"	
Apr. 27, 1763	48	12	30	30	9	
May 29, 1764	48	24			8	5
Apr. 27, 1765	48	24			10	6
Sept. 29, 1766	48	24			19	11
Oct. 20, 1767	50	24			12	7
Oct. 18, 1768	50	25			13	7
Oct. 18, 1769	50	25			15	7
Oct. 16, 1770	55	30			12	4
Oct. 16, 1771	55	30			12	8
Oct. 17, 1772	55	30			15	13
Nov. 7, 1773	56	30			18	11
Dec. 30, 1775	56	30			16	12
Oct. 6, 1776	56	30				

Whether Hildreth had a schoolmistress assistant from the beginning is not shown. In view of the size of the school and the teaching of both sexes, it is more than probable that he did have such help for most of the time, and that he met the expense out of his own income. In 1761 a schoolmistress was employed by the Vestry, who was to have charge of the girls in needlework.

183 S. P. G. Letter-book, B, 11, pp. 120–2; B, 13, p. 122; Journal, X, p. 170; Letter-book, B, 15, pp. 88, 120; B, 16, pp. 44, 54; B, 17, p. 98; B, 18, p. 100; B, 19, pp. 68, 70; B, 20, pp. 58, 59; Journal XIV, pp. 113, 214, Letter-book, B, 3, pp. 153–171.

They were still to come to Hildreth one hour a day for instruction in writing.[184] The duties of the schoolmistress were never clearly defined by Hildreth, but in frequent references to her it is certain that she remained in this work from 1761 until after the schoolmaster's death.[185] In addition to needlework she taught the girls to read only, these accomplishments with ability to write being held sufficient for girls. Further assistance was allowed by the Vestry in 1771. A former pupil was bound out to Mr. Hildreth for this purpose, according to a minute of the Vestry which is as follows: "Mrs. Wyley having agreed with the Vestry to bind her Son to Mr. Joseph Hildreth for four years to Act as an Usher or Assistant in the Charity School. It is resolved that this Corporation will allow and pay unto the said Mrs. Wyley the sum of Sixteen pounds p. Annum for the said four years to Commence from the first Day of January last and to Cloath her said Son in such decent manner as the Vestry shall from time to time think fitt."[186] In Hildreth's next report, this lad is thus spoken of: "The Vestry having been kind enough to allow me an assistant, a Lad brought up at my School, who has been a great help to me in forwarding the Children in their learning. He is a sober Youth and very assiduous."[187] There is a strong probability that this lad was a son of the schoolmistress, for a further entry in the minutes of the Vestry suggests that Mrs. Wyley is herself the assistant of Mr. Hildreth. It reads: "Ordered that Mr. Clarkson, Mr. Bache and Mr. Van Dam be a Committee to have the Charity School-House (in which Mrs. Wyley lives) repaired in such manner as they shall think proper."[188]

Until 1748 Hildreth found his own schoolhouse. This was a discouraging feature of his work and he pressed the matter both with the S. P. G. and before the Vestry.[189] When Trinity first took up plans for the building of St. George's Chapel as a second place of worship in the city, Mr. Hildreth took advantage of the opportunity. He petitioned for the assistance of the Vestry in building a schoolhouse which the latter forthwith agreed to. It

---

184 "The Vestry have also employed a School Mistress to instruct the Girls in Needlework, and those that can Read come to me an hour in a day to be taught to write." S. P. G. Letter-book, B, 3, p. 153, Dec. 21, 1761.

185 *Ibid.*, B, 3, pp. 155, 156, 157, 158, 163, 167; Journal XX, p. 656, and XXI, pp. 318–22.

186 Trinity Vestry Minutes, I, p. 353, March 21, 1771.

187 S. P. G. Letter-book, B, 3, p. 168, Oct. 17, 1772.

188 Trinity Vestry Minutes, I, p. 359, Aug. 30, 1771.

189 S. P. G. Letter-book, B, 16, p. 54.

was "Ordered that the Committee appointed for Considering of a proper place for Building a Chappell of Ease also Consider of Mr. Hildreth's Petition and make their Report thereon with all Convenient Expedition."[190] The report of the committee was ready at the next meeting in May 1748, and it was then "Ordered that so much of the Churches Ground adjoining to the Lutheran Church as the Church Wardens shall think proper be Appropriated for Building a Charity School."[191] Further progress in the building of a schoolhouse is shown in Hildreth's account sent the Society in the fall of the same year, in which, after giving the usual statistics concerning the pupils, he continued:

"Sometime in May last I drew up a Petition which I laid before ye Rector, Churchwardens, & Vestry of Trinity Church in this City, representing to them ye Circumstances of my School; . . . that if I could have a convenient House built on some of the Church's vacant ground it would be a great encouragement to me & my Successors in the faithful discharge of our duty and desir'd leave of his Excy the Honble George Clinton, Esq. our Governour, to go round with a Subscription paper, in order to collect ye Charitable donations of well disposed Persons towards carrying on ye said building of a Charity School, (the Vestry having granted a sufficiency of the Church's Ground near ye sam for a spacious House, Yard, & Garden) which his Excy not only granted but greatly encourag'd the same by his own Subscription as also did our Rector, wth ye Church Wardens & Vestry, with many others who are well wishers to our Church, so that I have rais'd a considerable sum toward the Building, wee have only laid ye foundation this fall, and intend to get all materials ready agast next spring to carry on ye Building which is to be of Brick 50 feet front & 26 ft. wide & 2 stories high, with a Cupola for a small Bell, the lower part to be for ye dwelling, wth a Kitchen adjoining, and ye upper Stores wch will be in one spacious Room for the School, wch by God's blessing I hope will be compleat by next fall. This Pious design being a thing so absolutely necessary as 'tis at prest *ye only Charity School* in this City (except a Dutch one) surely will be a standing Monument of the Society's Bounty, who were the first promoters

190 Trinity Vestry Minutes, I, p. 250, Apr. 15, 1748.
191 *Ibid.*, May 3, 1748.

and for so long time supported the same, to the immortal Honour of that truly Charitable Body."[192] And a letter of the same date from the Rector, Rev. Henry Barclay, adds this further information: "Mr. Hildreth also Discharges his Duty with fidelity, and for his farther Encouragement there has been a Subscription made of upwards of £300, to which the Vestry of Trinity Church will ad a Sum sufficient to Build a Handsome School & Dwelling House for the Use of the Societys Schoolmaster for the Time being, The foundation of which is Already finishd Being 50 feet in length and 23 in Bredth, and a Wing of 18 feet Square."[193] In March 1749 Mr. Hildreth had liberty to keep his school in the belfry of the Church till the schoolhouse was completed,[194] which was in the fall of that year. The cost of the building is not known but that it was more than £300 is proved by a Vestry order directing that "Coll. Robinson (Churchwarden) furnish and pay such Moneys as shall be necessary (over and above the Subscriptions) for Carrying on and Compleating the Building for the Public School."[195] The school building which Hildreth reported as being "one of the most beautiful edifices in this city,"[196] was occupied about November 1749.[197] In the following February it was destroyed by fire through some unknown cause.[198] The incident occasioned severe accusations against

192 S. P. G. Letter-book, B, 16, p. 54, Nov. 6, 1748. Italics not in original.

193 *Ibid.*, p. 55. The facade was "entirely of hewn stone." Hildreth to the Sec., Apr., 1, 1749, *ibid.*, 17, p. 98.

194 Trinity Vestry Minutes, I, p. 254.

195 *Ibid.*

196 S. P. G. Letter-book, B, 18, p. 100, Apr. 6, 1750; also B, 17, p. 116, which mentions the "large handsome School."

197 Trinity Vestry Minutes, I, p. 256.

198 The following account is from the New York *Weekly Post Boy* of February 26 1750: "Friday Morning last about 4 o'clock, a violent Fire broke out in the new Free School-House Kept by Mr. Joseph Hildreth Clerk of Trinity Church in this City; which got to such height before it was discovered as to render it impossible to save it from being entirely destroyed; . . . and tho' it stood at a considerable distance from the Church, yet the flames ascended so high, and carried with them such Abundance of Live Coals, as to put the Church in imminent danger, particularly the steeple; which was set on fire five several times, almost at the top, what little wind there was setting directly on it; notwithstanding which, by the good Providence of God, and the Diligence and Activity of a few Persons within who broke Holes through, it was happily extinguished, and preserved: There was scarce any thing saved out of the house, from the fury of the Fire; and we are assured besides a great deal of furniture and other things, the Records of the Church are Entirely consumed. The whole Loss sustain'd is supposed to be near Two Thousand Pounds Value." Printed in Dix, History of the Parish of Trinity Church, I, p. 252. Trinity Vestry Minutes, I, p. 257.

Hildreth which he felt called upon to defend in public.[199] If the charges had any basis in fact they stand out as the sole criticisms of the schoolmaster among a great number of testimonials to his praiseworthy characteristics as a man and a schoolmaster.[200] After the fire Hildreth's school went back to the Church steeple in which, said the schoolmaster, "I can make a good shift during the summer, but for want of a fireplace it will be too cold in winter."[201] The Vestry took immediate steps to rebuild and another subscription paper was circulated for the purpose. No record of this second amount is available. The rebuilding committee of the Vestry let the new contract "for the Sum of three hundred and Seventy five pounds certain and Twenty five pounds more when the whole is Compleated if it shall appear they shall deserve the same."[202] In October 1751 the new building was ready for occupancy and Hildreth was again commissioned to use it. At least he was given liberty "to keep his School in the School Room of the New Charity School House till further Orders."[203] In 1753, practically the entire use of the building was granted him, the Vestry having ordered "that the said Joseph Hildreth with his Family have the Care and Use of the Charity School House from the first of May next till further Order, he always taking Care and keeping Clean the Vestry Room in the

---

199 Hildreth sent the following to the editor of the *Weekly Post Boy* which was printed in the issue of March 5, 1750 together with the affidavit mentioned:

"Mr. Parker,
I desire you'll print the Affidavit herewith sent, in your next Gazette, that those who have either inadvertently or maliciously, aspers'd my Character, at a Time when I had lost my All, by the merciless Flames, and when it would have become them much better, to have assisted me and my poor Family, with their Charity; may judge whether the Calumny proceeded from the Envy some Persons in this Town had to my person, or the Station I was in. And I hereby beg all those who have been so ill-natured, as to cast a Blemish on my Reputation, and thereby added to my Affliction, if they can prove any of those gross Immoralities wherewith they have charged me, to do it as publickly and speedily as they can; otherwise let them take Shame to themselves, and endeavour to repair the great Loss I have sustained by Means of their False Aspersions.

Joseph Hildreth."

The accompanying document attested that Hildreth's family were out of town on the night of the fire and that Hildreth himself had stayed at the home of friends in the city. It concluded: "the Deponent saith, That while they were at Waters's as aforesaid, there was not any Gaming in their Company; and that he never saw or heard, that the said Mr. Hildreth did game, or that he was addicted to Liquor; but on the contrary, he believes him to be a very sober, diligent Man, he having been much with him during the Time Aforesaid; and further saith not." Printed in N. Y. Hist. Soc. Pub., 1870, p. 155.

200 The charges may have been the reflection of the bitter feeling toward the Church and Society, which in 1750 was acute.

201 S. P. G. Letter-book, B, 18, p. 100.

202 Trinity Vestry Minutes, I, p. 258, June 15, 1750. The additional £25 was voted on completion of the schoolhouse. *Ibid.*, p. 260.

203 *Ibid.*, p. 260, Oct. 3, 1751.

said School House."[204] In 1758 the school was presented with a bell by Mr. Thomas Randall,[205] and, to properly house it, the Vestry added a cupola to the building.[206] This schoolhouse continued to be used until 1768, when the Vestry decided to devote the school plant to a rectory. Accordingly it was "Unanimously Resolved and Ordered that the present Charity School House be altered and made into a neat and convenient Dwelling House and when finished That the Same together with the Yard and Garden thereunto belonging be appropriated and set apart for the use and dwelling of the Present Rector of the said Church and his Successors forever, free from the payment of any rent for the same, And that a New School House be erected on some other part of the Lands belonging to this Corporation to serve and be made use of for the Charity School instead of the Present one."[207] Proper lots for the third schoolhouse were selected and then it was found they could not be used for some time because of leaseholds.[208] To meet the difficulty a temporary structure was put up in compliance with the following: "Ordered that a Temporary School House of Fifty feet in front and Thirty feet deep be erected and built on some of the Lotts behind Trinity Church and that the same be built of Brick and Covered with Tile or Slate."[209] From this time until 1776 no further mention is made of a permanent schoolhouse by the Vestry Minutes or in other records examined. In 1772, however, it was voted to repair the "Charity School House" in which Mrs. Wyley lived, reference to which has been already made.[210] The same year steps were taken to secure the consent of the Common Council for the erecting a schoolhouse, church, parsonage house and burying ground "on a piece of land in the out ward of the city."[211] A second schoolhouse was eventually provided, because it is recorded that the great conflagration of 1776 destroyed "two Charity School Houses."[212] Therefore a new permanent building must have been erected on the designated lots, leaving the

204 *Ibid.*, p. 269, Apr. 5, 1753.
205 *Ibid.*, p. 258.
206 July 28, 1760, *ibid.*, p. 296.
207 March 25, 1768, *ibid.*, p. 333.
208 *Ibid.*, p. 334.
209 *Ibid.*, Apr. 18, 1768.
210 See p. 107.
211 *Ibid.*, p. 363; see also Dix, *op. cit.*, 1, pp. 348–9.
212 Trinity Vestry Minutes, I, p. 398.

"temporary schoolhouse" for the use of the schoolmistress; or else the old schoolhouse, which was burned in 1750, was repaired for that use. On three different occasions in 1768 the Vestry voted sums aggregating £2100 to the work of completing "the parsonage and Schoolhouse."[213] Such an amount would have been sufficient to defray the expense of the parsonage repairs, of the temporary schoolhouse, and of the ultimate construction of an adequate and permanent building for the school.

The events of 1776 in New York interrupted Mr. Hildreth's school for a time. Amongst other disasters the schoolhouse was again destroyed and the school had to be resumed in a private house. The quotation herewith is descriptive of Hildreth's plight: "My full complement of Scholars viz. 56 Boys & 30 Girls regularly attended untill the beginning of July last, from which time they by degrees dwindled to a small number. Immediately after the Declaration of Independence by the Congress, our Clergy shut up the Churches, this increased the persecution against Friends to Government most of whom were obliged to leave the City, to avoide being sent Prisoners to New England as many already were, for no other Crime, than that of being Loyal Subjects. We were then entirely in the hands of Rebels from New England. At this time I found it necessary for my own safety to retire, which I did, and a few days after the King's troops took possession I return'd but to my great Surprise and Grief I found the City in Flames, by which a great part was consumed, and among the rest, our Antient Beautiful Parish Church the Parsonage & School-House. So rapid and violent were the flames that nothing could be saved out of either. I have taken a vacant House, and am collecting my Poor Scholars together. I have at present 25 Boys & 10 Girls, but as the Inhabitants are now daily coming in, I expect in a short time to have my full number."[214] Not only Hildreth's, but the other schoolhouse, was included in Trinity Church's great loss, the value of these two alone being £2000.[215]

---

213 Apr. 22, July 7, Nov. 7, 1768, *ibid.*, pp. 334, 336, 338.

214 October 6, 1776, S. P. G. Letter-book, B, 3, p. 171.

215 Note the following report from the Vestry Minutes of June 9, 1777: "The committee that was appointed to Estimate the Damage this Corporation had sustained by the late fire, made a report in writing, in the words following (to witt)—

Pursuant to an order of Vestry of the 1st of April last to us directed, to Estimate the loss of the Corporation of the Rector and inhabitants of the City of New-York, in Communion of the Church of England, as by Law es-

Books continued to be supplied to Hildreth as to the preceding teachers and most of them were still of a doctrinal nature. In 1776 he wrote: "The greatest difficulty I meet with is the want of School Books, writing paper & Lewis's Catechisms, which I am extremely in want of;"[216] and in another letter, thanking the Society for books "sent for the school," he said: "Nothing could be more acceptable, as they were very much wanted and not a prayer book to be bought in this City, occasioned by the nonimportation."[217] In 1767 the S. P. G. voted the School "50 of Fisher's Spelling books & 30 primers."[218] Three times money was voted for the purchase of books.[219] In addition to these, specific grants of Prayer-books amounted to about 150, catechisms to about 200, and Lewis's explanation thereof to about 275.[220]

The scholars under Mr. Hildreth continued to attend the church services in a body. With the building of the new and larger church in 1764, more spacious quarters were assigned the school.[221] Hildreth took particular pains to teach his pupils psalmody, in consequence of which he wrote to the Society: They "can join with great decency, in singing the Psalms in

---

tablished have sustained by the late Fire which happened in the City of New-York on the 21st day of September last, do report, That the said Corporation have lost Twenty two thousand two hundred pounds in the four following Buildings, which was consumed by the Fire,—

Trinity Church, including the Organ	£17,500
Parsonage or Rectors House	2,500
Two Charity School-Houses & Fencings	2,000
Library	200
	£22,200

besides the loss to the Corporation of £536 p. Annum, the Annual rent of 246 lots of ground the Tennants' buildings being all Consumed by the fire. In Witness whereof, we have signed this report the 13th day of May, 1777.

ELIAS DESBROSSES, CHARLES SHAW, ANTHO VAN DAM, WILLIAM LAIGHT."

See also Rev. Mr. Inglis' account of the fire and the saving of St. Paul's Church and King's College. S. P. G. Letter-book, B, 2, p. 68, October 31, 1776.

216 *Ibid.*, B, 3, p. 159.

217 *Ibid.*, B, 3, p. 165, Oct. 16, 1770.

218 S. P. G. Journal, XVII, p. 231. Trinity Vestry's grant of such books has been noted before, see p. 104.

219 In 1750, £5 for "proper School Books for the Scholars;" in 1753, "50 sh. worth of Bibles, Psalters, & Ch. Catechisms;" in 1774, "small tracts to the amount of 40 shillings." *Ibid.*, XI, p. 244; XII, p. 292; XX, p. 66.

220 *Ibid.*, X, p. 112; XI, p. 38; XII, p. 152; XV, p 386; XVIII, p. 264; XX, p. 66.

221 "Resolved that a Gallery be Erected on Each side of the Organ above the present Gallerys for the use of the Charity Schollars and Ordered that the same Committee that are Appointed to build the New Church have power to do the same in such manner as they Shall think most Convenient and best." Trinity Vestry Minutes, Apr. 24, 1764, I, p. 312.

Church and always entertain the Congregation on the Grand Festivals and at Charity Sermons &c. with an Hymn suitable to the Occasion, which has given great satisfaction."[222] The children took part in other public functions. On the dedication of St. George's Chapel the entire school participated in the exercises of this occasion. The following is reported in a newspaper of that period:

"Last Wednesday (being the Day appointed) was open'd St. George's Chapel, upon which Occasion, the Rector, Assistant, Church-Wardens, and Vestry, of Trinity-Church assembled in the Vestry-Room, in the Charity School-House, where they were met by some of the town and Neighboring Clergy, and other Gentlemen of Distinction, from whence they set out in regular Form and Order, attended by the Charity Schollars, 40 Boys and 12 Girls, who walked before in Pairs, with their School-Master at the Head of them; and at the City Hall were join'd by the Mayor, Recorder, Aldermen, and Common Council."[223]

In like manner the scholars were called upon to act as a guard of honor on such solemn public occasions as that of the burial of the Governor. In announcing the burial of Sir Henry Moore, the New York *Chronicle* of September 14, 1769, thus referred to the part taken by the Charity School:

"The Governor's remains were interred the evening of the next day, in the Chancel of Trinity Church. The corpse was preceded by the 16th Regiment, the Charity-School-Boys, and the Clergy of all persuasions. . . . .

"The first part of the procession was as follows:

I.

"The 16th Regiment with their Arms Reversed.

II.

"Twenty Boys belonging to the Charity School.

III.

"Twenty of said Boys with lighted Flambeax."[224]

Other evidences of public approbation, outside of the circle of the Church, can be cited. One of these from the files of the New York *Mercury* will serve as an illustration:

"BY PERMISSION OF HIS HONOR THE LIEUTENANT GOVERNOR.

For the Benefit of the

CHARITY SCHOOL

By a Company of Comedians.

At the New Theatre in Chapel-Street, this Day,
being the 25th Instant, will be presented,

[222] S. P. G. Letter-book, B, 3, p. 163, Oct. 18, 1768.

[223] From New York *Weekly Post Boy*, July 13, 1752. Quoted by Dix, *op. cit.*, I, p. 260. f.

[224] Quoted in Dix, *op. cit.*, I, pp. 329-330.

A Comedy, call'd the
COMMITTEE:
or
The Faithful Irishman.
The Part of Teague to be perform'd by
Mr. HALLAM,
And the Part of Ruth to be performed by
Mrs. DOUGLASS
To which will be added a farce, call'd
A WONDER
An HONEST Yorkshireman!
The Part of GAYLOVE to be performed by
MR. QUELCH,
And the Part of Arbella, by Mrs. Morris.

Tickets without which no persons can be admitted to be had of H. Gaine, Printer, Bookseller, and Stationer, at his Printing-Office at the Bible & Crown in Hanover Square.

The Ladies and Gentlemen who chuse to have boxes reserved for them, are desired to send to Mr. Douglass."[225]

The troubles and losses of 1776 were a hard blow to Mr. Hildreth in his rapidly declining years.[226] Having reopened his school soon after the city was taken by the King's troops, he quickly collected his usual class of eighty-six. In the midst of preparations for getting thoroughly established Mr. Hildreth died.[227] The Rector of Trinity, Rev. Mr. Inglis, assumed charge of the school. On July 24, 1777, he wrote the S. P. G. describing his disposition of the scholars and his plan for the continuation of the school, as follows: "We were looking out for a more convenient House for the School than the one which Mr.Hildreth occupied after his Return, (the School Houses being destroyed by the great Fire in September) & every Thing promised well with Respect to the Charity School; but his Death has involved us in new Embarrasments. With the Consent & assistance of

---

225 The New York *Mercury*, April 26, 1762. Quoted in Dix, *op. cit.*, I, p. 297; see also p. 255. "On Monday last the Committee was acted at the Theatre, in this City, for the benefit of the Charity School, by which a handsome Sum was raised and delivered by Mr. Doughlass to the Church Wardens for that Purpose. This is the Second Play the Company has given this season to Public Uses; which, with their unblameable conduct during their residence here and the Entertainment the Town has receiv'd from their performances, has greatly increased the number of their friends, and Considerably Obviated many Objections hitherto made against Theatrical Representations in this City." The New York *Mercury*, May 3, 1762. Quoted in Dix, *op. cit.*, I, p. 298.

226 See letter of Hannah Hildreth to Sec., July 23, 1777, S. P. G. Letter-book, B, 3, p. 172.

227 May 10, 1777, S. P. G. Letter-book, B, 2, p. 71. "Last week died at his House in this City Mr. Joseph Hildreth, who for about 40 years past was Clerk of Trinity Church and had the care of the Trinity School here; He was always esteemed an upright, honest Man." The New-York *Gazette*, May 12, 1777.

the Vestry, I have placed the Charity Boys in two private Schools that are taught in the City; where the utmost Care is taken of them, & under our Inspection as formerly, & where they are to remain untill a Person whom I have engaged, arrives & takes Charge of them. The Charity Girls still continue under the former School Mistress. Several Persons, after Mr. Hildreth's Death, offered their Service to teach the School, & act as Clerk; but I was anxious that a Person of good Principles & Character, & otherwise well qualified, should succeed Mr. Hildreth. Such a Person I found in Mr. Amos Bull, who is a man of unblemished moral Character, of steady Loyalty, a good English Scholar, writes a fair Hand, is well skilled in Church Music, & has an excellent Voice. He had taught Psalmody in this City for some Years, & was instrumental in improving many Members of the Congregation in that Part of Divine Worship. Like many other Loyal Subjects, he was obliged to fly, when the Rebels had the Ascendency here; but when Sir Wm. Howe reduced the City, he returned; & for a present Support, took an office in the Commissary's Department & went to Rhode Island with the Troops that were sent there last Winter. I wrote to him there, & he has undertaken the offices of Clerk & Master of the Charity School. He is to be here next September, his Business not admitting of a speedier Return. I most earnestly request that the Society would be pleased to continue the same allowance to Mr. Bull, when he enters on those offices, that they have made to Mr. Hildreth; we never stood in greater Need of their Assistance; for the losses we sustained have been so great, that without their kind aid, we shall not be able to support Mr. Bull."[228]

Mr. Amos Bull succeeded to the charity school early in 1778 and began his labors on April first.[229] The boys had remained in the two private schools since Hildreth's death and it had proved a great tax on the Church.[230] Because of this expense the number which was being privately maintained, it appears, was reduced. Mr. Bull stated that he began with a small number.[231] By October 1778 the school was again up to the previous

---

228 S. P. G. Letter-book, B, 2, p. 71.

229 S. P. G. Journal XXI, p. 233; Letter-book, B, 3, p. 173.

230 Rev. Dr. Inglis to Sec., May 1, 1778, S. P. G. Journal, XXI, p. 318 ff.

231 S. P. G. Letter-book, B, 3, p. 173.

enrolment of 86, and according to Dr. Inglis it seemed never in a more prosperous condition. Especially was this true, it was said, "so far as relates to the care paid to the children's instruction." This afforded the Church "no small pleasure, when every other institution" about them was "either sinking or totally destroyed by the ravages of war."[232] "Many of the Boys are promising youths . . . & they are visited once a Month by the Trustees & carefully examined," wrote Mr. Bull.[233] The S. P. G. had voted Mr. Bull the schoolmaster's salary of £15 only.[234] Soon after his taking charge of the school, the Vestry settled the usual salaries upon him and undertook the task of providing a building for the use of the school and the schoolmaster's family. These facts are set forth in the following entry from the Vestry Minutes: "The Reverend Mr. Inglis from the Committee to treat with Mr. Amos Bull (now in town) to succeed Mr. Joseph Hildreth deceased late Parish Clerk and Master of the Charity School in this city reported that they had agreed with Mr. Bull for that purpose at the Annual Salary of Fifteen pounds as Parish Clerk and sixty pounds as Master of the Charity school and the Customary fees and perquisites over and above what maybe Allowed to him by the Society for the Propagation of the Gospel in Foreign parts, *Ordered* that the said report be confirmed and that the said Two Salaries commence this Day and be paid by the Churchwardens as usual; ordered that Mr. Bache Mr. Edward Laight and Mr. Ustick be a Committee to provide a proper house to Accomodate Mr. Bull's family and for the Charity School upon the best Terms they can."[235] Within the year Mr. Bull found the combined income insufficient and induced the Vestry to allow £40 more for the year 1779.[236] They further "Resolved and Ordered that until such time as the Ten pounds Sterling formerly allowed from England . . . as Catechist to the Negroes be remitted . . ." the Corporation would pay the amount, computing it "from the time his other Salary commenced."[237] In 1780 the Vestry was again called upon to

---

232 Quoted from letter of Dr. Inglis to Sec., in S. P. G. Journal, XXI, p. 394 ff.

233 Apr. 20, 1779, S. P. G. Letter-book, B, 3, p. 173.

234 Mr. Hildreth, it has been shown, was enjoying an addtional salary of £10 as the society's catechist.

235 Apr. 21, 1778, Trinity Vestry Minutes, I, p. 401.

236 March 30, 1779, *ibid.*, p. 406.

237 *Ibid.*

meet the depreciation in the purchasing power of the schoolmaster's income. This was done, as follows: "Mr. Amos Bull Clerk of the Parish and Master of the Charity School represented to the Board the Insufficiency of his present salary and perquisites for a Decent Support and declared that he could not subsist under an Additional Allowance of One hundred pounds. And the Board taking under Consideration the Extravagant Prices of every Article of Living at this Time, Resolved that Mr. Bull be Allowed and paid out of the Charity School Fund for this present year to commence from Easter Tuesday last the said Sum of One hundred pounds in Addition to his present Allowance, but it is expected that if Mr. Bull Intends leaving the School that he will give the Corporation Six Months Notice thereof that they may have an Opportunity of Providing a proper person to Succeed him, which he Engaged to Do."[238] The manner in which the Church met the crisis of exorbitant prices and kept the charity school open is interestingly told in a letter from Dr. Inglis to the S. P. G., in which he said:

"I have the Pleasure to inform you that our Charity School is in a very flourishing Way. Mr. Bull is attentive to his Duty the Children are very regular, & make a surprising Progress in their Learning. All the Necessaries of Life have arisen to more than treble their former Price in this City, The Expense attending the School has proportionally increased, & yet we have made but a small Reduction in the Number of Scholars—formerly we had 86—now we have 80 we should be under a Necessity of reducing the Number much Lower; but People contribute generously to the Support of the Institution, which is the only one that has survived the general wreck occasioned by this detestable Rebellion. The Commander in Chief, *Sir Henry Clinton*, has been so good as to assist us with some Fuel, & our Commandant, Major General Pattison, a gentleman distinguished for his Humanity & Politeness, has been pleased to exempt the School Houses from Billets which was a matter of the utmost Consequence to us, & otherwise to patronize this excellent Institution."[239] The reduction to 80 pupils was for a very short time. By the next spring 86 pupils were again reported and

[238] Apr. 11, 1780, *ibid.*, p. 414.

[239] Nov. 26, 1779. S. P. G. Letter-book, B, 2, p. 72.

this continued to be the number.[240] Writing in 1782, the Rector of Trinity again voiced the Church's pleasure over the successful operation of the school. He also urged the need of the Society's bounty, doubtless realizing that it must soon be withdrawn. Dr. Inglis said: "The Charity School never was in a more flourishing state than now & for some time past By the generous Contributions of the Gentlemen of the Army and Navy, & of the Inhabitants in general we have been enabled to keep up the old Number of Scholars, which is 86; although the Expence is near treble what it was formerly. But Contributions are uncertain & precarious; & should any Deduction be made from our Stated Funds, we should probably be under the necessity of diminishing the Number of Scholars at a time when the Institution was never more necessary, & when applications are made for many more (especially by distressed Refugees) than we can admit. I cannot for this Reason, forbear expressing my anxiety & earnest wish that the Salary of £15 Sterl. may be continued by the Society."[241]

During the war plans were begun for providing funds with which to rebuild the schoolhouse. It was proposed in 1780 to raise £2000 by means of lotteries,[242] but the matter did not get beyond this stage for years to come. In 1787 and 1790 Vestry committees were ordered to report on the expense of rebuilding,[243] and on January 10, 1791, the scheme was indefinitely postponed because "upon considering the present Exigencies of the Corporation, the Board thought proper to defer the Consideration of this Subject to a future Opportunity."[244] In the meantime the Church rented such suitable quarters for the school as it was able to secure. During the period of the war the school occupied quarters "in the Broad Way."[245]

After serving four years as schoolmaster, during which "he had discharged his Duty with great Fidelity,"[246] Mr. Bull resigned and the Vestry immediately filled the position by the

---

240 S. P. G. Journal, XXII, pp. 142, 172.

241 May 6, 1782, S. P. G. Letter-book, B, 2, p. 74.

242 Trinity Vestry Minutes, I, p. 414.

243 *Ibid.*, pp. 491, 492, 536.

244 *Ibid.*, p. 537.

245 "Ordered that the Seal of the Corporation be affixed to a bond to the Execution of Samuel Bayard for the ballance due them from the Corporation on account of the rent of a house in the Broad Way occupied during the War by the Charity School." Oct. 7, 1785, *ibid.*, p. 479.

246 S. P. G. Letter-book, B, 2, p. 74.

appointment of Mr. Ebenezer Street.[247] The Society was earnestly requested to continue the regular allowance to Mr. Street,[248] which it agreed to. But in doing so the S. P. G. submitted the following protest to Dr. Inglis, the Rector: "I believe that you have already been informed by Dr. Chandler, that the Society have complied with the desire of Your Vestry in granting the same Salary of £15 to Mr. Ebenezer Street, now School Master at New York, as Mr. Bull enjoyed. At the same time I must confess to you, that had it not been pressed by yourself, I don't think the Society would have adopted the measure so readily. Many members were of opinion, that so considerable a place did not want that assistance, & that it had been too long allowed by the Society. Something of this you will perceive in the Resolution of the Board 'That the Salary be allowed in consideration of the present unsettled state of affairs but that inquiry be made into the annual emoluments of the Schoolmaster, exclusive of the Society's bounty, as it appears extraordinary that any assistance should be wanting to support a School at N. York.' You will be so kind therefore as to give me some satisfaction on these points. Be assured of this, that the Society are always disposed to do everything in their Power for the promoting of Religion, & in the distribution of their benevolence would wish always to have it placed where it is absolutely necessary, & where it can be of most extensive use.

(Signed) Wm. Morrice Secretary."[249]

The Vestry's agreement with Mr. Street as to salary suggests, in an interesting manner, that the latter outclassed his predecessors in ability to drive a professional bargain. The agreement is given herewith:

"The Corporation agreed with Mr. Ebenezer Street . . . on the following Terms for the ensuing year:

"1st As Schoolmaster he is to be allowed a House and ten Cords of Oak Wood per Annum.

---

247 May 1, 1782, *ibid.*

248 *Ibid.*

249 Aug. 6, 1782. From a copy in Trinity Vestry Minutes, I, 428. In view of this letter the Vestry took action as follows: "It was thereupon ordered, That the Committee for Auditing the Charity Accounts, wait on Mr. Beach, & that they (with him if he can conveniently attend) do draw up an Account of the Institution, its Progress & Proceedings adjoining thereto a State of its Funds, & its Annual Receipts and Expenditures from its Institution to the present day, & that they report to the Vestry as soon as possible that the Society may have the information they request." Dec. 9, 1782, *ibid.* But this seems to have been all that was done, for the writer has been unable to find such an account or any further reference to it either in the Vestry Minutes or in the S. P. G. papers.

"2d Although the Sallary for the School Master is no more than £60 per annum, yet this Corporation in consideration of the dearness of living in the present times will allow Mr. Street at the rate of £200 per Ann^{m} New York Currency.

"3d In Consideration that Samuel Street, son of Mr. E. Street, is regularly to Attend as Assistant to his father in the said School, the Corporation have agreed to permit them to take twenty private Scholars provided that this indulgence shall not prevent their attentions to the public School.

"4th Mr. Street and his Son are to attend diligently to the Instruction of the Charity Children in Reading, Writing, Arithmetic, and Psalmody, and to be particularly attentive to the Morals and decent behavior of the Children and take them to Church whenever Divine Service is performed.

"5th As Parish Clerk the Corporation are to allow him at the rate of fifteen Pounds pr Ann^{m} New York Currency, being the usual Salary and he is to perform the duties and receive the Customary Fees appertaining to that office.

"6th As Mr. Street undertakes the office of Catechist to the Negroes in Consideration of that duty being duly performed, the Corporation agreed to pay him at the rate of ten pounds Sterling pr Ann^{m} and will recommend him to the Society for the Propogation of the Gospel for their usual bounty allowed to such Catechist."[250]

There remains no report of Mr. Street's school, so that it is not certain whether the innovation of private scholars was carried out or not. Presumably it was and caused dissatisfaction, since the Vestry imposed a rule on his successor, which stated that, "he is to conform in every respect to the rules laid down for Mr. Street excepting his taking in private Scholars in the day time which is not to be allowed."[251] In September 1783 Street informed the Vestry that he was obliged to leave the city and begged leave to resign. This was accepted and Mr. Edward Haswell was named as the schoolmaster, "till May next."[252] In April 1784 Mr. John Wood assumed charge of the school.[253] The Society's support, however, ceased with the work of Mr. Street. One payment of £15 was sent him,[254] after which all relationship between the S. P. G. and the work in New York City seems to have terminated.

---

250 Apr. 15, 1782, *ibid.*, p. 424. Street did not receive the appointment of catechist from the S. P. G.

251 *Ibid.*, p. 432.

252 *Ibid.*, Sept. 18, 1783.

253 *Ibid.*, p. 441.

254 Abstracts of the Society's Proceedings, Feb. 21, 1782 to Feb. 21, 1783.

CHAPTER VII

THE SOCIETY'S SUPPORT OF SCHOOLS IN WESTCHESTER COUNTY*

The Schools in the Parish of Rye

The beginning of the educational work of the Society in Rye was due to the initiative and enthusiastic aid of Col. Caleb Heathcote, whose country seat was in the parish of Rye.[1] In 1704 Heathcote set up a school in the parish and engaged as the schoolmaster, Mr. Joseph Cleator.[2] After a short period of teaching Cleator was called to England, whereupon Heathcote and the people used the opportunity to further urge the assistance of the Society. In a letter to the Bishop of London, Heathcote said: "I send your Lordship here inclosed copie of a short Letter wch went via Boston; this comes chiefly to accompany the bearer Mr. Joseph Cleator, who has lived about 4 years in this Province the greatest part whereof he has lived with me, & has always approved himself a very honest man & regular in his life, & being exceeding firm & zealous for the Interest of the Church, I recom-

* For this account the writer has consulted Bolton, *Hist. of the P. E. Church in Westchester County;* Baird, *Hist. of Rye Parish;* but it has been necessary to depend nearly altogether on the S. P. G. records direct.

[1] The Manor of Scarsdale.

[2] "I did in my last Acquaint you that I would put forward a School in Westchester County which I hope in a few months to inform you I have done, haveing the Promise of an extraordinary good man for a Schoolmaster, one who is not only very firm to the Church, but I am sure will be Indefatigable to Instill those Principles into the youth and Children of whom the greatest Hopes are I believe at first setting out. It will be attended with some Difficulties, that I beg the Favor of you to move the Society that they would be pleas'd (untill such time as we are able to carry it on wthout help to give us £15 a year or what they shall think Conven^{t}, towards maintaining of the Schoolm^{r} & I will take care wth the blessing of Almighty God to make it as Usefull as I can to the Church and that Satisfactory Accts shall be sent over how the same is Employ'd and w^{t} good is done for it & I pray for you likewise to move that some Catechisms and Pray^{r} Books be sent over for the Scholars. S^{r}, The People of the Westchester County are more Gen^{lly} English than they are in any County of the Gov^{mt} & Altho' there is not at present above 2000 souls in it, yett it contains a very great Body of Land & generally the best I have seen in any of these parts, that time will make it a Great Peopled County, that, were the Church wth Schools well settled in its Minority, It would in future ages probably bear no other ffruit." Heathcote to the Sec., June 1, 1704, S. P. G. Letter-book, A, 1, p. 174. In an earlier letter Heathcote had the project in mind, but his activity against Sabbath breaking and in behalf of the Church service raised a storm against him and made him defer for awhile. *Ibid.*, p. 182.

ended him to the Towne of Rye & Mamaroneck for their Schoolmaster & is ye same person I formerly mentioned to yor Lordship & ye Society, but before he had been very long in that Service he received Letters from his Friends in England, earnestly desiring his return to settle some of his private concerns, wch he is come to do; ye People & his Scholars are so fond of him, that his leaving them is a very sore affliction to them all & have in an uncom̄on manner pray'd me to use my utmost Endeavours that he may return to them again. I have desired Mr. Claytor to wait upon yor Lordship & do most earnestly beseech your Lordship in behalf of those people to use yor Interest with the Society that he may have some allowance from them to encourage his return & really my Lord when ye Society have been at never so much expence in sending Ministers a full half of the work must be done by good Schoolmasters, to root & fix ye principles of the Church in our Youth. I'm sure I need not use many Arguments in a matter so agreeable to yor Lordships Inclinations."[3] The letter was accompanied by the following petition:

"To the Rt Reverend Father in God Henry Lord Bishop of London—The humble address of several of the Inhabitants and Freeholders of the Towns of Rye & Mamaroneck in behalf of Themselves & ye rest of the Sd Inhabitants.

"We the Inhabitants and Freeholders of the Towns of Rye and Mamaroneck in ye Province of N. York out of the deep sense we have of that unparallel'd care & Tenderness yor Lordship has been pleased at all times to manifest for the Prosperity and welfare of this Province, are hereby emboldened to become most humble Supplicants to yor Lordship in behalf of Mr. Joseph Cleator ye Presenter hereof who did make a beginning to teach School in our Towns, but his own private Affairs requiring his immediate Attendance in England he could not continue long amongst us to our inexpressible grief he being a very sober man and good schoolmaster and not only indefatigable in Teaching our Children but in Catechising and otherwise Instructing them to our wonderful Satisfaction.

"We therefore most humbly pray yor Lordship to endeavour the procuring him such an allowance from ye Society wch with what we are able to give him might encourage his Return, amongst us, And as in Duty bound we shall ever pray for yor Ldps long life and Happiness."[4]

Acting on the above petitions, Cleator was appointed schoolmaster by the Society, March 2, 1704/5, with an annual allowance of £15.[5] He was not ready to return to Rye for more than a year after this, as the following minute from the S. P. G. Journal indicates: "Also that Mr. Joseph Cleator (whom the

---

[3] Oct. 23, 1704, *ibid.*, A, 2, p. 37.

[4] The copies of signatures here follow, *ibid.*, A, 2, p. 45.

[5] S. P. G. Journal, I, p. 186.

Society upon the recommendation of Col. Heathcote had appointed Schoolmaster at Rye, N. Y. at a salary of £15 per annum) has attended them & acquainted them that he was now going over to his post, & that the Committee had thereupon procured from the Lord Bishop of London a Letter to the Lord High Treasurer for the Queens Bounty of £20 to the said Mr. Cleator, and had moreover provided him with a copy of the Society's Instructions to Schoolmasters. Ordered Mr. Cleator's salary do commence from Midsummer last."[6] Still other delays were encountered after this, so that he did not sail from England until February 18;[7] and did not arrive at New York until three months thereafter,[8] much to the disquietude of the people of Rye.[9]

Speaking of the opening of his school, Mr. Cleator said: "On the Second of June I was put upon School Teaching. I have now above Sixty Scholars, small children, Boys and Girls not above eight, who can say their Catechism, but they are very improving children."[10] About two weeks afterwards Col. Heathcote thus wrote of the position of the schoolmaster in the life of the town: "He has entered upon his School teaching & with all the success which can be desired, for the people being exceeding fond of him most willingly commit their Children to his care to be trained up by him according to the Discipline of our Church, which with the assistance of Almighty God will be established on a Lasting Foundation in this Parish, & besides the care of his School, which trust he discharges with the utmost faithfulness, when Mr. Muirson is absent from the town of Rye, either to the extream of his Parish or otherwise for ye Service of ye Church. The people being called together after the usual manner, he reads the Prayers of the Church, to them, and a Lecture Morning and Evening, and the people come very readily to hear him."[11] Indeed the people expressed their appreciation in a material way, having agreed to give Cleator £20, "money of the Province" and "diet

[6] July 6, 1706, *ibid.*, I, p. (30).

[7] Much of the delay was, of course, due to the long waits between ships bound for America. But Cleator reported that storms delayed the voyage. S. P. G. Letter-book, A, 3, p. 15. Apparently he waited about three months on the English coast for a ship to New York. *Ibid.*, A, 3, pp. 21, 151.

[8] May 18, 1707, *ibid.*

[9] *Ibid.*, A, 2, pp. 164, 165; A, 3, pp. 86, 137.

[10] Letter of July 14, 1707, *ibid.*, A, 3, p. 151.

[11] June 18, 1707, *ibid.*, A, 3, p. 137. Also a letter from Rev. Muirson, Jan. 9, 1707/8, *ibid.*, A, 3, p. 168.

for this year," in addition to the Society's bounty.[12] For a few years thereafter this allowance from the town continued. Then it decreased to £12 and still later to £10 per annum.[13] There is more or less uncertainty as to what his "diet" signified, but it is reasonable to suppose that he referred to an old-time practice of "boarding round." The practice did not continue, probably because he brought his family over from England. His letters mention his family at various times and his wife was undoubtedly in England during the first year or two of Cleator's teaching.[14] In 1713, he definitely stated that he had the £12 local allowance only for "food, cloathes, laundry & lodging" in addition to the Society's support.[15] He officiated, many years at least, as Clerk of the Church,[16] for which the small salary of 20 shillings per year was allowed.[17] Once he acknowledged a special gratuity of £5 from the Society and also a bounty to his wife and family, the amount of which was not given.[18] It would be interesting to know how the money allowance from the parish was raised, since this is nowhere indicated. It must have been by means of subscription papers or tuition fees from those parents whose children attended the school. Certainly Cleator had no other income from the people than the above-mentioned allowances.[19]

Cleator for some years taught in three different places in the parish, giving four months time to each.[20] The towns of Rye and Mamaroneck were two of those places and the third, while not mentioned, was probably Bedford or White Plains. In 1710 he proportioned his time between two places,[21] and in the next year it was agreed that he should "teach constantly near the Church in Rye."[22] To explain the moving school which he first

---

[12] *Ibid.*, A, 3, p. 151. More than a year thereafter he reported the continuance of this stipend. *Ibid.*, A, 4, p. 77, Oct. 18, 1708.

[13] 1712, *ibid.*, A, 8, pp. 117, 171; 1713, Journal, II, p. 330.

[14] In February 1708/9 the Society's Treasurer was ordered to pay Cleator's salary directly to his wife. S. P. G. Journal, I, p. (50). From a town minute, it is certain that his family was not in Rye in 1708. See the quotation in Baird, Hist. of Rye, p. 174 (footnote).

[15] S. P. G. Letter-book, A, 8, p. 171.

[16] From 1711 to 1721, Rye Vestry Minutes, I, pp. 1, 4, 7, 9, 10, 11, 13, 15, 17. "So ffar Mr. Joseph Cleator performed ye office of Clerk of ye Vestry," Rye Vestry Minutes, I, p. 17, Feb. 28, 1720/21.

[17] *Ibid.*, I, pp. 1, 4, 7, 9, 10, 11, 13, 15. In a letter from the inhabitants of Rye, in behalf of Cleator, with 72 signatures, Sept. 22, 1717 (S. P. G. Letter-book, A, 12, p. 357), it was reported that he was serving as Clerk of the Church *without* salary.

[18] July 19, 1715, *ibid.*, A, 10, p. 199.

[19] *Ibid.*, A, 8, p. 171.

[20] *Ibid.*, A, 5, p. 150; A, 4, p. 133.

[21] *Ibid.*, A, 6, p. 135.

[22] *Ibid.*, Sept. 6, 1711.

adopted, he wrote: "The Inhabitants are so scatter'd that I teach in three Several places, 4 months at a place, so cannot have so great a Number at a time as If I were constantly settled in one place."[23]

Cleator began his service for the Society at the age of 53 years,[24] and continued until his death in March 1732,[25] being then 78 years old. During the entire time, then, he was too old for the work. For the first ten years his perseverance seems to have been commendable. Information of his lack of efficiency and inattention to duty began to reach the Society as early as 1714,[26] and was repeatedly given thereafter.[27] Admonished by the Society on several occasions,[28] the schoolmaster excused himself on the score of declining health.[29] In 1720 he reported the rapid loss of his sight, but pleaded his necessitous condition and his ability to continue the school. The S. P. G. retained him notwithstanding the handicap. In 1724 the Society's missionary reported, "ye Misfortune of our Schoolmaster's blindness wch has rendered him incapable of keeping School."[30] For twelve years Cleator was physically unfitted to perform the duties of his position and the School was attended by Daniel Chubb, who acted as Cleator's assistant and whose remuneration was arranged between them.[31]

The available reports of Cleator's school date between 1707 and 1720. During the time of the moving school his total enrolment in the different places ranged from 45 to 80 in the summer, with about half the attendance in the winter.[32] After the school was fixed at Rye town this irregularity was kept up. In the summer of 1712 only 30 are mentioned,[33] and within that

[23] 1708, *ibid.*, A, 4, p. 77.

[24] In Oct. 1717 he passed his 63rd birthday. *Ibid.*, A, 12, p. 352.

[25] S. P. G. Journal, VI, p. 54.

[26] "I have persuaded Mr. Cleator to a closer attendance and better order about his School and hope he will be more serviceable in his place." From the Society's missionary at Rye, Oct. 4, 1714, S. P. G. Letter-book, A, 9, No. 39, p. 164.

[27] *Ibid.*, A, 12, pp. 424, 431; A, 13, pp. 337, 345, 433; A, 12, p. 352. Journal, III, pp. 402, 405.

[28] *Ibid.*, A, 12, pp. 424, 353; A, 13, pp. 431, 433.

[29] "I can perform my part in ye School as well as ever except in ye Night; my sight being weakened by loss of my right Eye makes me write crooked." *Ibid.*, A, 14, p. 109, Jan. 12, 1719/20.

[30] *Ibid.*, A, 18, p. 191.

[31] Petition of Daniel Chubb to Society, June 15, 1733, *ibid.*, B, 1, p. 26. From this petition it might be inferred that Cleator retained the S. P. G. salary, and Chubb had the benefit of whatever money was raised in Rye.

[32] *Ibid.*, A, 3, p. 151; A, 4, pp. 77, 133; A, 5, pp. 10, 150, 151; Journal, II, p. 124.

[33] June 9, 1712, S. P. G. Journal, II, p. 242.

same year two other enrolments are given of 43 and 49, respectively,[34] giving an average attendance of 41. For the years of 1714 to 1720, there are eleven reports which show an average attendance of 51.[35] The children were young and capable only of very elementary education.[36] By the age of thirteen they left the school to engage, it would seem, in work for their parents. Not once is any reference made by Cleator as to apprenticing to trades, but it may be assumed that the practice was not unknown in Rye. In 1712 and 1714 the girls slightly outnumbered the boys,[37] while from 1715 to 1719 they amounted to about one-third of the class rolls.[38] The following is a copy of one of the first lists sent by Cleator:[39]

"Thoms & Eliza Bridge Children of Mr. Bridge	2
Ann daughter of Jonathan Hart	1
Jno Joseph Elisha Underhill & Hannah Budd, children of Captain Bud	5
Henry & Mary Children of Widow Straing	2
Josias Son of Francis Lecount	1
Isaac Samuel Hannah & Mary Children of John Lownsbury	4
David & Joseph Sons of Joseph Ogden	2
Martha Daughter of David Ogden	1
Phebe & Ann Daughters of Joseph Lyons	2
Susannah & Gertrude Daughtrs of Jos. Purdy	2
Hannah Daughter of Joseph Banks	1
Wm. Son of Saml Kniffin	1
Hannah Daughter of John Merrit	1
Ebenezer Eliza ffrancis & Sarah children of ffrancis Purdy	4
Jona Benjamin Ann Elizabeth & Sarah Children of Jonathan Kniffin	5
Joseph & Jemina Child. of Robt. Bloomer	2
Peter Son of Peter Clapham	1
Jonathan Son of John Haight	1
Charles Sarah & Susannah Children of Ebenezer Theal	3
Jonathn & Ann Children of Ebenezer Kniphin	2
Mary Daughter of Hathaliah Brown	1
Eunice Daughter of Deliverance Brown	1
Danl Son of Danl Strainge	1
Phebe & Hannah Daughters of Andrew Coo.	2
Susannah Travise Daughter of Philip Travise	1"

[34] S. P. G. Letter-book, A, 8, pp. 114, 117, 120, 168.

[35] *Ibid.*, A, 9, p. 137; A, 10, pp. 169, 199; A, 11, pp. 305, 337; A, 12, pp. 353, 380; A, 13, pp. 339, 470; A, 14, p. 114; Journal, III, pp. 289, 303.

[36] The children of his first class were not above eight years of age. At various times he stated that they were mostly small children. In 1717 none was above twelve and in 1718 the oldest was not thirteen. S. P. G. Letter-book, A, 3, p. 151; A, 8, p. 114; A, 13, p. 339; Journal, III, p. 289.

[37] S. P. G. Letter-book, A, 8, p. 114; A, 9, p. 137.

[38] See citations under average attendance.

[39] Nov. 4, 1712, *ibid.*, A, 8, p. 114.

The lists were nearly always in the form shown above. The one sent in October, 1717 varied from the others by including a full year's enrolment and by having the children grouped by sexes and according to their ability to recite the Catechism. It is shown below:

"Boys who can Perfectly say and answer the whole Catechism.

Mr. Christopher Bridge	Joseph Piordy
Jonathan Haight	Jonathan Palding
Charles Theal	Jonathan Ogden
Joseph Theal	Daniel Ogden
Elisha Budd	Caleb Brundige
Underhill Budd	John Brundige
Samuel Height	Nathan Kniffin
William Height	Delivarance Brown
Isaac Lownsbury	Solomn Purdy
Samuel Lownsbury	Edmond Weeks

Joseph Bloomer

21.

"Boys who cannot answer to the whole Catechism.

Joseph Haight	Nathan Purdy
Charles Haight	Caleb Haight
Roger Parke	Jonathan Horton
Thomas Kniffin	John Bloomer
Jeremy Lownsbury	Gilbert Bloomer
Stephen Williams	Ebenezer Brown
Daniel Williams	Joseph Green
Joseph Bancks	Isaac Anderson
Nathaniel Merritt	Jeremy Anderson
Jonathan Lyon	John Merritt
Andrew Kniffin	Ebenezer Kniffin
James Purdy	Ebenezer Purdy
Munmoth Purdy	Joseph Lyon

Joseph Anderson

27.

"Girls who can perfectly Answer to the whole Catechism.

Mrs. Elizabeth Bridge	Phebe Lyon
Mary Haight	Anne Lyon
Susanna Theal	Phebe Kniffin
Elizabeth Robinson	Hannah Bancks
Hannah Coo	Mary Brown
Sarah Ogden	Marty Brown
Sarah Brundige	Ruth Merritt

Martha Purdy.

15.

"Girls who cannot answer The whole Catechism.

Sarah Lyon	Abigall Banks
Amy Lyon	Mary Anderson
Susanna Purdy	Ruth Purdy
Gertrude Purdy	Sarah Kniffin
Martha Brown	Mary Steen Rod

Mary Banks.

11.

Whole Number 74."[40]

[40] List of children from Sept. 1716 to Oct. 14, 1717, *ibid.*, A, 12, p. 353. "Mr. Christopher Bridge" is intended for Christopher Bridge, Jr., son of the S. P. G. Minister of Rye. The writer has been told that such usage was customary in England, and is even now to be found, with reference to the children of the clergy.

Mr. Cleator found his own schoolhouse, as appears from two of his reports in 1713 and 1714.[41] This probably held true in the years of the moving school as well, though the owners of private houses may have been very willing to grant the use of rooms in lieu of his own accommodation to the children. In 1711 he brought his school nearer the church as a constant centre, and in 1713 he purchased a house both for a residence and for this purpose,[42] making use of it until 1716. He then moved the school two miles from his place of residence where he could have a great number of small children.[43] In 1718 again Cleator brought his school very near the Church and purchased a small house as a permanent location for it. In this move he had some assistance from the parish, in addition to his salary. The school thus located became permanently fixed for the remaining years during which Cleator had charge of it,[44] and so continued under his successors with but a slight break. There were other schools in the parish during Cleator's time, some of which it may be presumed were in the town. In 1728 Rev. Mr. Wetmore wrote the Secretary:

"As to Schools for teaching Children there are several poor ones in the differ^t parts of the Parish, while Mr. Cleator had his sight they tell me he kept a constant and good School, but now where a number of ffamilies live near together they hire a man or Woman at a Cheap rate subscribing every one w^t they will allow, some Masters get £20 per an^m & their Dyett, some £12 but there is no publick provision at all for a School in this Parish."[45]

Mr. Cleator first appealed for books in 1709, the lack of which he set forth as follows: "Books are very much wanted; if your Honours would be pleased to bestow 3 or 4 dozen on me would do me a great Kindness, primers, psalters, Testaments, Bibles, & Catechism, for here hath not these six months been either Testament or Bible to be got at N. York."[46] The S. P. G. immedi-

---

[41] S. P. G. Journal, II, p. 330; III, p. 6.

[42] *Ibid.*, II, p. 330.

[43] Apr. 16, 1716, *ibid.*, III, p. 218.

[44] "I have had more Constant Schollars this year than I have formerly given an account of, being I now teach near the Church, and in a small house I Purchased by their Honors Assistance (over and above my salary). I think I shall be removed no more this being for several reasons the most Convenient proper place in the Parish." Cleator to the Secretary, April 29, 1718, S. P. G. Letter-book, A, 13, p. 372. The writer was not able to find any other data concerning the details of this aid. Baird (Hist. of Rye Parish, op. cit., p. 176) says the schoolhouse was first mentioned in 1738. The Rye Vestryoccasionally used the Schoolhouse for a meeting place. Rye Vestry Minutes I, pp. 13, 14, 16.

[45] Feb. 29, 1727/8, S. P. G. Letter-book, A, 20, p. 207.

[46] *Ibid.*, A, 5, p. 10.

ately "directed the Treasurer to send over to Mr. Cleator the Schoolmaster at Rye by the first opportunity 200 primers, 50 psalters, 200 Church Catechism, 30 Common Prayer Books, 40 Testaments, and 20 Bibles for the use of his School."[47] In 1712 the schoolmaster reported that he was furnishing the children with books as they had need of them. He also desired Testaments, Psalters and Spelling books to be sent, since such were to be had only at great prices,[48] and suggested that he might have the advantage of selling them.[49] Such sales were against the orders of the Society, as he well knew,[50] but notwithstanding he may have taken advantage of the occasional opportunities to increase his income in this manner. Books were ordered out to Cleator in 1712, 1714, 1717, and 1718.[51] Besides the different kinds given above the Society in 1714 sent out two dozen horn-books for the use of the smaller children.[52] Two other packets were sent in 1724 and 1725 at the solicitation of the S. P. G. missionary.[53]

Cleator was succeeded in the school by Samuel Purdy, who had been recommended to the Society by the missionary at Rye.[54] The affair was a grievous disappointment to Daniel Chubb, the assistant to Cleator,[55] whose long years of service had been given in the hope of being appointed to the place. Purdy was allowed the previous salary of £15 per annum.[56] When appointed, he was holding some public posts which were not remunerative. Referring to them, Rev. Mr. Wetmore, the missionary, said: "Purdy is the foremost Justice of the Peace & one of the Quorum, & a chaplain of the Militia, but these places being such as rather require than make a fortune, he will accept a Mission from Soc., & the greater his interest in the people's esteem & affections he will the better be able to promote religion & Church, for which he has always had a good affection."[57] Later he was made one of the Judges of the Common

[47] S. P. G. Journal, I, p. (203).

[48] S. P. G. Letter-book, A, 8, p. 114.

[49] *Ibid.*

[50] *Ibid.*, A, 7, p. 201.

[51] *Ibid.*, A, 7, p. 201; A, 9, p. 225; A, 12, p. 427; A, 13, p. 433; Journal, III, pp. 6, 289, 402.

[52] S. P. G. Letter-book, A, 9, p. 225.

[53] S. P. G. Journal, IV, p. 314; V, p. 83.

[54] S. P. G. Letter-book, A, 24, p. 200.

[55] Petition of Chubb to the S. P. G. June 15, 1733, *ibid.*, B, 1, p. 26.

[56] S. P. G. Journal, VI, p. 54, Dec. 15, 1732.

[57] S. P. G. Letter-book, A, 24, p. 200.

Pleas and so served until 1737. A political upheaval in the town then displaced Purdy and he was left with the position of Town Clerk, the business of which was but small and the profits inconsiderable.[58] The office of Town Clerk he held for the years 1745 to 1753.[59] Furthermore, he had occasional work at surveying, and, at such times, employed an usher in his school. The surveying was said to be worth about £6 per annum, besides paying the usher. The people of Rye gave him about £20 yearly, in tuition fees.[60] As far as can be ascertained, therefore, Purdy relied on a better income than his predecessor.[61]

Mr. Purdy's first report gave a total enrolment of 44 for the year with "about 34 attending at one time."[62] Such irregular reports as succeed this show a smaller school than Cleator had, save in 1741 when there were 51 pupils,[63] and in 1751 when the number was as high as 50 again.[64] Within the decade Purdy reported 32 in 1744, 29 in 1746, 27 in 1747, 37 in 1748, and 42 in 1749.[65] There were two reasons for the decline in attendance. One was as follows, to quote from Purdy's report: "Such Children as grow up to be capable of Labor, their Parents will not afford time for further Instruction but take them away to business."[66] The other reason was the dissenters' growing objection to the teaching of the Church catechism in the school. Cleator had not been rigidly insistent on this, much to the annoyance of the S. P. G. missionary.[67] Purdy from the beginning was zealous in his attention to this particular,[68] and he continued to adhere to it. Children of dissenting parents were withdrawn from his school on account of it, and Independent teachers were encouraged to set up opposing schools. In 1746

[58] S. P. G. Journal, VIII, p. 4. But Baird claims he was Justice of the Peace for more than thirty years, *op. cit.*, p. 175.

[59] Rye Vestry Minutes, I, pp. 104, 106, 108, 110, 112, 114, 117, 120, 122. Purdy held also the honorary office of Churchwarden. Bolton, *op. cit.*, pp. 224, 233.

[60] Said Wetmore in 1738: "His Employers, some of whom are very poor, scarce pay him £20." S. P. G. Journal, VIII, p. 4. The few times that Purdy speaks of this allowance he states the same amount. In 1751 Purdy mentions "the perquisites of the Scholars that are able to pay." S. P. G. Letter-book, B, 10, p. 79.

[61] This income was sufficient to maintain Purdy and his family, consisting of a wife and two children, and to enable him to employ a servant. *Ibid.*

[62] Dec. 5, 1735, S. P. G. Journal, VII, p. 39.

[63] S. P. G. Letter-book, B, 9, p. 76.

[64] *Ibid.*, B, 19, p. 79.

[65] *Ibid.*, B, 13, p. 268; B, 14, p. 115; B, 15, p. 116; B, 16, p. 69; B, 17, p. 111.

[66] *Ibid.*, B, 7, p. 145, July 16, 1738.

[67] *Ibid.*, A, 12, p. 345; Journal, III, p. 405. While Cleator did not distinguish between children of the Church and of dissenters the inference is a fair one that both attended his School on about equal terms and in equal proportion.

[68] S. P. G. Letter-book, A, 24, p. 470.

and 1747 only seven dissenting children were reported.[69] In 1738 there were no schools within two miles of Purdy,[70] but in the following year a Presbyterian schoolmistress was established within one mile.[71] She was not able to maintain herself and soon gave up, but in 1741 a schoolmaster and schoolmistress both attempted schools for a time;[72] while in 1747 two were again under way, both of which were brought within a half mile of the Society's school.[73] Not until the failure of these last attempts do we find the scholars coming back to Purdy.[74] The number of children that were given free tuition cannot be ascertained, but it is certain that some were thus privileged. On one occasion only did Purdy, in such reports as are to be had, refer to the poor children. He then stated that such as were poor were taught gratis.[75]

The location of the school remained as it had been fixed by Cleator, that is, near the Church in the house built for that purpose.[76] In 1749, Purdy wrote the Society that the dissenters had lately given him much trouble and opposition, on account of which he had agreed to move his school some three miles from the Church.[77] The agreement, it appears, was not carried out, because the opposition subsided.[78]

Whether Purdy's succession to the school led to any marked improvement is debatable. He was inexperienced as a teacher. In thanking the Society for his appointment, he expressed the wish that he might be better qualified for the work, and especially for writing, which was his particular weakness. But with "such preparation as he had" he was "ready to teach the catechism and such other learning as he had, and to practice as much reading and writing and arithmetic as might serve the common occasions of vulgar people."[79] Yet his outside interest made him neglect the school. He was frequently absent, employing

[69] *Ibid.*, B, 14, p. 115; B, 15, p. 116.

[70] S. P. G. Journal, VIII, p. 4.

[71] S. P. G. Letter-book, B, 7, p. 147.

[72] *Ibid.*, B, 13, p. 268.

[73] *Ibid.*, B, 15, p. 116.

[74] In 1741 the proportion of the two groups of children was as 27 to 22; in 1746, it was as 22 to 7; in 1751 it was as 30 to 20. *Ibid.*, B, 9, p. 76; B, 14, p. 115; B, 19, p. 79.

[75] Dec. 10, 1751, *ibid.*, B, 19, p. 79.

[76] S. P. G. Journal, VIII, p. 4.

[77] S. P. G. Letter-book, B, 17, p. 111.

[78] Report of 1751, *ibid.*, B, 19, p. 79.

[79] Aug. 29, 1733, *ibid.*, A, 24, p. 470.

on such occasions, as he afterwards declared, "at a considerable Charge such masters as are more capable."[80] Some of the dissenters' opposition may have been caused by his irregularity in this respect. In the later years of his service he constantly maintained an assistant at his house, as the following indicates: "When the Independent in the Neighbourhood, (having got a teacher of their Sort among them) began to undermine my School and set up another in opposition, I took a Gentleman into my house better qualified than myself, whom I imployed under my care and direction, for several years, visiting the School and assisting myself as there was occation; and finding this method Satisfactory to the better people, I still Continue to Imploy a Gentleman well qualified, whom in a Good measure I maintain myself and allow him to Receive the perquisites by the Scholars that are able to pay; (Such as are poor, being taught gratise) I am at hand to observe the Master's Diligence and Childrens' Improvements, & do all I can to incourage both, and assist my Self as there is occation."[81] The gentleman here spoken of, we learn in an earlier report, was "a young Schollar Educated at New Haven."[82] He was, very likely, William Sturgeon, son of a Presbyterian minister, who had just graduated Bachelor of Arts from Yale and had become "an hearty Proselyte to the Church."[83] In 1746, or even earlier, Sturgeon had undertaken a school in the precinct of the town of Rye, it was reported.[84] This must have been Purdy's school according to his Notitiae.

Until Purdy determined on the constant employment of an assistant his school was undoubtedly neglected in favor of other affairs, in spite of the commendations given him by the rector of the parish. Reports from the neighboring parish spoke of his miserable neglect.[85] That he saw fit to improve conditions in the last eight or ten years was due, perhaps, to the competition of the dissenters which threatened his school, more than to anything else.

---

[80] *Ibid.*, B, 15, p. 116.

[81] Purdy to the Sec., Dec. 10, 1751, *ibid.*, B, 19, p. 79.

[82] Dec. 30, 1747, *ibid.*, B, 16, p. 116.

[83] S. P. G. Journal, X, p. 168, notes from a recommendation of William Sturgeon by the missionary at Rye, April 3, 1746. Sturgeon afterwards became the S. P. G. catechist at Philadelphia.

[84] *Ibid.* Bolton, *op. cit.*, p. 351, lists Sturgeon as one of the S. P. G. schoolmasters, which can be true only in the sense of an assistant to Purdy. For this he had no allowance from the Society.

[85] Rev. Thos. Standard to Sec., Westchester March 18, 1742, S. P. G. Journal, IX, p. 132.

One packet of 100 catechisms was sent out for the school and for distribution in 1740.[86] This was in response to a request of the parish missionary and not of the schoolmaster.[87]

Mr. Purdy's death on the 4th of March 1753[88] caused another vacancy in the school. The earlier opposition to him had apparently ceased and he died greatly esteemed by the community, according to the rector, Rev. Mr. Wetmore, who wrote: "His body was attended to Church on Ash Wednesday by a great concourse of people of all persuasions."[89] Upon receipt of the announcement, the Secretary of the Society sent the following condolence to Wetmore: "I heartily condole with you on the death of Mr. Purdy the Society's worthy Schoolmaster, & if you find the poor widow & Children in such circumstances as to require it, I will endeavour upon her Petition supported by your Recommendation to obtain for her a Gratuity of ten pounds from the Society."[90] In a letter of December 4, 1753, Mr. Wetmore urged the prompt filling of the vacancy. Furthermore, we learn in the following quotation from the proceedings of the S. P. G.: "He recommends his son Timothy Wetmore, a youth of 19 years, prudent temper, sober & virtuous & with a sufficient stock of learning, he having trained him up himself, & led him through most of the Latin Classics, & given him some instruction in Greek & Mathematicks, History, Logic, & Ethics, in wh., as he improves himself, he hopes he may hereafter become qualified for some higher employments; and Mr. W. will do his utmost to make his son a worthy Schoolm^r there."[91] Acting on the recommendation the S. P. G. elected the youth, Timothy Wetmore, the successor of Mr. Purdy at the reduced salary of £10 a year, the same to date from March 25, 1754.[92] Young Wetmore may have taken up his duties immediately upon Purdy's death for the value of such perquisites as the community afforded. Unfortunately we have no records from him until 1757, so that this is uncertain. Regarding tuition he wrote

86 *Ibid.*, VIII, p. 184.

87 No evidence could be found concerning the sending of other books or of a request for any by Purdy.

88 *Ibid.*, XII, p. 269.

89 *Ibid.*

90 S. P. G. Letter-book, B, 20, p. 37, Aug. 1, 1753. The Society voted a gratuity of £5 instead, Journal, XII, p. 270.

91 *Ibid.*, XII, p. 359.

92 May 17, 1754, *ibid.*

that "the Reward that way was but small," even when the attendance was high.[93]

The statistics of Wetmore's school are found in eight of his Notitiae between 1755 and 1765. In these years his pupils numbered from 34 to 63, the average being about 46.[94] Fully half of these were the children of parents not affiliated with the Church of England. Indeed in 1762 there were 24 belonging to the Church and 38 from the dissenters, the odd one being a Negro. In 1763, 1764 and 1765 also the latter considerably outnumbered the former.[95] The reason for the large proportion of non-Church children is perhaps explained in the same reports from the schoolmaster, since in the case of five of them it was claimed that there were no other schools within two miles of the S. P. G. school.[96]

Wetmore's school continued in the quarters which had been previously provided until about the end of 1765. Then he transferred his pupils to a room in his own house. The reason for this will appear shortly.[97] A few years after Wetmore undertook the work he adopted the precedent of his predecessors and engaged an assistant, who gave entire attention to the school and left him virtually in the position of an overseer. He wrote in 1761 as follows: "I think my Father sometime before his Decease desired the Salary might be fixed upon my Brother James Wetmore but as we have had no advice of his appointment it seems to me to be proper that I shou'd draw. If the Society have not yet made the Alteration if they shall think proper, if it remains as it is it will equally be Satisfactory to my Brother. My Brother has hitherto attended the School to good satisfaction, & I hope will continue faithfully to discharge his Trust."[98] Since the Society did not transfer the appointment to the brother, Timothy Wetmore's status remained the same as Purdy's had been. In the following year he wrote: "I herein inclose my *Notitia Scholastica* & beg this may serve as proper advice. My

[93] S. P. G. Letter-book, B, 3, p. 216a; Wetmore served as clerk of the Church for one year only, 1762, and was allowed one pound therefor. Rye Vestry Minutes, I, p. 147.

[94] 34 in 1775, 40 in 1757, 38 in 1578, 53 in 1761, 63 in 1762, 47 in 1763, 51 in 1764, and 42 in 1765. S. P. G. Journal, XIII, pp. 139, 284; XV, p. 95. Letter-book, B, 3, pp. 216 a, 217, 222, 224, 227.

[95] See citations immediately above for the years given.

[96] *Ibid.*, B, 3, pp. 216 a, 217, 222, 224, 227.

[97] See the quotations from his letter given on the two following pages.

[98] May 6, 1761, *ibid.*, B, 3, p. 215.

brother James Wetmore has the Year past tended the School, I hope faithfully & will continue so to do. I allow him the Salary in full & wish on his Account that it was larger. His family is large having Seven Children & living at this Time uncommonly expensive."[99] James Wetmore acted as schoolmaster assistant to his brother until 1764. For the next two years the school was put under the care of George Harris, "an European who gives good satisfaction" according to Wetmore's Notitia.[100] In 1766 the Society received complaints from one of its agents in New York City[101] to the effect that the school was badly neglected, and resolved that the salary should be withdrawn unless good satisfaction could be made.[102] The charge was confirmed by the new missionary to Rye, Rev. Ephraim Avery, and thereupon the Wetmores were discharged on January 7, 1767.[103] Timothy Wetmore wrote the Society at length in justification of himself and brother. His letter gives us the fact of the reestablishment of a dissenters' school and the consequent dwindling of his own. The account of it, together with his defense, is thus related by him: "I beg leave to justify myself as far as Truth will permit. I therefore assert that when I have kept the School never was the School more faithfully attended nor never was there any Scholars in Rye better taught. I am also bold to affirm that in the annual Letters I have sent to the Secretary I have endeavoured to represent the State of the School with strict Truth. I have in them informed that about three Years ago the School was kept by my Brother & notwithstanding his utmost Endeavours to please the people Yet the school being surrounded by Presbyterians & hereditary Enemies of our Family (for no other Reason that I know of but because we wou'd not be Tools to ruinous Measures to Church & State) they agreed with a Master to set up another School—I then went into the School myself—but they had been about privately & by Misrepresentations got the people to Sign to this Master so that my School was so small that it wou'd not support my Family. I therefore & to prevent a mischievous Division which I had seen the bad Effects of in Mr. Purdy's

[99] May 25, 1762, *ibid.*, B, 3, p. 216a.
[100] Apr., 4, 1764, S. P. G. Letter-book, B, 3, p. 224.
[101] Samuel Auchmuty to Sec., Oct. 24, 1766, *ibid.*, B, 2, p. 19.
[102] S. P. G. Journal, XVII, p. 199.
[103] S. P. G. Letter-book, B, 3, p. 232.

Time—thot it best (in which I took Advice of such as I tho't most proper) to agree with the School Master to come into my School which he promised to resign to me at the End of the Year & all the Scholars. But at the End of the Year he insisted that as the Stamp Act prevented him from collecting his Debts that if I turned him out of the School he wou'd set up another. I therefore tho't it most adviseable to let him remain, as he was remarkably industrious—But I have kept from that Time a School in a convenient Chamber in my own House which was handy to another Quarter of the Town & though I did not get so many Scholars as I expected yet I have generally taught 7 or 8 for which I have never recd 20s nor do expect to—besides several others & some Latin Scholars—this School I continued as low down as I have drawn to; this was the best I cou'd do & I believe was better than to have gone into the School & thereby in all probability occasioned another School House to be built which wou'd have made such a Division as wou'd have spoiled the School. From this Representation it appears that I have not entirely neglected the School; so far from it that I have earned the money I have rec*d*d; My Crime has been going out of the School House into my own Chamber which I am certain the Society if they had been on the Spot wou'd have advised to—I have also a good Right to call the other School mine—he entered by Agreement with me & has kept it faithfully & of this I have truly informed the Society—to employ School masters is usual."[104] Wetmore's conduct had the appearance of imposition on the Society. His school of seven or eight appears to have been more in the nature of a plausible continuation of his claim to the £10 salary, and his peculiar reasoning that the dissenting schoolmaster stood in the relation of Usher to him was for the same purpose. Indeed the George Harris mentioned in Wetmore's Notitia was perhaps this same Independent schoolmaster.

During the services of the Wetmore brothers, at least one packet of books was sent.[105] It consisted of one hundred catechisms and a quantity of prayer books and doctrinal tracts. Both Timothy and James Wetmore reentered the Society's

---

[104] Wetmore to the Sec., July 7, 1767, *ibid.* There is nothing further to show that he had "truly informed the Society." Baird quotes from New York Revolutionary Papers, p. 159, in confirmation of the hatred of Timothy Wetmore, "that arch-tory or enemy of his country." Baird, *op. cit.*, pp. 159, 177.

[105] Dec. 17, 1762, S. P. G. Journal, XV, p. 292.

service as schoolmasters. The former took up the practice of law in New York City until the war made it no longer remunerative to continue therein.[106] James Wetmore, on the other hand, probably continued as a private teacher for a few years, and was reappointed to Rye.

The school was vacant for nearly a year.[107] The Society meantime desired Mr. Avery the missionary to appoint a schoolmaster.[108] He suggested that the missionary be made schoolmaster as well and set forth his reason for it, saying "with humble submission to the venerable Society, beg leave to ask, whether it would be disagreeable to them that I should be appointed their School-Master (not that I would go into the School myself, neither could I because my publick Administration and Parish Duties are quite as much as I can manage). But my view in this Request is, in order to prevent the Society a great Deal of Trouble, on account of the frequent change of Masters which will undoubtedly be the Case, because the Income of the School will be so small, that no good Teacher would willingly continue long in it, especially if better Business presented."[109] The Society objected, however, to a combination of the two duties.[110] Avery was correct as to the uncertainty of schoolmasters. His first appointee remained in the school but one quarter.[111] "Another," said Avery, "in two days succeeded him, who continued likewise but one Quarter."[112] The name of the first man was not given, but of the second Avery said: "the Person was my Brother, a Man of a liberal Education but he has now left the School, & taken to Merchandizing: another Man upon his Removal immediately took charge of the School, how long he will continue I am not able to say, but conclude not long."[113] He did, however, continue longer than the two before him, so that Avery could write, in the spring of 1769, "a third took Charge of the School and as yet continues in it, tho' am afraid will not tarry long. Him I would now take the liberty

---

[106] In 1776 Wetmore advertized a "Day and Night School" to be kept by himself. See New York *Gazette* and *Mercury*, Dec. 30, 1776.

[107] From about Sept. 1767 to May 1768. S. P. G. Letter-book, B, 3, pp. 233, 234.

[108] S. P. G. Journal, XVII, p. 427.

[109] S. P. G. Letter-book, B, 3, p. 234.

[110] S. P. G. Journal, XVIII, p. 66.

[111] Avery to Sec., May 2, 1769, S. P. G. Letter-book, B, 3, p. 235.

[112] *Ibid.* This teacher began May 1, 1768, *ibid.*, p. 234. The Rector later mentions the time more definitely as, "about half a year," *ibid.*, p. 238.

[113] *Ibid.* John Avery was the brother referred to.

to recommend to the Venerable Society as their School-master; his Name is John Rand; was educated at Cambridge College New England, a sober, pious man & proposes shortly to take Holy Orders."[114] John Rand was accordingly appointed the S. P. G. schoolmaster at Rye on July 21, 1769,[115] with the usual £10 per annum; but by this time he had left the school. From Mr. Avery we learn that Rand was succeeded by John Avery. He thus reported the fourth change: "Mr. Rand immediately succeeded him" (Avery's brother) "& remain'd in the School till July 1769, when my brother, not prospering in his Views return'd & again took charge of it. The only Reason why Mr. Rand quited the School, was the People's not being pleased with his Method in teaching their Children."[116] Two years after this time John Avery quitted the school a second time and moved to Long Island.[117] Rev. Mr. Avery thereupon recommended that James Wetmore be returned to the school and his appointment was confirmed by the Society July 19, 1771.[118] The school was continued under his teaching until October 1776, when the belligerent state of the country about Rye brought it to a permanent end. On January 10, 1777 Wetmore wrote the Society as follows: "I beg leave to inform the Ven^ble^ Society that I diligently taught the school in Rye until the 23rd day of Oct^br^ last. For more than a year before the 23rd of Oct^br^ I was lookt upon as a Friend of Government & had Reason to expect continually to be made a Prisoner; I thought myself then under an absolute necessity of escaping, being detected in assisting a Number of Persons in escaping from the Rebels to the Kings Troops—I have one son carried 200 miles from me & closely confined for his Loyalty; part of the time in Irons. I have another son engaged in his Majesties Service. I have another son, two young for the Service with me. My wife and 6 children are in the power of the Rebels."[119] From 1777 to 1779 he continued to teach on Long Island with a fair degree of regularity. Between then and 1783 he was maintained on the salary list of

114 *Ibid.*, p. 235.

115 S. P. G. Journal, XVIII, p. 156.

116 S. P. G. Letter-book, B, 3, p. 238.

117 About May 1, 1771, *ibid.*, p. 239; the letter giving the information is incorrectly dated 1770. That it is an error is made certain by the fact that the context stated that salary had been drawn for two years last past as schoolmaster. Besides the Minute in the Journal makes certain that the date should be 1771.

118 S. P. G. Journal, XIX, p. 74.

119 S. P. G. Letter-book, B, 3, p. 248.

the Society, but he rendered less than a year of service,[120] and in 1783 he was formally dropped.[121]

Between 1767 and 1777 the Society did not receive full reports called for by the Notitia. In fact no Notitiae for this period are to be found. For the three last years only do we know what the school enrolment was, namely 56 in 1775, 71 in 1776, and "upwards of 60" in 1777.[122] But the number of children who enjoyed free schooling was reported for nearly every year. From 10 to 16 pupils were taught on the bounty of the Society during almost the entire period.[123] In 1775 Wetmore reported that of his 56 enrolled, he was receiving no pay for 34.[124] In 1768 we have the first definite information as to the actual number of charity children in the Rye school. Rev. Mr. Avery then stated in one of his reports to London, "there are now in the School eleven Charity Children, which number I propose to continue because the Bounty will just defray the Expense of so many at the Rate that the Master teaches other children."[125] The bounty being £10, the tuition was therefore in the neighborhood of 18 shillings per annum.[126]

The school was kept in the old schoolhouse, which in 1770 Mr. Avery had repaired, "being out of Pocket 3 or 4£" thereby.[127] The dissenter to whom Timothy Wetmore had granted the use of the schoolhouse probably found quarters elsewhere and continued his work. Such a school, at any rate, was mentioned by James Wetmore in 1775. "There is but one School in the Town," he said, "kept by a Dissenter from Ireland that has heretofore drew many of the Children of those that are able to pay, but at present is upon the decline."[128]

Thus far we have traced the history of the school originally set up by Cleator and serving the town of Rye primarily. But

---

[120] S. P. G. Journal, XXIII, p. 95.

[121] Feb. 21, 1783. "Mr. James Wetmore not having kept school from 1779 to present time, Salary discontinued." *Ibid.*, XXIII, p. 51.

[122] S. P. G. Letter-book, B, 3, pp. 244, 246, 248.

[123] *Ibid.*, B, 3, pp. 234, 235, 230, 238, 239, 240, 241, 243.

[124] *Ibid.*, B, 3, p. 244.

[125] *Ibid.*, B, 3, p. 234.

[126] On this basis Wetmore's 22 paying scholars which he gave in the 1775 report brought him nearly £20 a year in addition to his fixed salary.

[127] *Ibid.*, B, 3, p. 238.

[128] *Ibid.*, B, 3, p. 244. The teacher was doubtless George Harris, the European assistant to Timothy Wetmore. See p. 136. This Harris is mentioned in the Abstracts of the S. P. G. as having kept a private school opposite the Church at Rye, for many years. In the same record he is the reputed murderer of Rev. Mr. Avery, the missionary. See Abstracts for Feb. 1776–1777.

the S. P. G. was instrumental in the establishment of other schools in this parish. After Cleator gave up his moving school, the Society's missionary, Rev. Mr. Bridge, urged his superiors to allow bounties for two places remote from the Church. It was agreed to allow one bounty of £5 per annum towards the schoolmaster desired, with the provision that he should "teach Catechism Liturgy, & Certify that he teaches 30 children."[129] More than a year ensued before a satisfactory schoolmaster could be found. In March 1714/5 Bridge appointed Richard Cudney, who set up a school at White Plains and taught for 18 months.[130] His enrolment was "about 30 scholars."[131] Though most faithful in the discharge of his duty "he was forced to desist for want of necessary encouragement," having little or no help from the people. The Society voted £7–10 for the period of his teaching but did not see fit to make further provision for him.[132] In 1729, Rev. James Wetmore requested the Society to establish a school at North Castle. Concerning this place he said: "My Congregation is considerably increased at North Castle, a new Settlement in the woods where I go to officiate every fifth Sunday. The Dissenters there are all Quakers, and I have thought if we had a good Schoolmaster there, it might be of great Service to Religion, in some sort to supply the place of a Resident Minister, in Catechising and instructing the Youth and keeping the People from running Wild in their Principles and practice, as they are in great danger of doing by being among so many Quaker Seducers and men of no Religion."[133] His next letter represented that the "chief people" at North Castle had urged him to petition the Society for a schoolmaster to teach the children and to "read the Ch. prayers & holy Scriptures & good books on Sundays, & thus keep them from faithlessness." "They have no subscriptions at present," he continued, "but are confident that they will be able to raise full £20 p.a. for a Schoolmaster."[134] For this position Wetmore recommended an ex-schoolmaster among the dissenters, named

---

129 Oct. 10, 1712, S. P. G. Journal, II, p. 242.

130 *Ibid.*, III, pp. 198, 293. This was six miles from the Church.

131 *Ibid.*

132 *Ibid.* Failing in this, Bridge persuaded two women "that were in want," to teach school, one of them at White Plains. They also had, he said, "very mean encouragement from the People," S. P. G. Letter-book, A, 12, p. 372.

133 July 21, 1729, *ibid.*, A, 22, p. 342.

134 Nov. 5, 1729, *ibid.*, B, 1, p. 51.

Flint Dwight, in whose behalf it was stated: "He has had a liberal education at Cambridge in New England, & got his B.A. about 4 years ago. He is of a sober & exemplary life, & lately came over to the Church, & is willing to serve religion for a suitable encouragement and to accept of a Catechetical office, till he have opportunity to furnish himself for further service."[135] The S. P. G. decided to grant Dwight an annual allowance of £10 dating from midsummer 1729 "on condition that the people contribute £20 yearly according to their promise."[136] The clerkship of the church at Rye was also given Dwight, and with it an extra 20 shillings per year.[137]

The obstacles in the way of Dwight's success at North Castle were set forth in his letter to the Secretary, after two year's work there. He said: "My School in this place has been under some discouragements the year past, partly by reason of some contentions among the People relating to the Place for the School, and partly through meer opposition, one to another, for when some that dislik'd the place agreed upon by the Major part, refused to Join in paying my Salary, four of the Principal Men offered to pay the £20, and those that did not become engaged with them, were to pay to them according to what Children they sent at the usual rate per quarter, which some seemed discontented with, tho' they refused to be engaged for the £20 and for a long time they would send none, but of late they grow better reconciled and send their children, and I have a prospect of a very full School for the next year; but I believe they would be better agreed among themselves, if I had liberty to remove my School to some other part of my Parish with Mr. Wetmore's advice in case they dont show themselves forward to promote the good design of it."[138] In 1732 the S. P. G. ordered the missionary to reprove the people for their neglect of the school and, if necessary, to remove it. In spite of their failure to assist, the people were so unwilling to have Dwight removed from them that he urged further patience. In the same spirit Wetmore wrote of the situation: "The people are poor, & worse still, they are divided against one another. Those who chiefly encouraged

---

[135] *Ibid.*, A recommendation from Mr. Vesey enclosed with this, stated that Dwight taught a Latin School in New York for some time, and while there showed himself well qualified to be a schoolmaster and catechist.

[136] Jan. 16, 1729-30, S. P. G. Journal, V, p. 235.

[137] *Ibid.*, VIII, p. 4.

[138] May 15, 1731, S. P. G. Letter-book, A, 23, p. 231.

learning & religion, are either dead or removed within 2 years. Mr. Dwight says they are a poor unfortunate people deserving compassion, & as he hopes their affairs will mend, so he is willing to make a further trial among them if the Soc. will allow him, being urged by some new comers among them. After some trial he will acquaint Soc. with his success."[139] A year later conditions had shown no improvement and the Society ordered the school removed to White Plains.[140] Though the people were mostly Presbyterians here,[141] Dwight found much happier encouragement. A schoolhouse was begun and until its completion he was allowed to teach in the meeting house.[142] The people also paid for "his diet and horse keeping" and gave him £10 which was "at least equivalent to £20 per annum that currency."[143]

There are no statistics as to Dwight's school at North Castle. At White Plains, however, he had in 1735 between 20 and 30 pupils.[144] By 1738 the number had increased to between 30 and 40,[145] and in 1739 the last report of the school, in the form of a Notitia, showed a total enrolment of 46 scholars, of whom 27 belonged to the Church, 17 to the dissenters, and 2 were Negroes.[146]

In 1741 Dwight died and the school came to an end.[147] Sometime afterward Mr. Wetmore attempted to have the work revived and urged the appointment of a Mr. Lamson as schoolmaster, catechist, and assistant minister in the parish.[148] The Society ordered the matter to be considered later,[149] but it does not appear that further action was ever taken towards renewing the school.[150]

---

139 June 6, 1732, *ibid.*, A, 24, p. 200.

140 Dec. 21, 1733. S. P. G. Journal, VI, p. 114.

141 S. P. G. Letter-book, A, 26, p. 75.

142 S. P. G. Journal, VIII, p. 39.

143 *Ibid.*, VIII, p. 4.

144 Nov. 12, 1735, S. P. G. Letter-book, A, 26, p. 75.

145 Aug. 31, 1738, S. P. G. Journal, VIII, p. 4.

146 July 20, 1739, S. P. G. Letter-book, B, 7, p. 151. Reports for other years were not to be found.

147 Oct. 9, 1741, S. P. G. Journal, IX, p. 18.

148 May 1, and Dec. 13, 1744, S. P. G. Letter-book, B, 13, pp. 253, 255. It is evident, however, that Wetmore desired an assistant minister more than a schoolmaster.

149 S. P. G. Journal, X, p. 23.

150 Lamson or Lampson was ordained and served as an assistant to Wetmore in the capacity of catechist for North Castle and Bedford. He held the position for one year, 1745-1746, afterwards being transferred to New England. Classified Digest, *op. cit.*, p. 855.

There are evidences of instruction in secondary education by the agents of the Society, on two different occasions. Both of these were in the town of Rye. The first mention of it was in the year 1747, in a letter of Rev. Mr. Wetmore to the Secretary from which the following is quoted: "Here is a very worthy young Gentleman Mr. Thomas Bradbury Chandler educated at New Haven College who has lately declared himself a Conformist to our Church, and has desired me to present his humble Duty to the Honble Society and request that his Name may be remembered among the Candidates for Holy Orders designing to devote himself to the Service of the Church when of sufficient Age & the Honble Society shall be pleased to send for him. He is now about 21 years of age, and has made Uncommon Proficiency in Learning. He has undertaken to keep a Latin School in this Parish and for some small Encouragement is willing to undertake the Service of reading at Bedford and North Castle alternately, for three years after which he will become of Age for Holy Orders. And as I can think of no Young man that would perform that Service better, I would humbly Request that the Honble Society would allow ten pounds pr. annum to Mr. Chandler . . . If Mr. Chandler undertakes this service, besides the Perquisites of his School which will be about £30 a Year New York currency, I don't doubt but I shall be able to prevail with them to subscribe at least ten pounds pr. annum which I shall endeavour to do for his Encouragement, and I am much mistaken in my opinion, if he does not prove a Credit & Ornament to our Church."[151] The Society forthwith resolved that Chandler should become the catechist for North Castle and Bedford at £10 a year.[152] In the ensuing year he was transferred to the office of catechist at Elizabethtown, New Jersey,[153] so the Latin School, according to the facts ascertainable, had an existence of about two years. The other venture was carried on by Timothy Wetmore. His reference to it has been previously quoted.[154] For possibly three years, 1764–67, he conducted a Latin School in conjunction with his work in the elementary field. In 1774 there was "no grammar School,"[155] but in 1775

[151] Feb. 14, 1746-7, S. P. G. Letter-book, B, 14, p. 114.

[152] S. P. G. Journal, X, p. 252.

[153] May 20, 1748, *ibid.*, XI, p. 26.

[154] See p. 137.

[155] Quoted by Baird, History of Rye Parish, p. 176, and taken from President Adam's Works, II, p. 345.

Rev. Mr. Avery, the missionary, advertised the establishment of a boarding Grammar School with tuition at £22 per annum. This probably continued till his death in November 1776, if it was ever actually started.[156]

One other incident relating to the Society's support of schools in Rye parish should perhaps be included here. Among a large number of benefactions in support of the work of the church in New York Province, Mr. St. George Talbot of the city of New York was one of the foremost individual donors. Besides various gifts and legacies to churches in other places he made generous provision for the church in Rye. In 1759 he further "devised £500 for the use of Schools" in Rye parish, "& for clothing poor children."[157] This and other legacies were put under the direction of the S. P. G.[158] But the poor children of the school at Rye received no benefit from the bequest, nor in fact did the Society. Long years of ligitation followed Mr. Talbot's death, and the legacies were not available until the beginning of the nineteenth century.[159] No data have been found to show other provision of this kind for the poor children who were enrolled in the Society's schools.[160]

The Schools of West Chester Parish

The second missionary that the S. P. G. appointed for New York province was stationed at West Chester parish.[161] This was Rev. John Bartow. Before the Society began its support of schools in the parish, he provided, out of his own means, for the religious instruction of the children. "I take care," he informed the Secretary, "to Catechise the Children sometimes in the Church, and, to make amends for my Omission of that duty at any time, I allow a Schoolmaster 20 shillings per ann to en-

[156] New York *Mercury*, April 3, 1775; also Baird, *op. cit.*, p. 176.

[157] Wetmore to the Soc., April 7, 1759. S. P. G. Journal, XIV, p. 199.

[158] *Ibid.*, also XV, p. 167.

[159] Bolton, quoting from a minute of Trinity Vestry meeting on March 3, 1803, fixes the date of final settlement in that year. Bolton, Hist. of the County of Westchester, I, p. 25.

[160] Pratt, *op. cit.*, p. 114, includes Thomas Huddleston and John Carhart in the list of S. P. G. schoolmasters for Rye. His authority is Baird (*op. cit.*) and Bolton (*op. cit.*). The writer has already shown the relation of Thomas Huddleston Jr. to the Society. He has also indicated that the elder of that name was a private schoolmaster on Long Island in 1708. (See p. 77). If he taught at Rye, as Baird and Bolton contend, it was in a private school. He was never on the Society's roll, and neither was John Carhart as Bolton thinks (p. 126). The confusion of Huddleston was caused by a clerical error in the Abstracts of the S. P. G. which printed Huddleston of "Rye" instead of "New York." Carhart was Clerk of the Vestry of Rye. See Bolton, *op. cit.*, p. 235; also Rye Vestry Minutes, I, meetings between 1722–1744.

[161] 1702, Classified Digest, *op. cit.*, p. 58.

courage him to instruct the children in the Church Catechism."[162] How long this plan was carried out by Mr. Bartow cannot be determined, but in 1709 the direct assistance of the Society was sought. Bartow sent the following recommendation: "We want very much a fixed School at West Chester; If Mr. Daniel Clark, my neighbour now in England, shou'd wait upon you desirous of that employment I recommend him as a person worthy of it, being of good report, a constant Communicant, & being a clergyman's Son has had a pious and learned education."[163] No appointment followed, and after three years Bartow was joined by other clergy of the province in an appeal for schoolmasters,[164] who, said he, "are especially wanted at West & East Chester, for the people can give so little, that a good master will not stay long";[165] and "one at Yonkers would be of great use to teach the Dutch children English."[166] The Society "agreed to allow £5 p. anum . . . to a schoolmaster there (Yonkers) to teach Catechism & Liturgy, & certify that he teaches 30 children."[167] Not until 1714 was any action taken in behalf of West Chester. On December 17th of that year the Secretary acknowledged the petition of West Chester in behalf of "Charles Glover, Schoolmaster there," and was pleased to inform Bartow that the Society had agreed "to allow him £10 p.a. provided that he comply with the Soc's rules."[168] In their petition the inhabitants set forth their belief that Mr. Glover was "well qualified to teach their children according to the Church of England" and that he already had "more than 40 Scholars,"[169] the poor children being taught for a small recompense.[170] From about the middle of 1714 until June 1716 Glover acted as the Society's agent[171] with the exception of the winter

---

162 Dec. 1, 1707, S. P. G. Letter-book, A, 3, p. 184. This is the school, probably, to which Huddleston referred in his account of 1708. see p. 77.

163 Oct. 30, 1709, *ibid.*, A, 5, p. 103. Another testimonial for Daniel Clarke was forwarded by Col. Caleb Heathcote, who said that Clarke "formerly taught School on Long Island very much to satisfaction." *Ibid.*, A, 6, p. 98.

164 1712, S. P. G. Journal, II, p. 243.

165 June 9, 1712, S. P. G. Letter-book, A, 7, p. 209.

166 *Ibid.*

167 S. P. G. Journal, II, p. 243, Oct. 10, 1712.

168 S. P. G. Letter-book, A, 9, p. 246.

169 S. P. G. Journal, III, p. 2.

170 *Ibid.*, also S. P. G. Letter-book, A, 9, 7 fol. p. 97. (The paging of this volume is entirely different from the others, there being several sets of Ms. each starting with page 1.)

171 S. P. G. Journal, III, p. 192; Letter-book, A, 12, p. 273.

of 1714–15.[172] His school during the time numbered between 30 and 40. One certificate, bearing the date July 18, 1715, informed that he "instructed above 30 children to the parents satisfaction, not omitting Ch. Catechism."[173]

The school was vacant for the next year. On May 1, 1717, William Forster assumed charge of it at the request of Bartow and other inhabitants.[174] Forster in writing a brief sketch of his biography to the Society, tells us that his father, Marmaduke Forster, is an attorney at law and his uncle, Pexall Forster, is a clergyman and Rector of Eggscliff in the Bishopric of Durham; that he was educated under Rev. Mr. Burton, the master then there, and has since served three years at sea with "Her Late Majesty's Letter," and four years a midshipman; that after this he found there was not much advancement in the service, as there was an abundance of old soldiers to provide for, and not many ships at sea; and that he came hither intending to follow the sea but was desired to keep school, which, if he was not helped, he must leave, as a laborer got more by his daily work.[175] Petitions were sent desiring the bestowal of an annual bounty on Forster.[176] There was a delay in acting on this matter which may have been caused by the hazards in the transmission of mail. At any rate Forster did not come before the consideration of the Society till the October meeting in 1718, when he was voted £10 per year from the commencement of his teaching, and a packet of books was ordered to be sent him, consisting of: "2 Bishop Beveridge's Catechism, 2 Ostervald's Catechisms, 2 whole art of Catechising, 50 Catechisms broke into Small questions, and 50 abc."[177] In addition to the usual subjects taught, we learn that, "he Catechises them weekly in the School and makes the Quakers as well as other attend thereat, but does not ask the unbaptised any questions that are improper for them. On Sundays, when Bartow is away he catechises all

[172] "I cannot omitt to informe that last winter I did not teach here, better incouragement then presenting." S. P. G. Letter-book, A, 10, p. 194, July 18, 1715. This was from Oct. 29 to May 23, *ibid.*, p. 193. Bartow observed that it was difficult to get a fixed schoolmaster because there were "greater advantages to be made by other employments"; and he added: "The Husbandman earns 3 sh. p. day, & the joiner carpenter, mason, weaver, &c. 5 sh. or 6 sh. so that many prefer to be labourers & artisans to keeping a School—there was one lately at East Chester that turned weaver, & we have one now in W. Chester, that keeps School in winter & in summer is a Shephard & has done this for many years." Feb. 16, 1716, *ibid.*, A, 12, p. 273.

[173] *Ibid.*, A, 10, p. 266.

[174] S. P. G. Journal, III, p. 401; Letter-book, A, 12, p. 368.

[175] *Ibid.*, A, 12, p. 364, Nov. 2, 1717.

[176] *Ibid.*, A, 12, pp. 368, 411.

[177] *Ibid.*, A, 13, p. 434; Journal, III, p. 401.

children whether Scholars or not that attend the Church, & reads the Psalms, Hymns & Lessons & has had good success."[178]

Forster went to England to get his family about November 1718, having in the meantime given great satisfaction in the school, so that Bartow reported, "We all wish he would continue longer with us."[179] He returned in the ensuing fall taking charge again in April 1720. On departing for England he, of course, had not yet received notice of his appointment and allowance, and, it appears, another reason for his trip was to personally enlist the interest of the Society. In one of his letters he informed the Secretary, as follows: "After I had kept School here 18 months and had not had ye Hon^r^ of a Letter from the Honble Society, I Returned to great Britain as I desired to do all ye Service in my power for the Society and also for the people here. I delivered to the Society's Clerk, in order to be laid before them, a Certificate setting forth the satisfaction I had given by my method and Success in Teaching and also how earnestly the inhabitants of this place did in ye humblest manner request the Society's Encouragem^t^, For my return to them again. And I would have attended myself had I not been obliged to be in ye Country at ye time of their meeting. upon my return to Town the Clerk told me it was contrary to the Orders of the Society to send any Scoolmasters abroad but w^t^ was in Deacons Orders, but if I return'd, tho' they could not give me an Order, yet they would Continue the Salary, I told him I resolved to return and did accordingly the last fall but having my family to settle, and the winter being Extremely cold and no convent^t^ Schoolhouse then provided I did not then begin to keep school till the fourth of Aprill last past. I have here sent a Certificate signed by the principall inhabitants which will inform the hon^ble^ Society how much they desire I may be encouraged among them. . . . I hope the hon^ble^ Society will be pleased to Encourage me & as the people here are of abillity to do very little for me, I hope they'l be pleas'd to make some augmentation to the £10 per Ann. & take into consideration my expenses in removing my family, and for any assistance I shall be always very thankfull."[180] This being backed by letters from Bartow and

178 *Ibid.*, III, p. 401. Nov. 2, 1717.
179 Rev. J. Bartow to Sec., Nov. 18, 1718, S. P. G. Letter-book, A, 13, p. 395.
180 June 1, 1720, *ibid.*, A, 14, p. 115.

Heathcote, not only was the salary continued, but "the Committee agreed as their opinion that the Society be moved to make Mr. Forster a Gratuity of £10, and send him also 100 Church Catechisms, 100 broke into short Questions, 12 of Archbishop Wake's Catechisms, and 12 Common Prayer books, and that the Secretary acquaint Col. Heathcote herewith."[181]

While Forster was in England the school was continued by a substitute who met with very indifferent success. Mr. Bartow referred to this schoolmaster, saying: "I have set my hand to a Testimonial of one Edward Fitzgerald who kept School in Mr. Forster's absence one Year at West Chester; in the Summer he had upwards of twenty-five scholars, in the winter under 12, but attended the whole Year. I think he deserves a half Years allowance."[182] Forster, on the other hand, was unguarded in his account of the affair, which said: "Here is one *Edward Fitzgerald* who, during the time I was absent in England which was about twelve months, kept school in this Town, and he has by pleading poverty prevailed with Mr. Bartow and some others to signe a Certificate in his favour for a Salary for that Year: Which Certificate as I am informed only setts forth the time he kept School and that he instructed in the principles of the Church of England, neither mentioning the Number of his Scholars nor his diligence. But that you may not be in the dark as to this man's true character I give them this acct. which if desired shall be sufficiently testifyed: he is much given to drink and don't attend the Church, for Mr. Bartow does not remember he saw him above once there in the time he kept ye school here. On his request Mr. Bartow let him have some of the Books that were sent to me but I cannot find, tho' I have Examined all the Scholars, that he gave them any save one to a child where he lodged, and what use he put them to is not known; as to the Encouragmt he gave by his dilligence it was such that, from near thirty Scholars, they were before my Arrival reduced to Six."[183]

Forster was constantly commended in the earlier years of his service. His activity in both the school and the Church so pleased the S. P. G. that the following recommendation was

---

[181] Adopted by the Society Jan. 20, 1720-21, S. P. G. Journal, IV, p. 135. The Secretary also wrote: "The Society have agreed to allow you a Salary of £10 per annum from the time you began to teach School at West Chester, also a grautity of £10. Letter-book, A, 16, p. 254.

[182] Aug. 13, 1720, *ibid.*, A, 14, p. 121.

[183] Aug. 8, 1720, *ibid.*, A, 14, p. 120.

passed in 1724: "Whereupon the Committee in consideration of the extraordinary Services of Mr. Forster in makeing of a Collection for reparing the Church at Westchester, surveying of Glebes and otherwise besides the diligent teaching of his School, agreed that the Society be moved to increase his salary to £20 a year to commence from Christmas last and also allow him a Gratuity of £10 for his past services."[184] From this time on he enjoyed a bounty as great as that conferred on the schoolmaster in New York. Forster held the office of County Clerk from 1733 to 1746,[185] and enjoyed the perquisites of that office. He was also Recorder of the borough during some or all of this time,[186] with such extra emoluments as might be afforded by this means. In 1733 Rev. Mr. Standard, the successor of Mr. Bartow, severely attacked Forster because of his too great interest in politics, his taking on outside work, and his consequent neglect of the school.[187] The affair brought about an investigation by Mr. Vesey and others of the clergy. Forster was amply cleared for the time being. It was declared: "Forster's appointments are Recorder of the borough and clerk of the county: the first engages him one hour in a day, once a month, & that out of School time; & the other twice a year, at most 4 times, generally 3 days each. He was never Judge of the Common pleas (wh. Standard confesses to have been a mistake), & that the Bonds or writings Forster may do for people may generally be done at home—Mr. Forster never had the nominating of the Justices, & they believe the offices & trusts he now enjoys are very compatible, and that he discharges them justly & diligently, which together with his great humanity piety & civil deportment hath gained him esteem & respect from all good men, & they believe him to be accused by an uneasy ill-tempered envious and avaricious person—As to Mr. Forster's being Scrivener to Mr. Vesey &c., Forster has only drawn 4 or 5 Bonds for him, one of which was 15 years ago, & has delivered 6 or 7 letters for him, & 2 or 3 times spoke to people who owed Vesey Money—Altogether Vesey & other Clergy have known Forster for many years as a zealous promoter of the Church, ready to serve her Ministers and as a sober religious industrious man &

184 Feb. 19, 1723/4. S. P. G. Journal, V, p. 28–9.
185 Doc. re. Col. Hist. of N. Y., *op, cit.*, V, p. 978; Ec. Rec., *op. cit.*, p. 2140.
186 S. P. G. Journal, VI, p. 278. July 1, 1735.
187 *Ibid.*, VI, pp. 134, 192, 194. Letter-book, A, 25, p. 50.

well deserving of Soc's Salary."[188] Though Mr. Standard's conduct was unduly bitter and contentious[189] in the affair, he surely had some basis for complaint against Forster. The latter's irregularity in sending reports and his failure to have them properly attested soon brought forth the Society's protest.[190] Public business, too, called him away frequently, though he usually kept the school in session on such occasions by employing one of his former pupils to take charge.[191] In 1742 Mr. Standard again complained of Forster's school, and of the one at Rye. His letter declares that they "have been miserably neglected, the masters absenting themselves for days or even weeks together . . . none have been neglected like theirs, & therefore the intelligent part of the country are unanimously of opinion, that the Soc., had better save their expences on this head, & use it to better purposes."[192] After this, regardless of Standard's possible prejudices, the Society revoked the salary,[193] and Forster retired from the school in 1744.[194]

Seventeen reports of Forster's work at West Chester are available, much less than half of the number which the Society's rules required. They cover years between 1717 and 1742, the majority being for the decade 1730 to 1740.[195] In 1718 he had enrolled 82 pupils in fifteen months,[196] and in 1731 there were "60 during the year."[197] The lowest attendance shown was 20, recorded in 1723 and 1741;[198] the highest was 44 in 1734.[199] The average attendance was 35. The proportion of boys and girls was not given by Forster,[200] but four reports group the children

---

[188] July 1, 1735, *ibid.*, VI, p. 278. Gov. Cosby similarly defended Forster. S. P. G. Letter-book, A, 25, p. 60.

[189] The missionary was himself under a severe fire of criticism about this time. Hawks Transcripts, N. Y. II, p. 80, being a letter from Gov. Cosby to the Bishop of London, S. P. G. Letter-book, A, 25, p. 60.

[190] S. P. G. Journal, VII, p. 55; VIII, p. 88.

[191] *Ibid.*, VI, p. 192.

[192] *Ibid.*, IX, p. 132. Mar. 18, 1742.

[193] Apr. 15, 1743, *ibid.*, IX, p. 132.

[194] S. P. G. Letter-book, B, 13, p. 336. This document from the Church and people of West Chester includes this quotation: "Wm Forster, Soc's late Schoolmaster, by reason of his practising surgery & other employments, has left the school." It is dated Apr. 5, 1744.

[195] Mr. Standard in 1742 charged Forster with exaggerating reports, S. P. G. Journal, IX, p. 132. But Standard's animosity towards Forster was such as to make his claim doubtful.

[196] *Ibid.*, A, 13, p. 382.

[197] *Ibid.*, A, 23, p. 349.

[198] *Ibid.*, A, 17, p. 228; B, 9, p. 63.

[199] S. P. G. Journal, VI, p. 192.

[200] With this exception: In 1718 he adds, in speaking of his scholars, "Several of them being young men and women." S. P. G. Letter-book, A, 13, p. 382.

of dissenters and those of the Church, as follows: In 1723, 23 were of the Church, 5 were Quakers, and 5 were dissenters; in 1739, 17 of the 32 were classed as non-Church children; in November of 1739, 16 out of 36 were so classed; and in 1741, 6 out of 20.[201] Reports from 1737 to 1739 inclusive are the only ones that give the number of free children. Their proportion is from 45 to 62 per cent.[202] Paying scholars, however, did not materially increase his income for we have his own declaration that the people paid him but little on account of the school.[203] In the quotation following he thus describes his work: "I shall take care to Comply with the Society's Standing orders and in Order thereunto Do thereby inform them that my method is the same as sett forth in my former Letters That the Number of my Scholars is uncertain being sometimes more and sometimes less as the people can spare their children from their Country business, but the greatest number has been between Thirty and fforty and the fewest about Twenty but then in the Winter sometimes twenty or more Young people come to School in the Evening which come not in the day. I bless God my Success in the Instruction of my *Scholars* has been to the Content of their Parents and Severall of *Scholars* are not only qualified for Country Employments but for other business; for I teach all the Rules of Vulgar and Decimal Arithmetick, and Mr. Bartows eldest son is now about to learn Geometry, Trigonometry Surveying and other branches of the Mathematicks."[204] But, at a later date, he says: "The Number of my Scholars at present is 31 and the reason there are no more, is my teaching them Quick, and as they generally learn no further than the double Rule of Three or Practice, one Sett goes off, before another is grown up fit to come."[205]

The schoolmaster provided his own schoolhouse at first. In 1724 he reported: "This summer they are building a new School House;"[206] and in 1726 he wrote that he had "kept School in the new School-house" all the past winter and that it was "built

[201] *Ibid.*, A, 12, p. 364; B, 7, pp. 115, 157; B, 9, p. 63.

[202] 18 or 19 out of 40 on June 6, 1737; 22 out of 38 on Nov. 18, 1737; 20 out of 32 on June 14, 1738; 26 out of 40 on Feb. 16, 1738-9; and 20 out of 32 on Oct. 19, 1739. S. P. G. Journal, VII, pp. 239, 257, 302; VIII, pp. 88, 144; Letter-book, B, 7, p. 115.

[203] Oct. 14, 1724, *ibid.*, A, 18, p. 193.

[204] May 18, 1723, *ibid.*, A, 17, p. 228.

[205] July 10, 1728, *ibid.*, A, 21, p. 348.

[206] S. P. G. Letter-book, A, 18, p. 175.

big enough to hold 60 scholars."[207] We learn from another source that the schoolhouse was "100 yds, from the County Hall."[208] Forster did not employ an usher regularly, but on the occasions when other business occupied his time he did hire assistance. In 1734 we have the word of Thomas Bartow, son of the earlier missionary, to the effect that three years before and "now lately" Forster had employed him in his school several times, paying him for it, sometimes 3 shillings a day.[209] On the same date John Bartow stated that, whenever the Schoolmaster "was called away on business last autumn," he taught the school and that he did this a little before the election.[210] Forster made no reference to the matter when reporting to his superiors. To judge from his increasing absence for outside business, the Bartow boys were frequently called on in the later years of his teaching. Such books as were sent to Forster for the use of the school were contained in the packets already mentioned. Apparently he did not send requests for any others.

In January, 1745, Basil Bartow, another son of the deceased missionary, was made the S. P. G. schoolmaster.[211] The Church and people of the town had urged his selection by the Society, in which Forster himself had joined.[212] Commissary Vesey also wrote in his behalf from New York City, and said of him: "Mr. Bartowe is 23, a single man, of good temper, prudent, and sober & pious in life and conversation, well affected to the present Government, conformable to the doctrine & discipline of the Church, and in his opinion, exceedingly well qualified for teaching children."[213] On appointing him the Society voted a salary of £10 only, which, it was ordered, was to "commence from Michaelmas last."[214] From this it may be inferred that Bartow had taken up the duties of Schoolmaster as early as September 1744, so that, perhaps, no break of any length occurred in the school. Besides fees he had no other emoluments at the out-

---

207 *Ibid.*, A, 19, p. 388.

208 *Ibid.*, A, 25, p. 49.

209 Aug. 27, 1734, *ibid.*, A, 25, p. 77.

210 *Ibid.* And Vesey wrote: "Sometimes the public business . . . calls upon him in school time, yet he has substituted one or other of Mrs. Bartow's sons to serve in his stead on those occasions." August 28, 1734, S. P. G. Journal, VI, p. 192.

211 Jan. 18, 1744/5, S. P. G. Journal, IX, p. 348.

212 S. P. G. Letter-book, B, 13, p. 336.

213 Sept. 24, 1744, S. P. G. Journal, IX, p. 348.

214 *Ibid.*

set.[215] In 1747 he was made Clerk of the Mayor's Court,[216] which he held until 1752 at least and, presumably, during the remainder of his schoolmastership.[217] Bartow made two attempts to get his salary restored to the former amount. In 1746 he declared: " . . . in this luke warm Age it seems as if Parents (Dissenters in particular) were quite Negligent of their Children's Christian Education—there is many poor Children here that I believe would be wholly without Education if it was not for the Society's Charitable bounty. The Charity of the people here is so Small (many of them poor) that as I make the School my whole Employment the income which I have is not sifficient [*sic*] for my Support."[218] The Society met the appeal to the extent of agreeing "to give Mr. Bartow a gratuity of £5 to encourage him to persevere diligently in his duty."[219] In 1748, he appealed the second time for the allowances of his successor without which he felt he could not continue.[220] His condition was vouched for by the Rector of Trinity, as follows: "I also recommend Mr. Basil Bartow to the Honble Society's Favour, he being one of the most useful Schoolmasters in their Employment and his Stipend altogether Insufficient for his Support. I have been informed by some Gentlemen of this City who frequently visit Westchester, that he is very Diligent and Conscientious in the Discharge of his Office, and they are affraid it would prove a Detriment to the Interest of Religion, if he should betake himself to some other Employment."[221] Information was returned that the S. P. G. was not then in a condition to augment salaries,[222] and Bartow continued in charge of the school without urging the matter again. On account of "bodily infirmities" which prevented "his working any longer," he resigned at the end of 1761.[223]

Between 1745 and 1761 there are thirteen reports of Bartow's school; in fact, for every year save 1754–57 inclusive. All but

---

[215] S. P. G. Letter-book, B, 13, p. 337.

[216] *Ibid.*, B, 15, p. 107. "As to my being Clerk of the Mayors Court, it is no hindrance to me in the School, the Court being opened only the 1st Tuesday in Every Month to fulfil our Charter, And then its seldom that a Writt is Returnable." *Ibid.*

[217] His Notitiae did not mention the office after 1752, but doubtless he let it be taken for granted thereafter.

[218] Sept. 29, 1746, *ibid.*, B, 14, p. 119.

[219] Apr. 10, 1747, S. P. G. Journal, X, p. 242.

[220] *Ibid.*, XI, p. 118.

[221] Rev. Henry Barclay to Sec., Jan. 2, 1748, S. P. G. Letterbook, B, 16, p. 71. Barclay had succeeded Vesey as Rector of Trinity and Commissary of the Province.

[222] Sec. to Bartow, *ibid.*, B, 17, p. 199a.

[223] Dec. 14, 1761, S. P. G. Journal, XV, p. 202.

three of them are in the form of Notitiae. His average enrolment during the different years was 43, the lowest being 33 and the highest 61.[224] Up to 1754 there were more of the dissenters' than Church of England children, the proportion being as 58 to 42 per cent;[225] while after 1758, there was 36 per cent only of dissenting children.[226] In explanation of the enrolment Mr. Bartow wrote in 1745 that he did not have the number of pupils in the list at one time. The most, he said, attended in winter when there were 23. Some of these were men who "in spring had to go to husbandry." In early summer there came in a set of small children who could not attend in cold and snow. This seasonal change may of course be applied to other years. Regarding sects Bartow said: "Tho' part of the Children are of dissenting families, I teach them the whole Catechism, except the parts relating to Baptism & the Lord's Suppor."[227]

From 1753 to the end of his work Bartow employed an usher whose sole time was given to the children. The Society records state that, "being of a weakly condition, he had, by advice of his friends, taken in an Usher, & will take care that the School be duly attended."[228] For the first years and until 1752, the reports specifically stated that no other schools were in the town. Thereafter no answer was made to this question of the Notitia, yet his silence is a fairly safe inference that his own school, located in the town schoolhouse, was the only one during the period.

Though the Society promised the usual assistance for a successor to Mr. Bartow,[229] it was three years before the missionary could report the securing of a satisfactory schoolmaster.[230] Meanwhile the schoolhouse had been occupied by another master

---

[224] 42 in 1745, 33 in 1746, 36 in 1747, 46 in 1748, 46 in 1749, 44 in 1750, 61 in 1751, 55 in 1752, 51 in 1753, 38 in 1758, 34 in 1759, 34 in 1760, 36 in 1761. S. P. G. Letter-book, B, 13, p. 337; B, 14, p. 119; B, 15, p. 107; B, 16, p. 61a; B, 17, p. 109; B, 18, p. 120; B, 19, p. 84, B, 20, p. 62–3; B, 3, p. 275; B, 8, p. 276; Journal, XII, p. 341; XIV, p. 165; XV, p. 202.

[225] In 1750 there were 22 of each group, in 1753 there was as wide a difference as 18 Ch. of Eng. and 38 dissenters. S. P. G. Letter-book, B, 18, p. 120; Journal, XII, p. 341.

[226] See citations above for these years.

[227] Oct. 28, 1745, S. P. G. Letter-book, B, 13, p. 337.

[228] S. P. G. Journal, XII, p. 341. The usher is referred to later in 1759 and 1760. S. P. G. Letter-book, B, 3, p. 273.; B, 8, p. 276.

[229] *Ibid.*, XV, p. 224.

[230] Presumably on account of the S. P. G. requirements, the missionary reported many unsuitable offers and added: "It has not been in my power to procure a Schoolmaster as yet tho' I have taken all the usual methods of advertising & enquiry." S. P. G. Letter-book, B, 3, p. 284.

who taught for a year, if not for longer.[231] The missionary at West Chester finally appointed Nathaniel Seabury who entered upon his work September 25, 1764,[232] at the age of nineteen years.[233] He served the school for the following three years and, "having entered on another Scene of Life, had come," we are told, "under such Engagements, that he tho't he could not attend the School, so as to do Justice to it, & therefore declined it."[234]

The school declined perceptibly under Seabury, though it was not altogether his own fault. The dissenters who could pay tuition were making other arrangements for educating their children. So, too, were the better families among the Church adherents. The following is an example of such provision: "Mr. George Youngs who has officiated as Clerk to the Churches, since I have been in the Mission, & has taught school for three or four families of sober pious People . . . about two miles from hence, for several Years past, to their very particular Satisfaction, & who supports a very good Character, is a Communicant, & very well known, both to me & the People."[235] Young Seabury had only 18 or 20 pupils in the summer and about 14 in the winter.[236] Of these but 3 or 4 were taught gratis, others paying "at the Rate of one Spanish Dollar the Quarter."[237] So far from being a charity school the Society was told at one time that it had become shamefully neglected and of no manner of use.[238] The S. P. G. was on the point of withdrawing the salary, but refrained from doing so in view of other representations. The situation was thus described by a brother of the schoolmaster, who had become the Society's missionary at West Chester: "The Schoolmaster is my Brother, and since I have been in the Parish has lodged at my House, and I can honestly affirm that he hath not neglected the School the year past. I have also enquired of those People who were most likely to inform me of his former Conduct, especially of those

231 From the winter of 1763–4 to about Sept. 1764. S P. G. Letter-book, B, 3, p. 289. The name of the schoolmaster was not mentioned.

232 *Ibid.*, S. P. G. Journal, XVI, p. 299. This was confirmed with salary of £10. Feb. 15, 1765. *Ibid.*

233 S. P. G. Letter-book, B, 2, p. 165.

234 Rev. Samuel Seabury to Sec., Oct. 1, 1768, *ibid.*, B, 2, p. 159; also B, 3, p. 291.

235 *Ibid.*, B, 2, p. 159.

236 *Ibid.*, B, 2, p. 172; B, 3, pp. 289, 290.

237 *Ibid.*, B, 2, p. 172. The Spanish Dollar was equivalent to eight shillings. This would have made the yearly tuition £1-12 sh.

238 Samuel Auchmuty to the Sec., *ibid.*, B, 2, p. 19.

who had Children at the School, and have heard of no Complaint. Notwithstanding I do not think the School is of so much use as the Society may reasonably expect. Those children that are poor, and the proper Objects of the Society's Bounty are the hardest to go to School. Their Parents are either careless and suffer them to grow up in Idleness, or they keep them at Home to labour; so that not more than three or four have been to School, and those not Constantly. . . . By this Account the Society will see, that the Number of Children is so small that if they withdrew their Salary the School should cease. This I should be sorry should happen. I should also be sorry to see their Bounty productive of so little good. Tho' therefore I cannot urge them to continue their Salary, yet I can assure them that if they continue it, either to my Brother or any other Person, I will do everything in my Power to make the School useful, and will myself also see that the Master does punctually conform to such Directions as the Society shall give."[239]

A year after Nathaniel Seabury retired from the school, Rev. Mr. Seabury prevailed upon George Youngs, the private schoolmaster, to open it, as the engagement with his patrons had expired.[240] "This he consented to do," wrote Seabury, "upon my promising to recommend him to the Society & endeavour to get him appointed their schoolmaster. Mr. Youngs is to begin the school in two or three Days; & as he is very agreeable to the People, & I believe every way qualified & disposed to do Justice to the School, & answer the Society's Expectations, I hope they will be pleased to appoint him their Schoolmaster here."[241] Youngs was accordingly appointed "with £10 p.a. from Michaelmas last."[242] As an assurance to the Society, Seabury promised a close inspection of the school, saying: "I have informed him that I shall frequently visit the School, & that he must teach such Children as I shall nominate to him upon the Society's Account. I tho't it best to take that Matter into my own Hands, & shall after proper Inquiry among such People as I can depend upon, nominate such as I think the Society's Bounty will be best bestowed upon; & shall make it a Condition with the Parents or Friends, that the Children shall be sent constantly to School

239 Dec. 28, 1767, from Rev. Samuel Seabury to the Sec., *ibid.*, B, 2, p. 172.

240 *Ibid.*, B, 2, p. 159, Oct. 1, 1768.

241 *Ibid.* The school reopened about Oct. 3, 1768.

242 S. P. G. Journal, XVIII, p. 84.

& not be kept at Home, one half of their Time; That they shall moreover regularly attend Church & Catechising and I hope in due Time to give the Society such Accounts of this School, as shall be agreeable to them."[243]

Youngs also officiated as Clerk of the Church and enjoyed such perquisites as that position might afford. His enrolment in the first year increased to 26[244] and in the years 1770 and 1771 there were 41,[245] ten of whom were taught on the Society's bounty. In 1769, 16 were children of the Church, the others being dissenters and Quakers. In 1770 he had 28 of the first with 5 dissenters and 8 Quakers; and in 1771 he had nine Quakers in addition to the Church children.[246] As a means of better serving the community Youngs proposed to set in operation the following interesting plan, which, unfortunately, was not allowed to materialize. In reporting on his work in 1771, he informed the Society: "I shall by Desire (if God permit) open an Evening School about two Miles and an half from where I now keep and will be conducted in the same manner as the School is in the Day, the said evening School will be opened on the fourth Day of November next at 6 of the Clock every Evening and to continue till 9 at Night During the Winter Season, for the Conveniency of those that can't attend the School in the Day time. This Evening School will Consist of 20 Scholars, of which some will be of the poor, that can't attend in the Day for they must be to their Business, having no other Support. Notwithstanding this, the School in the Day will be continued and kept to Daily as usual."[247] Just previous to the sending of the above, Rev. Mr. Seabury forwarded the following unfavorable account: "I must in Faithfulness to the Society inform them that the Conduct of their Schoolmaster here has not been so Satisfactory to me, the last Year, especially the latter Part of it, as formerly. He is become an Encourager of Conventicles, admitting stroling Independent and Methodist Teachers to hold forth at his House. He is by Several Persons accused of neglecting his School, & maltreating the Scholars, & by some of drinking too freely; tho' I do not imagine that this last article

[243] S. P. G. Letter-book, B, 2, p. 159.
[244] Notitia of 1769, *ibid.*, B, 3, p. 294. Five of these were taught gratis.
[245] *Ibid.*, pp. 295, 296.
[246] See citations above for these years.
[247] *Ibid.*, Oct. 15, 1771.

can be directly proved upon him. When I sign his Notitia I shall acquaint him, that my signing any more after this Year, will depend intirely upon his good Behaviour & such Directions as I receive from the Society."[248] The attitude of the missionary seems more narrowly partisan than justifiable and is to be regretted. He doubtless did reprimand Youngs in the manner indicated, which the latter must have resented. Some three weeks after this Youngs "abruptly quitted the Place, & went to New York."[249]

Another long vacancy in the school followed. Not until 1774 did Seabury procure a schoolmaster who could meet his approval. Writing on January 3, 1775 that he had been trying to find a proper person ever since the departure of Youngs, he announced further that "about 8 months ago, Mr. George Gott, a single man, born in England, who had been an Usher in a school at N. York, offered for the employment," and was accepted. "He came well recommended," continued Seabury, "& has behaved with great propriety & diligence, & the children improve greatly."[250] Mr. Gott we learn elsewhere opened his school May 9, 1774,[251] but scarcely could he have learned of his acceptance by the London office before he gave up the work. He left the school May 23, 1775, which "want of health obliged him to relinquish," and returned to England.[252] Regarding his schoolmastership, Mr. Seabury said: "He conducted himself in the most unexceptionable manner; & the Children made a very considerable Improvement under his Instruction. Those Children whose parents were unable to pay for their Schooling were admitted & properly attended to by him. I am really sorry to part with him, & the people, who are duly sensible of the favour of the Society & desire to return their Thanks for it, are a good deal disconcerted, but hope the Society will still continue their bounty, when a proper person can be found to take charge of their School."[253] With the departure of Gott, the Society's school at West Chester came to an end.[254]

---

[248] Oct. 8, 1771, *ibid.*, B, 2, p. 182.

[249] About Nov. 1, 1771, *ibid.*, B, 2, p. 184.

[250] S. P. G. Journal, XX, p. 328. His appointment was approved by the S. P. G. March 17, 1775, *ibid.*

[251] S. P. G. Letter-book, B, 2, p. 187.

[252] *Ibid.*

[253] *Ibid.*

[254] The Abstracts of Proceedings have listed George Youngs as the schoolmaster until 1778. How misleading this is has been shown by the actual records. What the abstracts intend to convey is probably this: that the S. P. G. carried an open account for the school until 1778, bounties being allowable pending any appointments; and clerical carelessness kept repeating Youngs name.

The Society's resolution to assist in setting up a school at Yonkers has been referred to.[255] This action was taken in 1712, but no schoolmaster was found upon whom the bounty could be conferred. Rev. Mr. Bartow wrote in 1714 that the people at Yonkers were mostly Dutch, who came generally to church when he preached there, and added: "I hope their Children will be educated in ye Church way wn we can get an English Schoolmaster of the Church."[256] He followed this with the suggestion that "if Soc. would send over one of the poor youths of the Hospital wth £5 p.a. to teach the children sometimes at Yonkers & sometimes at East Chester, the people would contribute £20 p.a. (that country money)."[257] In reply the Secretary represented that the Governor of Christ Church Hospital had been discoursed with on this matter, but would give them no answer.[258] Yonkers was again alluded to by the missionary in his letter of February 1716/7, from which the Secretary has made the following note: " . . . nor could they ever get a Schoolmaster for Yonkers, wherefore Mr. Noah Barton, a Justice of Peace, who dwells in the outer-most part of Yonkers desired him to request Soc. to grant one half of the five pounds, granted to Yonkers, to a Schoolmaster to instruct the children of the adjacent families at Miles Square and the other half to be for the other part of Yonkers, when they can get a Schoolmaster; which he submits to the Soc's pleasure, but observes the difficulty to get a fixed Schoolmaster because there are greater advantages to be made by other employments; yet says a small encouragement from Soc. will oblige them to attend so long at least, annually, as to teach the children the Ch. Catechism, & to read their Mother tongue."[259] This ended Bartow's interest in behalf of Yonkers. With the sanction of the Society, as to Miles Square,[260] he found a candidate upon whom he bestowed the bounty of 50 shillings. "The people there," said Bartow, "have a Schoolmastr one Samuel Jones an inhabitant of the place who with the assistance of his wife when he is about his necessary business in the field does instruct the children of the

[255] See p. 146.
[256] S. P. G. Letter-book, A, 9, p. 225.
[257] S. P. G. Journal, III, p. 2.
[258] S. P. G. Letter-book, A, 9, p. 246.
[259] S. P. G. Journal, III, p. 288.
[260] *Ibid.*; also Letter-book, A, 12, p. 428.

place to the satisfaction of the Parents."[261] But Jones "continued his service for one Year and no longer" and then "left off to keep School."[262] In 1718 Mr. Bartow urged that East Chester be given the balance of the allowance voted for Yonkers, inasmuch as "Justice Noah Barton & others of the Inhabitants of East Chester" had desired him to pray the Society to grant "50 shillings per. ann. to a Schoolmastr at East Chester, Mr. John Gifford."[263] The request, evidently, did not receive the Society's consideration. In 1729 James Delpech, a former Society schoolmaster at Narragansett,[264] was teaching at East Chester but there is nothing to indicate that he was then under S. P. G. auspices.[265] Finally Rev. Mr. Standard made an unsuccessful appeal to the Society in 1733, in behalf of the appointment of a Mr. Child at East Chester.[266]

The Society's first missionary at New Rochelle, in 1711, reported having set up "a School for young people," whom he made to read the Psalms.[267] It did not, however, have any material support from London. In 1727 and the following year there was "no school nor Schoolmaster" there,[268] but in 1729 one school had been established in which both French and English were being taught.[269]

There are slight evidences of any secondary education carried on by members of the Society. Accessible records show that Forster in 1720 had some Latin scholars besides his elementary pupils. This work he mentioned on one occasion only,[270] so that we are left in doubt as to whether it was more than a temporary arrangement on his part. Again, after a long lapse of years, we learn that the S. P. G. missionary of the parish, Rev. Samuel Seabury, when hard pressed by the troubles of 1776, set up a Grammar school. Concerning it, he said: "To extricate my self from some Debts, which it was my Misfortune & not my Fault to contract I opened a Grammar School at West

261 Nov. 18, 1718, S. P. G. Letter-book, A, 13, p. 395.
262 From 1718 to 1719. Bartow to the Sec., July 2, 1719, *ibid.*, A, 13, p. 463.
263 *Ibid.*, A, 13, p. 395.
264 *Ibid.*, A, 22, pp. 45, 159, 160.
265 *Ibid.*, B, I, p. 50.
266 *Ibid.*, A, 24, p. 480; Journal, VI, p. 134.
267 May 18, 1711, S. P. G. Journal, II, p. 37.
268 Rev. J. Stoupe to Sec., S. P. G. Letter-book, A, 20, p. 198; A, 21, p. 349.
269 Rev. Mr. Standard to Sec., *ibid.*, B, 1, p. 50. New Rochelle was a French settlement originally.
270 June 1, 1720, *ibid.*, A, 14, p. 115.

Chester, which for two years past brought me in nearly £100 a Year this Currency, & in another Year I should have been freed from my Incumbrances. But my School is broke up, & the Profits of the past Year must go for the Support of my Family, as the Salary from the Parish which will be due on New Years day, has never been assessed."[271]

[271] Dec. 29, 1776, *ibid.*, B, 2, p. 190.

CHAPTER VIII

THE SOCIETY'S SUPPORT OF SCHOOLS ON STATEN ISLAND

The first appeal for the aid of the S. P. G. on Staten Island was made by Rev. Eneas Mackenzie, missionary, as early as 1705.[1] Upon the receipt of it the Society took prompt steps to supply a schoolmaster, as the following minutes show: "Mr. Townsend attending was called in and acquainted that the Society had agreed to send him as a Schoolmaster to Staten Island with an allowance of £20 per Annum to commence from Lady day last in order to instruct the Children of such poor people in the Said Island in reading, writing, & the principles of the Christian Religion, as are not able to pay him for the same. . . . Agreed that the sum of £5 be allowed for Catechisms & other books for the use of the Scholars under the direction of the said Mr. Townsend according to the discretion of the Committee."[2] Mr. Townsend did not avail himself of the offer but remained in England and the order was countermanded the next year.[3] In 1708 there was still no school on the island, as we are informed by William Huddleston.[4] In the year following, however, Mr. Mackenzie succeeded in getting two schools under way and so wrote to London: "I have at last, with much adoe got two English Schools sett up upon the Island, but the children of the poor are not the better for it, for the Schoolmasters, having no set Salaries, but so much for each Scholar, they teach none but such as are able to pay 'em the Stated ffee, which the poor cannot afford. If the Society was pleased to allow the £20 that was once alloted for a Schoolmaster upon this Island to be divided between these two now teaching, they shou'd be obliged thereby each of

[1] Nov. 8, 1705, S. P. G. Letter-book, A, 2, p. 116.
[2] Apr. 19, 1706, S. P. G. Journal, I, p. (18).
[3] July 18, 1707, *ibid.*, I, p. (84).
[4] Previously cited p. 77; S. P. G. Letter-book, A, 4, p. 58.

them to teach so many poor children and besides it would be a considerable ease and encouragement to all."[5]

Before the approval of the Society could be ascertained, these two men had retired and the missionary repeated his proposal in behalf of other candidates. "You desire me, Sir," he said, "to be more explicite in my proposals concerning the two Schoolmasters upon our Island, to give their Names, an account of the places they teach in, of those they teach &c. One Adam Brown, a young man teaches children in the South side of the Island, where there is a mixture of almost all Nations under heaven—And one Benjamin Drewit, a Man of 30 years of age, teaches in the ffresh Kilns about the center of the Island within a Mile of the place where we are a building of our Church and where most of the Inhabitants are ffrench. The Schoolmasters we had there last year, wou'd serve no longer, their encouragement was so small and these two I named I have engaged to stay for a year in hopes the Society will be pleased to allow ten pounds p. Annum to each. I fear it may be thought an Act of Presumption & imprudence in me that I should engage these Schoolmasters in any Assurance of this money, till I was first inform'd that the Society wou'd allow it. But the want of a School (without wch the youth are incapable of any Spiritual Instruction) is so deplorable a want I wou'd run a great Risq to have it supplyed; and besides I took some encouragement from Mr. Chamberlayne desiring an Account of his Schoolmasters Names, and that the Society was pleased once before to settle £30 a year upon a Gentleman that was designed thither to teach School. In Short, I have so far assured the Schoolmasters of the Society's Bounty that it will fall heavy upon me every way to meet with a disappointment in it, but if thereby I have done myself a prejudice, I shall have this satisfaction to support me under my punishment, that I did it with a design to Serve the Church; for there's such a diversibility of languages in the Island, that except they be taught English, their Conformity to the Church can't be expected."[6] Whereupon Brown and Drewitt were formally appointed by the Society with £10 each per year to commence from midsummer 1710.[7]

[5] June 13, 1709, *ibid.*, A, 5, p. 18.

[6] July 28, 1710, *ibid.*, A, 5, p. 148. Brown's Christian name was Symon and not Adam. The mistake was later corrected. *Ibid.*, A, 7, p. 190.

[7] S. P. G. Journal, I, p. (306); II, p. 70.

Brown opened his school on July 27, 1710[8] and continued in this work, teaching in the south precinct of the island, until about February 1714.[9] In just two reports that could be found we are told that he "has 35 Scholars many of whom have been taught according to the intent of the Society to read, write, & cypher with the Catechism & the explanation thereof to such as are capable, together with the use of the Common prayer, & that 24 of them have been publickly catechised in the church by Mr. Mackenzie."[10] Drewitt was disliked by the people and Mackenzie after about a year displaced him and appointed in his stead two schoolmasters, Francis Williamson for the middle or west precinct and a Mr. Dupuy for the north precinct.[11] It was mutually agreed that the £10 allowed Drewitt should be divided as their allowance from the Society.[12]

Nothing regarding Dupuy is known beyond his appointment. Williamson sent a report in March 1712 that he began teaching Nov. 20, 1710 and still continued, having 15 children.[13] He was superseded within a month after the above report by Thomas Potts.[14] Through the arrangement made by Mr. Mackenzie, Potts was to have the full £10 heretofore divided between the north and the west precincts, and from now on these two positions were combined according to the previous terms made with Drewitt.[15] A letter from Potts to the Secretary, in April, 1713, represents that he has kept school for a year at the Freshkills in the west of the county (Richmond) where he was settled by Mr. Mackenzie and the people there. He had 23 children, and several of them according to the Society's bounty he had "taught to read & some to write & Cypher & Ch. Catechism."[16]

Potts served for one year and his place was taken by Benjamin Miller in April 1713.[17] Miller served two and a half years for the S. P. G. In 1715 he taught "above 30 Children with what poor

---

[8] *Ibid.*, II, p. 239.

[9] *Ibid.*, III, p. 3; Letter-book, A, 8, p. 323.

[10] March 1712 and April 1713. S. P. G. Letter-book, A, 7, p. 196; A, 8, p. 160; Journal, II, pp. 239, 330.

[11] Reported Feb. 27, 1711/12 S. P. G. Letter-book, A, 7, p. 190; Journal, II, p. 237. The change was made about Nov. 20, 1710, Letter-book, A, 7, p. 197.

[12] S. P. G. Letter-book, A, 7, p. 190; Journal, II, p. 221.

[13] S. P. G. Letter-book, A, 7, p. 197.

[14] S. P. G. Letter-book, A, 8, p. 172. Potts began in April, 1712.

[15] *Ibid.*; also, A, 8, p. 156; also Sec., to Mackenzie, Dec. 18, 1713, *ibid.*, A, 8, p. 323.

[16] Apr. 10, 1713, *ibid.*, A, 8, p. 172.

[17] *Ibid.*, A, 9, 10 fol. p. 97; Journal, III, p. 3.

have been sent."[18] In October 1715 Miller went to England bearing Mackenzie's testimonial of his having served to the satisfaction of the people. "He designs," added the missionary, "to return to his post early in the spring. . . . Most of the Church people here are willing if Soc. agrees that the whole or £15 of the £20 allowed for teaching School here be settled on the bearer to encourage him to return & settle here. For tho' the benefit of £20 divided between the two as at present may be more extensive, yet experience proves that £10 with what more he can make is not enough to encourage a good schoolmaster & this has occasioned a frequent change among them."[19] In accordance with the proposed change, and upon Mackenzie's recommendation of Miller, "the Society resolved to allow £15 p.a. to a Schoolmaster in Statten Island, & that Mackenzie should choose whom he would." His salary was to begin when he commenced work.[20] If Miller ever returned to the Province, he did not enter into the service of the S. P. G. With him ended the attempt to maintain more than one schoolmaster by means of the bounty.

Following Brown in the south precinct the work had been taken up by Charles Taylor who began teaching for the Society February 17, 1713/14 in expectation of the former bounty of £10.[21] After teaching more than two years on this bounty, and being the only S. P. G. schoolmaster on the island Mr. Mackenzie advised that he had agreed that Taylor should be allowed the increased salary, as previously voted.[22] From 1714, then, until his death in May 1742,[23] Taylor continuously served the Society on Staten Island. He taught in the south precinct up to 1724 and then moved to the west precinct.[24] In 1735 he reports that he has again kept school "this last half year in the south part of Richmond County,"[25] from which time any other changes he may have made are not recorded. The bounty of the Society and tuition fees constituted his income, for on two occasions he

[18] S. P. G. Journal, III, p. 92, report dated Apr. 18, 1715.
[19] Mackenzie to Sec., October, 1715, S. P. G. Letter-book, A, 10, p. 214.
[20] *Ibid.*, A, 11, p. 366.
[21] S. P. G. Journal, III, p. 70; Letter-book, A, 10, p. 214.
[22] Oct. 29, 1716, S. P. G. Journal, III, p. 269.
[23] May 27, 1742, S. P. G. Letter-book, B, 10, p. 83.
[24] *Ibid.*, A, 18, p. 185.
[25] *Ibid.*, A, 25, p. 55; Journal, VI, p. 269.

reported no other employment than that of schoolmaster;[26] and the school occupied his evenings, as well as his days, up to 1725 at least.[27] If he served as Clerk of the Church, he has not indicated it in such reports as are now accessible.

Though Taylor spent twenty-eight years in the school at Staten Island, there are but ten reports of his work. He undoubtedly sent many more, which seem not to have been preserved, as nowhere do we find a reprimand for negligence in this respect. None of the reports are consecutive, save those for each year between 1722 and 1725 inclusive, and for nine years, between 1725 and 1735, there is not a single report. Up to 1735 the enrolment averaged above 40.[28] Afterwards it barely exceeded 30, except in September 1739 when it was given as 37.[29] In 1739, 1740 and 1741 from one-third to one-half of the pupils were from the families of dissenters.[30] Previous reports did not give the proportions. The specific number taught gratis was never mentioned, but those so privileged were usually reported as "some" or "several."

Taylor furnished his own schoolhouse and does not seem to have employed an assistant. Other schools were not reported by him until 1739.[31] In that year we are told: "One schoolmaster teacheth English School at the Northside, Andrew White."[32] He further reports that there are "other transient Schoolmasters that travel and hire themselves in familys for a small time and then go away to other places."[33] In 1741 there were two other schools, both being of the Church of England.[34] It has been already stated that Mr. Taylor taught in the evenings. This can be assumed to hold true, at any rate, of the decade 1720–1730, since in his accounts for the period he in-

---

[26] In 1739 and 1741. S. P. G. Letter-book, B, 7, pt. 2, p. 149; B, 10, p. 107.

[27] S. P. G. Letter-book, A, 16, p. 216; A, 17, p. 220; A, 18, pp. 169, 185.

[28] Thirty-eight in 1715, 48 in 1722, 43 in 1723, 42 in 1724, 36 in Sept. 1724, 41 in 1725, and 42 in 1735. *Ibid.*, A, 10, p. 138; A, 25, p. 55; B, 1, p. 107; and citations immediately above.

[29] In 1740, it was 31 and in 1741, it was 32. *Ibid.*, B, 7, pt. 2, pp. 149, 151; B, 10, p. 107.

[30] Negroes are listed in half of the accounts, their numbers being given as from 2 to 6.

[31] This was because of his first using the Notitia, which included the question among others.

[32] *Ibid.*, B, 7, pt. 2, p. 149. He was confused in the name and referred to Andrew Wright, soon to become his successor. Moreover it seems certain that there was another private school at this time. *Ibid.*, B, 10, p. 84.

[33] *Ibid.*

[34] *Ibid.*, B, 10, p. 107. One of these was Wright's, and the other was kept by Peter Prefontaine, who for several years had "kept a private school, having been regularly educated in England." *Ibid.*, B, 10, p. 84.

cludes the following: "I have taught Several of them upon Accot of ye Venble Societys bounty without any other Consideration & upon ye same Accot I keep night School, for teaching of Negroes & of such as canot be spared from their work in the daytime."[35]

On the death of Mr. Taylor the Church officials sent the following petition for the appointment of Andrew Wright, one of the private schoolmasters: "Mr. Taylor died on the 27th inst. His application & endeavours tended much to the advancement of piety, catechetical knowledge & the principles of common learning among great numbers of poor children, who must otherwise have been utterly wanting in these advantages. There are many such here now, & the Petiters ask Soc. to continue the salary, & recommend Mr. Andrew Wright, an inhabitant of this place, & who is thoroughly well qualified. He is an Englishman, has lived here sevl years, & bears a good character, has a large family, & only a small school to supply it with."[36] The other private teacher, Peter Prefontaine, also petitioned to become Taylor's successor,[37] but Mr. Wright was given the appointment.[38] He was voted the same salary of £15, which the Society agreed should begin from September 1742.[39] As in the case of the former schoolmaster, Wright received tuition fees from a majority of his scholars. His income must have been fairly encouraging, for in the first year of his service in the S. P. G. school we are told that he "built a schoolhouse at his own charge in the midst of a poor neighborhood."[40]

Since the salary voted Wright was to begin in September 1742, we may conclude that he had started on his work at that time or even before, so that there was not a long break in the school as a result of the change. There are very little data concerning Wright's schoolmastership. He was in charge of the school for five years and upwards, in which time there are but two reports of his pupils and these are of a brief nature. In 1746 he wrote as follows: "For the year pass'd I have taught

[35] March 8, 1721/2, *ibid.*, A, 16, p. 216; also A, 17, p. 220; A, 18, pp. 169, 185; B, 1, p. 107. It cannot be supposed that many availed themselves of the evening work though the Negro enrolment is the only data on which to base conclusion.

[36] June 5, 1742, *ibid.*, B, 10, p. 83.

[37] S. P. G. Journal, IX, p. 100.

[38] *Ibid.*, Dec. 17, 1742.

[39] S. P. G. Letter-book, B, 10, p. 196.

[40] S. P. G. Journal, IX, p. 296. He may have served as Clerk of the Church also.

forty Children most of them very small, and may of them on the Honourable Society's account without any other Consideration; five of them Cypherers, Twelve Writers, the others Read in their Testaments several of them are well acquainted with the Common prayer books the Church Catechism, and the Prayers set forth in the Venerable Society's Instructions, all which I diligently Teach."[41] Another letter dated October 20, 1747, acquainted the Society that he was teaching "42 Children to read and to repeat the Church Catechism" and that 14 of them were learning to write and 4 to cipher.[42] News of Wright's death reached the society in July 1748,[43] but the letter announcing it is marked "undated" in the S. P. G. Journal, and it is impossible to know definitely when the school came to an end. However, since a successor had been provided by March 1748, and Wright had reported on the school as late as the October preceding, there was probably only a short interval of delay.

The next schoolmaster was Nicholas Barrington, whose first work in the school was thus announced by the minister of the parish: "The Decency & Seriousness of my Catechumens in their Devotion has already had an happy Effect even upon the Elder, who labour under the Infelicity of not having a like early Instruction. And I hope wth Gods blessing that ye rising Generation will have a more lively sense of their Duty & keep clear of y^{t} Slovenly behaviour too prevalent in most Country places, during the time of Divine Worship; ano^{r} Advantage arising from this Lecture, is the Introducing of Psalmody wch now is carried on wth a far greater Decency than w^{n} I first settled upon the Island for this I am greatly indebted to Mr. $Nich^{s}$ Barrington, A Sober, diligent & *a capable Schoolmaster who* began to Teach the Youth last March, upon Promise of my Recommending him to the Society, & in humble hopes of their taking him into their service: his previous Instruction greatly promotes my Design and I most humbly entreat the Society may grant him such a Salary as may induce him to stay amongst us."[44] In adopting the recommendation above, the salary was reduced

---

[41] Nov. 10, 1746, S. P. G. Letter-book, B, 14, p. 141.

[42] S. P. G. Journal, XI, p. 10.

[43] *Ibid.*, p. 38.

[44] Rev. Richard Charlton to Sec., Oct. 5, 1748, S. P. G. Letter-book, B, 16, p. 48.

to £10 per annum,[45] which with the tuition fees made up Barrington's income from the school. We learn definitely that Barrington also acted as Clerk of the Church during the entire time he was schoolmaster.[46] But even with any additions that this office could bring Barrington was dissatisfied with his emoluments and represented them as entirely inadequate.[47]

On several occasions Barrington's work was commended by Rev. Mr. Charlton, the minister of the Church of England, who reported that blacks as well as whites attended his school and were instructed with no small pains.[48] There is, though, but one meagre report from him to the S. P. G.[49] This does not give his enrolment. In it he states that he has taught nine poor children on the Society's bounty and in a few days expects four more. Besides this he was teaching upwards of twenty Negroes at times.[50] He probably made use of the schoolhouse formerly built by Wright, although there is no certainity of this. In the fall of 1752 Barrington left the school and went to New York to open a private school.[51]

Mr. Thomas Price was appointed to succeed Barrington with the same salary of £10,[52] which was "to commence from Michaelmas last, if it should appear by Certificate . . . that he hath taught the School & behaved well from that time."[53] Price opened the school about March, 1753[54] and had charge of it until about April, 1760.[55] No details of the work of this school-

---

[45] April 21, 1749, S. P. G. Journal, XI, p. 120. By this resolution his salary was to date from March 25, 1749, but the 1748 salary was voted to him later. *Ibid.*, XII, p. 163.

[46] S. P. G. Letter-book, *ibid.*, B, 20, p. 73. This record makes it very probable that both Taylor and Wright before him were also clerks.

[47] *Ibid.*

[48] March 26, 1750, S. P. G. Letter-book, B, 18, p. 115; see also B, 19, p. 85; also B, 20, p. 73, being a testimonial from townspeople.

[49] For March 26, 1750, *ibid.*, B, 18, p. 117.

[50] *Ibid.*

[51] He gave up the Staten Island school about September 26, 1752, *ibid.*, B, 20, p. 73. The following is an excerpt from a printed notice of Barrington's venture in New York City, which he started on the above date: "Nicholas Barrington lately mov'd to this City, has open'd a School near St. George's Chapel, in Beekman's Street, and teaches Reading Writing, and Arithmetick, both vulgar and decimal, as also Navigation and Merchants Accounts, where good Attendance will be given at the usual Hours. N. B. has begun his Evening School and intends to teach Youths to sing Psalms, Also recites for Gentlemen between Schools, Bills, Bonds, Indentures, Leases, Deeds of Sale, Wills, &c. at very reasonable Rates." This notice was attached to one of Barrington's letters to the Society, *ibid.* For newspaper notices of Barrington's private school, see New York *Mercury*, May 19 and Dec. 29, 1755.

[52] Apr. 19, 1753, S. P. G. Journal, XII, p. 247. Though Gov. Clinton and Rev. Mr. Charlton requested a salary of £15 for Price, no advance was made. *Ibid.*; also Letter-book, B, 20, p. 71.

[53] Sec. to Charlton, Aug. 1, 1753, *ibid.*, B, 20, p. 38.

[54] Price to Society, S. P. G. Journal, XII, p. 379.

[55] Charlton to Society on Apr. 10, 1760 reported that Price had a severe attack of smallpox, *ibid.*, XV, p. 4. His death followed on the 13th of May, Letter-book, B, 3, p. 61. He drew for salary to March 29, *ibid.*

master can be given beyond the fact that he was frequently commended by Mr. Charlton for his diligence in the school and in behalf of the Church's Negro catechumens.[56] Regarding the loss of the schoolmaster's assistance to him, Mr. Charlton reported: "The want of his assistance for the present season will be a sensible loss to my Catechumens, especially the Negroes, whose improvements in Psalmody must meet with a considerable check, and what is yet worse I have it not in my power to pitch upon one of suitable morals and Capacity, that I can recommend to the Venerable Society, as his Successor."[57]

In the following December a satisfactory candidate had been found and installed in the school. In his behalf Mr. Charlton sent the following recommendation: "I have now the great satisfaction of most humbly requesting an appointmt for Mr. John Watts, mentioned in mine of ye 21st of June last, to succeed Mr. Price as Society Schoolmaster in this Island. His known Qualifications make me very desirous of having him an instructor of both Setts of my Catechumens. As such men are not easily met with I must entreat yr interest to have the former salary increased, which may be an inducement to a person duely qualified to accept of the place and continue in the Servis; and it must be a great misfortune to the imployed that when the Expences of living increase, Salaries do not in proportion rise; however this is most humbly submitted to the Charitable Society. He has promised to open School next Monday."[58] John Watts was, therefore, appointed by the Society at the former salary in April 1761.[59] Before the formal appointment could be made, however, he had quitted the work, and another suitable person was not found until 1763.[60] In March of that year Tunis Egberts was appointed by Mr. Charlton and forthwith entered upon his duties.[61] In the interval the Society had agreed that the salary should be increased to £15 a year.[62] Between 1763 and 1776 various testimonials and reports were sent

---

[56] S. P. G. Journal, XIII, pp. 185, 241, 285; XIV, pp. 106, 268 Letter-book, B, 3, p. 61.

[57] S. P. G. Letter-book, B, 3, p. 61, June 21, 1760.

[58] Dec. 13, 1760, *ibid.*, B, 3, p. 62. Watts, said Charlton, *had been lately* a Schoolmaster in Staten Island. *Ibid.*, B, 3, p. 61.

[59] S. P. G. Journal, XV, p. 77.

[60] See letters of 1761 and 1762, S. P. G. Letter-book, B, 3, pp. 64, 68.

[61] March 15, 1763, S. P. G. Letter-book, B, 3, p. 70.

[62] Feb. 19, 1762, S. P. G. Journal, XV, p. 190.

by Charlton and Egbert which indicate a faithful performance of duty on the part of the schoolmaster. Other than this they gave no information regarding the school. Whether his service continued after 1776 is not known. As in the case of Wetmore of Rye, it seems that his name was retained in the list of schoolmasters during the period of the Revolution and after the school had disbanded. Finally on March 21, 1783, the Society ordered that Tunis Egberts, schoolmaster on Staten Island, be left out of the next Abstract.[63]

In 1773 Mr. Charlton mentioned a schoolmaster from "about 2 miles off," who had greatly aided him and had also assisted Mr. Egberts. For this person Charlton desired some recognition from the Society.[64] Indefinite as such information is, it is the only notice to be found indicating that assistants were ever employed for the Staten Island school. The presumption is that they were not and that the one exception represents a temporary arrangement of short duration.

Such books as were intended for the school were forwarded to the missionaries on a few occasions. Packets of prayer-books were ordered sent in 1709 and 1711,[65] and again in 1747 and 1749 packets of books included upwards of 300 catechisms.[66] Furthermore, books for school use may have been included in the regular £5 gift of books allowed each missionary. Primers were not requested and were not sent, being supplied doubtless by the parents of the children.

That the S. P. G. should have tolerated the inadequate reports from these schools for the thirty and more years is peculiar, in view of the resentment of such neglect in other places. It is, of course, possible that protests were made, but, in any case, they are not now to be found. It may have been that, because of the Society's very high opinion of Rev. Mr. Charlton, it was felt sufficient to receive his favorable confirmation of the progress of the school, even though the method did not adhere to the standing rules.

---

[63] *Ibid.*, XXIII, p. 66.
[64] Oct. 15, 1773, *ibid.*, XX, pp. 38–9.
[65] *Ibid.*, I, p. (207); II, p. 33.
[66] *Ibid.*, X, p. 323; XI, p. 119; Letter-book, B, 17, p. 199a.

CHAPTER IX

THE SOCIETY'S SUPPORT OF SCHOOLS ON LONG ISLAND

THE SCHOOLS IN HEMPSTEAD PARISH

Rev. John Thomas became the S. P. G. missionary for Hempstead in 1704. He thus described conditions which had to be contended with in the beginning of his work: "My parish consists of a large Tract of Ground, the Inhabitants much scattered, visiting of them often necessarily requisite. I wish with all my heart the Honble Society were truly informed, how much care & Industry is necessary to be bestowed to rescue them from their degeneracy into Atheism & Infidelity & Corruption in Morals & good manners long since contracted. To convert a heathen to Christianity is a very good & pious work, but to reconcile the English, in a great measure sunk into paganism & Infidelity, to the principles of the Christian faith, is with humble submission, I imagine, a far worthier employment, especially since I find the one feasible & practicable, the other morally impossible, for our Indians are wholly given up to drink & Sottishness, Rum & strong liquor being the only Deities they now care or are solicitious to worship. This was the state of my Parish before my Settlement here; by the people's own confession, Quakerism & paganism triumphing as Conquerors for some years past."[1] As soon as possible he took steps to establish a school without calling on the Society for assistance. Concerning his early efforts he wrote the Secretary in 1707 as follows: "I have raised a School in ye Towne since my coming and allow towards it in Conjunction with ye Inhitants £20 a year. Wee are now a building a School house and settling a piece of Land upon it, which I have Contributed unto, a good precedent of that nature I presume is the most moving Rhetorick I can use to persuade those whose In-

[1] June 12, 1709, S. P. G. Letter-book, A, 5, p. 4.

tellectuals are so mean and earthly that they cannot discern the Advantage worth, and Excellency of education for their Children's present and future wellfare. In vain I preach to them the Superstructures of Christianity when they are destitute of the Ground works and Fundamentals of Religion by Educacon. I have bought Catechisms to give away among the Children and hope in some time to have a set of Catechumens."[2] The venture lasted for a short time and had to be disbanded for reasons thus set forth by Mr. Thomas: "You desire an Account of the State of our Schools; Wee had a Schoolmaster settled among us for two years & a half, now we are destitute, the people being utterly weary of the Subscription I had engaged them in; I hope in God's due time to induce them to settle another; I shall not be wanting to contribute towards it both by purse & persuasion as heretofore."[3]

In 1712 representation was made to the Society that the school could not be resumed without assistance.[4] An allowance of £8 or £10 was asked for, which, being united with the office of Clerk of the Church, and with what the townspeople could add, it was felt would be sufficient.[5] A salary of £10 per annum was accordingly allowed, when a proper schoolmaster should be found.[6] On December 1, 1713 the school was started with Thomas Gildersleve as schoolmaster.[7] Gildersleve had been Clerk of the Church since the arrival of Mr. Thomas at Hempstead,[8] and recommendations sent by the inhabitants declared him to be "a good man, and qualified to teach the necessary subjects of reading & writing English, and the Rudiments of Arithmetic."[9] With the fixed salary and the occasional perquisites belonging to the office of Clerk, Gildersleve received additional assistance from the fees of those children who were able to pay. His fee in 1728 was, we learn, "five shillings per Quarter for

[2] Apr. 22, 1707, *ibid.*, A, 3, p. 67. The schoolmaster was Alexander Beard of whom Huddleston spoke in his reports of 1708. See p. 77.

[3] June 12, 1709, *ibid.*, A, 5, p. 4.

[4] The chief reason given was that the people were distant from one another and too poor to board out their children. *Ibid.*, A, 9, p. 162.

[5] Thomas to Society in behalf of the people, Feb. 20, 1711-12, *ibid.*, A, 7, p. 141.

[6] Oct. 10, 1712, S. P. G. Journal, II, p. 232; Letter-book, A, 7, p. 274.

[7] S. P. G. Letter-book, A, 9, p. 162.

[8] S. P. G. Journal, III, p. 47. He served gratis, according to Thomas, up to the beginning of the school and probably continued without salary.

[9] S. P. G. Letter-book, A, 9, p. 162.

each Scholar"[10] which is about the tuition rate noted elsewhere.[11] Other than these fees he had no benefactions from the town.[12]

Though Mr. Gildersleve was schoolmaster for about 26 years there are almost no details of his school. In 1714 he was teaching many poor children gratis.[13] In 1717 and 1718 he reported that the school was "Very full."[14] Finally in 1729 he gave the following information: "My School has been for the most part of thirty & sometimes forty scholars, sum reeders sum Righters and sum sypherers."[15] Since he probably saw fit to specify the number enrolled on this one occasion it may be doubted if he had even thirty pupils as a rule. At least half of them were very poor and taught gratis, as he affirmed.[16]

Gildersleve was clearly inefficient as a teacher. His recommendation in the first place was not made on any ground of competency previously shown, but was rather based on the fact that he was an exceptionally zealous assistant to Mr. Thomas in the pioneer work of getting the Church organized.[17] When a change of missionaries occurred, an attempt was made to have Gildersleve removed, which the people had hesitated to do before, because of their kindly feeling for Mr. Thomas. In 1728 a number of the inhabitants petitioned Rev. Mr. Jenney to advise a change of schoolmaster. They said: "It is Notorious Sr, that Mr. Gildersleve being in the Post has been a very great Detriment to the Town by hindring a Person qualified for it from coming; in which he has been a great hindrance to our Youth and a Lett to the Groweth of Religion."[18] He was further charged with keeping school in the summer only, when the sons of poor parents could not be spared from the farms; and with general incapacity as a teacher,[19] which his letters confirm. The affair was submitted to the Society by Mr. Jenney, after which

---

10 *Ibid.*, A, 21, p. 339.

11 See p. 156. But with his paying scholars and the Society' sbounty the school was "scarcely a Competency." S. P. G. Letter-book, A, 9, p. 162.

12 *Ibid.*

13 *Ibid.*,.

14 *Ibid.*, A, 13, p. 368; Journal III, p. 399.

15 Dec. 1, 1729, S. P. G. Letter-book, B, 1, p. 47.

16 *Ibid.*

17 "From a rigid Dissenter he is become a zealous Ch. man," wrote Thomas. S. P. G. Journal, III, p. 193. He was recommended because of his great pretences of being a Churchman, declared the inhabitants to Rev. Robt. Jenney, Thomas' successor. S. P. G. Letter-book, A, 22, p. 57.

18 June 7, 1728, *ibid.*, A, 21, p. 387.

19 *Ibid.*, A, 21, p. 323.

two schoolmasters of the town were urged as the successor.[20] In answer to the Society's letter Gildersleve acknowledged that his age and infirmities made him less capable in the school. The severe winters and the poor condition of the schoolhouse, which was not kept in repair, were responsible for his neglect, he explained.[21] Doubtless fearing dismissal, he proffered his resignation.[22] No action was taken on it by the Society, nor on the petitions for a successor. Gildersleve therefore remained at his post until his death,[23] to the certain detriment of the school.[24] Regrettable as this must have been, however, the fact remains that the Society's school offered the best opportunity for regular schooling which the town afforded in that period. "There is nothing more unconstant than schools here," wrote Mr. Jenney, "Excepting those from the Honble Society. The Usual Custome is for a Set of Neighbors to Engage a Schoolmaster for one year: 'tis Seldom y^t^ they keep ye same longer and often they are without for Several years."[25] Soon after the death of Gildersleve, Thomas Temple was installed in the school[26] and, on the joint recommendation of the missionary and the parishoners he was voted the former salary of £10 which was to commence from midsummer 1739.[27]

Temple's school was not large. The first available report showed an enrolment of 26.[28] The next summer he had 20 and a year later there were 32.[29] In January 1744 there were 27 while the two following reports sent in the summer of 1744 and 1746 showed but 14 and 18 respectively.[30] In December 1746

[20] Gerhardius Clowes, vouched for by a long list of the inhabitants; and John Young, endorsed by Mr. Jenney. Each party opposed the other candidate. *Ibid.*, A, 22, p. 54; B, 1, p. 45.

[21] This is the only reference to a schoolhouse by the Society's schoolmasters in Hempstead. It was probably the town schoolhouse built as early as 1705, if not before, and used by Gildersleve and his successor. The S. P. G. Abstracts for 1905 report that Hempstead has built a schoolhouse. Pratt (*op. cit.*, p. 94) quotes from the town records of Dec. 12, 1709 the following: "The school house is let to Isaac Jarmin for a year except the leanto which is reserved for the use of the school at any time when a schoolmaster presents, for £4-18 to be p^d^ the church wardens; and if the town shall hire a schoolmaster, then he shall go forth of said house at a quarter's warning."

[22] Nov. 22, 1729, *ibid.*, B, 1, p. 48; Dec. 27, 1729, *ibid.*, A, 22, p. 53.

[23] Midsummer, 1739. S. P. G. Journal, VIII, p. 172.

[24] The failure of the S. P. G. to change Gildersleve seems accountable only on the ground of the strong objections raised to the two candidates proposed.

[25] June 27, 1728, S. P. G. Letter-book, A, 21, p. 339. Quoted in Moore, Hist. of St. George's Church, Hempstead, p. 58.

[26] S. P. G. Journal, VIII, p. 172.

[27] Temple therefore probably took up the school at about that time. *Ibid.* According to his Notitiae he was not made Clerk.

[28] Dec. 14, 1741, S. P. G. Journal, IX, p. 34.

[29] S. P. G. Letter-book, B, 10, p. 91; B, 13, p. 243.

[30] *Ibid.*, B, 13, p. 243; B, 13, p. 245; Journal, X, p. 172.

he reported that the school was "less frequented."[31] This was owing to the opposition of dissenters, for one reason, and to his own infirmities for another.[32] Nearly half of the pupils were the children of dissenters.[33] Of those taught gratis there were from four to six of the white children, besides two or more Negroes, and an Indian. For the accommodation of pupils who could not attend during the day Temple started a night school during the winter of 1741–42, if not before. At that time the night pupils were ten in number.[34] Though specific mention of such work was not thereafter made, the fact that he reported eight hours daily attendance on the school[35] may perhaps be fairly good evidence of it.[36]

In 1747 the Society empowered Temple, in view of his physical condition, to employ an assistant.[37] It does not seem to have been done, since the school declined so much that Rev. Samuel Seabury, reporting in 1748, said of it: "Mr. Temple's school hath been quite broke up for the full space of a year, Nor has he offered me any Notitia Scholastica for more than two years past."[38] Out of extreme compassion the Society patiently tolerated the distressing conditions, again acquainting both Mr. Seabury and the schoolmaster that an assistant should be procured.[39] Apparently the request continued to be unheeded.[40] After waiting until 1753 for promised improvement in the situation at Hempstead, the Society dismissed Temple,[41] and gave no further support to the school within the town. What effect this withdrawal of bounty had is not known. Evidently no subsequent appeals were made to the S. P. G.

---

[31] S. P. G. Letter-book, B, 14, p. 135.

[32] By 1744 the dissenters were encouraging a school three miles from Temple's and during that year a second one had been set up. *Ibid.*, B, 13, pp. 243, 245. In 1746 he was severely injured by falling from a horse, and it brought on deafness. *Ibid.*, B, 14, p. 135.

[33] At least through 1744, after which the proportion was not given.

[34] S. P. G. Letter-book, B, 10, p. 91.

[35] *Ibid.*, B, 13, pp. 243, 245; Journal X, p. 172.

[36] Six hours being the customary length of the day school, he probably taught for two hours in the evenings.

[37] S. P. G. Journal, X, p. 254.

[38] Letter to the Sec., March 25, 1748. S. P. G. Letter-book, B, 14, p. 135.

[39] July 15, 1748, S. P. G. Journal, X, p. 40.

[40] It does not seem tenable to suppose that both of these proffers failed to reach Hempstead; and if satisfactory assistance were not to be found, it would be reasonable to expect word to be sent the S. P. G. to that effect. There are two letters from Temple thereafter, but neither refer to the matter at all.

[41] Apr. 19, 1753, S. P. G. Journal, XII, p. 248.

In 1768 the Society's help was again sought for a school without the town. On behalf of this section the missionary, Rev. Leonard Cutting, wrote as follows: "To the South of Hempstead for severall Miles are great Numbers of Inhabitants, in general in very indigent Circumstances; they say they cannot procure Conveniences to come so far to Church. I frequently on Week Days go amongst them to officiate; I find large Numbers of them assembled: they appear glad of my Services & willing to be instructed but are totally illiterate, great Part of them not being able to read; nor have they Abilities, or opportunity to get their Children instructed; a School there would be a real Blessing."[42] Mr. Cutting was informed that he had liberty to employ a teacher if a worthy man could be procured,[43] to which he replied: "You was pleased to inform me Sr that the Society, in Compassion to the Situation of the People, to the South of Hempstead, had generously determined to endeavour to draw them from Darkness and Ignorance, by kindly assisting them to procure Instruction for themselves and Children. The benevolent Intentions of that venerable Board, I immediately communicated to proper Persons but as the Season was something advanced before I received your Commands, nothing of effectual can I fear be done till towards Spring. They are however raising Money by Subscription to build a Schoolhouse, and as soon as the weather will permit, we shall endeavour to fix upon the most proper Place for it."[44] In 1769 Mr. Cutting found a properly qualified person and the school was opened in the new building.

The following information was sent to London concerning the schoolmaster: "His name is William Leahy, born in Ireland, but has been an Inhabitant in New York many Years; he marryed there & has a Family; He was formerly engaged in Trade, but a Series of Ill Success, obliged him to decline Business. Since that he has kept School in different Places, with a good character. On hearing of Encouragement from the Society, He presented himself here; and was willing to undertake it, and Wait for farther Orders from that Venerable Board. The People appear very Thankfull for the favour that is con-

[42] Jan. 7, 1768, S. P. G. Letter-book, B, 2, p. 143.
[43] Apr. 15, 1768, S. P. G. Journal, XVII, p. 488.
[44] Dec. 28, 1768, S. P. G. Letter-book, B, 2, p. 144.

ferred on them, And I am in Hopes they will act in such a manner as to answer the Intention and deserve in some Measure the Bounty of the Society. As the Society has been pleased to confirm the appointment of a Master I think it necessary to inform you Sr that the School was opened on the 22d of June last."[45] A salary of £10 was thereupon conferred on Mr. Leahy by the Society[46] to which about £10 sterling was added by means of tuition fees.[47]

"The Schoolmaster," it was reported, "is much liked in the Neighbourhood and is generally praised for his Sobriety Diligence, and carefull attendance on the children under his Care. He has indeed one Difficulty to Struggle with, and that is the Humour of the Parents, who unacquainted with the proper Regulation of a School, and unused to restrain their Children themselves, do not sufficiently attend to the Necessity of a decent Subjection; But I am in Hopes this will soon be overcome; and that by prudent Management, the School will answer the Charitable Designs of the Society. But few can take advantage of the Charity during the Severity of the Winter as their Circumstances will not permit them to furnish their Children with proper Cloathing to Support the Inclemency of the Weather; but as the intense cold is not of long continuance it will but little retard their Progress; every School in the Country is extremely thin, for two Months in the Winter."[48] Mr. Leahy did not give the number of his pupils, but he did report that he taught "twelve poor children entirely at Society's bounty."[49] After struggling with an inadequate income for himself and large family for above a year, Leahy gave up the school.[50] To explain his sudden departure, Mr. Cutting announced: "I am sorry to inform you that Mr. William Leahy whom the Society had been pleased to appoint as their Schoolmaster, to the South of Hempstead, has resigned the School—He was in Esteem amongst the People, and his Character unexceptionable. But he had a large family of young Children; and an infirm Sickly wife; the Bounty therefore of the Society, with what he got from the People were

[45] August 23, 1769, *ibid.*, B, 2, p. 145.
[46] Dec. 15, 1769, S. P. G. Journal, XVIII, p. 260.
[47] S. P. G. Letter-book, B, 3, p. 213.
[48] Jan. 22, 1770, *ibid.*, B, 2, p. 146.
[49] *Ibid.*, B, 3, pp. 212, 213.
[50] In Sept. 1770, *ibid.*, B, 2, p. 147; B, 3, p. 214.

not sufficient to supply him and his helpless family, with the common Necessaries of Life, Several of which he was to my Knowledge sometimes destitute of. And as a good School to the North of the Plains of Hempstead amongst some Wealthy Farmers, unexpectedly presented, his Circumstances obliged him to embrace the opportunity immediately, as he had not above twenty four Hours to consider."[51]

The school was left without a regular teacher for two years before Mr. Cutting could find a proper person to recommend. Meanwhile opponents of the Church attempted to open the school, their behaviour being thus described: "The School at South is now vacant, as no proper Person has offered we have been retaxed in our Enquiries, by the ungenerous Behaviour of a few of the Inhabitants there; who from a Party Spirit have thrown a temporary Obstacle in our Way. They are disaffected to the Church, and though they acknowledge the Advantage, & Generosity of the Society's Donation; Want to have the Management in their own Hands to Answer their Purpose. Accordingly some Time after the Departure of Mr. Leahy, though the School House was built entirely by the Labour, and at the Expence of the Friends of the Church, they without consulting any proper Person privately thrust a Man into the School; in Hopes of his Obtaining the Bounty and did send a Petition to me, to recommend him to the Society. This I could take no notice of, as I knew him to be very unfit for the Care of the Children, and by no Means qualified for the Favour, of that venerable Board. The poor who felt the Advantage in Mr. Leahy's Time have made frequent Complaints to me, but as the present Master is employed but by few, and approved of by fewer He cannot subsist there without the Bounty of the Society of which he is totally unworthy; He must therefore soon quitt and I hope if a proper Person offers I may be allowed to admit him, With the same Encouragement the Society was pleased to grant to Mr. Leahy as I am convinced it will be of real Service to the People, to the Church, and to Religion in general."[52] The person "admitted" was John Leffert, "a Young Widower without Children, A Sober well disposed Man & a Church-man from Principle."[53] He

[51] *Ibid.*, B, 2, p. 147.
[52] Mr. Cutting to Sec., Jan. 8, 1772, *ibid.*, B, 2, p. 148.
[53] *Ibid.*, B, 2, p. 149.

opened the school in September 1773,[54] continued a quarter in it, then, meeting with opposition, left it.[55] After the beginning of the war Mr. Cutting said of the school: "I cannot now by any means attempt to supply it with a proper person, the carelessness of the Inhabitants of South has discouraged me."[56]

During the war Hempstead was made headquarters for troops and the school buildings were made use of. Schools were therefore "to no purpose."[57] The following from the Society's proceedings shows the final action taken in behalf of Hempstead: "Mr. Cutting flatters himself he now has an opportunity of supplying the long vacant school at Hempstead with advantage. Mr. Wetmore (son of the Rev. Wetmore formerly missionary at Rye, bred to the law & of an unexceptionable character) having been driven from his estate & practice, & all his property being in the hands of the Rebels, has, for some time, been very disagreeably circumstanced, within the King's lines. He is now reduced to keep a small school in the country, & struggles with great difficulties. If nothing more advantageous offers (which at present seems little likely) he would be extremely happy to serve the Society in that Capacity & Mr. Cutting is convinced the Church & people would reap considerable benefit from his service or if, unexpectedly, this Mr. Timothy Wetmore should be otherwise provided for, there are 2 or 3 other worthy & well qualified refugees, who would rejoice in such an appointment. Mr. Cutting will be glad to receive the Society's commands on this subject as soon as may be, it being of the utmost consequence in these parts & these times that education should not be wholly neglected. Agreed that as Mr. James Wetmore is at present in the Society's service, and was by his last letter destitute of a school, it will be proper to offer the school at Hempstead to him; but in case he is provided that Mr. Timothy Wetmore may be appointed."[58]

The S. P. G. records for the town of Hempstead show that between 1709 and 1747 ten or more packets of books were given

[54] *Ibid.*

[55] *Ibid.*, B, 2, p. 150.

[56] *Ibid.*

[57] *Ibid.*, B, 2, p. 153.

[58] Apr. 20, 1781, S. P. G. Journal, XXII, pp. 230–1. Evidently nothing was ever done as a result of the Society's decision. The two Wetmores mentioned were the persons formerly included among the S. P. G. schoolmasters.

by the Society to the church and the school.[59] In these packets there were many doctrinal tracts but most of the books by far were prayer books, catechisms, and expositions thereof. More than half of them were designed for the school. Once, in1718, a set of 50 A B C. primers was forwarded.[60] In the ensuing year a special consignment for the use of the school was included in the packet,[61] some part of which may have been of a non-doctrinal nature. Any books sent after 1747 are not a matter of record at the present time, and, presumably, they were not sent.

Secondary education was offered in the town of Hempstead by two of the Society's missionaries. Rev. Samuel Seabury, 1742–1764, kept a Grammar school in the town during the years of his pastorate.[62] In 1762 the following notice appeared in one of the New York papers:[63]

> "A Card—The Rev. Mr. Samuel Seabury, of Hempstead, in order to enlarge his school, had engaged a young gentleman as usher, who is candidate for orders. Mr. S. will entertain young gentlemen at his own house in a genteel manner at £30 per year, schooling, washing and wood for school-fire included."

Elsewhere we learn that "this school obtained much repute, and its advantages were appreciated by many of the principal families of New York City and all over Queens County."[64] Rev. Leonard Cutting who succeeded Mr. Seabury continued the Grammar school. Mr. Cutting was educated at Eton and Cambridge, and had acted as a "public Tutor" at King's College.[65] He had begun his service to the Society as a missionary at New Brunswick, New Jersey, and had, in addition to ecclesiastical functions, attempted a Grammar school there, which was not successful. In 1766 he was transferred to Hempstead,[66] and while yet in New Brunswick wrote the Secretary, saying: "I have great Expectation of a good Latin School at Hemp-

---

[59] *Ibid.*, I, p. 195; III, pp. 71, 399; IV, p. 179; V, pp. 121, 229; IX, pp. 72, 207; X, p. 226; Letter-book, A, 13, p. 477; A, 16, p. 260. The full amount was about 650 separate books and pamphlets besides three or more instances where amounts were not specified.

[60] S. P. G. Letter-book, A, 13, p. 433; Journal, III, p. 399.

[61] S. P. G. Letter-book, A, 13, p. 477.

[62] *Ibid.*, B, 24, p. 292.

[63] New York *Mercury*, March 27, 1762.

[64] Moore, Hist. of St. George's Church, Hempstead, p. 103.

[65] Commissary Barclay to Sec., July 22, 1763. S. P. G. Letter-book, B, 2, p. 52.

[66] *Ibid.*, B, 24, p. 296. He was missionary there from 1766 to 1782.

stead."[67] In 1775 he referred to the school, on which he was quite dependent for properly supporting his family.[68] The school was once more mentioned in his letter of December 28, 1779, from which the following has been entered in the S. P. G. proceedings: "His prospects are still gloomy, for, as Hempstead will probably still be the winter-quarters for the Light Horse, their distress must needs increase every year. Several of the inhabitants are going to remove, as they can enjoy neither their houses, barns, nor farms. His house indeed by the kindness of the commanding officer, is at present free from billets; but the exhorbitant price of provisions, & the village being occupied by troops, prevent gentleman's children being sent thither as usual for education: consequently his school, which was a great help to him, must diminish. If this school should continue to diminish, as it is to be expected it will, he is afraid he shall no longer be able to subsist, where he now is, but must retire to his glebe. But this will be his last resource."[69] From the above facts it is seen that the Society was indirectly instrumental in providing Hempstead with opportunity for secondary instruction for a period covering possibly more than thirty-five years.

A school under the auspices of the S. P. G. was opened at Oyster Bay in 1727. For the work Mr. Daniel Denton was recommended by Rev. Mr. Jenney as a person "well qualified as to reading writing & Arithmetick," who "makes Divinity ye main reading," and who was desirous to be engaged either as schoolmaster or catechist.[70] With the Society's assurance of an allowance of £10 per year as schoolmaster for Oyster Bay,[71] Denton set up his school in the following January. Strong opposition on the part of some of the people attended this venture from the very beginning, and it proved a decided handicap to Denton.[72] The cause of the trouble was explained in part of the following document, which was forwarded to the London office:

---

67 July 26, 1766, *ibid.*

68 S. P. G. Journal XX, p. 327.

69 *Ibid.*, XXII, p. 112.

70 Jenney to Sec., July 1, 1726, S. P. G. Letter-book, A, 19, p. 167.

71 Sept. 16, 1726, S. P. G. Journal, V, p. 100.

72 Denton to Sec., March 26, 1727, S. P. G. Letter-book, A, 20, p. 179.

"These may Certifie the Honourable Society for Propagating the Gospel &c. That when Daniel Denton first came into Oyster bay to keep School he met with a Violent opposition grounded on these Reasons.

That the Rev. Mr. Jenney should endeavour to Settle a Schoolmaster in the Town without their consent, but we do verily believe that the cause of the difference and opposition that the said Denton met with in his coming in the town is in a great Measure made up, and we do desire that the said Denton may be continued in the said Town of Oyster bay Schoolmaster and we do verily believe that for the future he will meet with great encouragement and be of great use and Service to the Town.

Witness our hands in Oyster bay 17th January 1729.

JOSEPH WHITE TOWNSEND,
PETER UNDERHILL,
THOMS UNDERHILL."[73]

The differences were not smoothed over, however, and Denton was unable to secure enough income through tuition to support his family.[74] This forced him to resort to other means and in consequence he seriously neglected the school. Severe complaints were entered against him in 1731, and, after an inquiry conducted for the Society by Commissary Vesey and Rev. Mr. Jenney, Denton was dismissed from the school.[75]

The school enrolled, according to Denton's reports, 30 for the year 1727 and 29 for the next two years.[76] These were not in constant attendance as he later admitted,[77] and Jenney, on visiting the school in December 1727, found only 20 present.[78] Denton found his own schoolhouse being "obliged to teach two for a House to teach in."[79]

The Society appointed Thomas Keble as Denton's successor, most of the people of the town having signed a petition in his favor.[80] The new schoolmaster had kept school for nineteen years at various places in Hempstead parish and, when chosen, was so engaged in Oyster Bay.[81] He was, "A sober industrious man, beloved & respected in the Townspot, even tho' the people were of different opinions in Religion."[82] As in the case of Denton his income was derived from tuition fees and the usual

---

[73] *Ibid.*, A, 22, p. 68. But the antagonism of dissenters may have also had a hand in the affair.

[74] *Ibid.*, A, 22, p. 66. In 1729 he offered to teach "all who came if he could be given £24 per annum, but he could not get near that sum." S. P. G. Journal, VI, p. 41.

[75] June 12, 1732. S. P. G. Journal, VI, p. 41.

[76] S. P. G. Letter-book, A, 20, pp. 179, 205; A, 21, p. 363; A, 22, p. 65.

[77] S. P. G. Journal, VI, p. 41.

[78] S. P. G. Letter-book, A, 20, p. 205.

[79] *Ibid.*, A, 22, p. 67.

[80] S. P. G. Journal, VI, p. 41.

[81] He was teaching "in the schoolhouse near the Church at the time of his appointment." *Ibid.*

[82] *Ibid.*

salary of £10.[83] But he had use of the town schoolhouse,[84] and nearly all of his children were able to or did pay "a small consideration,"[85] so that his condition was somewhat more satisfactory than was that of neighboring schoolmasters.[86]

Keble began his service for the Society about the end of 1732, the exact time not being given. There are yearly reports of this work from 1733 to 1744 save for three years, 1736 to 1738 inclusive. His enrolment ranged from 19 to 37, the average being 26.[87] Attendance in the winter was usually 20 or less.[88] Of his pupils four or five only were taught free. Up to 1735 all the white children paid something, and four freed Negroes were allowed gratis. After this date Negroes did not attend.[89] In 1734 Keble reported that he had given public notice of his intention to teach "free negroes and poor gratis,"[90] yet the proportion thus privileged remained the same. As regards the religious grouping of the children, the reports were vague. While dissenters patronized the school, most of the children were from families more or less identified with the Church of England.[91] In the last report of 1744 he was more specific and showed that 7 of his 29 pupils were dissenters and 8 of them were Dutch.[92] Keble's Notitiae from 1739 on showed one other school within the "Townspot" and from three to five in the outer parts of the township, at a considerable distance from his own.[93] In fact

[83] He had no other employment than the school as affirmed by him frequently. S. P. G. Letter-book, B, 7, pp. 145, 155; B, 9, p. 78; B, 10, p. 105; B, 11, pp. 130, 133; B, 13, p. 321. However he served as Reader in the Church without pay. *Ibid.*, B, 10, p. 105.

[84] *Ibid.*, B, 10, p. 105; Journal VI, p. 41.

[85] S. P. G. Letter-book, B, 1, p. 14; Journal VI, p. 123.

[86] The significance of the S. P. G. support was indicated by his statement that he could not otherwise subsist. "Most of the people of this Place," he added, "are very bad pay." S. P. G. Letter-book, B, 9, p. 78. Some became indebted to him for ten years schooling of their children which made it impossible to collect without suing. *Ibid.*, B, 10, p. 105.

[87] 30 in 1733, 31 in 1734, 37 in 1735, 26 in 1739, 19 in Nov. 1739, 25 in 1740, 20 in 1741, 22 in 1742, 25 in 1743, 29 in 1744. S. P. G. Letter-book, A, 25, p. 39; A, 26, p. 94; B, 1, p. 14; B, 7, pp. 145, 155; B, 9, p. 78; B, 10, p. 105; B, 11, pp. 130, 133; B, 13, p. 321.

[88] *Ibid.*, A, 26, p. 94; B, 11, p. 133; B, 13, p. 321.

[89] See citations for different years.

[90] S. P. G. Letter-book, A, 25, p. 39.

[91] Keble gave the number *baptized* in the Church only; and, providing he took pains to ascertain, there were few of these—namely, from two to eight.

[92] S. P. G. Letter-book, B, 13, p. 321.

[93] "One at Jericho about 6 mls, one at Musketoe Cove about 6 mls., 1 at Cedar Swamp about 6 mls., 1 at East Woods about 5 mls., & 1 at the West end of this town." He did not know what denomination they were "for most of the people are so infatuated with Enthusiasm & infidelity, that some seem to be against all religions." Report of 1741; and similar reports in other years, see citations above. Speaking of the schoolmasters of the different places, Keble said: "The Masters generally that teach are necessitous Travelling Persons, that there is seldom a school kept above a quarter of a year or half a Year at a Place." S. P. G. Letter-book, B, 7, p. 155. The children in these schools were largely Dutch and Quaker. *Ibid.*, B, 7, p. 145.

Keble moved his own school to East Woods, another part of the township, in 1744 and it is uncertain whether or not he ever went back to the town.[94]

Between 1744 and 1748 Mr. Keble became utterly incapacitated for further service through a mental break-down.[95] He was dropped from the Society's roll,[96] and interest in the school at Oyster Bay ceased.[97] A son of Rev. Samuel Seabury, however, reopened the school June 6, 1749,[98] in expectation of the usual assistance. Young Seabury had already been appointed S. P. G. catechist at Huntington, Long Island,[99] and the Society took no step to provide additional allowance for this work. Since further reports make no mention of the school, it is fair to suppose that he retired on failing to secure the bounty.

After being driven from Rye, James Wetmore set up a school for the Society at Oyster Bay and was teaching there in 1777.[100] He reported 40 scholars under his tuition.[101] In the summer of that year he removed to Mosquito Cove and founded a school with upwards of 50 enrolled.[102] In 1778 he reported as follows: "I continue to teach a School at Musquito Cove on Long Island. The Number of Scholars has been the Summer past between forty & fifty—the pay very small, especially when the enormous price of Provisions is considered—which is at four Times as much in general as before the horrible Rebellion."[103] His next report, which was sent in May 1779, stated: "I have at the present 40 Scholars at £6 Currency per Quarter. I cou'd afford my Family but little relief were I not assisted by the Ven^ble Society."[104] But this attempt to maintain a school in the midst of the serious condition of the country was doomed to failure. He was soon forced to retire and gave as a reason the following: "I continued my School at Musquito Cove on Long Island untill

---

[94] *Ibid.*, B, 13, p. 321.

[95] S. P. G. Letter-book, B, 16, p. 40.

[96] S. P. G. Journal, XI, p. 40, July 15, 1748. Keble died on Dec. 26, 1748. *Ibid.*, p. 128.

[97] Three packets of books had been sent to the school between 1728 and 1742. These included 150 catechisms and 50 expositions thereon. *Ibid.*, V, p. 197; VII, p. 25; IX, p. 71.

[98] S. P. G. Letter-book, B, 17, p. 105.

[99] S. P. G. Journal XI, p. 91.

[100] S. P. G. Letter-book, B, 3, p. 249.

[101] *Ibid.*

[102] Nov. 15, 1777. S. P. G. Journal, XXI, p. 265.

[103] Nov. 1, 1778, S. P. G. Letter-book, B, 3, p. 250.

[104] May 1, 1779, *ibid.*, B, 3, p. 251.

the 1st of Augst last—to the Satisfaction of my Employers—But a number of my Neighbours being captivated by the Rebels & I very Providentially escaping—& the Loyal Inhabitants being obliged to Lodge in the Fields for Safety—I have thought it Consistent with my Duty & prudent to quit the School, & am at present unsettled. My wife & a Number of my younger Children barely subsist between the Lines living in continual Fear & subject to frequent Depredations."[105] Finally in 1780, 1781, and 1782 we learn of his intention to resume the school. This he was unable to do with the possible exception of the winter of 1780–81.[106] In the meantime he opened a school at Flushing in May 1780 and had 30 scholars. This was broken up after three months by the King's troops, which encamped around the schoolhouse.[107] At length he made a final attempt at Newtown, Long Island. In a letter, dated May, 1, 1783, he announced having kept school there for the preceding six months to the people's satisfaction.[108] By this time Wetmore had been retired by the Society.

The School in the Parish of Jamaica

The first petition in behalf of a school, which the S. P. G. received from Jamaica, is shown in an excerpt from the proceedings which states:

> "The Sec. also reported from the Com^ee^. that they having read the petition of Alexander Davidson a Schoolmaster to them presented setting forth his misfortunes & every hard circumstances and as an addition to which that Mr. Lynn dec^ed^ the Attorney of the late Rev^d^ Mr. Urquhart having placed the said Mr. Urquhart's Son to be Boarded and Taught by him, for which the Exc^rs^ of the said Mr. Lynn not only refuse to pay the arrears due, but also to take the child off his hands; in all wch he prays to be relieved: The Com^ee^ agreed to lay the same before the Society: Then the said Petition was read and referr'd to the Com^ee^ to state the case of the said Mr. Urquhart and his child."[109]

It was decided that the petition was not "subject for the Society."[110] Nothing further is noted until 1730, when Mr. Joel Burroughs was urged as deserving assistance. Burroughs was "the son of a gentleman of N. York, & a trustee & con-

[105] Nov. 1, 1779, *ibid.*, B, 3, p. 252.
[106] S. P. G. Journal, XXII, p. 162; Letter-book, B, 3, pp. 253, 254.
[107] S. P. G. Journal, XXII, p. 219.
[108] *Ibid.*, XXIII, p. 95.
[109] April 20, 1711, S.P. G. Journal, II, p. 22.
[110] May 18, 1711, *ibid.*, II, p. 36.

siderable benefactor to the Ch. there."[111] Through misfortune, he had been so reduced that he was seeking bread by teaching school, and, after having done this "above 5 years," he was unable to maintain himself and family.[112] Having lived long amongst the people of Jamaica he was known to be "in every way qualified to teach a school there."[113] As in the previous instance, the Society took no action on the petition, notwithstanding the established policy of encouraging all ventures of this kind.[114] With the appointment of a new missionary, Rev. Thomas Colgan, efforts were renewed, which were this time crowned with success. In his petition for the Society's favor Mr. Colgan said: "A good schoolmaster is more wanting here, than in any part of N. America, the youth being very corrupt in their principles & manners, & at the age of manhood are utter strangers to the fundamentals of religion."[115] He therefore recommended Mr. Edward Willet, "a man of exemplary life, modest sober conversation, & every way capable of discharging that office."[116] Other missionaries voiced the happy qualification of Mr. Willet, who, it was said, "is willing to undertake it, if the small encouragement he expects from the spot, be raised by the Soc's bounty to a comfortable subsistence."[117] Willet was thereupon agreed upon with an annual allowance of 15 pounds,[118] from September 1733.[119]

Willet opened his school November 1, 1733[120] and served continuously until September 29, 1741, when he was obliged to move away, his income being insufficient for the support of his large family.[121] Tuition fees from paying scholars did not amount to much, for the pay was poor, and there were many children unable to pay anything, who were received gratis. In 1736 Willet told the Society that what he received from the people did not provide common necessities; that, furthermore, in the six

[111] S. P. G. Letter-book, B, 1, p. 66. March 2, 1729-30.

[112] *Ibid.*

[113] *Ibid.*; also A, 22, p. 69.

[114] The long quarrel between the missionary, Rev. Mr. Poyer, and his opponents, heretofore referred to, may have led the Society to believe the time inopportune for attempting a school at Jamaica.

[115] May 22, 1733, S. P. G. Journal, VI, p. 92.

[116] *Ibid.*

[117] S. P. G. Letter-book, B, 1, p. 37.

[118] Aug. 17, 1733, S. P. G. Journal, VI, p. 92.

[119] *Ibid.*, VI., p. 177.

[120] *Ibid.*

[121] *Ibid.*, IX, p. 22; Letter-book, B, 9, p. 67.

months immediately preceding he had not received as much as half his house rent for that length of time.[122] To improve conditions he started "a small shop of European goods," which he declared was attended by his wife.[123] The shop was being kept in 1738 and 1739 at least, and may have been begun much earlier, but the profits from it were not enough to tide over his difficulties.

The school in the summer of 1734 had 20 poor children enrolled.[124] By the end of that year there were 61 pupils, of whom 20 (the same number as before) were taught free.[125] For the years 1735 to 1739 inclusive the enrolment decreased from 59 to 38 and the free pupils from 24 to 21.[126] In the report of 1739 Willet, for the only time, classified the children as, one Negro, 5 from dissenting families, and 32 from those of the Church of England.

It may be assumed that Willet occupied a schoolhouse belonging to the parish. He did not mention any but elsewhere it is noted that the church in 1761 sold the "Old school house" for £3.[127] An assistant was employed in the school in the summer of 1738. While Willet was absent in New England the assistant acted as substitute and diligently supplied the place.[128] Evidently this was the only occasion of such assistance. As to other schools, there are two references to them among the Society's papers for this period. In 1738 Mr. Colgan reported: "there is no other School in the Town but his" (Willet's), "and but one near unto it, which is taught by a Poor Widow."[129] The

---

122 S. P. G. Journal, VII, p. 54.

123 S. P. G. Letter-book, B, 7, p. 123.

124 June 12, 1734, S. P. G. Letter-book, A, 25, p. 58. This first report from Willet did not specify the paying pupils.

125 Nov. 12, 1734, *ibid.*, A, 25, p. 78. In a copy of Rev. Mr. Colgan's certificate which is in the Journal of Proceedings (VI, p. 251), the enrolment is given as 63 with 23 free. A clerical error has occurred in one of two places and probably in the latter.

126 59 in 1735 with 24 free; 51 in 1736 with 22 free; 45 in 1737 with 23 free; 45 in 1738 and April 1739 with 21 free; 38 in 1739. S. P. G. Journal, VII, pp. 40, 54, 246; VIII, p. 6; Letter-book, A, 26, p. 70; B, 7, pp. 121, 123.

127 Onderdonk, Antiquities of the Parish Church, Jamaica, p. 62. This item appears in a list of subscribers to a fund for repairing the church-building and enclosing the church-yard.

128 Rev. Mr. Colgan to Sec., Oct. 10, 1738, S. P. G. Journal, VIII, p. 6.

129 *Ibid.*

next year Willet reported three schools in the parish taught by women, "all of ye Independent persuasion."[130]

Mr. Willet's withdrawal from the school was very unfortunate, based, as it was, on the people's lack of support. His success in the instruction of his pupils and his zeal in carrying out the desires of the Society were frequently attested. "He is singularly diligent to the satisfaction of everybody," wrote Mr. Colgan in 1734.[131] In 1738 another testimonial from the minister is thus recorded in the proceedings: "He writes also, that he hath received the Secretary's of the 28th March concerning the Conduct of Mr. Willet the Society's Schoolmaster in that town and the state of his School. As to Mr. Willet's Behaviour (which is the first thing enquired into) he must say that it is good and unblamable. He (Mr. Willet) is a man of a well order'd life and conversation, sober and Religious, he has always closely attended the Business of his School."[132] The vacancy was immediately filled by the appointment of Mr. John Moore, B.A., pending the action of the Society.[133] Moore, we are told, was about twenty-five years of age and was educated at Yale, where he had "made good proficiency in learning"; and he hoped, when occasion offered, to engage in the ministry.[134] Moore had charge of the school for about two years. In 1743 he was given permission to vacate the position long enough to go to England, as the following letter sets forth: "The Society hath granted your Request of coming to England for a Short time, you taking care to have the School Supplied in your absence, and they will be very ready to recommend you to Holy Orders (provided you shall be found worthy) that you may be the better qualified to promote their pious Designs."[135] With Moore's departure the

[130] S. P. G. Letter-book, B, 7, p. 123, Aug. 25, 1739. Schoolmasters known to have been in Jamaica parish before this time are: Henry Lindley and Thomas Huddleston, licensed by Gov. Cornbury 1705 (Pratt, *op. cit.*, pp. 91, 92); Alexander Davidson 1711 and Joel Burroughs 1729 (cited above); and Thomas Temple and a Mr. Rock about 1731 (Onderdonk, *op. cit.*, p. 37). The S. P. G. missionary, Rev. Mr. Poyer, reported to the Society in 1724: "There are Schools in each Town in the Parish but the Masters and Mistresses of them are some of them Presbyterians and others Quakers." Doc. Hist. of New York, III, p. 186.

[131] S. P. G. Letter-book, A, 25, p. 78.

[132] S. P. G. Journal VIII, p. 61. The Society was petitioned by Vesey, Jenney and Colgan to add to the salary but, feeling further responsibility rested with the people, it very justly determined not to do so. *Ibid.*, VII, p. 54.

[133] Moore began teaching forthwith, Sept. 1741. *Ibid.*, IX, p. 23. He was approved by the Society in April 1742. *Ibid.*

[134] *Ibid.* Moore was one of the first of the College graduates and prospective missionaries for whom positions were to be provided, pending ordination.

[135] Sec. to Moore, June 14, 1743, S. P. G. Letter-book, B, 10, p. 194a.

the support of the Jamaica school came to an end.[136] In 1745 a final reference to it was made in a letter from Mr. Colgan to the Society which said in part: "One great disadvantage the Church here lies under is the want of a good Schoolm[r] to instruct the youth in the sound, most rational, & Orthodox Principles of the Ch. of Eng. as some daily strive to instil notions destructive of good manners & of all religious & civil Gov[mt]. As Soc. has for several years past allowed £15 p.a. to a proper person to undertake that office he hopes they will continue it, when such an one offers for the purpose."[137] There are no records to indicate further events. Though the S. P. G. funds were in an embarrassing condition shortly before this time,[138] it is a question whether the Jamaica school was refused further assistance or whether the difficulty was continued inability to find a suitable person to conduct it.[139]

The Schools at Southampton and Brookhaven

Between 1732 and 1735 the Society allowed a bounty to a schoolmaster in the town of Southampton. This support was the result of a petition from some of the inhabitants, asking that a salary be granted to Mr. Edward Davies, who had been there "as Schoolmaster several years."[140] The petitioners affirmed that Davies had "taught many children to read & write, & the principles of Christianity." He had also "instrtucted negroes & Indians, many of whom desired to be instructed."[141] In an accompanying testimonial Commissary Vesey and the missionaries at Hempstead and Jamaica vouched for the good character of Davies, setting forth his industry and ability, and his great usefulness in the promoting of religion.[142] Davies was accordingly chosen the Society's schoolmaster and an annual salary of £10 was agreed upon.[143]

---

[136] There are no available reports of Moore's service in the school. After ordination he was appointed to Bermuda and resigned the school. *Ibid.*, B, 11, p. 136.

[137] Sept. 30, 1745, B, 13, p. 233. The Society recorded the letter without comment or action.

[138] See p. 101 in reference to Hildreth.

[139] The writer was unable to find either request for, or any special grants of, books to the Jamaica school. Various packets were dispatched to the successive missionaries but none of them seem to have been designed for school use.

[140] Undated petition received Oct. 20, 1732, S. P. G. Journal VI, p. 40.

[141] *Ibid.*, Letter-book, A, 24, p. 203.

[142] S. P. G. Letter-book, A, 24, p. 205.

[143] Oct. 20, 1732, S. P. G. Journal, VI, p. 40.

In the subjoined letter, which is given in full, we have Davies' report of his service during the first year:

"Bridghampton belonging to the Town off Southampton on the Island of Nassaw in the Colony of New York In North America November 6th 1733.
Revd Sr.

I have recd an Order from the Honble Society by the Revd Mr. Vesey appointing me School Master of Southampton and villages belonging thereunto for which please to return my most Humble Thanks to that Venerable Body—And I hope that the Future Accts that I shall give of the Increase of my School and the Improvemt of my Scholars in the Knowledge of Christian learning will in some measure please the Honble Society and evidence the Necessity of their charitable Bounty to these Parts. And in order to Forward this good work I humble Intreat that Honble Body to send me over some Catechisms with Explanation thereof and some of Mr. Tho: Dyches Spelling Books to Enable me to Instruct the children comitted to my Charge in the True rules of Spelling and such other good books, as they shall think most helpfull to discountenance Vice and Incourage Virtue. Inclosed is a Certificate according to your Instructions.[144] Since that was Signed there are more children added to my School upon the Accot of the Bounty, and the last Summer I Taught Twelve white Children on said Bounty and since the beginning of October I teach all the Negroes and Indians that are Inclineable to come, and can be spared by their Masters, the time of Teaching them is in the night, by reason of their being confined all the day to their Labour.

"I observe by the Instructions I am ordered to send Accot of the progress I make in the School every Six months to the Honble Society. I hope that Honble Body will please to Excuse me as to the Time. for I Live one hundred and near Twenty miles from New York therefore I cannot easily know when Vessels goe from thence to London. I will observe as often as I can get an opportunity send an accot to that Honble Body. I have humble presumed to Draw upon Wm Tryon Esqr or the Treasurer for the Time being of the Venerable Society Bounty for my years Salary Ending In July Last. I hope it will not be Taken amiss of me for so doing—

I am with Dutiful Regard,

Revd Sr Your Most obliged obedient Humble Servt.

EDWARD DAVIES."[145]

A summary of his report for the ensuing year dated November 12, 1734, is thus entered in the Society's proceedings: "He has made considerable progress with the Children under his care this last year; he had from 12 to 22 children, as they could be spared by their parents, & as weather permitted, some living 2 mls. away. Most of them can read tollerably well in the Bible & most of those from 7 to 13 years can write a fair hand to the great likeing of all who visit the school, which is very frequent. Last winter from Oct. to the middle of March he instructed from 10 to 20 negroes & Indians, & sometimes more as they could be spared by their masters. He is obliged to teach them from sun-

---

144 Not now among the S. P. G. Papers.

145 S. P. G. Letter-book, B, 1, p. 9. In compliance with his request, a packet containing "100 Sticht Catechisms, 12 Lewis's Exposition & 30 Dyche's Spelling Books" was dispatched to him. S. P. G. Journal, VI, p. 124.

set to 9 at night, as they work all day, & cannot come at all in summer; with much difficulty he has taught some to spell, some to read, & some to write, as well as could be expected considering the brokenness of their speech & age, most of them being grown to manhood—He hopes this winter to make a greater progress than last."[146] His letter of this date, moreover, states that, "Some of the children begin in their letters in the Primer, some in the Psalter, & some in the Testaments."[147] In the summer of 1735 it was reported that Davies had grown tired of the place and desired to be removed to Brookhaven. The S. P. G. missionary at Brookhaven urged that this be done, since there were few of the Church of England at Southampton, and it was at least fifty miles from any church.[148] But the Society would take no action without the recommendations of the other missionaries on Long Island.[149] Without waiting for final action in the matter, Davies left the school in the fall of 1735 and went to England. There he waited upon the Society and "declared his intention of not returning."[150]

One other instance of the Society's assistance to schools on Long Island remains to be noted. In 1733 Isaac Browne petitioned for an allowance on the ground that "by request of Rev. Mr. Johnson" (afterwards President Johnson of King's College) he had taught school in the interest of the Church of England, and had catechised children and read prayers "at Westerly in Naraganset, Brookhaven on Long Island, and Horseneck and Greenwich in Connecticut." The people being poor he had not received enough to support him and had spent his own money.[151] In appreciation of his service the Society made Browne a gratuity of £30.[152] Browne was a Yale graduate and one of the prospective candidates for Holy Orders while engaged in this work, the details of which it has been impossible to ascertain. Following his ordination, in the same year, he was appointed the Society's missionary at Brookhaven.[153]

---

146 S. P. G. Journal, VI, p. 208.

147 S. P. G. Letter-book, A, 25, p. 40.

148 *Ibid.*, A, 26, p. 38.

149 S. P. G. Journal, VI, p. 263.

150 *Ibid.*, VI, p. 278, Oct. 17, 1735.

151 *Ibid.*, VI, p. 96; also Rev. Samuel Johnson to Sec., Oct. 9, 1732, Letter-book, A, 24, p. 143.

152 *Ibid.*, VI, p. 95.

153 *Ibid.* VI, p. 99.

CHAPTER X

THE SOCIETY'S SUPPORT OF SCHOOLS IN THE UPPER PROVINCE

With the exception of the assistance allowed to schoolmasters and catechists among the Mohawk Indians, the educational work of the S. P. G. was of no great consequence in the northern part of New York Province. The Society did, however, maintain a number of missionaries in this section and through them there were occasional attempts to give encouragement to religious instruction in the schools that were carried on within their jurisdiction. In 1712 the Society received a petition on behalf of six hundred families of Germans on Hudson River.[1] "These people," it was declared, "stand in great need of qualified persons to educate their children in English reading, & writing, & Christian religion, & as there are now 2 able German Ministers, they only need Schoolmasters at present."[2] A plan was at once presented to the Society for meeting the situation, which, it appears, got no further than this. It may have been considered an undertaking beyond the limit of present resources, or else a responsibility to be assumed by the Crown and such agencies as brought about the migration. The proposed scheme was the following:

"A proposal to make the Settlement of Palatines at N. York more complete by appointing English Schoolmasters to instruct the children.

The Settlement consists of 5 towns, & it is proposed:

1. That 5 Englishmen be sent to N. York by Soc. & one in each town keep a free school to teach reading, writing, English & Arithmetic.
2. That they be good men, & with sufficient knowledge of the Ch. of Eng. Doctrine, as to be able to instruct the children therein.

---

[1] S. P. G. Letter-book, A, 7, p. 68. These Germans had emigrated to New York about 1710 and were settled in about five towns centering about Newburgh. They were usually referred to as the "Settlement of the Palatines." Doc. Hist. of N. Y. III, p. 339; S. P. G. Letter-book, A, 7, p. 68; A, 17, p. 232; A, 18, p. 44.

[2] S. P. G. Letter-book, A, 7, p. 68.

3. That the nearest missionaries visit these Schools at least once a year to see that the Masters are not remiss in duty.
4. That the Books & papers be provided for the use of these schools.
5. That this be done for at least 2 years from Christmas 1712 at Soc's. Expence."[3]

The S. P. G., however, sent missionaries among the Palatines and later to New Windsor and Newburgh.[4] Rev. Mr. Haeger, the first of these,[5] asked for some assistance for the English and German children of his congregations. He said: "I have been several times resolved to make my humble application to the Honorable Society for Prop. the Gospel about some encouragement for a schoolmaster to teach my children English and German, and this would contribute a great deal to propagating the Gospel and in time to turn them into English and good members and I will hope the Honorable Society will take it into consideration."[6] Another appeal on behalf of the "poor Palatines" was sent the Society in 1723, as follows: "I look upon them as true Lovers of our happy Constitution and Nation and think it is a Pity they should be soe bewildered in a state of Ignorance, their Inclinations bend them to have an Education in English, but their ability will not allow them to Entertain a person qualified to Assist them. It is humbly requested that you move in their favour and State their Case to the Honble Society to see if there may be any assistance from them to Support so good an Inclination. Sr They entertaine thoughts of being Supplyed wth books proper to Train up Youth in the English Tongue and what else can be allowed by the Charitable Society to carry on their good designs."[7] In 1747, Rev. H. Watkins wrote: "And as there are abundance of Children here who belong to poor Families, I could also wish for some Church Catechisms to give them of different Sizes for the different Capacities of the Children; being much wanted."[8] Five years later there is another report, referring to the education of the children in the following manner: "There are a great many Children, and youth in my Mission, which belong to Families of the Church of England and I am endeavouring as fast as I can, to implant in Them the Principles

[3] *Ibid.*
[4] Classified Digest, *op. cit.*, pp. 61, 855f.
[5] 1710–1718.
[6] S. P. G. Letter-book, A, 12, p. 341; Ec. Rec., *op. cit.*, p. 2118.
[7] James Ogilvie to Sec., June 5, 1723, S. P. G. Letter-book, A, 17, p. 232.
[8] *Ibid.*, B, 15, p. 101.

of our Holy Religion according to the Capacity while in their youth—To this End I have distributed to them upon my own account 4 Doz. of Lewis's Church Catechisms; and I have advised the Masters and Mistresses of the little Schools in my mission, and also the Heads of Families, who are of the Church, Carefully to see that the Children and youth learn this Catechism thro as fast as they can. And as I am from Time to Time visiting my People, I examine Those Children myself, both in those Little Schools and in private Families—And there are several of Those Children who have got this Catechism almost thro by heart."[9] Just at this time a tract of five hundred acres was granted by Letters Patent for the benefit of the Church of England minister and a public school.[10] As soon as the matter was determined, Newburgh took steps to erect both Church and school buildings, and to establish a school. The Society was memorialized on this occasion by means of the document herewith given:

To the Right Honourable and Reverend the Society for Propagating Christian Knowledge.

The Memorial of Alexander Colden and Richard Alberston, Trustees of the Parish of Newburgh in behalf of themselves and the Inhabitants of the said Parish and Places adjacent. Humbly showeth.

That the Inhabitants of said Parish and Places adjacent Consists of Persons Originally of Different Nations, Languages and Perswasions.

That there is no School for the Education of youth any where near Hudsons River above the City of New York, a very large Country above one hundred and fifty Miles in extent and full of Inhabitants, whereby the Youth are brought up and remain in Great Ignorance.

Towards the Supplying of this great want the Inhabitants of said Parish have Obtained a Grant of Letters Patent of Five Hundred Acres of Land for the Use of a Church and School as will more particularly appear by a Copy of said Patent herewith Sent so far as relates to the Use of the said Five Hundred Acres.

That the said Five Hundred Acres of Land are pleasantly Situated on Hudsons River in a most healthy part of the Country about half way Between the Cities of New York and Albany capable of great Improvements as a ship of any Burthen which can come into the Harbour of New York may come likewise to this place. But as the Expence of the necessary Buildings for the Church and School, and for the Minister and School-Master and giving Proper Encouragement to able Persons to officiate greatly Surpasses the ability of the Inhabitants.

We must therefore Humbly pray the Charitable Assistance of the Society and by their Intercession of other Charitable Persons in Order to Carry the Intention of his Majesties grant into its design'd Effect.

---

[9] June 12, 1752, *ibid.*, B, 20, p. 77.

[10] This was a tract or glebe originally given by Queen Anne to a Lutheran minister at Newburgh. By 1752 the Germans, by death or removal, had so decreased that the glebe became useless, for which reason the new grant was made. S. P. G. Journal, XIX, pp. 449-454. For copy of petition to Gov. Clinton, see S. P. G. Letter-book, B, 20, p. 89. For the Governor's order for a patent, see Doc. Hist. of N. Y., III, p. 359.

Unless this School can be properly Established the Rising Generation over a large Extent of Country may be involved in Gross Ignorance, And if it be promoted the Principals of Religion and Virtue probably will be Established and Propagated among them and many become good and Usefull Members of the Society who otherwise will be lost.

We Humbly therefore hope that the Encouragement of this Pious Design will Deserve the Serious Attention of the Society and which is most humbly pray'd and Submitted by The Right Revd & Honble Society's Most obedt and most humble Servts

Newburgh	ALEXR COLDEN	Trustees of
June 4, 1752.	RICD ALBERSTON	the Newburgh.[11]

During the entire period the Society, according to the records, adhered to its early policy of not assisting in the maintenance of schools in and about Newburgh. A school was established later and was partly supported from the tract of land. But the dissenters increased rapidly at Newburgh, came into control of the land and the school, and administered both for their own interest,[12] in spite of protests from the missionaries.[13]

The first English schoolmaster affiliated with the Church, who was commissioned to Albany, was probably George Muirson (1702). But, as we have seen,[14] he was retained at New York. In August 1706 Mr. John Humphreys sailed from England in company with Capt. C. Congreve of the Army, in expectation of receiving the Society's assistance as schoolmaster at Albany.[15] Both of these men were captured and carried into Spain, and it was 1709 before they reached America,[16] after which Humphreys was appointed a schoolmaster at Burlington, New Jersey, by the S. P. G. minister there.[17] In 1707 Rev. Thomas Barclay was sent out as Chaplain at Albany at a Royal bounty of £50 per annum.[18] On the recommendation of the Bishop of London, Mr. Barclay was in 1709 appointed the Society's missionary and school master for both Albany and Schenectady, with an allowance of £50 annually.[19] Schenectady got little benefit from his services, save a sermon once a month and his influence in getting an English school erected there in 1710.[20] Nor did he personally

[11] S. P. G. Letter-book, B, 20, p. 84-5.
[12] S. P. G. Journal, XII, p. 407; XV, p. 153; XIX, pp. 449-54.
[13] *Ibid.;* also Letter-book, B, 3, pp. 307, 308.
[14] See p. 71.
[15] S. P. G. Journal, I, p. (1).
[16] S. P. G. Letter-book, A, 5, p. 145.
[17] *Ibid.*, A, 5, p. 19.
[18] *Ibid.*, A, 11, p. 26.
[19] S. P. G. Journal, I, p. (189).
[20] S. P. G. Letter-book, A, 5, p. 176; Doc. Hist. of N. Y., *op. cit.*, III, p. 540.

establish a school at Albany. In addition to his ministration to the garrison he conducted the regular Church services. To fulfill the functions of schoolmaster, Barclay concentrated his efforts at first upon the encouragement of the teaching of the catechism and prayers of the Church. For this purpose he frequently visited schools and divided his charity collection into small stipends which he presented to the masters as an encouragement. He wrote of his method in 1710, as follows: "As I did begin from my first coming to Albany, so I go on to catechise the youth, and it hath pleased God to bless my weak endeavors that way, for a great many Dutch Children, who at first arrival, were altogether ignorant of the English tongue, can distinctly say our Catechism and make the responses at prayer, I explain some part of the catechism in as plain and familiar a way as I can, shunning all controversies, teaching them such fundamental doctrines as are necessary and tend most to promote piety and a good life. I have taught the scholars the prayers appointed for charity schools, and I have used all possible methods to engage the children to their duty, both by the giving of small presents to the most forward and diligent, and by frequently visiting their schools; and for encouraging the School Masters I give them what charity is collected in our Church, obliging them to bring their Scholars to the Public prayers."[21] It would be interesting to know how many and what schools Barclay was thus co-operating with. Possibly one was the school of the "Soldier belonging to the Garrison" of which Huddleston made mention in 1708.[22] If he had access to Dutch Schools,[23] they were certainly those outside of the control of the Dutch Church, for he reported being opposed in his work "by Major Myndert Schuyler & his brother-in-law, Petrus Vandrissen, Minister of the Dutch Congregation."[24] The very small minority of the population that the English must have represented[25] would hardly lead one

---

[21] Sept. 26, 1710, S. P. G. Letter-book, A, 5, p. 176; Doc. Hist. of N. Y., *op. cit.*, III, p. 540.

[22] See p. 77.

[23] He sometimes instructed in Dutch. S. P. G. Journal, III, p. 28; Letter-book, A, 9, 30 fol. p. 97.

[24] *Ibid.*, III, p. 28, June 29, 1714; also Letter-book, A, 9, p. 158, Oct. 22, 1714.

[25] At least he reports the proportion in Schenectady as 16 English families to 100 of the Dutch, outside of the garrison there, and we may infer that Albany was as predominantly Dutch at this time. S. P. G. Letter-book, A, 5, p. 176. In 1742 also the Society was informed that "in the city & county of Albany are 10610 whites, & 1110 slaves, Communicants 64 white 58 Indians, professors of Ch. of Eng. 170, 2 independent Companies, & 500 Indians." S. P. G. Journal, IX, p. 70.

to expect more than one English school, yet there were at least two of these in 1713, Barclay having in that year referred to "the English Schools."[26] It is therefore possible that his work with the children was done through these schools and that, in his reports of encouraging schoolmasters, he has the English schools only in mind. Indeed he declared in a letter of 1713 that he had distributed to the most deserving in the English schools, the Bibles and prayer books sent by the Society; and that "to encourage the principal Schoolmaster" he was paying him £8 per year out of the Church money.[27] Whatever the schools, it is certain that the Dutch children were receiving his instruction in the catechism of the Church which, we have already seen, he tactfully handled by avoiding controversies and teaching the more generally accepted fundamental doctrines. Most of his 70 children in 1713 were of Dutch extraction.[28] In 1716 Barclay's salary from the Society was withdrawn. This was done, the proceedings state, through a desire to retrench excessive expenses, and in view of the missionary's bounty from the Crown.[29] After this he still continued to report diligent attention to the work until 1722.[30] In 1719 Mr. Barclay was instrumental in setting on foot a Latin school in Albany. Of this he said: "I am at present Employ'd in gathering of a Latin School for one Mr. Willson, who arrived here last November from Ireland, a Man of sober Conversation and has a competent skill in the Latin and Greek tongues."[31] But no further mention was made of it.

Between 1728 and 1736 Rev. John Miln acted as the Society's missionary to Albany and the Indians. During the time, and even before Miln's arrival, a schoolmaster was affiliated with the work of the Church in Albany. In 1728 we learn that fifty children were brought by their schoolmaster to the minister twice a week to give account of their catechism, the parents allowing them to do this chiefly on account of the language.[32] A

[26] *Ibid.*, A, 8, p. 165, Apr. 17, 1713.

[27] *Ibid.*

[28] *Ibid.* There is a fair indication in the above that Dutch prejudice against English influence was breaking as early as this in Albany. Furthermore, Mr. Barclay reported as an offset to the opposition of the Dutch minister, that he had the encouragement of Col. Killian van Ranslaar and Col. Peter Schuyler, as well as English gentlemen. S. P. G. Journal, III, p. 28.

[29] *Ibid.*, III, p. 127.

[30] S. P. G. Letter-book, A, 12, pp. 290, 375, A, 13, p. 452, A, 16, p. 206.

[31] *Ibid.*, A, 13, p. 452.

[32] *Ibid.*, A, 21, p. 412.

report was sent in 1730 with the additional information that John Beasley the schoolmaster "also instructed near 20 Negroes in the Catechism."[33] Reports from both Mr. Miln and Beasley were sent in 1731, 1732 and 1734 describing similar work,[34] and seeking the Society's allowance as catechist for the Negroes in Albany.[35] In consideration of his efforts the Society voted two gratuities of £10 each.[36] It was even resolved to allow him an annual salary as catechist in conjunction with his work as schoolmaster, but a later report of available funds for that purpose caused the withdrawal of the plan.[37] Succeeding missionaries did not refer to schoolmasters. Since nearly all of them were commissioned to the Indians as well, a large part of their time was given to that work, and their letters usually made brief reference to Albany. The following excerpt from a letter of Rev. John Ogilvie in 1751 is evidence of the fact that the Dutch children continued to be instructed in the Church catechism by the missionaries. It reads: "At Albany the Church is much the same only that my Catechumens of the dutch Children are increased to near 150, this I hope will tend in some Measure to Introduce the English Language more universally and Lessen their Prejudices to our excellent Liturgy."[38]

The S. P. G. missionary at Poughkeepsie, Rev. John Beardsley, in 1767 sought aid for a school there. "Could the venerable Society," he said, "think proper to Lend their aid in Settling a School according to our Constitution, I am very sure it would be of Excellent purpose in this country, as the original Settlers were chiefly Dutch and therefore have been under but low advantage (in general) to obtain an English Education."[39] This favor was desired for some 50 children whom he was regularly

[33] S. P. G. Journal, V, p. 294; Letter-book, A, 22, p. 85. Beasley's teaching at Albany dated back to 1725 or "more than 6 years before" 1732, according to his own statement, *ibid.*, A, 24, p. 164.

[34] Nov. 2, 1731—10 of the negroes instructed by Beasley were baptized by the missionary, *ibid.*, A, 23, p. 345; May 1, 1732—12 of his negroes "and hopes to have as many this year," *ibid.*, A, 24, pp. 164, 199; 1733,—8 of his negroes (6 grown up and 2 children), *ibid.*, A, 25, p. 19; 1734,—5 of his negroes (grown up), *ibid.* An accompanying certificate from the mayor and other officials was sent in 1734 to the Society, *ibid.*, A, 25, p. 20. Rev. Joseph Hooper, in his History of St. Peter's Church, Albany p. 71, dates Beasley's work from 1732, "continuing several years." He thus relies on the S. P. G. Abstracts which have not a complete record of his services.

[35] Beasley stated in 1733: "there are about 300 people in this city, & not less than 400 negroes." *Ibid.*, B, 1, p. 6. A certificate from the Mayor and others vouched for the 400 Negroes, *ibid.*, A, 25, p. 20.

[36] S. P. G. Journal, VI, pp. 46, 51.

[37] *Ibid.*

[38] Apr. 14, 1751, S. P. G. Letter-book, B, 19, p. 71.

[39] Sept. 5, 1767, *ibid.*, B, 3, p. 25.

catechising.[40] In return the Society resolved "to appoint a schoolmr at Poghkeepsie, when a proper person shall be well recommended."[41] The next reference to the matter is in 1769, when Mr. Beardsley reported as follows: "I beg leave to inform the venerable Society that I have found a proper person Mr. Austin Beardsley for keeping a school agreeable to the laudable Design of their Charitable Institution. He hath been strictly educated in the Rules of our Chh reads and writes Plain English and is firmly attached to the british Constitution both in Chh and State; For confirmation of which I beg leave to refer to his recommendation from the Revd Doctor Auchmuty,[42] by whose approbation he is to open a School in Poughkeepsie after Christmas Holy-Days in hopes of Patronage from the venerable Society. I shall take care that the School be fixed on the Parsonage Land where we have an old House convenient for that purpose, which is Situated in a Neighbourhood of poor people who in general, are unable to pay their Children's Schooling and that Nothing be introduced but what is agreeable to the Rules of our Ch. and (as I observed in a former letter to the Society) I am fully persuaded a thing of this kind among us in the present State of the Country would as completely answer ye Intention of Such an Institution as the bestowment of their Charity on the Savage Indian Tribes."[43] Evidently, then, Mr. Beardsley did not learn of the resolution of the Society up to the time of writing the letter, and probably for some time thereafter. In the meantime, if Austin Beardsley actually opened a school about January 1770, as stated, he seems to have retired from it by 1771. There is strong probability that no school had been started up to that time, according to the following letter from the missionary: "I have in Sundry of my Letter to ye Society mentioned the great Necessity of a School at Poughkeepsie, & begged ye Assistance of that venerable Board and I have long since learned by Doctor Auchmuty that the Society are disposed in favour of the Scheme; and that whoever he shall approve the Society will appoint as a Master, all which I hope by this Time is settled,

---

[40] *Ibid.*

[41] S. P. G. Journal, XVII, p. 428.

[42] Rector of Trinity Church, N. Y., and Commissary of the Bishop of London. Austin Beardsley may have been a kinsman of the missionary though it is not so stated.

[43] Dec. 3, 1769, S. P. G. Letter-book, B, 3, p. 29.

& that ye person he recommended (Mr. Eli Emons) is accepted by the Society and that he will soon have Directions to open the School."[44] No further reference to the school or to Emons is to be found save the entry made in the S. P. G. minutes, on receipt of the information from Beardsley. The entry was to this effect: "Agreed that Mr. Beardsley be informed, that Dr. Auchmuty has not sent any recommendation of Mr. Eli Emons; that, if that shall arrive Soc. will appoint Mr. Emons Schoolmr at Poghkeepsie."[45] Since the Abstracts of Proceedings do not include any mention of school support at Poughkeepsie, it may be fairly assumed that the intentions of the Society were not carried out.

It has been pointed out that the Rev. Mr. Barclay was commissioned as schoolmaster to Schenectady in conjunction with his other numerous functions.[46] This was in 1709. Soon thereafter Mr. Barclay sent word that he had got an English school erected at Schenectady and hoped the children would soon be fit for catechising.[47] His relation to it was in an advisory capacity only. His visits to the town were once a month when he conducted Church services and catechised the children. This is the only indication available to show a relationship between the work of the Society and elementary instruction in the town. Years later, however, a Latin school was conducted by two of the missionaries. From 1771 to 1773 Rev. William Andrews kept such a school, not at the direction of the Society but to increase his inadequate income.[48] While the purpose was primarily that of a Latin school Mr. Andrews included elementary instruction in the curriculum. In explanation of the purpose of the school, he wrote to one of the foremost members of the Society in the Province: "I have very lately opened a Grammar School in this Town, and that I may make it more generally useful, I shall give instruction, in Writing, Reading, and Arithmetick—At present I have Ten Scholars and as the Prices are moderate I have the Prospect of getting more daily."[49] Before two months had passed, three scholars had been added, and we

[44] Apr. 26, 1771, *ibid.*, B, 3, p. 32.
[45] S. P. G. Journal, XIX, p. 76.
[46] See p. 197.
[47] Sept. 26, 1710, S. P. G. Letter-book, A, 5, p. 176.
[48] *Ibid.*, B, 3, p. 3. Jan. 21, 1772; also B, 2, p. 93.
[49] Andrews to Sir Wm. Johnson, Doc. Hist. of N. Y., IV, p. 466.

learn that Mr. Andrews had determined on an expansion of the curriculum and the establishment of an academy for both day and boarding pupils. His plan was thus described to the aforesaid member: "I lately took the Liberty of acquainting You, that I had opened a Grammar School in this Town, and since that, I have determined on forming it into an Academy, and propose giving Instruction in Reading, Writing, Arithmetic, Geography and History to those who may be designed to fill the Stations of active Life, exclusive of those who may be taught the Learned Languages—Bookkeeping, and Merchants accompts to fit them for Business, or the Mechanic Arts.—At present I have Thirteen Scholars, and as the Prices are moderate for teaching, and receiving Boarders, I have a good prospect of getting more daily. I hope, Sir, it may merit your Countenance and Encouragement, as it shall be conducted with the greatest Care and Attention, and that you will be good enough to patronize this Plan which may prove very useful to this Place, and may enable me to continue in this Mission."[50]

After two years Mr. Andrews surrendered the mission and retired from the academy to take up less burden some duties in Virginia.[51] The mission was immediately filled by the appointment of Rev. John Doty, who conducted it until 1777, when he became a refugee in Canada.[52] Mr. Doty took up the care of the school as well as the Church.[53] The following excerpt concerning the Latin school is taken from a letter of the Churchwardens and Vestry to the Society: "Thirdly, as the School began by Mr. Andrews not only laid a Foundation of Improvement to our Posterity, but promised an Addition to the Members of our Church, which has visibly declined in Mr. Andrew's Absence & of which our Neighbours of another Denomination have availed themselves by setting up a school and by various Artifices drawing away our Children with a View to their being educated in different Principles, which must inevitably happen not only to them, but to many Adults of our Congregation, unless we can have the Mis-

---

[50] Nov. 5, 1711, *ibid.*, IV, p. 470.

[51] "Finding it impossible to continue in this Mission upon the Society's Salary & the Subscriptions of the Congregation without teaching a school which has much injur'd my Health, I have therefore relinquish'd it, as thro' the Recommendation of Sir William Johnson procur'd a Parish in Virginia." Nov. 25, 1773, *ibid.*, B, 3, p. 11.

[52] Classified Digest, *op. cit.*, p. 855. For his appointment see S. P. G. Journal, XX, p. 85.

[53] Doty to Sec., Dec. 19, 1773. S. P. G. Letter-book, B, 3, p. 13.

sion revived in the person of Mr. Doty, as he is both from Character & Abilities peculiarly calculated for the Care of the Parish & School, both which he is willing to undertake."[54] Mr. Doty doubtless maintained the school as long as conditions permitted. Finally Rev. John Stuart attempted to open a Latin school in the summer of 1781. Writing to the Society on October 13 from Montreal, the missionary reported his ill-treatment by the Rebels, including the confiscation of his property and his confinement to the town of Schenectady. There, as a last resource, he "proposed to open a Latin School" for the support of his family, but "this privilege was denied on pretence that, as a Prisioner of War," he "was not entitled to exercise any Uncertain occupation in the state."[55]

In May 1768 the Society requested Sir William Johnson to provide a schoolmaster for the recent settlements of Johnstown.[56] Accordingly Mr. Edward Wall was appointed to the place and began instructing the children about November of that year.[57] In December Sir William wrote to the Secretary: "I have likewise established a fit person who received a Liberal education in Europe at Johnstown near this place who has at present near 40 children Whites & Indians, and his school daily encreases."[58] The name of the schoolmaster he said was Edward Wall, to whom he had advanced a half year's salary, and he proposed soon to draw for the amount.[59] For some reason the letter did not reach the Society until the meeting of May 18, 1770, at which time the appointment was allowed, with such salary as Sir William thought proper to allot to him "agreeably to the discretion-

---

[54] Dec. 10, 1773, *ibid.*, B, 3, p. 12.

[55] *Ibid.*, B, 2, p. 204. Mr. O'Callaghan, Doc. Hist. of N. Y., IV, p. 513, calls in question the truth of Stuart's ill-treatment and of his plan to open a school, on the ground that he contemplated emigrating as early as Nov. 1780. Judging from the context of documents quoted by O'Callaghan (*ibid.*, pp. 511-513) as well as from the assertions above, which are taken from an original letter of Stuart, it seems necessary to the writer to accept the missionary's statement of events.

[56] S. P. G. Journal, XVII, p. 511. Sir William served as His Majesty's commissioner of Indian affairs from about 1746 to 1774, and in 1766 was made a member of the S. P. G. About 1760, he established his seat at Johnson Hall. In this neighborhood Johnstown developed from about 40 families in 1760 to 260 in 1773 (Letter of Sir William to Sec. Letter-book B, 2, p. 94.) The town owed its development to the encouragement of Sir William who among many benefactions presented it with a handsome stone church "near 90 feet in length with the Steeple & Chancel" and added "a Neat Organ that cost £100 Sterl." *Ibid.*

[57] See reference to a letter from John Wetherhead to Sir William, introducing Mr. Wall, dated Nov. 17, 1768. Calender of Sir William Johnson's Manuscripts, p. 406.

[58] Dec. 10, 1768. S. P. G. Letter-book, B, 2, p. 90.

[59] *Ibid.*

ary power given him, by order of the Board in March 1769."[60] The salary was eventually fixed at £25 per annum.[61] Among Sir William's papers there is the following list of Mr. Wall's pupils, which, though it has no date, is presumably the enrolment of the school some time during the first year.

"List of Scholars at the Free School Johnstown

Richard Young
Peter Young
Hendrick Young
Richard Cotter
Hendrick Rynnion
James Mordon
Daniel Cammel
Samuel Davies
Renier Vanisclan
Jacob Veder
Randel M'Donald
John Foilyard
Peter Rynnion
Peter Potman
Jacob Doran
Jeromy Doran
David Doran
Adam M'Donald
Abraham Boice
Caleb M'Carty
Hendrick Callinger
Jacob Servos
John Servos
John Miller
James M'Gregar
George Binder
Christian Rider
Bernard Rider
Simeon Scouten
Francis Bradthan
John Everot
Sarah Connor
Luny Rynnion
Betsey Garlick
Baby Garlick
Rebecca Vanisclan
Caty Cammel
Caty Garlick
Mary M'Intyre
Peggy Potman
Eve Waldorff
Caty Waldorff
Leny Waldorff
Margaret Servos
Catherine Servos

Males & Females—45"[62]

The school had almost doubled this enrollment by 1772, Sir William reporting as follows: "The School here is extremely promising, and encreases very fast, the last return made to me by the Schoolmaster of the Number of Scholars, was Eighty six."[63] Other statistics are not to be found. Though Whites and Indians were enrolled, the proportion is not given and the list above does not aid us in this respect. The names seem to be those of English and Dutch children, 14 of the 45 being girls.[64] Evidently none of the children paid tuition. It was in reality a free school and the small salary given by the Society was added to by

[60] S. P. G. Journal, XVIII, pp. 371-2. In the first instance, the Society had agreed to allow £10 as salary. Sir William did not at first exercise his discretionary power and increase it.

[61] S. P. G. Abstracts, 1770-1 to 1774-5.

[62] Doc. Hist. of N. Y., IV, p. 416.

[63] Oct. 18, 1772, S. P. G. Letter-book, B, 2, p. 93.

[64] Both Indians and half-breeds are doubtless in the list, since European names were being used among the Six Nations.

the generosity of Sir William. In 1773 he wrote to the Society as follows: "By these actions the new Settlers, who were very poor and ignorant and of various Denominations, are now become much improved in their Manners, & Members of our Church, whilst the Free School, I erected near the same, contributes to enlarge ye understanding & confirm the faith of the rising generation, the prospect of which affords me much Satisfaction; I have promoted it hitherto as far as was in my power, and am heartily sorry that the circumstances of the People does not as yet enable them to lessen the charge they are to the Society, & to myself."[65]

That Johnstown possessed a schoolhouse for Mr. Wall's use, is shown in the very interesting quotation herewith subjoined.

". . . The next thing I mean to refer to, is the Building of a new Free School house nearly in the Centre of the Free-School-House Lot in the form of an Academy; with a conveniency at the top, for a little Bell of the Hall; if this was to be done, the present School House might be removed upon one of the vacant lots in Town, and answer the End of a dwelling-house—as it would not be proper for to have the New Free School in the least incumbered, but to have the whole Lott fenced in neatly and Suitable Trees planted round the whole square. If these things was done, (which is of far greater Consequence than the Building of Blockhouses in Town) your Honour would then engage the attention of people, and perhaps them who live in the remotest part of his present Majesty's Dominions."[66]

Mr. Wall gave general satisfaction as schoolmaster and the fact was certified to by Sir William and by the missionary at Johnstown. "The Schoolmaster," reported the latter in 1773, "is a very able and diligent man."[67] The minister went once a week to examine and catechise the children.[68] By June 1775 Wall had left the school and gone to a place called "German flats."[69] His place was taken by a man named Rose of whom there is but one report to this effect: "There is a certain Mr. Rose who has had the Charge of the School at Johnstown; and as far as I can judge he discharges that Trust with Care & Fidelity. The Children under his Care, are catechized regularly in

---

[65] Dec. 3, 1773, S. P. G. Letter-book., B. 2, p. 94.

[66] John Cottgrave to Sir William, Johnstown, May 18, 1772, Doc. Hist. of N. Y., IV, p. 474.

[67] Rev. Mr. Mosley to Sec. May 19, 1773, S. P. G. Journal, XIX, p. 479.

[68] *Ibid.*

[69] June 8, 1775, Calender of Sir William Johnson's Manuscripts, p. 536. In October 1772 Wall asked permission for John Thompson and himself to sell dry goods to the Indians. *Ibid.*, p. 511. It does not appear to have been allowed by the Indian Commissioner and his retiring from the school may be related to that incident.

Church."[70] The death of Sir William Johnson in 1774 occasioned a decline of the Society's interest in the school and no appointment was made after the retirement of Edward Wall. Whether Wall took charge of instruction elsewhere cannot be stated, but it is certainly questionable. Until 1778, however, his name is listed as schoolmaster at Johnstown with an apparent compensation of £7 10sh. from 1775 on.[71]

The Society's support of schools among the Indians is next to be noted. Conversion and civilizing of the American Indians began with the Jesuits of Canada at an early date and continued with tremendous zeal until after the French and Indian War. Scarcely an Indian settlement of the eighteenth century from the St. Lawrence to the Mississippi could have been found without evidences of the work of these assiduous priests. The Dutch gave the Indians little consideration save in the ordinary avenues of trade, and practically nothing of consequence was done by the English up to 1700.[72] The Crown, in the eighteenth century, paid for some time a small salary to the clergymen at Albany.[73] In the first decade of the eighteenth century Rev. Mr. Freeman, a Dutch minister at Schenectady, translated a great part of the English liturgy, the morning and evening prayer, Athanasian creed and several chapters of the Old and New Testament into the Indian language.[74] The Indians received the attention of the S. P. G. from the first, and the latter came to realize at once that the difficulties of their civilization would be great. Most regrettable of all was the fact that neither their savage natures nor their wandering habits were such stumbling blocks as the bad lives of so many of the Europeans about them. The seeds of death had been well sown in the seventeenth century. "Their numbers daily diminish by drinking rum," wrote Rev.

---

[70] Rev. John Stuart to Sec., Oct. 27, 1775, S. P. G. Letter-book, B, 2, p. 203.

[71] See S. P. G. Abstracts for the different years. As in other instances they may be unreliable regarding this data.

[72] Save perhaps the earlier work of the Society for Propagating the Gospel among the Indians of New England.

[73] To Rev. Thomas Barclay and afterwards to his son Rev. Henry Barclay. This was in all from about 1707 to 1746. S. P. G. Letter-book, B, 13, p. 8. Rev. Henry Barclay was appointed Rector of Trinity, and soon after this Col. William Johnson (from 1755, Sir William, see Doc. Hist. N. Y. II., p. 703), took charge of Indian affairs.

[74] Mr. Freeman to Sec. May 28, 1712, S. P. G. Letter-book, A, 7, p. 203. These papers for which the government promised him £75 per year, were by this letter put at the Society's service. At the same time, he declined the S. P. G. offer to appoint him to the Indians. *Ibid.* "The Indians," he said, "have a great veneration for the English Liturgy, especially the Litany, at which they frequently trembled." *Ibid.*

Mr. Freeman.[75] "As to the Indians, the natives of the country, they are a decaying people," wrote the Rev. G. Muirson of Rye in 1708. "We have not now in all this parish 20 Families, whereas not many years ago there were several Hundred. I have frequently conversed with some of them, and bin at their great meetings of *pawawing* as they call it. I have taken some pains to teach some of them but to no purpose, for they seem regardless of Instruction—and when I have told them of the evil consequences of their hard drinking &c. they replyed that Englishmen do the same: and that it is not so great a sin in an Indian as in an Englishman, because the Englishman's Religion forbids it, but an Indian's dos not, they further say they will not be Christians nor do they see the necessity for so being, because we do not live according to the precepts of our religion, in such ways do most of the Indians that I have conversed with either here or elsewhere express themselves."[76]

In the beginning of Queen Anne's reign some of the leading Sachems made touching appeals for religious instruction, and these were backed by similar representations from the Governor and other officials in the government of New York. The matter was laid before the Society with the result that Rev. Thoroughgood Moor was sent to Albany to undertake this mission to the Indians.[77] Mr. Moor was not acceptable to the Indians and remained only a year.[78] The work of caring for them was assigned in 1709 to Rev. Thomas Barclay, in conjunction with the mi sion at Albany. Very soon after the appointment of Mr. Barclay, four Sachems of the Iroquois tribe visited England to lay a special appeal before the Queen. Considerable enthusiasm was aroused in England. The matter was again referred to the Society and the result was the passing of the resolution,[79] heretofore alluded to, which came very near to limiting the work of the Society to work among the Indians. Fortunately, however, it did not.

In response to the favorable recommendation of the Crown and the direct appeal of the Sachems, the S. P. G. undertook the

---

[75] *Ibid.*

[76] *Ibid.*, A, 3, p. 168. Italics not in the original.

[77] Indeed the Society tried to engage the services of two Dutch ministers, Rev. Mr. Lydius and Rev. Mr. Dellius, who had done praiseworthy work among the Five Nations. S. P. G. Journal, I., June 18, Aug. 20, Oct. 15 1703; Mar. 17, 1704, Jan. 18, 1706; Godfrey Dellius to Bishop of London, Oct. 11, 1703, Fulham Archives.

[78] Report in S. P. G. Abstract 1706, p. 52.

[79] See p. 31.

obligation of supplying the Mohawks with a special missionary. This was Rev. William Andrews, who began his labors in 1712 at the Mohawks Castle at Onondage.[80] The "Castle" was only a short distance west of Schenectady and at the beginning of Mohawk Valley. Coincident with his coming, the French busied themselves to offset any possible influence that Mr. Andrews might build up. A story was started to the effect that instructions had been found, driven ashore from the English fleet in the "Canada river," in which plans were laid for the destruction of all Indians.[81] And the traders, who feared an interruptions of their gains, had it that Andrews was coming to claim a tenth of the Indians' possessions.[82] In the beginning, therefore, Andrews found it necessary to disabuse their minds of these fears, and he seems to have done it fairly well, being received with more than usual enthusiasm by the Mohawks and Oneidas.[83]

Mr. Andrews was to serve in the double role of minister and schoolmaster. He discovered that the Indians refused to have their children instructed in any but their own language.[84] With the Indian language as the sole medium of speech, Andrews was required to have two interpreters—one to translate into Dutch, and, since that one did not know sufficient English, another to serve between the interpreter and himself. He employed for the second interpreter Mr. John Oliver, former Clerk of the Albany Church, and put him, as assistant, in charge of the school.[85] The cumbersomeness of this triangular method may be easily realized. It involved a heavy expense and was a burden which the Society put up with in a truly commendable manner. Andrew's salary allowance was £150 a year,[86] the interpreter was allowed £60, and the assistant £20 and afterwards £30 per annum.[87] In 1716 a representation was sent to the King

[80] S. P. G. Letter-book, A, 8, p. 252. This person was not the Rev. William Andrews who was later at Schenectady.

[81] *Ibid.*, A, 7, p. 214.

[82] *Ibid.*, A, 8, p. 143.

[83] Though, as Governor Hunter said, "what was done by the Indians own desire & by their own request" they were so given to vacillating that he was not certain of the possible attitude which Andrews might meet. But he hoped they would "be wiser than to contradict" their interests and desires. *Ibid.*, A, 8, p. 252.

[84] Because the Indians believed, said Andrews, that "those who speak English & Dutch are the worst, because they learn the evils of the traders & soldiers." *Ibid.*, A, 8, p. 182.

[85] Dec. 17, 1712, *Ibid.*, A, 8, p. 125.

[86] From the time of his assumption of duties. From the date of his appointment till then he was allowed at the rate of £80 per annum. *Ibid.*, A, 7. p. 102.

[87] *Ibid.*, A, 8, p. 329; Journal, II, p. 361; III, p. 127.

setting forth the unusual expense of the work and asking that it be put upon a government foundation.[88] The proposal was not adopted, possibly for political reasons, and the Society retained the responsibility.

In 1713 Mr. Andrews made the first report of the school in which he said: "The Indians have built a school 30 ft. long & 20 ft. broad, & 40 boys & girls come to it, & they expect many more, for there are a great many children—some of 16 & 18 years come—Mr. Oliver the Interpreter assistant is willing to undertake the school & serve the Interpreter for £30 p. a. he writes well, & knows the ways of the Indians."[89] The work of schoolmaster was impossible for Andrews himself to perform, he declared, because he had so much else to do, but he would see that it was well done and was sure the Society could not more usefully employ a schoolmaster than there.[90] In less than a year from this time he reported that the school did not succeed as well as he expected when he began, that after three or four months most of them grew weary and their overfond parents did not oblige them to learn against their inclinations. But he hoped that when they saw the progress of the constant scholars, "some of whom begin to read their language & write," they would be more steady in attendance. Furthermore he was teaching three or four of them English, and had taken two of them into his own house.[91] His next report informs the Society that about twenty children are fairly regular at school, some of whom read fairly well, the best scholar being a young man, who is too lame to hunt with the others. The chief expedient to keep them regular in attendance, he finds, is to feed them, especially asthey fare very poorly in summer, having little else but wild roots, dried fish, and a little corn.[92] In 1716 only five or six children were in attendance and even these were irregular. As a reason for this Andrews charged the traders with decrying learning, which would take the Indians from hunting and do them no good, and with saying that, if they went to school, the Society ought to maintain them. "Whatever Andrews' success," wrote Governor Hunter, "he spares no pains," but, to convert the

[88] May 3, 1716, *ibid.*, A, 11, p. 34. This is the copy of the representation.
[89] Sept. 7, 1713, *ibid.*, A, 8, p. 182.
[90] Andrews to Col. Nicholson, Dec. 1, 1713, *ibid.*, B, 1, p. 158.
[91] Andrews to Society, May 25, 1714, *ibid.*, A, 9, 18 fol. p. 97.
[92] July 12, 1715, *ibid.*, A, 10, p. 185.

Indians to civilized life, "there ought to be schools erected among them to teach the younger ones our language & religion."[93] Again Andrews reported towards the end of 1716: "Not more than 8 or 9 come to School."[94] Even the promise he made, "to write for blankets & shirts for those who attended school constantly," proved to be of little use in making them come.[95] In fact, the Society had in 1713 acted on the advice of Mr. Andrews and dispatched £5 worth of trinkets as an encouragement to induce attendance. The invoice of this curious consignment is subjoined:

"Invoice of Sundrys shipt on Board the Drake John Tucker Mr. for New York on the proper account and Risque of the Honble and Revd the Society for propagation of the Gospel in foreigne parts and goes consigned to the Revd Mr. Wm. Andrews Missionary at the Mohawks Castle Vizt.

A Box and Cord					1	
It. N.	1.2 Bundles bla & Green beads				4	6
	2.2 Bundles last Cristal & Amber &	Amber				
	Colars	at 3s. 6d.			7	
	3.4 Bunches of Small Red	at	8		2	8
	4.4 Do Larger		10		3	4
	5.4 Do Larger		14		4	8
	6.6 Doz. Sortd					6
	7.2 Doz. Large Do	at	22		3	8
	8.2 Doz. bone haft knives & some fork		14		2	4
	9.2 Doz. Boyes knives		18		3	
	10.4 Doz. Roch Belly'd Do		12		4	
	11.2 Doz. pr painted haft Do	3	8		7	4
	12.2 Doz. Spring knives	2			4	
	13.1 Doz. Do Large				2	6
	14.1 Doz. Small looking glasses in frames				3	
	15.2 Doz. Do Large	3	6		7	
	16.3 Doz. 8 Sqr Leather Guilt Do	at	6		18	
	17.2 Doz. pictures in Guilt frames		18		3	
	18.2 Doz. Small Stone Rings		6		1	
	19.2 Doz. Large Do 3 Stones		12		2	
	20.2 Doz. Do Coloured Stones		14		2	4
	21.4 Doz. Bath Mettle Rings		18		6	0
	22.3 Cords Coulored Sleeve Buttons		6		1	6
	23.3 Do with stones		8		2	0
				5:	1	10
	Custo ffees & all charges on board				6	0
	ffrat prind on Bills of Ladcing				6	
				5:	13:	10
	Commission at 2½ per cent.				2	8
				5:	16:	6

Except Errors p Rowld Tryon.[96]

[93] Oct. 2, 1716, *ibid.*, A, 12, p. 238.
[94] Oct. 11, 1716, *ibid.*, A, 12, p. 239.
[95] *Ibid.*, Journal, III, p. 291.
[96] Feb. 1, 1713, *ibid.*, A, 8, p. 306.

At the beginning of Andrew's labors the Society took steps to meet the great need of books in the Indian language and for this the translations offered by Mr. Freeman and others made by Andrew's interpreter were made use of. The manuscripts for a series of books were submitted to the Society in 1713 by Andrews.[97] Of the first 180 or 200 were desired, and as many Indian hornbooks. With these he asked that there be sent "2 or 3 dozen of English Hornbooks, & as many primers, 2 or 3 reams of writing paper . . . 6 doz. Inkhorns, & 6 doz. penknives."[98] The Society ordered the prayer books printed in New York, but decided that the hornbook, "to show respect to the Indians," should be printed in England.[99] From the Society's annual report for 1714–1715 we learn that "They have paid likewise an impression of Hornbooks in the Indian language and sent with them several dozen of Gilt Primers, Leathern Inkhorns, Pen Knives, Paper of several sorts, etc. as proper and engaging instruments for them to work with in the School, and have returned a manuscript Copy of Prayers for their Use, to be printed in the Indian Language also, at New York, where the Exemplars are likely to be more perfect than if worked off in Europe."[100] The account of the series of books prepared in New York certified to by Governor Hunter was forwarded to the Society in 1715, and duly allowed. It is as follows:[101]

July 1	The Rev. Mr. Wm. Andrews	Dr.		
		£	S	d
1715	To printing 18 sheets of the Common Prayer &C. in ye Mohawk Indian Language at 35s p. sheet	31	10	0
	To 10 Rheam of Paper at 16s	8	0	0
	To 1 Rheam of Paper at 25s	1	5	0
	To paper printing and making up 150 spelling books	1	0	0
	To making up 150 Indian Catechisms		6	0
	To binding 150 Indian Common Prayers at 12d	7	10	0
	To making 50 ditto of five Paper		4	6
	To 2 boxes to pack them upon		4	6
		50	0	0

[97] *Ibid.*, A, 8, p. 187. The series when printed comprised: (1) Portions of the Prayerbook with family prayers and several chapters of the Old and New Testaments. (2) Horn-book, primer or spelling-book, and catechism with Prayers. Classified Digest, *op. cit.*, p. 800.

[98] *Ibid.*

[99] March 4, 1713-14, S. P. G. Journal, II., p. 361. The horn-books Andrews received in July 1715 and duly acknowledged them. Letter-book, A, 10, p. 185.

[100] Abstracts of Proceedings, 1714–1715.

[101] S. P. G. Letter-book, A, 10, p. 239. According to the Treasurer's acct. this amounted to £33-6-8 sterling. *Ibid.*, A, 10, p. 40.

This more than ample provision of books the Society determined to increase. In ordering the payment of the previous bill it was also agreed "that Andrews be directed to have printed in Quarto a number of Catechisms & following prayers in the said Collection now sent over from fo. 1 to 21. interlineary for use of the Indan Children, & that he have printed a small Vocabulary Indian & English to be annexed to this—the whole charge not to exceed £20 ster."[102] But these were never printed. "While the Indian children care so little for school," replied the missionary, "it would be useless to print more books or continue Schoolmasters, so will defer printing the Catechism & Vocabulary till further Orders."[103]

In discouragement Andrews advised that the schoolmaster-assistant be dismissed, that the Society might thereby be saved a needless expense, after which he would be able to assume charge of teaching those few that come.[104] Whereupon the suggested retrenchment was ordered.[105] The reports from Andrews for the following two years showed no improvement in the state of affairs and the abandonment of the mission was recommended.[106] The opinion of Governor Hunter, as to the usefulness of the mission and school, was sought by the Society. He replied by stating that the work was a failure, not, however, through any "want or care or attendance on Mr. Andrews's part."[107] The mission was abandoned in 1719[108] and Mr. Andrews on quitting the Mohawks wrote thus to the Society: "I have left with the Interpreter the Manuscript in the Indian Language vizt. St. Mathews Gospel, Expositions of the Church Catechism 2, one large and the other short, and Sermons &c. to give to the Indian Lad (but he was not at home when I came away) who has learn'd to write as well as to read, & can, and which is all that has learn'd to write he can read those Manuscripts very well and may make a good use of them to himself and others, if both are so well disposed and both for him and four Girls which are all that can read have left to each severall of the Books that were printed

[102] Oct. 21, 1715, S. P. G. Journal, III, p. 95.
[103] Apr. 20, 1716, S. P. G. Letter-book, A, 11, p. 317.
[104] Oct. 11, 1716 *ibid.*, A, 12, p. 239.
[105] Sept. 20, 1717, S. P. G. Journal, III, p. 291.
[106] S. P. G. Letter-book, A, 12, pp. 310, 325, 327, 337.
[107] Nov. 4, 1718, *ibid.*, A, 13, p. 356; Journal, IV, p. 27.
[108] S. P. G. Journal, IV, pp. 27, 78.

in their own Language: more than they will ever make use of, if as the Interpreter tells me they will soon forget all again, that they have learn'd, as he says those did which Mr. Freeman a Dutch Minister formerly Taught to read, and indeed I perceive already that it is like to be so, for they take not delight in their Books and learn'd only for the sake of what was given them for their Encouragement, the rest of the printed books in ther language which are twelve dozen and three or four more, and allsoe the venerable Society's Books which I brought out of England both which I have left with Mr. Jenney Chaplain to the Garrison at New York, his Receipt of them is here Inclosed."[109]

Disappointment over the failure of Mr. Andrews' venture did not deter the Society from further effort to civilize the Six Nations. When Rev. John Miln assumed charge of the mission at Albany,[110] he undertook to care for the Indians, receiving therefore an additional salary of £10 a year from the Society.[111] In 1735 Henry Barclay, son of the former missionary, was especially commissioned as a catechist or schoolmaster, as is seen in the accompanying quotation from the S. P. G. proceedings: "Also a letter from Mr. Vesey & others of Clergy of N. York, N. Jersey & Connecticut, Nov. 20 1734, stating that by a letter from Mr. Miln sent them by Mr. Vesey they are informed of the inclination of the Mohawks to receive the Gospel, & that the present Interpreter at Fort Hunter is not qualified for this work. Also that young Mr. Barclay has spent 4 years & taken his degree at Newhaven College, but not being yet of age for priest orders would willingly be employed as catechist or schoolmaster among them, learn their language, & be thus able more effectually to instruct them. Soc. heartily agree that this is a good work among Indians not only for propagating the Gospel among them, but also to secure them to the English interest & make a strong frontier barrier—Agreed to allow Barclay £20 as Catechist or Schoolmaster among Mohawks for one year from Michaelmas & the end of which Soc. will expect an account of his progress."[112] Mr. Barclay's reports show the encouragement with which he

[109] July 2, 1719, S. P. G. Letter-book, A, 13, p. 465.

[110] 1728–1736, Classified Digest, *op. cit.*, p. 855.

[111] S. P. G. Journal, V, p. 294.

[112] April 18, 1735, *ibid.*, VI, p. 233. The interpreter was a man under encouragement from the Assembly, which allowed £30 per annum for his work. *Ibid.*, III, p. 196. For letter of Mr. Miln to Mr. Vesey, see Letter-book, A, 25, p. 42.

entered upon this work. From his letter of August 31, 1736, the Secretary has noted the following: "From Henry Barclay to Sec. Fort Hunter, N. York. enclosing a certificate from the Commissioners for the Management of Indian Affairs for New York province (in the absence of Mr. Miln) for his diligence & success in the Instruction of the Mohawk Indians. He has resided above 18 months among the Indians & has met with good success. He has made himself master of their pronounciation & performs divine services every Sunday which they constantly & devoutly attend, & understand him very well. He daily teaches above 40 young men and children to read & write in their own tongue, & most of them make great progress. . . . he finds the language very difficult without an interpreter, & if suitable encouragement were offered the interpreter employed by Mr. Andrews might easily be persuaded to reside at Fort Hunter for 2 or 3 years, during which time he (Barclay) might master there (*sic*) tongue, he has drawn on Treasurer for £20 for his year's allowance this is very insufficient for his support, his necessary expences at Fort Hunter being double that—his board being £15 p. a. and he must keep a horse to get to the upper Town, 200 mls. away, as the Indians there expresses as great a desire of Instruction as they of the lower Town. He must give many trifles to them & must sometimes send 20 mls. for an interpreter at his own charge, so that he is still a great burden to his parents. He knows that the Soc's former & unsuccessful charges in this work has made them cautious, but unless he saw a good prospect he would not undertake so laborious & difficult a task."[113] In 1736 the Albany mission became vacant and Mr. Barclay was appointed to the combined post of missionary to the Mohawks and Albany.[114] To each of these he gave half his time,[115] but his personal ministration to the Indians seems to have been carried on through Church service rather than the school. Barclay's influence over the Indians was, however, very great. Born and reared in the neighborhood, he soon acquired a knowledge of the Indian language, which gave him the necessary efficiency and made him acceptable to the Mohawks.[116]

---

113 S. P. G. Journal, VII, p. 85.

114 Jan. 20, 1737, *ibid.*, VII, p. 207.

115 *Ibid.*, VIII, p. 34.

116 *Ibid.*, VI, p. 236. Indeed, the difficulties experienced by Andrews were in part due to a lack of these advantages.

Mr. Barclay, in 1740, petitioned for leave to appoint Indian schoolmasters to work among their own people. "I cannot omitt observing," he said, "the Absolute Necessity there is of having a School Master amongst them. I am much affraid that the Honble Societys Bounty will not have that good Effect which they hope for unless some means could be found to instruct the Youth (upon whom my greatest hopes are Built) to read their own language—I have tried several ways to get an Allowance for that purpose, but have not succeeded, and must at last have recourse to that Charity which has done so much for them already. No people have ever greater need of It and perhaps in nothing so much as in this Affair. There are several Indians well qualified for that Office and I believe would be prevailled with to undertake It."[117] Having the approval of the Society, Mr. Barclay, "with the advice of the Lieut. Governor Clarke and the Indian Commissioners" appointed Indian schoolmasters at two of the Mohawk towns, "Cornelius, a Sachem, at the Lower, & Daniel at the Upper Town," with a salary of £10 each New York money.[118]

From 1742 until his transfer from the mission to the Rectorship of Trinity Church in New York City, Barclay sent various faithful reports of the schoolmasters. From some of these the following abstracts are found in the Society's minutes: (1) May 31, 1743, "The Indians still continue their good dispositions, & behave exceedingly well, and attend the School very steadily, and make a great proficiency under the Schoolmaster who is very diligent, and takes great pains to teach them."[119] (2) November 4, 1743, "The 2 Schools, under the 2 Indian Schoolmasters, are carried on with great diligence and no less success, particularly at the Lower Town, where the Master, besides his attendance on his School, instructs several young men and women, & is much beloved of his brethren, & reads prayers to themin the absence of Mr. Barclay."[120] (3) July 4, 1744, "He has drawn Bills for £15 St. for a year's expence of the 2 Indian Schools, viz. £10 that Currency to each of the 2 Indian Schoolmasters, for

---

[117] Oct. 18, 1740, S. P. G. Letter-book, B, 7, p. 141.

[118] Nov. 17, 1742, *ibid.*, B, 10, p. 112; Journal, IX, p. 133. The first town Onondage or Mohawks Castle has been given before, the "upper town" was Conajohare. According to the Abstracts of Proceedings the salary of each amounted to £7–10 sterling.

[119] S. P. G. Journal, IX, p. 199.

[120] *Ibid.*, IX, p. 232.

pen ink & paper £2–15–0, for house rent 10s for a writing table £1–0–0, for trifles given to the Indian children by way of encouragement £1–16–0 in all £26–1–0 that currency, which at 75% exchange leaves a balance of 4s out of £15 st. to be carried on to next years account."[121] In 1745 and 1746 the work fell upon evil days again. As a result of vicious reports circulated among them, the Indians became restless and suspicious. They were filled with the fear of a proposed massacre of all their tribes.[122] Mr. Barclay was also slandered. Referring to this he said: "I acquainted you in my last of some strong prejudices instill'd into their minds against my Person, by one Lydius an Indian Trader; especially with Regard to the Schoolmaster's Salary; I am sorry to find that no mention has been made of that affair in that last abstract of the Society's Proceedings. This same wicked man has not ceased ever since to make me as odius to the Indians as possible by instilling New Jealousys into their minds telling them I had an annual allowance of £100 Sterling in Goods to be Distributed among them, all which I had converted to my own use So that I pass'd the Two last Years in a very Disagreeable manner and have been able to do but little Good amongst them."[123] As a result of the agitation, the two schoolmasters left their respective schools.

In order to provide books for the school, Mr. Barclay was granted £5 in 1737 "for procuring translations of parts of Scriptures &c. in the Mohawk's language instead of the usual tracts," to which £2 was added in 1740.[124] Again in 1741 the sum of £20 was given to enable him to complete the translation of other books.[125] Packets of books were also dispatched from England.[126]

Rev. John Ogilvie followed Mr. Barclay in the mission, and officiated from 1749 until 1763.[127] This included the period of the French and Indian War. "The advantage of the mission to

121 *Ibid.*, IX, p. 347. The "£15 st." spoken of at the end of the excerpt has reference to a benefaction of £50 donated by an "unknown person" in England to the work among the Mohawks. *Ibid.*, VIII, p. 216. Two other benefactions of five guineas each were given directly to Mr. Barclay for this work. S. P. G. Letter-book, B, 10, p. 196; B, 13, p. 38.

122 *Ibid.*, B, 13, p. 316. The Indians were told that Barclay was in the plot.

123 Dec. 2, 1746, *ibid.*, B, 14, p. 95.

124 S. P. G. Journal, VII, p. 207; VIII, p. 232.

125 "At least one of the Gospels & the Bp of Man's Essay towards an Instruction for the Indians." *Ibid.*, IX, p. 27.

126 In 1740 and 1743, S. P. G. Letter-book, B, 7, p. 141; B, 10, p. 196.

127 Classified Digest, *op. cit.*, p. 856.

the English," it has been asserted, "became apparent to al during the wars in which the country was involved, the Mohawks joining the British troops, and being 'the only Indian nation' which 'continued in our interest.'"[128] On the recommendation of Col. William Johnson, the Indian Commissioner, a schoolmaster was once more appointed for the upper Mohawk town in 1750. Col. Johnson's letter announced that the Indian, Petrus Paulus, had already undertaken to teach the youth of that place and, if the Society would allow him a salary for continuing in the work, it would be counted a great favor to both "Castles."[129] Petrus Paulus was, in view of these facts, voted a yearly bounty of £7-10.[130] No appointment was made for the lower town at this time. Petrus Paulus served only a short while and the nature of his work is not known. Mr. Ogilvie reported, in 1753, that he had been dead for some time.[131] In his place, Ogilvie recommended another Indian named Paulus, for the upper town, which recommendation the Socitey confirmed and voted the previous salary.[132] During these changes, the loyalty of the Society to the cause did not wane. Its attitude was well defined by the Secretary who sent the following letter to the Rector of Trinity in New York. "The Society are much concern'd," he said, "at the present disorderly State of the Mohawks & have at heart the Instruction of their Children & I have particular Orders to desire you & Mr. Ogilvie to advise with Colonel Johnson & to propose to the Society what you shall judge to be the most proper Method for their Education, & at the same time to inform the Society whether any assistance may be hoped from the Government of New York towards bearing the Expense."[133] Mr. Barclay returned word that he had delivered the suggestion regarding the Indians to the Lieut.-Governor, who promised to lay it before the Assembly, but that nothing had been done.[134]

---

[128] *Ibid.*, p. 73.

[129] S. P. G. Letter-book, B, 17, p. 118.

[130] S. P. G. Journal, XI, p. 259. His father, Sachem Abraham, was at the same meeting voted a gratuity of £5 for reading prayers to the Indians for several years past. *Ibid.*

[131] *Ibid.*, XII, p. 308. July 19, 1753.

[132] *Ibid.*, Dec. 21, 1753.

[133] Aug. 1, 1753, S. P. G. Letter-book, B, 20, p. 341; also Journal, XII, p. 136.

[134] June 5, 1754, *ibid.*, XII, p. 3.

Mr. Ogilvie, on his visits to the Indian village in 1754 and 1755, found the school in satisfactory condition. He so reported, desiring at the same time that a school be again started at the lower town. It is entered in the Society's minutes as follows: "Paulus is very diligent, & teaches above 40 children daily—sevl begin to read, & some to write they learn the Ch: Catechism & have made considerable progress in Psalmody—The Indians of the lower castle, having signified their desire to have a Schoolmaster, as they formerly had, Mr. Ogilvie thinks it would be of considerable service, as there are a large number of promising children."[135] Power was given the missionary to secure another schoolmaster as desired, but this was not carried out until after the war. Paulus on the other hand continued in the school at upper town, but his attendance on the work was not regular. The fortunes of war at times made this impossible.[136] But when he could have attended to the school, he was so taken up with war parties, it was complained to Mr. Ogilvie, that he had greatly neglected it.[137] In 1761 the school was still in existence but it is not certain whether Paulus or another Indian was in charge.[138] In 1762 an abstract of a letter from Rev. Mr. Oel, assistant to Mr. Ogilvie for the upper Indian Country, refers again to the school. Mr. Oel indicates, in a fairly clear manner, that the person then in charge was not Paulus. He says: "His (Mr. Oel's) congregation formerly more than 30, is by the war & disease among the Indians & other accidents, reduced to 12 or 13, but hopes it may be recovered by erecting a school for young & old under the care of a young Indian, who reads & writes that language elegantly, & has a zeal for propagating the Gospel—He has already above 30 Scholars, but Mr. Oel fears he will not be able to attend the school & his other labours without some supply. He asks that Soc. will add to the salary he draws for once in 2 years, wh. he will faithfully bestow on the sd Indian teacher. The Treasurer informed that Mr. Oel has drawn £22–10 more than his salary, it was agreed that Mr. Oel is not to draw for any more, till that debt be paid, wh. will not

[135] Dec. 27, 1755, *ibid.*, XIII, p. 183.

[136] More than once during the war "the Mohawk River was a Scene of all the Horrors of War, with continual Circumstances of the most horrid Cruelty." Mr. Ogilvie to Society, 1758. Abstracts of Proceedings, 1758–1759.

[137] S. P. G. Journal, XIV., p. 186, Feb. 25, 1759.

[138] *Ibid.*, XV. p. 203—abstract of a letter from Rev. Mr. Oel to Sec. mentioning "a certain Indian who teaches in it."

be till mid-summer 1764. Commee recommended a small gratuity to be given to the Indian lad, who is so useful to Mr. Oel, Agreed, and that it be such as Dr. Johnson shall think proper, not exceeding £5."[139] Dr. Johnson wrote in reply to the Secretary, September, 1762, that he had made "what inquiries he could at that distance," and could get no information about Paulus, but supposed he might be keeping a little school in one of the small clans.[140] On the other hand the name of Paulus recurs among the list of schoolmasters in the Society's abstracts of proceedings until the year 1769.[141] The writer is inclined to question whether he performed very much service after 1759.

With Paulus the attempt to educate the Indians exclusively in their native tongue came to an end, and the subsequent schoolmaster of the Society maintained English schools. This change, it appears, met with the approval of the Indians, who now began to show a great desire to learn the English tongue. Early in 1762 a memorial was received by the Society in behalf of the appointment of Mr. Cornelius Bennet as catechist and schoolmaster to the Mohawks. This was from Dr. Johnson of the New York College and it contained the following extract: "But what I chiefly aimed at in writing, was to give you an account of a worthy gentleman of Boston Government, whose name is Bennet, & was lately with me. He seems inspired with an earnest desire of doing his Utmost towards converting the Mohawks & Senecas & other Tribes of Indians, & came to be directed by Dr. Barclay & me in pursuit of that design having been well known to us both many years ago. He was bred & graduated at Newhaven College. After which he kept a School at Stratford, & resided with me: & having never been baptized, was then baptized with me, & has been a very serious person ever since. He was many years Master of Mr. Kay's Grammar School at Rhode Island, & is a very good Grammarian & would teach the Mohawk Children, which would give him opportunity (in pursuance of the Society's Design you mentioned to me of educating some Indian Lads at this Colledge) to look out some & prepare them to be sent hither for further Education. He is

[139] From a minute of the meeting of Dec. 17, 1762, *ibid.*, XV, p. 294. This schoolmaster was very likely Philip Jonathan, who was teaching in Canajohare in 1764. See his letter to Sir Wm. Johnson, Doc. Hist. of N. Y., IV, p. 339.

[140] Sept. 16, 1762, S. P. G. Letter-book, B, 2, p. 92.

[141] See Abstracts for the various years.

about 50 years old, but seems to have a firm Constitution. however being so far advanced, he declines going so far for orders, & chuses to act only as a Catechist under the Minister of Albany. He has a little Competency of an Estate, which he would have left with his Family, & desired only so much Salary, as may be sufficient to Support his own person in his undertaking."[142] The Society at once took the proposal under consideration, pending more adequate reports from their agents then in the field.[143] After waiting for a year Mr. Bennet made an appeal for assistance to the missionary at Cambridge in New England, by which means his design became known to the New England Society. From both Church people and the non-Church Society Bennet received sufficient encouragement to warrant his initiating the work at Mohawk Castle, which he did about September 1763.[144] The generosity of the New England Society is shown in the subjoined document:

At a meeting of the Commissioners of the Society for propagating the Gospel among the Indians in New-England and Parts adjacent in America 22 July 1763.

Mr. Cornelius Bennet of Middleborough having offered himself to go as a Catechist to the Mohawks, and been in treaty with the Revd Docr Johnson and Docr Barclay about going, Voted that the Commissioners will allow Twenty pounds lawfull Money for one year for his encouragement in the Service, and advance one quarter's Salary to enable him to prepare for and prosecute his journey to the Mohawk Castle provided the Revd Dr Johnson and Dr Barclay shall approve hereof.

And that the Treasurer write to Docr Johnson and acquaint him that the Commissioners have not officiously engaged in this affair, but as it has been Mentioned to them from his Excellcy the Governor and the Revd Mr Apthorp they readily fell in with the proposal to manifest their desire of uniting with them in propagating our common Christianity among the Indians. And that whenever the Docr shall think fit that Mr Bennet should proceed, the Treasurer advance the Quarters salary as aforementioned.

A. Oliver,
Treasr.[145]

On receiving information of the above action, the Society conferred on Bennet a salary of "£40 for 1 year to commence at the same time with that allowed him by the Commissioners,"[146] and subsequently continued it.[147] A gift of 20 copies of Fisher's

142 Extract from Dr. Johnson's letter of Oct. 9, 1761, enclosed in a letter to the Archbishop, Feb. 27, 1762. Lambeth Archives 1123, III, p. 250.

143 S. P. G. Journal, XV, p. 190.

144 Lambeth Archives, 1123, III, p. 317. He was stationed at the lower town.

145 S. P. G. Letter-book, B, 23, p. 412.

146 Oct. 28, 1763, S. P. G. Journal, XVI, p. 6.

147 *Ibid*, XVI, pp. 149, 330.

"Childs Christian Education & 12 small common prayer books" was also made.[148]

Mr. Bennet's first report was forwarded in March, 1764. It was set forth the following facts: ". . . A letter is enclosed from Mr. Bennet, Catechist to the Mohawks, that he has begun instructing the Indians, & has a fine company of lively pretty child en, boys & girls, who, though ignorant of learning at their first coming, are very ingenious & orderly—They hear prayers morning & evening, learn to read English, are catechised in the Mohawk tongue, are taught obedience to their parents, the observation of the Lord's day, respect to their superiors, & a courteous civil behaviour. This is the only English School ever known here, & by a divine blessing may in some measure soothe & mollify their wild fierce tempers. The parents are so well pleased with their children's improvement that they send them for instruction from Indian town 30 miles up the river, & it greatly concilates their minds towards the English. As there is no Doctor near, Mr. Bennet visits the poor Indians, when they are sick & infirm."[149] In November, 1764, the schoolmaster returned to New England[150] for reasons explained in the accompanying letter, which was the second and last report of his work among the Mohawks: "After some Gentlemen in Boston had Subscribed towards my Support as a Catechist, and a Schoolmaster among the Mohawks for a Year; and the Commissioners had made a Grant to me of Twenty Pounds New England Currency for the same time; as soon as I could prepare my Self I set out on my journey and arriving at Sir William Johnson Seat was kindly received by him. And the Indians being informed of my design met me there. When the reason of my coming among them, being minutely examined after their way, was well approved, Then Lodgings and a School was provided for me & Boys & Girls Sent to me and Sometime young men and young women as their Hunting and other Business allowed, where I have diligently instructed them in Reading, Writing, and the Church Catechism, in the English Tongue and Civilizing their ways and Manners. They seem forward and willing to be taught

[148] *Ibid.*, p. 149.

[149] Abstract of Bennet's letter inclosed with one from Rev. Mr. Apthorp, March 12, 1764, *ibid.*, XVI., p. 148.

[150] S. P. G. Letter-book, B, 22, p. 71.

and passively obedient in School. their parents use me kindly and Sir William Johnson well approves of the Scheme. The season of Hunting began in October and will continue till January and almost the whole Tribe are gone out with their Familys and the Small pox being likely to Spread among the remaining Indians and Dutch people there: hath induced me to return to New England for sometime where I shall endeavour to do what Service I am able among the Narraganset Indians or elsewhere until I can safely return to the Mohawks again who have manifested a desire for it and also to have a Missionary in their Tribe and I humbly beg leave to offer it as my opinion that if they had one who would kindly and tenderly use them and diligently and affectionately Instruct them in our holy Faith and Charity, they would forsake their evil practices and be an Example for the other Tribes to follow. I am Learning their Language and Composing a Vocabulary & Nomenclature which if effected will be Serviceable to the Six Nations."[151] Regarding Bennet's efficiency, it was reported that Sir William Johnson was extremely well pleased. The Indians, too, liked him and were desirous for his return, but after a long illness he died early in 1766.[152]

By 1765 the Society seemed inclined to rely, for the future, upon such service as the missionary at Albany could render among the Mohawks.[153] But through the earnest representations of Sir William Johnson and certain missionaries in both New York and Pennsylvania, renewed activity was soon set on foot. Indeed this was partly due to another cause. The New England Society, which had, since 1748, given some attention to tribes on the Mohawk river, became unusually active after the war. The leader in this movement was Rev. Dr. Wheelock, who introduced a number of missionaries and schoolmasters, in the hope of reclaiming the Indians.[154] Headquarters were established at Lebanon, Connecticut, where a school was erected.[155] From this place Wheelock sent his agents into the west to instruct the Indians and to serve as feeders to the Lebanon school. The following information regarding the Wheelock plan was given the Society: "A Society of Gentlemen in N. England have

---

151 *Ibid.*, B, 22, p. 72. The letter is undated.

152 Feb. 25, 1766, *ibid.*, B, 22, p. 73.

153 S. P. G. Journal, XVI, p. 330.

154 Doc. Hist. of N. Y., IV, pp. 505–6.

155 See correspondence between Wheelock and Sir William. *Ibid.*, pp. 314 ff.

set up an Indian School under the direction of Mr. Wheelock, a dissenting preacher—Young probationers are sent from their Colleges into the woods, where they stay till they have prevailed upon the Indians to send some of their children to this school with whom they return, & then others are sent. Mr. Barton saw one of these Missionaries at Sir W. Johnson's returning from the Indian country with 5 or 6 Indian Boys, which appears to be the most plausible method to civilize these rude & barbarous creatures, & to prepare them for the reception of knowledge & religion, & is highly worthy of imitation."[156] The scheme at once appealed to the Society's interest, and word was sent that every plan for the instruction of Indians was highly approved and every opportunity would be taken to promote it. In the meantime the Society desired to have pointed out what particular method could best be pursued. A plan was accordingly submitted by a Pennsylvania missionary, the outline of which is shown in the abstract following:

From Rev. Mr. Barton, Lancaster, Pensyl.

In answer to Sec's letter of May 26, he proposes 3 schools for Indians, each consisting of at least 10 boys. The first school to be set up in the Mohawk River & to be incorporated with the Free School, which Sir W. Johnson intends to erect & endow near Johnson Hall, for the use of his tenants, & the master to be subject to Sir Wm's direction. The second to be at Fort Pitt, under the protection of the Commanding officer there for the time being, subject to such rules as the Soc. may think conducive to the prosperity of it. The third to be placed in the back parts of S. Carolina, under the care of the superintendent of Indian affairs for the Southern district. These 3 schools, supposing them to consist in all of 30 boys will not exceed the following expence.

	£		
To dieting & lodging each boy £7–0–0, 30 boys	210	0	0
To clothing Do 2–0–0	60	0	0
To books & paper for Do 1–0–0	30	0	0
To the Master of each School 50–0–0	150	0	0
In all for 3 schools	450	0	0

He would willingly hope this heavy expence will not fall entirely upon Soc. The civilizing & instructing the Indians ought to be a public concern, as it will be a public benefit. For till the fierce & cruel tempers of these poor barbarians are softened, & subdued by knowledge his Majesty's American subjects can never expect a lasting peace with them. Nothing but extending the light of Knowledge to them will ever conciliate them to us, or secure effectually the Frontier Settlements from their blood-thirsty designs—European missionaries residing in their country can expect to do but little service among them when Missionaries from amongst the Indians themselves, by being accustomed to their modes & manner of living, by being able to attend them in their long excursions, & to instruct them in their own language, may

[156] From Rev. Mr. Barton, Lancaster, Pennsylvania, to Society, S. P. G. Journal, XVII., pp. 77–8.

do a great deal. Such missionaries would in a little time persuade their wandering tribes to incorporate with civil Society, & to settle to village and the cultivation of their lands—Could they once be brought to this, every difficulty, that now lies in the way of their instruction & conversion from a wretched & destructive idolatry to the religion of Jesus Christ, would soon vanish. And there appears to him no scheme more likely to accomplish this most desirable end, than that of erecting Indians Schools, which would soon supply the Society with proper persons to carry the glad tidings of Salvation to the deluded Heathen. The difficulty of finding Masters, who understand the Indian language, & are men of prudence & good morals, He hopes Sir W. Johnson will be able to remove.[157]

The proposal was approved, to the extent of one school as a beginning. The Society by resolution, "Agreed that an Indian School for 10 Indian boys be established on the Mohawk River under the direction of Sir W. Johnson & that the Soc. will contribute towards the expence of the said School, what Sir Wm. shall find necessary not exceeding the sum of £150 p. a. & that Sr. Wm. be desired to provide a proper Schoolmr."[158] The plan of Sir William Johnson was forwarded to the Society about this time, and was adopted in preference to the Wheelock scheme of segregation in boarding schools, which Mr. Barton advocated. Sir William wrote as follows: "Mr. Wheelock's plan seems a laudable one, but give me leave to remark that many of these Schemes which had their birth in N. England have soon appeared Calculated with a View to forming Settlements so obnoxious to the Indians who have repeatedly declared their aversion to those who acted on such interested principles. All the good lands in N. England being thick Settled they are extremely desirous of Migrating and have created much disturbance by attempting it. Another objection is, that those brought up under the care of Dissenting Ministers become a gloomy race, and lose all their abilities for hunting &c. spending their time in idleness and hanging upon the Inhabitants for a wretched subsistence, having lost those qualities which rendered them usefull to us, without acquiring any others in their place worthy the name of Christians, to which indeed they have little or no pretensions, all which discountenance Religion with the rest of the Indians. I have just heard from the Revd Mr. Auchmuty of N. York on the Subject of the Society's intentions, and I am on that head of opinion that a Mission established at the lower Mohawks, with proper help would draw the Oneidas and others

[157] Nov. 10, 1766, *ibid.*, XVII, p. 281f.
[158] *Ibid.*, p. 287.

thither for Learning, . . . but constant residence and an exemplary life must be expected from him to insure success. This Mission might indeed be established at the Upper Mohawks or Conajohare, but what is stil an object of more importance is the Conversion of the Senecas who exceed 1000 men, & their Neighbours are much more numerous to the Westward who would follow their example. To this end a Mission, or schools should be established under some good Divine about Oneida or Onondaga to either of which the Senecas &c. might conveniently come; this Divine to be assisted by a good Catechist and as there are some Mohawk Lads who are in some Measure qualified to act as Ushers their presence would encourage the rest, to resort thither so that in a short time some would be qualified to take Orders & return with Abilities & natural interest to promote the aith amongst the rest. This is a rough Sketch on which I shall enlarge at some other time, and with a View farther to promote it."[159]

With prompt concurrence the Society resolved to provide missionaries and assistants.[160] Difficulty arose, however, in procuring suitable persons who were willing to undertake the work at the remote localities. Especially was this true of missionaries.[161] But in 1770 Rev. John Stuart, a native of Pennsylvania and graduate of the College of Philadelphia, was ordained and commissioned solely to the Mohawk Indians. Here he ministered to the neighboring tribes until in 1778 he became a prisoner of war.[162] The selection of the schoolmaster was put in the hands of Sir William Johnson with the power to fix a salary not exceeding £25 or £30.[163] The satisfaction that this co-operation gave Sir William is observed in the following: "I

[159] Oct. 8, 1766, S. P. G. Letter-book, B, 2, p. 86. Writing somewhat later Sir William again declared that the primary thing to be done for the Indians was, to quote his own words: "to establish on some regular system proper Missionaries & Schools in most of their Towns which is the only effectual means of Converting & Reducing them to Order. A few straggling Missions or Schools out of their Country will never answer the end proposed the more distant Indians being extremely averse to sending their Children abroad for Instruction, and if they did, they are too apt to relapse afterwards, of which I have seen examples amongst the best of them sufficient to Justify my opinion." Apr. 26, 1770, *ibid.*, B, 2, p. 92. This observation of Sir William has been justified time and again in the experience of Indian schools generally.

[160] S. P. G. Journal, XVII, p. 225.

[161] "The dificulty of procuring able and Conscientious Missionaries for the Indians, I fear will be very great. I will try what I can do here, and hope you will do the same." Rector of Trinity to Sec., May 1, 1767, S. P. G. Letter-book, B, 2, p. 23.

[162] Classified Digest, *op. cit.*, pp. 73, 856; Doc. Hist. of N. Y., IV, pp. 428, 507.

[163] S. P. G. Journal, XVIII, p. 90, Jan. 20, 1769.

have still the Honour of Corresponding with Sir William Johnson upon the Subject of Indian Schools, No Man can be warmer in the Interest of the Church than this most worthy Gentleman. It seems to be his constant wish to see the Plan of Indian Schools properly carried into Execution."[164]

In March 1769 Mr. Colin McLeland was put in charge of a school at the lower town by the Commissioner, who thus informed the Society: "I have fixed a Worthy, honest Man as a Schoolmaster at the Mohawks who tho' there only since the 24th of March has already 30 Indian Children under his Tuition, who improve very fast, and their Numbers will be shortly augmented. . . . The Name of . . the School Master is Colin McLeland."[165] Sir William's information concerning the enrolment was based on the list of children forwarded to him by McLeland at the end of August, 1769. According to it the school opened in April, and soon after was being attended by the Indians whose names are herewith given:

Mohawk School at Fort Hunter.
Begun to open School April ye 17th, 1769.

Augt 28th 1769	A list of The Indians Children belonging to the Free School at Fort Hunter near the Mohawk River in the County of Albany and Province of New York with their Tribes.	
Bear Tribe	David, David, Abraham, John, Jacob, Peter, Joseph, Adam, Brant, Kreenas, Johannes, Peter, Nellithe, Nellithe (Females)	15
Wolf Tribe	Thomas, Paul, Jacob, John, Daniel, Catherine, Susanna, Catherine (Females)	8
Turtle Tribe	Isaac, Joseph, Daniel, Jacob, Thomas, Christianna, Catherine. (Females)	7
Total		30

Pr Colin Mc(Leland) Schoolmaster Sr Accordinging to your Direction I have sent your Honour this List.[166]

---

[164] Rev. Mr. Barton to Sec., S. P. G. Letter-book, B, 21, p. 18.

[165] Dec. 10, 1769, *ibid.*, B, 2, p. 90. It may be pointed out that the Johnstown school admitted Indians as well and may therefore be thought of as a part of this work. It is further stated in the Abstracts for 1769–70 that "The Society has given encouragement to Mr. Hall, a graduate in the college at Philadelphia, to go to Conajohare, there to learn the Indian language, that he may be qualified to be Catechist and schoolmaster in that place, till such time as he shall be able to come over for Holy Orders." Mr. Hall was recommended to the Society May 26, 1770, (*ibid.*, B, 21, p. 266) and he was accordingly voted "£40 a year for his support in going among the Indians" (Aug. 17, 1770, Journal XVII, p. 396). But a letter of June 20, 1771, says that Mr. Hall seems to decline his appointment at Conajohare (Letter-book, B, 21, p. 24.). On the other hand the Indians of that upper town complained that they were given no school and were thus neglected. To prevent this Sir William at his own expense, maintained a schoolmaster for them from 1772 until his death, 1774 (*ibid.*, B, 2, p. 94.). Sir. William's schoolmaster may have been the Indian, Philip Jonathan (Doc. Hist. of N. Y., IV., p. 339).

[166] Doc. Hist. of N. Y., IV, p. 417. The Bear tribe shows fourteen and not fifteen names.

From the missionary at Albany we have a report of the school in 1770. It says: "Two Days following, on my return to Albany I waited on the Sachems of the Lower Castle, & visited the Indian School, which I can assure the Society is in a very promising way. The Schoolmaster is universally beloved by the Indians, & their Children are making considerable Proficiency under his care, both in Reading & Writing."[167] The final report of the school and the only available report from McLeland himself is one which he forwarded to the Society in 1775. It is possible that he did not make regular reports to the S. P. G. directly, as the following would seem to indicate: "During the life of the late worthy Sir William Johnson, I gave in yearly to him an account of the Number of Schollars and their Proficiency and he took my Draughts on the Society, for which he gave me Cash. Since his Decease I have continued My Attendance on the School as usual, and as I have had no particular Instructions from the Society to make my Returns to any other Person; I have presumed to write to that Venerable Body. The State of the School is as follows, I have Twenty four Schollars four of which Read in the Bible and the rest are in their Spelling Books and learn very fast. I attend school from Eight o'Clock till twelve, and from One till five in the afternoon. I live in Harmony with the indians as I understand their language."[168] Mr. McLeland remained at his post for some years after this, but the nature of his school is not known. With the serious struggles that the Mohawk country witnessed during the Revolution, the loss of Sir William's encouragement, and the subsequent flight of the missionary, little could have been hoped for in the way of education. The Society continued, however, to honor McLeland's bills until 1782.[169]

Though no record of the fact has been found,[170] suitable English books were doubtless transmitted from London. Sir William Johnson about 1769 provided a second and enlarged edition of the earlier Indian prayer-book. This edition was

---

167 Rev. Harry Munro to Sec., Sept. 25, 1770, *ibid.*, B, 3, p. 271.

168 Apr. 20, 1775, *ibid.*, B, 3, p. 342.

169 "Ordered McLeland's bills be paid to 1782 only." March 21, 1783, S. P. G. Journal, XXIII, p. 171.

170 With this exception: In reply to Mr. Johnson's letter of 1773 announcing the want of proper books, the Society agreed to send primers and psalters when he should indicate what sort were most wanted. *Ibid.*, XX, p. 83.

printed by Mr. Hugh Gaine at his New York Press.[171] In the Society's abstracts for 1774–75, we find one other reference to books, as follows: "The Indians frequently complain of the want of books in their own language. In order to supply this want Mr. Stuart was encouraged by the late Sir William Johnson to undertake a translation of a part of the New Testament, which Sir William promised to print at his own expense, and with the assistance of an Indian who understands English, Mr. Stuart hath prepared a Mohawk translation of St. Mark's Gospel, a large and plain exposition of the Church Catechism, and a compendious History of the Bible. But now having lost the generous encourager of this and every good work he applies to the Society for their assistance and will not fail of obtaining it, when they are assured of the fidelity of the translation."

What has been given herewith, covers the actual achievement of the Society among the New York Indians. It seems advisable to the writer to add to this some evidence of a comprehensive and far-reaching policy for the civilizing of the Indians which the Society, its agents, and its friends attempted to have supported by the government and people of Great Britain. This will occasion a reference back to the proposal made by Sir William Johnson, the King's Indian Commissioner, and its adoption by the Society. That such a scheme could not be carried to completion by the Society single-handed was well realized in England as in America. When the Society had taken the first steps in this plan, Rev. Charles Inglis, the assistant rector of Trinity Church, wrote the Society, as follows: "After the Appointment of Mr. Stuart with so large a Salary from the Society tho' not larger than necessary & of a Schoolmaster, . . . I concluded the Society would not, from the low state of their Funds, have it in their Power to do any more towards erecting new Indian Missions. In this opinion I am confirmed by your last Letter. We must therefore turn our Eyes to Government for what may be done further."[172] Somewhat before this Sir William Johnson expressed a similar view, to wit: "Two or Three People from New England have collected Ten or Twelve Thousand Pounds Sterling for Mr. Wheelock's Schools and the Government has allowed a Bishop to the Canadians, and as I

171 Classified Digest, *op. cit.*, p. 800.
172 March 8, 1771, S. P. G. Letter-book, B, 2, p. 66.

hear established a French Missionary lately in Nova Scotia at £100 stg. pr. Annum, I can therefore hardly think from these Instances in favour of other Persuasions that a proper application to his Majesty for his Royal Patronage & assistance in favour of a Plan of such great and extensive Utility could fail of success, and I should likewise think that thro' the Interest of his Grace, of Canterbury, the Bishop & the Society, this might not only be effected, but a handsome Sum collected in England, for these truly laudable purposes."[173]

Measures were immediately taken by these gentlemen and other friends of the movement to memorialize the government of England in behalf of all the nations of the Iroquois. During its preparation the advice and co-operation of the S. P. G. was sought by means of the following letter:

"One princpal Reason for my going to Sir William Johnson's where the Mohawks requested Dr. Cooper & me to write to the Society in their Favour, was to converse with Sir William about the State of the Indians." . . . . "Dr. Wheelock collected large sums in England for his School some thousands of Pounds by his own Confession. Can it be supposed that well-disposed People would be less liberal to this Scheme, when under the Direction of so respectable a Body as the Society, & attended with so many promising Circumstances? Especially if proper Measures be taken to lay them before the Public, & to collect Money. I humbly conceive that some vigorous effort of this Sort is necessary to draw the attention of People. A single Mission in the old, beaten Way makes no noise. Few regard it. But an extensive Plan, with the Society at its head, supported by Sir William Johnson's Influence here, & attended with the greatest Probability of Success; would not fail I imagine, to command Notice & awake the slumbering Charity of many Christians. Many just objections be against Dr. Wheelock's Scheme. It is too contracted, injudiciously formed, & inadequate to the Design of Christianizing the Indians, to say no worse Yet it serves the Ends of the Dissenters well enough, to make Bustle & will gain Credit, If no better Scheme is set on foot.

I request that you, Good Sir, would be pleased to consult the Society & let me know their Sentiments of this Affair. My intention is to represent the State, Number, Situation, & some other Circumstances of the several Tribes of Indians, bordering on this Government; to propose the Plan laid down by Sir William Johnson for the Conversion of the Indians, which appears the most rational & judicious I have yet seen, & obviate the objections that may be made to it; to remove some popular Errors that have been propagated by Dissenters of late with Regard to the first Emigrants to America, as if they had been all Dissenters who fled from Episcopal persecution; . . . & to place in as strong a Light as I can the several Circumstances which now concur to insure success to such an attempt at converting the Savages.

This is, in a few words, the Plan I have in View. If the Society approve it, I shall proceed & after Sir William Johnson has inspected my Papers, which he has promised to do carefully & give all the Assistance he can to correct them, I shall send them to the Society for their Perusal, & to do with them whatever they think proper Should the Society disapprove the design, & judge its unpracticable I shall desist."[174]

---

[173] Apr. 26, 1770, *ibid.*, B, 2, p. 92.

[174] Rev. Mr. Inglis to Sec. *ibid.*, B, 2, p. 65.

The memorial, carefully drawn up and elaborately prepared, was presented in 1771 to Lord Hillsborough,[175] bearing with it recommendations from the Governor of New York and Sir William Johnson, as well as from the Society and the prelates of the Church of England. From the document we quote only the six measures which the plan proposed should be taken to improve and civilize the Indians:

I. That two Missionaries, men of good character, abilities, and prudence, and in the orders of the established Church of England, be sent to the Iroquois, one to reside at Conajohare, the other at the old Oneida Town. Most of the Indians at both these villages have been baptised, and even profess Christianity; all are willing to be further instructed. Each of these Missionaries should have a Salary of £150 sterling a year at least, to enable them to shew some marks of favor to the more deserving Indians, by making small Presents to them from time to time. This will be expected from them, and if judiciously managed, will have a good effect in conciliating the affections of the Indians. If these Missionaries had some knowledge of Physic, so as to be able to assist the Indians in sickness, it would also increase their influence, and make their Spiritual Labors more successful.

II. That a Schoolmaster be fixed at each of those Villages, viz.: Conajohare, and the old Oneida Town; another at Onondaga; one at the principal village of the Cayugas, and two among the Senekas. These Schoolmasters, for whom admission and protection may be easily procured, should be prudent, and virtuous young men, and such as have had a liberal education. Their business will be to teach the Indians, to read and write. They ought also to apply themselves diligently to learn the Indian Language, by which they will be better qualified to act as Missionaries afterwards, should their behaviour and merit entitle them to that office. Schools, if properly conducted, will be of infinite service. The Indians are all willing that their Children should be taught to read and write; and Youth is the properest season to instill principles of Morality and Religion, which the Schoolmasters will have constant opportunities of doing. Of these they ought to avail themselves; and gradually unfold the Principles of the Christian Systems to their pupils. Each of those Schoolmasters ought to have a salary of £40 Sterl. a year, which might be increased according to their industry and success. They also, as well as the Missionaries, should be furnished with Prayer-books, and such other Tracts in the Indian language as can be procured; which will be necessary to teach the Indians to read, and instruct them in the principles of Religion.

III. That Smiths be placed at some of the most convenient Indian Villages. These would be of great service to the Indians, and therefore very acceptable; and probably some of the Indians, from a sense of their utility might be induced to learn their Trade. Their wives might also be engaged to teach such of the Indian women as are willing to learn Spinning, Sewing, and other Branches of female Industry. The Government formerly allowed Smiths at several of the Indian Villages, with a competent salary. These Mechanics would now be of much service in promoting the general design, and might be had at a trifling expense. The Spaniards have employed mechanics, and do still, for the same purpose to great advantage.

---

[175] See "A Memorial concerning the Iroquois or Five Confederate Nations of Indians in the Province of New York," in Doc. Hist. of N. Y., IV, p. 1089. This Memorial, we are told, having been "copied out fair in a good Hand, and in a quarto size, and having a Marble cover, with Col. Johnson's accurate and neat Map prefixed, made a handsome looking Pamphlet." *Ibid.*, p. 1090.

IV. That the Missionaries and Schoolmasters employed in this Scheme be appointed, or at least approved, by the Society for the Propagation of the Gospel in Foreign Parts. The Superintendency of those matters naturally belongs to that Venerable Body, not only by reason that they coincide with the design of their Incorporation, and with their connections on this Continent, but also because the Society have with great fidelity discharged the important trust reposed in them, and have already done much towards Converting and Civilising the Iroquois. It is therefore proposed that they have the Care and Direction of the Missions specified in this Plan; that the Missionaries and Schoolmasters shall regularly transmit to them accounts of their respective charges from time to time, in the same manner as those Missionaries and Schoolmasters in the Society's service do at present; to be annually laid before the Public, with their other Transactions. That the Missionaries, Schoolmasters and Mechanics however, be under the immediate inspection of His Majesty's Superintendent of Indian Affairs for the time being. His Station and Authority among the Indians will enable him to promote the execution of this Scheme. He will be the properest Person to direct the several Measures that shall be necessary on any new emergencies; and through him, in conjunction with the Society, applications to Government should be made, in matters relative to those Missions. It will be proper that the Superintendent of Indian Affairs should be thus concerned in the Management of those Matters, because it will be of Utility to the general Design; and also that he may see that such steps be taken as are consistent with the Interests of Trade, and the Views of Government respecting the Indians.

V. That a set of Rules and Instructions be prepared by the Society for the Regulation of the Missionaries and Schoolmasters in the Discharge of their Respective Duties, which Rules and Instructions however shall, for the reasons already mentioned be inspected and approved by His Majesty's Superintendant of Indian Affairs, previous to their Establishment. In drawing up these Instructions, particular Care should be taken to caution the Missionaries and Schoolmasters to be prudent in their Conduct, and to avoid whatever might give offence to the Indians, or awaken their Jealousy. Diligence in their Station, Sobriety, Gentleness, Condescension, and a disinterested Regard to the Welfare of the Indians, should be recommended, and that they sedulously inculcate Principles of Loyalty among their Hearers, Converts and Pupils.

VI. The last Article I shall mention as necessary to compleat this Plan, and make it more extensively useful, is the erecting a College or Seminary in the old Oneida Town, where the Young Indians who are distinguished for their Genius, may repair for a more enlarged Education, and be fitted for the Ministry. Very few of the Indians can be prevailed on to let their Children go any great Distance for Instruction, and when they are persuaded to it, the Children always go with Reluctance. They are continually anxious to return to their Parents and Brethren, which is an Obstruction to their literary Progress; and when they return to their own People they generally run into the greater Excesses for their former Restraints.

It is therefore a mistaken Notion that Seminaries at a Distance from the Indians and only among Christians, are fittest for the Education of Indian Youths. Besides the Difficulty of bringing them to such Seminaries, and the small Degree of Improvement they carry from them, it serves to raise their Jealousy, and the Transition is too great and too sudden, from their former mode of Life, to that which they must hereby enter upon. Any Change in the Manners of a Savage People, who have an high Sense of liberty, like the Iroquois, should be gradually effected. It should in some measure be the Result of their own Choice, as being apparently expedient, not of any Violence; which will not fail to rivet them firmly to their Customs, and shut their Minds against Reason and Conviction. The Indian Country is evidently the properest Place to fix a Seminary for this Purpose, where the Parents can frequently see their Children; by which all Uneasiness would be removed from both, and those other Inconveniences avoided. It would also be pleasing to the Indians in general. They would look upon it as a Mark of our Regard, and Confidence in them. This would serve to reconcile them to the Instructions and Discipline of a College; and induce them to encourage the Institution, even from a Principle of Gratitude. But I shall not enlarge on this Head, as this Seminary is not immediately necessary. It must be the Work of Time; after the other Parts of the preceding Plan are carried into Execution, and a considerable Progress is made in each.

The political situation of the period made it hopeless to expect any results on the part of the government, and the memorial was soon forgotten. But it served to emphasize that regretful policy of governmental indifference to the Indian, which began with the British in the colonial period, and continued for a shamefully long time thereafter.

CHAPTER XI

THE SOCIETY'S CATECHISING SCHOOL IN THE CITY OF NEW YORK, AND THE ALLIED NEGRO SCHOOL OF THE BRAY ASSOCIATES

There was no phase of the colonial work in which the Society evinced greater interest than in the religious instruction of the slaves, and none which met with more drawbacks in the Plantations. With few exceptions slave owners did not look favorably upon any plan of instruction, believing that it would develop insubordination on the part of the subjected race. The officials of the Society were extremely concerned in the evangelization of these benighted creatures, though at no time did this sympathy arouse any sentiment for their emancipation. In fact the followers of the Church and the agents of the Society were frequently included among the owners of slaves. The legal and economic status, being altogether a political issue, was not called in question. But the excluding of any persons from the enjoyment of its benefactions because of race or color, was ever repudiated by the Society.

The instruction of the Negro and Indian slaves was an explicit charge early resolved upon by the Society and repeatedly made to missionaries and schoolmasters.[1] The Society attempted to secure a Parliamentary Act by which owners of slaves would be *obliged* to provide them with religious instruction.[2] Failing in this, other means were resorted to. In 1726 when the movement had declined in the colonies, the Lord Bishop of London prepared for the Society a "Letter to the Masters and Mistresses in the English Plantations abroad, earnestly exhorting them to encourage and promote the Instruction of their Negroes in the Christian Faith"; and a similar letter to the missionaries, ap-

[1] See previous instructions, p. 58.
[2] Classified Digest, *op. cit.*, p. 64.

pealing for their active co-operation in influencing the aforesaid masters and mistresses.[3] These were distributed throughout the Plantations to the number of 12,000 copies,[4] and served to increase interest among Episcopalian slave-owners. The emphasis given the subject in England resulted in a number of special grants to this particular branch of work. Various benefactions, ranging from £50 to £1,000, are recorded in the Society's minutes between 1729 and 1750. In 1744 this special fund was more than £2500, in cash and "old So Sea Anny Stock."[5]

In the Province of New York the Society devoted considerable labor to the care of the slaves as well as to the Indians and the colonists. The missionaries generally took pains to catechise the slaves in so far as they were able to do so with their other duties. A number of catechists were employed during the century to assist the missionaries in some of the extensive parishes. It was their duty, in nearly all cases, to instruct the Negroes in the Church catechism and prayers, and to hold services in the different parts of the parish, in lieu of the missionary. For the most part the catechists appointed in New York were thus engaged. Their instruction was usually given on Sunday, and was hardly more than the oral reciting of the prayers and catechism, until these were thoroughly known by the catechumens. Occasionally the work of the catechist was combined with that of the schoolmaster, as has been noted in earlier chapters. But in some of the larger cities of the colonies, for instance, New York, Philadelphia, and Charleston, distinct "Catechising schools" were opened in which training in reading was added to the usual *memoriter* work. Because of the latter activity, it seems advisable to the writer to include the school in New York City. He does this on the ground that, in its operations, it was sufficiently differentiated from the purely religious services to warrant such a course. On the other hand, it should be pointed out that encouragement in reading was wholly incidental to the main purpose of the catechising school, and found a place there only because it contributed in an essential way to that purpose.

---

[3] March 17, 1726–7, S. P. G. Journal, V, p. 119.
[4] *Ibid.*, V, p. 125.
[5] *Ibid*, IX, p. 240.

The catechising school was opened in the city of New York in 1704 by Elias Neau.[6] Mr. Neau was a native of France. For confessing the Protestant faith he had been several years confined in prison there, after which he had been forced to serve in the galley for seven years.[7] He then settled in New York as a merchant.[8] His interest in the work of the religious societies began with the S. P. C. K. In 1701 he corresponded with its officials concerning affairs in the Province,[9] and later with members of the S. P. G. Mr. Neau's particular sympathy was for the slaves, which occasioned the society to offer him the appointment of catechist for the Province.[10] Rev. Mr. Vesey was strongly opposed to him, and this,[11] together with Neau's inadequate knowledge of English, made him decline the position.[12] In 1704 he was finally prevailed upon to accept the office for the city of New York alone, through the renewed urging of the Society and Lord Cornbury.[13] The Society's allowance for the position was £50 a year.[14] Licenses were issued to Mr. Neau by Lord Cornbury in August 1704, and by the Bishop of London at a subsequent date.[15] The Governor's license authorized Neau to catechise children generally and other persons who might come. It reads as follows:

"*To the worthy Mr. Elias Neau, greeting:*

"Reposing special trust and confidence in your ability, prudence and integrity, have nominated, constituted and appointed, and do hereby nominate, constitute and appoint you, the said Elias Neau, to be catechist in the city of New York, and do hereby give and grant unto you full license and power to catechise all children, Indians, negroes and other persons within the said city. Given under my hand and seal at Fort Anne in New York this twenty-fourth day of August 1704.

"CORNBURY."[16]

---

[6] About August 1704, S. P. G. Letter-book, A, 2, p. 19.

[7] *Ibid.*, A, 2, p. 21; Lambeth Archives, 841, fol. 18 ff. Classified Digest, *op. cit.*, p. 63.

[8] *Ibid.*, A, 2, p. 40; Lambeth Archives, *ibid.*

[9] Allen and McClure, *op. cit.*, pp. 120–21.

[10] S. P. G. Journal, I, p. 98. Jan. 15, 1702–3.

[11] Vesey to Sec., S. P. G. Letter-book, A, 2, pp. 20, 40, 26, Mr. Vesey was acting on his own interest herein; for he desired an assistant in the Church, which Neau could not accept, not having been ordained. *Ibid.* Ill feeling between the two men existed for many years. And Neau charged Vesey with veiled antagonism to the school. *Ibid.*, A, 4, p. 68; Journal, II, p. 243.

[12] *Ibid.*, I., p. 167; Letter-book, A, 2, p. 1.

[13] Neau to Sec., S. P. G. Letter-book, A, 2, p. 19, Aug. 29, 1704.

[14] S. P. G. Journal, I, p. 108.

[15] *Ibid.*, I, p. 194; Letter-book, A, 4, p. 68, May 18, 1705.

[16] From Mss. Deeds in the office of the Sec. of State, X, p. 27—quoted by Pratt, *op. cit.*, p. 91.

The Bishop's license enpowered him to act as "Schoolmaster & Catechist of the Negroes & Indians in New York."[17]

In order to devote his entire time to the work, Mr. Neau gave up active management of his business, and left the French Church, where he had been an Elder, to conform fully to the Church of England.[18] Speaking of the qualifications of the catechist, Rev. John Sharpe, chaplain of the Fort, declared him "the best qualified for it of any could be found."[19] His unwearied activity and earnestness of purpose are so thoroughly indicated in his letters to the Society, and so well attested by others, that it is doubtful if the Society ever engaged a more devoted agent in all its colonial work. Said Mr. Sharpe: "He is a person of great humility which is the foundation of all virtue. He can condescend familiarity to discurse with those poor slaves who are put to the vilest drudgeries & consequently esteemed the scum and offscouring of Men. . . . He is a person of great zeal for this pious Work; It was this which prompted him at first to the Undertaking upon the base allowance of £50 p^r^ Ann. when in the way of trade being a Merchant and in Considerable business he could have cleared three times that sum yearly. Yet he willingly divested himself of this secular affair that he might better attend on this. . . . He has taken great pains in collecting out of such as have wrote on the Church Catechism and digesting into form the Historical part of the Scriptures for the use of his Catechumens. . . . No doubt his being a confessor in the Gallies and prisons for the faith he labours to instruct them in gives him great advantage. . . . Lastly, his Resolution and perseverance in the work has been truly wonderful, they see him hated, ridiculed and even spitefully used by his Christian Brethren for this Work's sake. . . . They find him constantly attend his stated hours of Instruction be there many or few that come to hear him. . . . They see him creeping into Garrets, Cellars and other nauseous places to exhort and pray by the poor slaves when they are sick; and . . . that his house is full of hospitality and good works."[20]

---

[17] S. P. G. Journal, I, pp. 192, 194.

[18] S. P. G. Letter-book, A, 2, p. 21; A, 3, p. 80.

[19] Lambeth Archives, 841 fol. 18.

[20] From a paper proposing, "A Publick School," "A Publick Library" and "A Catechising Chappel" in the city of New York, by Rev. Mr. Sharpe, March 11, 1712–13. Lambeth Archives, 841, fol. 18 ff.

In 1705 Mr. Neau reported to the Society in the following words: "Mr. Vesey himself read a Note . . . in the Church in Form of an Exhortation to the masters and Mistresses to take care to send me their Slaves every Wednesday Friday and Sunday at Five o'clock in ye Evening, to the end that I may teach them ye Principles of our Holy Religion, they send me to the Number of Thirty as you will see by the List of ye Catechisms that I have distributed among them, the which I send here inclosed. These People come in such great Numbers, Sunday only: Wednesdays and Fridays there comes but Eight or Ten sometimes more & sometimes less."[21] In the list, which is shown herewith, we may see to what a preponderant extent the school catered to the Negroes.

The names of the Masters & Mistresses that have sent me their Blacks to Catechise and to whom I have given Catechisms & other good Books as follows.

My Lord Cornbury	1 Mulatress I gave her		2 Catechisms &	2 other Books
Mr Vesey	2 Negroesses		2 Do	2.2 Letters
Mr. Wm. Leaths	2 Negress's	1 Indian	3 Do	3.3 Do
Mr. Rbr Wandil	1 Negress		1 Ditto	1 Do
Mrs. Widow Keep	1 Negress		1 Ditto	1.1 Do
Capt Trevet	1 Negress		1 Ditto	1.1 Do
Mr. Stanton	1 Negress		1 Ditto	1.1 Ditto
Mr. Joseph Smith	1 Negress		1 Ditto	1.1 Ditto
Mr. Dudols	1 Negress	1 Negro	2 Catechisms	2.2 Letters
Mr. Crook	1 Negress	1 Negro	2 Do	2.2 Do
Mr. Skenlour		1 Negro	1 Ditto	1.1 Do
Mr. Mool		1 Negro	1 Dirto	1.1 Do
Mr. Daniel Cromelin	1 Negress		1 Ditto	1.1 Do
Mr. Wilson Sheriff		1 Negro	1 Ditto	1.1 Do
Mrs. Jourdain	1 Negress		1 Ditto	1.1 Do
Mr. Francorier	1 Negress	1 Negro	2 Ditto	
Mr. DeNeak		1 Negro	1 Ditto	
Mr. Burgins		1 Negro	1 Ditto	
Mr. George Milan		1 Negro	1 Ditto	
Mr. Boarn Bown		1 Negro	1 Ditto	
Mr. Abraham Keep	1 Negress		1 Ditto	
Mr. Brodfurt	1 Negress	1 Negro	2 Ditto	
Mr. Vandain	1 Negress		1 Ditto	
Mr. Morin	1 Negress		1 Ditto	
Mr. Allaire	1 Negress		1 Ditto	
Mr. Isaac Nephtaly	1 Negress		1 Ditto	
Mr. Henry Shephers	1 Negress		1 Ditto	
Mrs. Blockgross	1 Negress		1 Ditto	
Mr. Richard Laurins	1 Negress		1 Ditto	
Col. Depatris		1 Negro	1 Ditto	
Col. Morice		1 Negro	1 Ditto	
Mr. Bloom	1 Negress		1 Ditto	
Mr. Mindar	1 Negress		1 Ditto	
Mr. John Vincent	1 Negress		1 Ditto	
Mrs. Van Vosse		2 Negroes	2 Ditto	
Mrs. Harcomb	1 She Indian	2 Indians	2 Ditto	
	Women 28	Men 18	46 Books.[22]	

[21] Oct. 3, 1705, S. P. G. Letter-book, A, 2, p. 124.
[22] *Ibid.*

One month later Mr. Neau said, in writing: "I had a good Number of Scholars, that made me hope I should be forced to bring them to Church under ye Tower, because my Room could not hold them all, which was what Mr. Vesey and I resolved to do, but instead of ye Numbers increasing it has been much diminisht for ye most that come on Sundays are between 12 & 20 and Wednesdays and Fridays 6, 8 or 10."[23] In fact Neau at first went from house to house to instruct and afterwards gathered them at his own house. Col. Heathcote said of this: "As for my Thoughts of the Society having appointed that good man Mr. Neau as Catechist to ye Negroes & Indians 'tis undoubtedly a very good work & he is wonderfully industrious in the discharge of his Duty & ye truth is takes more pains than he needs by going from House to House to perform that office & I believe he would find it as affectual to gain ye End & not ye fourth part of ye trouble to himself, to appoint set times in having them together at ye English Church or at least so many at once may be proper & Catechise & instruct them."[24]

By 1706 the masters of slaves began to show great fear lest, through the act of Baptism, the slaves should be made free. Neau found it necessary to urge legislation on this subject to prevent a complete withdrawal of his pupils. As a result the Assembly decreed in the fall of 1706, that the legal status of the slave should be in no way altered by his evangelization.[25]

The effect of the legislation was seen at once, for in 1707 Neau reported: "I must begin in telling you Sr that last Autumn I took the Liberty to send you two samples of the Act of Assembly, in favour of the Instruction of Slaves, since that time the number of my catechumens is mightily augmented, so that I have now above 100 altho' they never come all at a time, I have furnished the second story of my Lodgings with Forms for their use; The Room Sr is 48 foot long and 22 broad, so that in Summer it will hold conveniently 200 Persons and in Winter above 300. what is most inconvenient in this, I am obliged to receive them every night by the Candle because they work all day long, except on Sundays at which time they come after the Second Sermon,

---

[23] Nov. 15, 1705, *ibid.*, A, 2, p. 125.

[24] *Ibid.*, A, 2, p. 117. The Church was not used for the work, save the steeple. The former had to be kept clean for the congregation, Mr. Sharpe reported.

[25] Col. Laws of N. Y., I., p. 597; S. P. G. Letter-book, A, 2 p. 167; A, 3, pp. 80, 81.

altho' in the Winter, that is also by Candlelight, as well as on the other days I have changed the Method I took in the beginning a little, or rather changed nothing, but have added a few things as Prayers & Singing of Psalms, that encourages both them and me, for I represent to them that God plac'd them in the world only for his Glory and that in praying and singing those divine Praises one doth in part obey his Commands, I observe with pleasure that they strive who shall sing best." . . . "Catechising days are Wednesdays, Fridays, & Saturdays. I would Catechise them much oftener, but their masters desire me not to keep them long; I keep them always two hours in Summer, but longer in Winter."[26] In the fall of that year the number had increased to 200, "of both Sexes & all ages."[27]

In 1710 Mr. Neau reported that about twenty young people of the town, "apprentices and young Boys and Girls" were coming to him daily and had done so for three months; and, there being too many at a time, he found it necessary to appoint two days in a week for the girls.[28] With the exception of the indifferent attitude of masters, satisfactory reports continued to be sent until 1712, when an uprising of Negroes in the city almost broke up the school. Bitter prejudices were created by charges that the school had been the main cause of the trouble. Mr. Sharpe thus described these events:

The late barbarous Massacre attempted by the slaves April 1712 gave strength at first to this clamour which had a full run for many days. The School was charged as the cause of the Mischief, the place of Conspiracy and that instruction had made them cunning and insolent.

The Catechist and all that were known to favour this design were reproached, and the flagitious villany was imputed to the Catechumens yet upon the strictest inquiry and severest tryal, where the bare affirmation of infidel Evidence who are not capable of any other tye to veracity was sufficient to fix the guilt, there were not any found Actors or Accomplices in the Conspiracy who had duly attended the Catechetical instruction, but two were accused one of which had been formerly baptised and he dyed protesting his innocence, and was, (but too late for him) pityed and declared guiltless even by the Prosecutors. The other had made some proficience, but was not admitted to Baptism thro' the reluctancy of his Master whom he had often solicited for it. He was an eminent Merchant and with his son were both murdered in the Streets. This Negro was hung in chains alive. I went to see him after he had hung five days he declared to me he was innocent of the murder with

[26] July 24, 1707, *ibid.*, A, 3, p. 128. Neau reported about 1,000 slaves in the town in 1706, *ibid.*, A, 2, p. 167.

[27] *Ibid.*, A, 3, p. 181.

[28] July 5, 710, *ibid.*, A, 5, p. 134. In 1711 he "had not so many apprentices as he had but this varies very much according to the pleasure of the youth." *Ibid.*, A, 6, p. 87.

a seeming concern for his Masters misfortune. He was often delirous by long continuance in that painful posture thro' hunger thirst and pain but he then answered directly to what I enquired and called me by my name so that I might conclude he had some intervals of the exercise of his reason.

One would believe that such a happy instance as the innocency of the few who frequented the School should take away this prejudice but it still remains and was last winter improved by imaginary plotts contrived on purpose by some ill men to hinder the good work which was by amusing the people to keep them within in the Evening which is the only time they are at Liberty from their Masters employ to attend on the School. The Devil finds his kingdom of darkness invaded and rages because his time is but short, 'tis no wonder therefore that he stirs up his instruments to oppose it.[29]

At the time the poor catechist could not venture out of his house, but the Governor and the clergy came to his defense and he was able to resume.[30] In 1713 the school continued "in spite of opposition,"[31] and Mr. Neau requested to be supplied with two hundred A. B. C's with the CH. Catechism" for his catechumens.[32] His next letter acknowledged the books. Having distributed these he desired others. It would be very advantageous if he could have the additional books, he declared, "because the children of the Masters who came to School teach their Negroes the Creed & Lord's Prayer by reading sometimes in the English Catechism, which also serves for an A. B. C. and to learn to read."[33] At the close of 1714 Mr. Neau sent the following curious enrolment of slaves, giving an incomplete list of those instructed by him during his ten years of service. The list does not include the white boys and girls, many of whom were still in attendance.[34] As arranged by the catechist, it is given below:

"The Names of ye Masters and Mistresses of ye Slaves which have been to my School from ye year 1704, till now and notice must be taken where it is said had, signifies they come no more or that their masters or they themselves are dead."

---

[29] Lambeth Archives, 841, fol. 18 ff.

[30] S. P. G. Journal, II, p. 233; Letter-book, A, 8 p. 224.

[31] *Ibid.*, A, 8, p. 173.

[32] *Ibid.*, A, 8, p. 174.

[33] Apr. 12, 1714, S. P. G. Journal III, p. 7. "I have visited Mr. Neau's School and am glad to acquaint that the good man is faithful in the discharge of his duty & ye Slaves are well instructed—he hath likewise several apprentices and white children in his School." Rev. Thomas Barclay to Sec., Oct. 22, 1714, S. P. G. Letter-book, A, 9, p. 158.

[34] Nov. 16, 1715, S. G. P. Journal, III, p. 67.

		Negro men	Negro women	Indian men	Indian women
All Baptised	His Excellency my Lord Cornbury had		1		
	His Exccy Coll. Robt Hunter	3	1		
	The Revd Mr. Vesey our Rector had	1	2		
All Baptised	Mr. Wm. Leathes had		2	1	
	Mr. Wm. Keat	1	1		
	Mr. Travet had	1			
	Mr. Stampton had	1			
	Mr. Joseph Smith		1		
1 Baptised	Mr. Gabriel Ludlos had	1	1		
	Mr. Sikulour	1			
	Mr. Mowl had	1			
	Mr. Daniel Cromelin	1	2		
Baptised	Mr. Ebenezer Wilson had	1			
	Mrs. Jourdin had	1	1		
	Mr. ffauconnier had	1	1		
	Mr. De Neak	1			
	Mr. Burgnis	1	1		
	Mr. Millard	1			
	Mr. Bueno had		1		
1 Baptised	Mrs. ffeurt	1	1		
2 Baptised	Mr. Vandan		2		
	Mr. Peter Morin had	1			
	Mr. Mephtaly had		1		
2 Baptised	Mr. Alexander Alaire had	1	2		
	Mr. Henry Sheppard had	1			
	Mr. Benjamin Blackgrosshad	1			
	Mr. Paul Richard	1	1		
1 Baptised	Coll. Abraham Depoyster	1			1
	Mrs. Horn Bloom		1		
3 Baptised	Mrs. Christiana Venvoss hath constantly	3	1		
	Mr. John Vincent	1			
	Mrs. Marcomb had	0	1	1	1
	Mr. Abraham Jouneau	1	1		
Molato	Mr. Carbell had				1
	Mr. Philipe	1			
	Mr. John Barbarie had	1	2		1
	Mr. Lagrane had	1			
	Mr. Wm. Tellor	1			
Baptised	Mr. George Natten	1			
	Mr. Leipinars had	1			
	Mr. John Keipt had	1	1		
	Coll. Whinam had			1	1
	Mr. Theobalds	1	2		1
	Mr. Havit had	1	1		
	Mr. Saml Moen had	2	2		
	Mr. David Jemminson had		1		
	Mr. Woolley had		1		
	Mr. David Provost had	1			
	Mr. Robert Walter		1		
	Mr. Hogland	2			
	Mr. Derick de Neack had	1			

			Negro men	Negro women	Indian men	Indian women
	Mr. Jacob Morrice	had		1		
	Mrs. Helena Cooper			1		
	Mr. John Cazal	had				1
	Mr. Eleans	had		1		
	Mrs. Susanna Tooet	had		1		
Baptised	Mr. Thomas Robert		1			
1 Baptised	Mr. Cornelius Depoyster		1	1		
1 Baptised	Mr. John Vanhorn		1		1	
	Mr. Joseph Baker	had		1		
	Dr. Pattison	had		1		
	Mr. John Ellison	had	1		1	
	Mr. Elias Nesearan	had	3	1		
	Mr. Glincross	had		1		
	Mr. Aspinwal	had		1		
	Mr. Clark	had			1	
	Mrs. Gerse	had		1		
	Mr. Hoatman	had		1		
	Mr. Palmiton			1		
	Mr. Hemet	had	1			
1 Baptised	James Neau	had	1	1		
	Mrs. Haran	had		1		
Baptised	A ffree Negro Woman Margaret			1		
Baptised	A ffree Indian Woman Janston					1
Baptised	Mr. Isaac Depyster		1			
	Mr. Stilwell		1			
Baptised	Mr. Boinot	had	1			
	Mr. ffraineau		4			
	Mrs. Vansure		1			
1 Baptised	Mr. Abraham Vanghorn		2			
	Mr. Stephan				1	
2 Baptised	Mr. Alexander Moor			1	1	
Molatto	Mrs. Marett					1
	Coll. Bayard	had	1			
1 Baptised	Mr. Elias Jamin	had	1	1		
	Mr. Cornelius Low		1			
	Mr. Thomas Gifield	had	1			
Baptised	Mr. Peter Chapneau		1			
Baptised	Mrs. Mary Lawrence			1		
	Mr. Maston	had		1		
	Mr. Thomas Bayeux		1	1		
	Mr. Benjamin Harette		1			
	Mr. Daval	had	1			
	Mr. Minville		1			
	Mrs. Davis	had	2			
Baptised	Mrs. Droyer			1		
	Mr. Dupuy		1			
	Mr. John David		1			
	Mr. Renehet		1			
1 Baptised	Mr. Thomas Tarpy		1	1		
	Mr. John Van Noreden		1			
1 Baptised	Mr. Boarn Bonn		2			
Baptised	Mr. Boarn Rindell		1			
2 Baptised	Mrs. Glaivis			2		
All Baptised	Mr. Vaneliff		1	3		
Baptised	Mr. Lancaster Syms			1		
Baptised	A freeman Peter the Porter		1			

		Negro men	Negro women	Indian men	Indian women
	Mr. John Bristick	1			
	Mr. Samuel Bristick			1	
	Mrs. Thotel		1		
1 Baptised	Col. Heathcote		1		1
	Mr. Henry Swift		1		
Baptised	Jannote a Mollato man			1	
		85	*45	10	10
			*69		

If I had not left off from taking their names I should have more.

ELIAS NEAU.

New York. Ober ye 6th 1714."[35]

In March, 1718, Mr. Neau was suddenly dismissed by the Society on the ground of his being engaged in trade.[36] The action was seemingly induced by some of the old enemies and doubtless had the sanction of Mr. Vesey. Mr. Huddleston was asked to take charge of the work. But prompt testimonials from the Governor, missionaries and other gentlemen caused an immediate reversal of the order.[37] In the interval, however, Neau forwarded an additional list of his slaves, as follows:

"An Accot of ye Number of my black Catechumens since and beside the list Ive Sent to Mr. Taylor on the 19th of Nov. 1714 which ought to be added to yt former accot because Severall Negroes baptized & unbaptiz'd do constantly Come to School here be also the Same Masters name of Several because they have more Slaves or their young are fitt to be instructed and by yt I am oblidged to write ye name but not ye Same Servant.

---

[35] S. P. G. Letter-book, A, 10, p. 220. Correction not in original.

[36] S. P. G. Journal, III, p. 348.

[37] *Ibid.*, IV., p. 43; Letter-book, A, 13, p. 491. For one of the memorials in defense of Neau, see *ibid.*, A, 13, p. 44.

Masters & Mistresses Names	Negro Men	Negro Women	Negro Boys	Negro Girls	Mulato Men	Mulato Women	Indian Men	Indian Women	
Mr. Gairard Comfort	1								
Mr. Sam^{ll} Suing							1		
Mr. Nichs Rosbell	1								
Mr. Isaac Keep	1								
Mr. John Hardenburg Jun.		1						1	
Mr. Jacob Harstead							1		
Mr. Ripp Vandam			1						Baptized
Mr. Abra^{m} Plainters	1								
Mr. Jno. Vanderhill					1				
Mr. Abr Laftrus		1							
Agara free Black woman		1							Baptized
Mr. Thos. Clark		1						1	
Mr. Jno. Right	2								Both Baptized John & James
Mr. La grange	1								
Mr. Alex. More			1	1			1		
Mr. John van forest	1								
Mr. Joseph Read	1								
Mr. Nathl Maston		1							Baptized Eliz.
Mr. Simon Saurman		1							Baptiz'd
Mr. fanconnier Junr					1				
Mr. Jno. Read	1								
Mr. fanconnier Sen		1							Baptiz'd Eliz.
Mr. Jno. More		1							
Mr. Jno. Cock	1								
Mr. Benj. Charitte			1						Baptized aigur
Mr. Charles Oliver	1								
A free negro woman		1							Baptized Mary
A free negro		1							
Mr. John Cazle	1	1							
Mr. Antony White	1								
Mrs. de Kay	1								
Mrs. Robert		1							
Mr. George Clarke	1								
Mr. John Barbery	1								
Mr. Thomas Norson							1		
Mr. Vesey	1								Baptized 25 yrs old
Mrs. Gravenratt					1				Baptized John 20 yrs old
Mr. Justice Bush	1								
Mr. John Mead				1					Baptized Eliz.
Mr. John Harris							1		
Mr. Living Stone	1								
Mr. Charles Cremelain			1						
Mr. John Bachan			1						
Mr. Jno. Tinch	1								
Mr. John Vaughan	1								
Mr. David Jennison			1						
Mr. Dick Dyforl	1								

Masters & Mistresses Names	Negro Men	Negro Women	Negro Boys	Negro Girls	Mulato Men	Mulato Women	Indian Men	Indian Women	
Mr. Johanis Myer	1								
Mr. John Wail	1								
A free Mollato					1				Baptized John 20 yrs old
Mr. John Ball				1					
A free negro woman		1							Baptized
Mr. Abram Evans			1						
	25	13	*6	3	4		5	2	
			*7						

Mr. Vesey hath baptized severall Children but I do not Take the account of them because they don't Come to School. This is only the Catechumens I have since my last acc^{t} but I have as much more again of the old Catechumens who come constantly to be instructed.

New York may the first 1718. ELIAS NEAU."[38]

"My School," wrote the catechist in 1719, "doth enlarge dayly now, since I receiv'd the copy of y^{r} last letter. I have severall new Scholars of all ages, and the old comes cheerfully to me to be instructed, so my School is in as good a prospect as before it has been."[39] It was still made up of whites and blacks. The latter numbered 83 in constant attendance. His list, when classified by approximating the ages, shows us a preponderant proportion of adults,—there being 65 to 18 children. For example

"A List of the Catechumens Slaves which come constantly to my School since I am reinstated in the office of Catechist besides the white apprentice boys and girls.

[38] May 2, 1718, *ibid.*, A, 13, p. 422. Correction not in original.

[39] Oct. 8, 1719, *ibid.*, A, 13, p. 479.

Masters & Mistresses Names	Negro Men	Their Ages by Guess	Negro Women	Their Ages by Guess	Negro Boys	Negro Girls	
Coll. Depeyter	1	45 yrs.	2	50, 35 yrs.			the Negr Man Bap. & Comt.
Capt. Isaac Depetyr	1	30 yrs.					He is Baptised Anthony
Mr. Jacobus Vincross	3	20, 25 yrs.	1	50 yrs.			ye Men Bap. Jephty Robt & Jno.
Mr. Dr. Cromelin	1	24 yrs.			1		
Mr. Vandam	1	30 yrs.	2	40 yrs. 30	1		The women & boy Bapt. Susannah Lillie & Jacob
Mr. Philip Scuyler			1	25 yrs.			A communicant.
Mr. Glaves			1	35 yrs.		1	Both Baptized
Mrs. Rattray			2	45, 24 yrs.			Both Commts Mary, Sarah
Mrs. Narett			1	22			Baptized Annah
Mr. Hardinbourg	1	20					Baptized Cesar
Mary black free woman			1	45			Baptized
Aigar Do			1	40			Baptized
Mr. Th. Robert	1	25					Baptized
Magdalin free womn			1	25			Baptized
Mr. Catale	1	26	1	25			Woman Baptized
Mr. Minville	1	35	1	50			Woman Baptized
Corne Depetyr	1	30					Baptized
Mr. Vanhorn	1	30					
Andr Fanecan	1	30					
Dr. Dupey	2	30, 28	2	25, 40			One man Baptized
Abrah. Vanghorn	2	65, 30					One Communicant
Mr. Bone	2	28, 30					Both Baptized
Mr. Rindell	1	26					Communicant
Mr. Alex. Moore			1	22			
Mr. Sim. Soumin			1	30			Baptized
Mr. Harrison					1		
Mrs. Droyer			1	25			Baptized
Mr. Wright	2	35, 30					Baptized John & George
Mr. Drick de Neack	2	30, 27					Baptized Jno & Oliver
Mr. Jno. Read	1	35					
Mr. Jos. Read	1	30					
Annah free bl. Wn			1	45			
Mr. Conardao Comfort	1	22					
Mr. Bachan					1		
Mr. Gerr Vanhorn			1	35			
Mr. Ed. Elsward			1	25			Baptized Dorothy
Mr. Bayeur	1	40	1	35	2	1	All Baptized
Mr. Renehett					1		
Mrs. Marit					1	1	
Mr. Abrh Evans					1		
Mad. Ingoldhoes	1	28					
Mr. Governour						2	
Mrs. Bloom						1	
Mr. Derick Defort					1	1	
Mr. Amilton	1	28					
Henry Lane	2	30, 26					
Cornel Vanhorn	1	20					
Jacobus Courland	1	35					
Adoph Philip	1	40					
Dr. Couling			1	35			
Mr. Congrove			1	30			
Mrs. Dekey			1	40			
Mr. Vanderhill	1	24					
Mr. Jno. Roswell						1	
Mr. Jer. Reading	1	27					
Dec. 23, 1719	*37		*28		*12	8	Elias Neau S."[40]
	*38		*27		*10		

[40] Inclosed in Neau's letter Jan. 22, 1719–20, *ibid.*, A, 14, p. 141. Corrections not in original.

The last reports of Mr. Neau's work were sent shortly before his death in 1722.[41] In April he reported: "My School dos prosper by ye Blessing of God for the Number of my Catechumens increase daily in both Sexes Men & Women I thought to have some Baptized at Easter but their Masters declin'd to give their Consent I have put them off, for Whitsunday week during wch time I hope to prepare more of them more poor Black Creatures, I would be much obliged to the Venerable Society if they were pleased to order 300 or 400 Copies of ye Church Catechism to be sent to me for the use of my Catechumens *with the alphabet in it* because ye Children of their Master reading once or twice ye Creed & the 10 Commandmts with the Lords Prayer every day they will learn ye sooner & that doth incourage their Masters to give their approbation to their christning & even their own Children learn our Church Catechism ye sooner by that."[42] To the above he added, in what appears to be his last report: "Several Negroes learn at home ye Catechism, & some learn to read."[43]

The Society made generous gifts of books to the school. Not only responding to the requests already noted, several packets of Catechisms, two hundred in each, were dispatched.[44] In the case of many of his catechumens, he once reported, there was "nobody in their Master's houses to teach them, a deficiency which he desired his school to make up by the supply of proper books.[45] Hence his various requests for books combining the features of primer and catechism. From such evidence as the writer has been able to review, it does not seem possible to hold that the technique of reading had a regular place in the catechising school. It was encouraged as far as possible by means of providing books adapted to that purpose, and, as is highly probable, occasional attention was given to it by the catechist. It is evident, too, that reading was practiced. The ultimate goal was, of course, to learn the prayers and the catechism by heart, but, as an aid to this, books were frequently opened for the additional stimulus of the printed page.

---

[41] Mr. Vesey on Oct. 4, 1722, reported Neau's death. It therefore occurred in the summer or fall of that year. *Ibid.*, A, 16, p. 209.

[42] *Ibid.*, A, 16, p. 196. Italics not in original.

[43] May 22, 1722, *ibid.*, A, 16, p. 204; Journal IV, p. 249.

[44] *Ibid.*, I, pp. (91), (103), (133).

[45] Feb. 28, 1708-9, S. P. G. Letter-book, A, 4, p. 121a.

The presence of the white apprentices, no doubt, added to the proficiency of the work. It is unfortunate that more details have not been given regarding these apprentices, for it would be interesting to know whether they were the former pupils of Mr. Huddleston, who, having been discharged and apprenticed to trades, were coming to Mr. Neau for religious ministration. If this was the case, they had already acquired the ability to read. On the other hand, some of these white children apparently could not read. In one of Neau's requests for the A B C catechisms, he specifically stated that they were for the English catechumens.[46] The writer is inclined to believe that there was a group of apprentice children receiving instruction from Mr. Neau for the first time, and distinct from the scholars in Mr. Huddleston's school, which could not possibly have attended to all of this kind of instruction. Again, the writer believes, that apprentices from the charity school also attended Mr. Neau for the religious features of his service. It seems indeed that at this time there was no religious service to which the slaves and apprentices of the Episcopalian adherents were admitted, except the catechising school. The records of Trinity Vestry show no assignment of seats in the church for either class, as such, or for Mr. Neau's pupils; whereas they do for the pupils of Mr. Huddleston. Furthermore, Neau complained of Mr. Vesey's attitude towards the Negro catechumens, saying that "he would not suffer any of them to have a place in his Church."[47]

For two years after Mr. Neau's death, Mr. Huddleston took charge of the School, "following Neau's Methods of Instruction," and attended it with the diligence and earnestness characteristic of his other service.[48] Mr. Vesey, in the meantime, renewed his efforts to secure for the position a man in Holy Orders, who might also be made an assistant to the Rector. The plan met with the approval of the Society and Rev. James Wetmore was assigned to the position.[49] He received a joint salary from the Society and Trinity Church. From this time until 1764 the

[46] S. P. G. Letter-book, A, 8, p. 174.

[47] *Ibid.*, A, 11, p. 294. But Mr. Vesey and the Church eventually allowed the negro catechumens to attend the "publick service of the Church." *Ibid.*, A, 21, p. 376, Dec. 23, 1728.

[48] "My Spouse comonly had in his Evening School 50 or 60 Negro Slaves & sometimes more, besides Children & Servts." Mrs. Huddleston to Sec., *ibid.*, A, 19, p. 411.

[49] Feb. 21, 1723-4, S. P. G. Journal, IV, p. 295.

work was carried on by a succession of missionaries, whose chief duty seems to have been the parochial work of the Church. The catechising school continued to be held as usual on Wednesday, Friday, and Sunday evenings at Mr. Wetmore's house, and in the Church steeple before evening service on Sunday.[50] Sometimes there were "200 children and Servants" whom he instructed in the catechism and "commonly" added "some practical discourse suitable to their Capacities joined with some devotions."[51] But the enterprise did not have the enthusiasm of Mr. Neau to support it. It was not the primary object of the missionary-catechist. When in 1726 Mr. Wetmore was transferred to Rye, he reported the following decline of the school: "My Catechumens are now very few & as for the Negroes their Master choose to instruct them at home rather than venture them into Companies together." "Nor can I think" he added, "the necessity of a Missionary so great in this place as in many other parts of the Country."[52]

In petitioning for a successor to Mr. Wetmore, the need of a catechist was emphasized on the ground that there were fourteen hundred Negro and Indian slaves in the city, which made the position "as important as ever."[53] However, in addition to increasing the parochial duties he was to assume, it was stated that if he had inclination to teach a Latin school, he might find a very good account in the discharge of that office.[54] From Mr. Vesey's viewpoint, if any function was to be slighted, clearly it was the work among the slaves and catechumens. In November 1726 Rev. Thomas Colgan was appointed to the place by the Society.[55] He served until 1731.[56] Reporting in 1727 he said: "I have about 50 Catechumens most of wch are white Children but hope in a short time to have the number of Slaves augmented."[57] Through his own personal interest he did succeed in bringing into the school additional Negro catechumens. In 1728 these were about sixty in number and, as "many of them

---

[50] *Ibid.*, V, p. 29.
[51] *Ibid.*
[52] June 24, 1726, S. P. G. Letter-book, A, 19, p. 395.
[53] Vestry to Sec., July 5, 1726, *ibid.*, B, 1, p. 73.
[54] *Ibid.*
[55] S. P. G. Journal, V., p. 107.
[56] *Ibid.*, V., p. 315.
[57] S. P. G. Letter-book, A, 20, p. 185.

could read," he desired "Common Prayer books to be disposed of to such as are capable of making use of them."[58] The proficiency in reading was largely due, we may assume, to the encouragement of Elias Neau and Mr. Huddleston. The methods of Wetmore and Colgan could have included little in the way of encouraging reading ability, for they had no need of primers or such helps.

From 1731 to 1746 Rev. Richard Charlton was the catechist and assistant of the Church.[59] He evinced great interest in the work with the catechumens and was commended for his diligence and effectual care therein.[60] His early reports mention many more attending him in the summer than in the winter, but they are not explicit. "Several Negroes improve, tho' slowly," he states.[61] In 1740 the Society was told that he was "training up more than 20 Negroe children and near as many Adults in the Christian Faith . . . and besides these a great number of white Children and servants" that "diligently attend."[62] Charlton segregated the catechumens about 1741, if not before, setting aside Friday for the whites. He had ninety of these in 1742, and seventy Negroes. He reports that he had persuaded Mr. Clemm, the organist, to teach forty-three of them Psalmody, which was being done "thrice in the week in the Church";[63] but whether they were taken from one or the other group, or both, cannot be determined. In 1743 he announced that all his catechumens, especially the Negroes, greatly improved in spiritual knowledge, "the Prayer books &c sent out" having "induced several to learn to read."[64] The catechist induced Mr. Hildreth to assist in the teaching of the Negroes in 1745, and twelve were sent to him daily for that year and fifteen for the next.[65] This was the beginning of Hildreth's evening class for Negroes, which he conducted for all of ten years, and for which

---

[58] *Ibid.*, A, 21, p. 376; Journal, V, p. 197.

[59] Appointed Nov. 19, 1731, *ibid.*, V, p. 315. Became missionary at Staten Island 1747. Classified Digest, *op. cit.*, p. 855.

[60] Vesey to Sec., S. P. G. Letter-book, B, 7, p. 71.

[61] *Ibid.*, B, 1, p. 27; A, 26, p. 310.

[62] S. P. G. Journal, VIII, pp. 185–6.

[63] Oct. 30, 1741, *ibid.*, IX, p. 21; Letter-book, B, 9, p. 62. "Agreeable to your Request I send you the Number of your Catechumens that are taught Psalmody by me in the Church three Times a Weeke, which Consists of Fourty three . . . William Clemm." *Ibid.*

[64] March 28, 1743, S. P. G. Journal, IX, p. 196.

[65] S. P. G. Journal, X, pp. 112, 170.

the Society made him extra allowance.[66] His pupils were those sent to him by the catechist, being the more promising of the catechumens. Meantime Mr. Charlton reported improvement in the results of his own work. "The singing a psalm after Catechizing," he wrote, "hath produced a very good effect for it hath engaged many of the Negroes to give a closer attention in learning to read and enables them to engage in that part of the worship."[67] But he qualified this encouraging indication somewhat by saying in his next letter: "Their ignorance of the English tongue is such as will not admit of a speedy improvement."[68]

The Society made various gifts of books to Charlton's catechumens. Most of them were books for their use in the school and at the Church service, and were similar to those being given to the lay schools.[69] Simpler books were supplied through the benefaction of Trinity Church Vestry. A reprint of one of the early catechisms was ordered, and "between 2 and 300" of these were donated to Charlton.[70]

Rev. Samuel Auchmuty was appointed the Society's "Catechist to the Negroes" in 1747 at the same time taking up the functions of assistant Rector of Trinity Church.[71] He was one of the most zealous of all the S. P. G. missionaries, in respect to his work as catechist no less than in other fields. The church had grown rapidly and his time could have been wholly occupied as assistant. In the face of it, he attempted to include "all of the children of the parish in his catechising work" and, commendable as this was from the Church point of view, it necessarily involved a partial withdrawal from the Society's original intention. "I have now under my Care," he reported, "not only the Slaves which are numerous, but also the Children belonging to the Parish."[72] The slaves were assembled on Sunday only for a while,[73] but after 1750 Mr. Auchmuty visited Hil-

---

[66] See p. 102.

[67] March 26, 1746, S. P. G. Letter-book, B, 13, p. 219.

[68] Sept. 29, 1746, *ibid.*, B, 14, p. 107.

[69] S. P. G. Journal, VI, p. 133; VIII, pp. 141, 231; IX, pp. 21, 196; X., p. 222; XIII, p. 40.

[70] Charlton to Sec., July 15, 1740, *ibid.*, VIII, p. 186.

[71] July 1747, *ibid.*, X., p. 271. Mr. Auchmuty was born and educated in New England, being the son of Hon. Robert Auchmuty, Esq., Judge of the Court of Admiralty at Boston. *Ibid.*

[72] March 30, 1748, S. P. G. Letter-book, B, 15, p. 80.

[73] In his report of 1748 Auchmuty said they were not able to attend on any day but Sunday, *ibid.*, B, 16, p. 59. This was true as regards assembling during the day.

dreth's Negro class on Wednesday evenings and gave catechetical instruction to the pupils and to as many of his black catechumens as could be spared by their masters.[74] A third session was arranged still later in the new chapel of St. George's. This was "for blacks and whites."[75]

Up to 1760 his black catechumens numbered between thirty and forty as a rule.[76] To encourage them in reading he secured proper beginning texts from the Society. "If the Society," he wrote in 1751, "would indulge me so far as to send me a few Coppys of the Catechism explained for ye use of Children in a private parish in Gloucestershire, with a few more Spelling Books, I could dispose of them to my Young Blacks who I trust in God would make a good use of them."[77] To further facilitate their instruction, he "divided the blacks into 2 classes," one of which was given "Lewis' Exposition" and the other the Catechism itself.[78] In 1756 he reported: "Many of them can read very well, & are desirous of being instructed."[79]

The opening of a lay Negro school by the associates of Dr. Bray, in September 1760,[80] was an event of great importance to the Society's work among the catechumens. The most significant result was the division of the instruction between this new enterprise and the catechist. Thereafter the Negro catechumens were assembled for the usual service and catechetical exercises. To the school was assigned the work related to lay instruction. The catechist in the capacity of an overseer or inspector, visited the school frequently, hearing the pupils read and say the prayers, and giving them instructions and advice. They attended his exercises on Sunday, when he catechised them and the adult catechumens together.[81] The Negro school caused a considerable addition of young catechumens. By 1762 he reported to the Society an enrolment of between sixty and seventy in constant attendance, besides many more who occasionally

---

74 *Ibid.*, B, 17, p. 116.

75 S. P. G. Journal, XII, p. 331.

76 S. P. G. Letter-book, B, 18, p. 99; B, 20, pp. 56, 57; Journal XII., p. 245.

77 S. P. G. Letter-book, B, 20, p. 57. Fifty of the first and twent -five of the second were accordingly allowed him. Journal, XII, p. 104.

78 S.P. G. Journal XII, p. 331, Nov. 23, 1753.

79 *Ibid.*, XIII, p. 204.

80 *Ibid.*, XV, p. 169.

1 S. P. G. Letter-book, B, 2, p. 2; B, 2, p. 8.

attended.[82] They continued to increase, "and in general," said Mr. Auchmuty, "there appeared among them a greater desire for instruction" than he had observed at any previous time.[83]

Mr. Auchmuty was chosen Rector of Trinity in 1764.[84] He retained the office of catechist until 1770 when, on his advice, it was added to that of the charity schoolmaster.[85] Once a week the catechumens were assembled by the schoolmaster, where they listened to his explanation of the catechism and of suitable parts of the Scriptures. Besides this they recited the catechism with a view to perfecting themselves therein. But it was distinctly a service which Mr Hildreth conducted, designed especially for the great number of adults (about 100) who attended.[86] After Hildreth's death in 1777 the Society's support of the work was withdrawn. But since, from the year 1760 on, the "school" features of the original catechising school were so absorbed by the enterprise under the patronage of the Bray Associates, and since this was so closely allied to the activity of the Society, the writer deems it advisable to include a brief description of that school.

The founding of the Associates of Dr. Bray in 1723 was mentioned by the writer in the first chapter, as also the benefaction of Mr. D'Alloune in behalf of the instruction of Negroes, which originated the movement.[87] Many years elapsed before the association could add enough to the proceeds from the above to undertake the support of schools in the Plantations. Until such time, the Associates agreed that the method, which appeared to them "the most effectual of pursuing Dr. Bray's Intentions," was, "in their present circumstances, that of sending Books to the Missionaries in the manner which the Dr. himself, did, thereby to enable and encourage them to undertake the Conversion of the Negroes, within their respective Parishes."[88] In the following minute we have an illustration of the way in which this plan was carried out: "Mr. Verelst acquainted the Associates that he had sent to the care of Mr. Canston at Savannah in Georgia three Parcels of Books containing in

[82] *Ibid.*, B, 2, p. 4.
[83] Sept. 29, 1763, *ibid.*, B, 2, p. 6a.
[84] *Ibid.*, B, 2, p. 8; Journal XVI, p. 221.
[85] See p. 102; also S. P. G. Letter-book, B, 2, p. 35; Journal XVIII, p. 432.
[86] S. P. G. Letter-book, B, 3, p. 168, Oct. 17, 1772; p. 169, Nov. 7, 1773.
[87] See p. 15.
[88] Associates Minute-book, 1729–1735, p. 6. about July 15, 1730.

each 3 Bibles, 30 Primmers, 30 small spelling Books, 30 Horn Books, 20 Testaments, & 30 Psalters Directed to Mrs. Hague, Mrs. Drayton, & Mrs. Bryan at Charles Town in South Carolina for Instruction of their Negroes, for him to send by the first opportunity."[89]

With the exception of some assistance in Georgia, nothing was done for schools until the second half of the century. In preparation for them, activity was begun in the year 1753 according to the following evidence:

"Ordered that the foll. acct. of the Associates be published in the London & Whitehall Evening Posts, and afterwards in the Public Advertiser, viz., within a week in the London Evening Post, a fortnight after in the Whitehall Evening Post, & occasionally in the Public Advertiser & Evening Posts. That the Assoc^ts^ are entrusted with a small Fund for converting negroes in the British Plantations, & will be very thankful for contributions to more effectually prosecute the design. The advantageous influence which religious principles may justly be supposed to have upon the negroes, the indispensible duty incumbent upon all Christians to set forward the salvation of others, & the particular obligation upon wealthy merchants & planters to sow spiritual things to them by whose servitude & labour they reap so much temporal gain: these, with other arguments seem to deserve most serious attention. The Soc. pays besides occasional gratuities £25 p. a. to Mr. Ottolenghe in Georgia. Catechists may be sent to any of our Colonies, whose province might be the Instruction of Negroes, or greater encouragem^t^ may be given by books or otherwise to the parochial clergy there. But the Assoc^ts^ will pursue any other method wh. should be judged more conducive to this great end."[90]

In 1758 the fund was sufficient to warrant establishing a few schools, and the city of Philadelphia was chosen as the best location for the first one. In November 1758, therefore, a school was opened, and put under the direction of the S. P. G. missionary, Rev. William Sturgeon.[91] Shortly afterwards the members of the association came to the further resolution "that 3 negro Schools be opened with all convenient speed in some part of the British Plantations; . . . also that Mr. Franklin be informed of this & the favour of his assistance on settling these schools be requested."[92] In pursuance of Dr. Franklin's recommendation the locations were fixed at the ensuing meeting. In the recorded minutes we are informed as follows:

[89] *Ibid.*, p. 70, Nov. 4, 1734.

[90] Associates Minute-book, 1735–1768, p. 84, Aug. 17, 1753.

[91] *Ibid.*, p. 124; also letter of Mr. Sturgeon to the Sec. of the Associates, June 12, 1759, in the archives of the Bray Associates.

[92] Jan. 2, 1760, *ibid.*, p. 129. The reference is to Benjamin Franklin, an active member of the associates. In 1761 during his residence in London, Franklin was the presiding officer at their meetings.

"Mr. Franklin declared that he thought N. York, Williamsburgh in Virginia, & Newport, in Rhode Is. the most proper places for the negro schools. Mr. Franklin recommended Dr. S. Johnson President of the College, Rev. Mr. Barclay Minister of Trinity Church & Rev. Mr. Auchmuty at N. York.—also Wm Hunter Esq. Postmaster Rev. Dr. Dawson President of Wm. & Mary College, & the Minister of the Church at Williamsburgh also Rev. Mr. Pollen of Newport Rhode Is. as proper persons to be requested to take the care & management of the sev[l] Schools in the aforesiad places.

Agreed that one school for 30 negro children be opened with all convenient speed at each of N. York, Williamsburgh in Virginia, & Newport Rhode Is., & that the salary in each do not exceed £20 St. p. a. Agreed also that Mr. Franklin be desired to write to the above gentlemen for their kind assistance in establishing these schools, & that they would as often as they judge convenient visit & inspect them, & transmit home an acct of their proceedings & the progress of the children, & the reception the design meets with from the people in general. Agreed also that 3 parcels of books for the schools be immediately prepared, & that Sec. procure from the S. P. C. K. such as may be neceassry & are not in tne Assoc[ts] store."[93]

With the sincere co-operation of Dr. Johnson and Mr. Barclay and with the enthusiastic support of Mr. Auchmuty, the catechist, steps were immediately taken to set up a school in New York City.[94] Both sexes were to share in the benefaction, and were to be taught reading, while the girls were also to learn sewing and knitting. Difficulty was experienced in finding a properly qualified schoolmistress[95] for the undertaking, and the position was advertised. The following appeared in the New York *Mercury*, August 4, 1760:

"WANTED immediately, a sober Woman, of a fair Character and Qualifications, necessary to keep a school, for the instruction of Thirty Negro Children, in reading, sewing, &c. Such a Person by applying to any one of the Clergy of the Church of England in the City, may be informed of the Terms which are advantageous.

"N. B. The intended School will be chiefly supported by a Charitable Society of worthy and well disposed Christians in England: It is therefore hoped that such Persons as have a regard for the Souls of their poor young souls, especially those born in their house, will be ready to assist in forwarding and promoting this Laudable Undertaking."[96]

Having secured a woman of "fair Character and Qualifications," another notice was issued, to the inhabitants by the same newspaper on September 15:

---

[93] Jan. 17, 1760, *ibid.*, p. 130. April following a benefaction of "200 childs first books" for the use of the four schools was reported. *Ibid.*, p. 135.

[94] Dr. Johnson to Sec. of the Associates, July 28, 1760, Archives of the Associates.

[95] *Ibid.*

[96] Quoted by Dix., *op. cit.*, I, p. 294. It was impossible to provide "a suitable Mistress for the undertaking," wrote Mr. Auchmuty, "under £20 sterg. which considering the great Rents that are paid for Houses in this City & the greatly increased prices of every Article of Provision since the War, is reckoned very reasonable." Letter to Sec. of Associates, Apr. 4, 1761. Archives of the Associates.

"This is to inform the Public, that a Free School is opened near New-Dutch-Church, for the instruction of thirty Negro Children, from 5 years old and upwards, in reading, and in the Principles of Christianity, and likewise sewing and knitting; which School is entirely under the inspection and Care of the Clergy of the Church of England in this City: Those Person therefore that have the present usefulness, and future Welfare of the young Slaves at heart (Especially those born in their Houses),are desired to apply to any one of the Clergy, who will immediately send them to the aforesaid school, and see that they be faithfully instructed.

"N. B. All that is required of their Masters or Mistresses is that they find them in wood for the Winter. Proper Books will be provided for them Gratis."[97]

The schoolmistress selected by the committee was Mrs. Lowner. In his first report to the associates Mr. Auchmuty said: She "faithfully discharges her trust. She began with two Scholars to which thirteen more have since been added, & others dayly coming, so that I make no doubt, but that the Number mentioned in your Letter will soon be compleate. I have hitherto visited and do intend if blessed with Health, to continue my visits to the School."[98] Four months later he wrote: "The Negro School is full & would the plan allow of it, as many more might in a few days be added to it."[99] In another report sent in October we learn that the children were "clean & orderly," and had begun to "read sew and say their Catechism as well as could be expected in the time." And, added Mr. Auchmuty: "I have cautiously avoided requiring too much from the Mistress at first therefore, have not as yet required her Attendance with her Scholars, at Church on Prayer Days; for, after the School is out she has her Self & Children to take care off: & victuals to prepare which she cannot do, while the Scholars are about her, besides some of the Children begin to be useful at Home, are able to lay a Cloth, to wait on the Table, therefore should I detain them till Prayers are over at Church, I fear it would occasion some uneasiness and grumbling, wch I would chuse to avoid."[100] Accompanying the report was the following list of slaves which shows 9 boys and 21 girls:

---

[97] Quoted by Dix, *ibid.*, p. 295. Mr. Auchmuty definitely announced, in writing the S. P. G., that the school opened Sept. 22, 1760. Letter-book, B, 2, p. 2.

[98] Apr. 4, 1761, Auchmuty to Sec. of Associates, Archives of Associates.

[99] Aug. 8, 1761, *ibid.*

[100] Oct. 7, 1761, *ibid.*

Names	Owners	Age	Improvement	When Admitted
1. Isabella	Mr. Cockraft	10. Bap.	Reads, works &c.	October 29–1760
2. Flora	Mr. Vanhorne	11. N.B.	Learning to spell &c.	December 1760
3. Mercy	Mr. Romer	11. Bap.	Do	Febry 17 1761
4. Rosannah	Mr. Rinders	10. Bap.	Do	Febry 19 1761
5. Judah	Mr. Rinders	9. Bap.	Reads well &c.	Febry 19 1761
6. Thomas	Do	7. Bap.	Learning to spell &c.	Do
7. Flora	Do	5. Bap.	Do	Do
8. Sarah	A free child	11. Do	Do	January 1761
9. Rachel	Do	8. Do	Do	Do
10. Nancy	Mr. Cockrafts	7. Do	Do	Febry 1761
11. Susanah	J. Cruger Esq.	6. Do	Do	October 27
12. Mary	Mr. Wendethams	6. Do	Do	Octr 29 1760
13. Hannah	R. Nicholls Esq.	8. Do	Reads very well &c.	
14. Dinah	Mr. Ludlows	6. N.B.	Learning to spell &c.	May 27 1760
15. Cloe	Dr. Johnsons	7. Bap.	Do	May 1761
16. Sally	Mr. Devoot	6. Do	Do	Janry 1761
17. Mercy	Mr. Governeur	6. Do	Do	Novr 3 1760
18. Andrew	Do	5. Do	Do	Do
19. Elizabeth	Mr. Kittletask	5. Do	Do	Nov. 3 1760
20. Mary	Mr. Banckers	5. Do	Reads well &c.	Septemr 22 1760
21. Polly	Mrs. Shavers	6. N.B.	Learning to Spell &c.	Do
22. William	Mr. Fells	9. Bap.	Do	May 5 1761
23. Jack	Mr. Montanies	6. Do	Do	
24. Jack	Mr. Astines	6. Do	Do	Janry 1761
25. Samuel	Dr. Bards	5. Do	Do	Do
26. Aeneas	Mrs. Elistons	10. Do	Do	July 18 1761
27. Cuffee	Mrs. Moone	6. Bap.	Learning to spell &c.	April 8 1761
28. Richard	Mr. Banckers	5. bap.	Do	October 1760
29. Marian	Mr. Schuylers	7. bap.	Do	Do
30. Sylvia	Free Child	8. bap.	Do	May 1761."

The Associates evinced the greatest satisfaction over the success of the school and resolved to refer the future management entirely to Mr. Auchmuty.[101] Between 1762 and 1768, inclusive, an average of two reports per year were made and these are now preserved in the archives of the Associates, but reports for the ensuing three years have been lost. Besides these, three subsequent reports for 1772 and 1774 are to be found. They uniformly certify to the marked success of the undertaking. As soon as any left the school others took their places. In 1765 the school was allowed to exceed the usual complement. Said Mr. Auchmuty: "There are now no less than thirty seven Scholars. The reason of exceeding the Number is that some of the oldest will leave the School this fall; and the Mistress has interceded with me to permit her to take all that at present offers, which will more than fill up their places. Those that are

[101] Minute-book, 1735–1768, p. 168. January 1762.

to leave the School are well instructed in reading & sewing and say their Catechism & prayers perfectly well; & what is is very commendable, & pleasing are very sober & orderly Children."[102] "The school succeeds beyond my Expectations, and is a great blessing to the poor Slaves," it was stated in the next report but one.[103] Regarding the pupils he reported: "The Scholars improve every day in reading, Spelling, & Working . . . I seldom miss hearing them read & say their Catechism once a week, & can with great pleasure assure you, that they dayly improve. I have put several of them to learn Lewis' Catechism and propose the rest shall begin with it, as soon as they are perfect in the Church Catechism."[104] And again he wrote: "Many of them are very notable at their work, and read extremely well."[105] In 1767 he said of them: "Those that have left the School after proper Instruction, attend every Sunday Evening . . . with the Adult blacks, & are Catechised and I have the pleasure to inform you that I have not heard of one among them, that has turned out bad."[106] In 1762 psalmody was added to the curriculum, and this in turn, added to the delight of the slaves. It was provided for them once a week. "I have also prevailed upon the Master of our Charity School," the Catechist announced, "to instruct them and the black Adults in Psalmody, in which they soon became proficient."[107] The schoolmistress Mr. Auchmuty found to be a really deserving woman, who conscientiously discharged her duty.[108] "I must do the Mistress Justice to say," he wrote, "that she is faithful and diligent. She takes a great deal of pains and employs her whole time to her business."[109] Furthermore, she was "very clever at her business,"[110] and seemed to be "very happy with her employment."[111]

It seems certain that Mrs. Lowner was constantly supplied with books by the Associates. As we have seen, it was publicly

[102] Auchmuty to the Sec. of the Associates, May 31, 1765.
[103] *Ibid.*, Dec. 22, 1766.
[104] *Ibid.*, Apr. 19, 1763.
[105] *Ibid.*, Oct. 20, 1763.
[106] *Ibid*, May 1, 1767.
[107] *Ibid.*, Oct. 18, 1762.
[108] *Ibid.*, May 18, 1762.
[109] *Ibid.*, Oct. 20, 1763.
[110] *Ibid.*, May 1, 1767.
[111] *Ibid.*, May 9, 1768.

announced that all books would be furnished. The incomplete records at present available show three consignments only, to wit: a box of books in 1760;[112] "Psalters, Testaments, Common Prayers & Bibles," in 1761;[113] and in 1765, "Spelling books & suitable Catechetical books."[114]

The school was probably abandoned by the Associates about the year 1775. No further records of it are found from that time.[115] In the minutes of the Associates there is an abstract of Mr. Auchmuty's reports in 1774. It represents the final available document relating to the New York school, and is as follows:

> "Dr. Auchmuty in a list, Sept. 28, 1774 says the negro school continues full, several of the children read very well & know the whole of their catechism. They attend Church constantly on Sundays & often on week days. The mistress continues her usual diligence, but is in a very declining state of health, he fears they shall soon lose her. Upon enquiry he finds that those who have been brought up in the school behave remarkably well. In a 2nd Letter Oct. 20 1774 he says the School-mistress died on the 19th & adds she was faithful in the discharge of her duty & a good Christian. He says he would by no mean throw any obstacle in the way against continuing the school, but his conscience obliges him to inform the Associates that the possessors of slaves in N. York are opulent & well able to put their children to school & pay for it. He believes some will do so, though not perhaps generally. The future welfare of the poor negroes has been one of principal objects of his attention for a number of years—from 10 communicants he found, when he first took charge of them he can now see at one time near 60; besides a Sunday evening lecture for the benefit of the negroes he has at the request of a number of good christians set on foot another at the house of an amiable man, & Mr. Beckman an opulent merchant, on Thursday evenings, & this Dr. A. attends occasionally. In his absence one of the blacks, a sincere good man, reads such part of the Church Service as seem best adapted to their capacities & by this means therefore thinks that if, instead of reviving the school, this method were adopted & part of salary formerly given were bestowed upon some honest good Christian, who would constantly attend upon the poor slaves at their meetings, read for them, visit them when sick, & inform him of everything relating to the conduct of those who are christians, it might answer the design of the Associates better than a school, because the blacks thus blessed with an able instructor would as many of them now are, soon be qualified to instruct their own children. Agreed to ask Dr. A. to consider whether it may not be most eligible to appoint some serious good Christian man to be a schoolm^r for such negro children, as shall appear to him to be most proper objects, & who may also instruct the adult negroes on Thursdays at their meetings, visit the sick &c. provided the Salary does not exceed £20 p. a. This is submitted entirely to Dr. A's judgement, & that he be asked to adopt such a plan as he shall think best answers Associate's intention."[116]

---

[112] Dr. Johnson to Sec. of Associates, July 28, 1760.

[113] Minute-book, 1735–1768, p. 152.

[114] *Ibid.*, p. 239.

[115] The same is true regarding the schools in Newport, Williamsburgh and Philadelphia. Their records cease in 1775. Philadelphia's school, however, was resumed in 1783 and continued until 1836 if not longer.

[116] March 2, 1775. Minute-book, 1768–1808, p. 72.

Provided a successor to Mrs. Lowner was appointed, the school must have suffered the same interruption as the charity school during the calamities of 1776; after which it could not have been revived. In view of the marked success of the work of the Bray Associates, it does not seem unfair to suppose that, with its fine record still fresh in the minds of many of the citizens, this Negro school served as a decided stimulus to the gentlemen who, in 1787, instituted the "New York African Free School."[117]

[117] See, Andrews, Hist. of the New York African Free-Schools, p. 7.

CHAPTER XII

THE ROUTINE AND CURRICULUM OF THE SOCIETY'S SCHOOLS

The records of the Society have few documents which refer to school routine. Those that are available show adherence to the usual school programs of that period. Sessions were continuous throughout the year. The time Mr. Bartow "took to himself" was a fortnight at Christmas, a week at Easter, a week at Whitsuntide, and every Saturday afternoon.[1] It is probable that this represents a somewhat more generous allowance than schoolmasters generally made for themselves. Frequent Holy Days at that time interspersed the school calendar. To offset the objection to so many interruptions, Chaplain Sharpe of New York sent the following proposal to the Society: "That every Holy day they meet to go to Church in a body, and in the afternoon of the same day an hour at School be spent in Catechetical exercises. This will help to retrieve the Honour of these days so profanely perverted in this wicked age to Idleness and Ryoting. I have heard the parents often complain of the Multitude of Holy days presented at Schools by which their children lost much of their time, yet I am persuaded were the days religiously observed they would not gruge those appointed by the Calendar which would give them only a moderate relaxation, but no indulgence to licentiousness."[2] Since no order followed the suggestion of the over-anxious clergyman, let us hope that the innovation was not carried out. The length of the school day was from five to eight hours. Where, as in Westchester County, the scholars were scattered, the hours were five in winter and six in summer;[3] on Long Island and in New York City, they were six and eight respectively.[4]

---

[1] S. P. G. Letter-book, B, 13, p. 337.

[2] Lambeth Archives, 841 fol. 18 ff. March 11, 1713.

[3] See reports of Forster, Bartow and Purdy, previously cited.

[4] Reports of Temple, Keble and Huddleston.

The early curriculum of the schools included for all the children reading and church catechism with the explanation thereof. Since nearly all of the reading was based on the Scriptures, it is apparent that the inculcation of religious doctrine was of the greatest possible consequence, to which all other work was subsidiary. But for those more promising pupils advancement to writing and then to ciphering was made possible when some degree of proficiency in reading was once attained. In 1717 William Forster had seventeen learning "to read and spell," primers being used for this when they could be had for his beginners, after which they were advanced to the psalter, prayer-book, testament, and Bible.[5] Nine scholars were in writing, and six in arithmetic—"3 in reduction, 1 in multiplication, 1 in addition and 1 in practice."[6] At the same time he taught Rev. Wm. Bartow's son grammar, an interesting detail since the subject does not again occur until Mr. Bull's appointment in New York City.[7] Mr. Forster was likewise accommodating in the subject of arithmetic. In 1723 he wrote: "Severall Scholars are not only qualified for Country Employments but for other business for I teach all of the Rules of Vulgar and Decimal Arithmetic and Mr. Bartow's eldest son is now about to learn Geometry Trigonometry Surveying and other branches of the Mathematicks."[8] That this was not Forster's regular custom is explained in his letter of 1728: "The reason there are no more, is my teaching them Quick, and as they generally learn no further than the double rule of Three or Practice, one Sett goes off before another is grown up fit to come."[9] Other mention of spelling besides Forster's is made by 1730.[10] Purdy in 1733 was offering his pupils "Ch. of England Catechism as also what other learning he has to render them able to know their duty to God by reading the Scriptures"; in addition, "as much reading & writing & arithmetic as may receive the common occasions of vulgar people, which is the most people will aspire to."[11] For

---

5 S. P. G. Journal, III, p. 401; Letter-book, A, 12, p. 364.

6 *Ibid.*

7 That is, as shown by the records. But it seems certain that grammar was not in the elementary curriculum during the eighteenth century, save in a few exceptions like this one.

8 S. P. G. Letter-book, A, 17, p. 228.

9 *Ibid.*, A, 21, p. 348.

10 *Ibid.*, A, 23, p. 82.

11 *Ibid.*, A, 24, p. 470.

writing we learn that, through his own deficiency, he procured "copies writ by the best Masters," and found the scheme answered well.[12] Spelling was seldom mentioned except by Mr. Hildreth,[13] but it was part of the curriculum in most of the schools, as an adjunct to the technique of reading. It hardly had a distinct place for the purpose of developing perfection in spelling ability. To write well was much more to be desired than to spell correctly in that day.

The eighteenth century was not far advanced when both writing and arithmetic came into great demand and schools responded to the new need. As early as 1713 Mr. Sharpe pointed out that, on account of the convenient situation of New York City, the people were principally interested in trade; and that, in consequence of this, there was a far greater demand for writing and arithmetic than there was for letters.[14] Courses in "Merchants Accounts" were added to the usual work in arithmetic. In advertising, schoolmasters made specific mention of their attention to this matter, and soon offered other branches, such as navigation, surveying, mensuration, and even astronomy. The following from one of the New York City papers is a typical illustration of the above:

> "Writing, Arithmetick, Merchants Accounts, Navigation, Surveying, Mensuration, Gauging, Dialing, and Astronomy, etc. regularly taught by James Bragg, at the foot of Pot-Baker's Hill, in one of Mr. Peck's new houses; Where there is a commodious Room for Young Gentlemen, to be instructed in any of the Branches of the Mathematics, retired from those that are only taught, Reading, Writing and Arithmetick. Due Attendance will be given to Young Gentlemen and Ladies at their Houses if required. Gentlemen Sailors and others, are taught Navigation in a short time and reasonable."[15]

Whether the Society's schools in general added to the arithmetic of th earlier curriculum is questionable, but in the city itself Mr. Hildreth introduced "Merchants Accompts" for his young scholars as one of the essentials for their preparation for trade.[16] In 1769 he reported "Arithmetick and several Branches of the Mathematicks."[17] The singing of psalms was a feature of the schools where the S. P. G. schoolmasters were able to con-

[12] *Ibid.*
[13] *Ibid.*, B, 3, pp. 158, 159.
[14] Lambeth Archives, 841, fol. 18. See previous quotation p. 68.
[15] New York *Weekly Post-boy*, March 31, 1755.
[16] S. P. G. Letter-book, B, 3, pp. 158, 159, 163.
[17] *Ibid.*, B, 3, p. 294.

duct it. This was mentioned by Mr. Huddleston and Mr. Forster at an early date.[18] It seems to have received considerable attention from Mr. Hildreth. In 1739 Trinity Vestry voted him the "Sum of five pounds for his Care and pains in having the Children taught to Sing Psalms." He instructed such as were capable, so he reported, in Psalmody on three days in the week.[19] Mr. Bull also instructed in it.[20] On three occasions the Trinity organist was allowed goodly sums for composing music for the charity scholars.[21] Psalmody was also part of the curriculum of Mr. Young's school in Westchester in 1769.[22] Mr. Bull added English grammar to the program of the charity school of the city when he succeeded Mr. Hildreth.[23] It is the only instance of it to be found save the special instruction in it, which Forster introduced for a while. On the whole the curriculum confined itself pretty closely to the three R's with assiduous and constant religious teaching. Even Quakers and dissenters who attended were compelled to submit to this, though they were usually spared the most rigorous parts of the orthodox faith.

There is no indication that the program was altered in any way for the girls, except in the city of New York. But we may assume that they were not given much instruction in writing or arithmetic. They were not supposed to need these subjects to any extent.[24] As to arithmetic, this seems to hold true of the entire period of the Society's labors, and up to about 1760 it appears to be the case with writing. In reading and religious teaching they received equal advantages with the boys; and besides this, their education was about complete when they could be made skillful in needlework, an art which they at first acquired in the home. When Mrs. Huddleston assisted her husband, she may have taught needlework to the girls, though it has not been so reported. However, when a schoolmistress was added to care for the girls of Mr. Hildreth's school, she taught them both reading and needlework.[25] By 1766 they

---

[18] 1716, *ibid.*, A, 12, p. 244; 1717, *ibid.*, A, 12, 364; Journal, III, p. 401.
[19] *Ibid.*, B, 3, pp. 163, 294, 295.
[20] S. P. G. Journal, XXII, p. 142.
[21] 1767, 1772, 1773, Trinity Vestry Minutes, I, pp. 332, 362, 371.
[22] S. P. G. Letter-book, B, 3, pp. 294, 295.
[23] S. P. G. Journal, XXII, p. 142.
[24] Memoirs of an American Lady, by Mrs. Grant, p. 27.
[25] S. P. G. Letter-book, B, 3, pp. 155, 157.

were learning "Needlework, Spelling & reading" with the schoolmistress.[26] When the girls had acquired a knowledge of reading they went to Mr. Hildreth for an hour every afternoon to be taught writing.[27]

The development of the principal subjects of the schools is best described by one of the Pennsylvania schoolmasters and will be given below. It represents, perhaps, the method of a teacher of more than ordinary ability, yet the writer believes it is fairly illustrative of a majority of the S. P. G. schoolmasters. Writing to the Society from Chester, Pennsylvania, June 17, 1730, Mr. Rowland Jones thus described his work: "Sir, you required an account of my method of Instruction in school. I endeavor (for beginners), to get Primmers well furnished with sylables, vizt, from one to 2, 3, 4, 5, 6, 7, or 8. I take them several times over them till they are perfect by way of repeating according as I find occasion and then to some place forward according to their capacity and commonly every two or three leaves, I make them repeat perhaps 2 or 3 times over, and when they get the Primer well I serve them so in the Psalter and we have some Psalters with the Proverbs in at the latter end. I give them that to learn the which I take to be very agreeable and still follow repetitions till I find they are masters of such places. Then I remove them, into such places as I judge they are fit for either in the new or old Testament and as I find they advance I move them not regarding the beginning or ending of the Bible but moving them where I think they may have benefit by. So making of them perfect in their vowels, consonants and dipthongs, and when they go on their reading clean without any noising, singing or stumbling, with deliberate way, then I set them to begin the Bible, in order to go throughout. And when I begin writers I follow them in the letters till they come to cut pretty clean letters and then to one syllable and so to 2, 3, 4 and to the longest words and when they join handsomely I give them some sweet pleasing verses, some perhaps on their business, some on behaviour, some on their duty to Parents, &c.; of such I seldom want them at command and when they come to manage double copies readily I give them some delightful sentences or

[26] *Ibid.*, B, 3, p. 159.
[27] *Ibid.*, B, 3, pp. 157, 158, 159.

Proverbs or some places in the Psalms or any part of the Bible as they are of forwardness and also to other fancies that may be of their benefit. And when I set them to cyphering I keep them to my old fancy of repeating and shall go over every Rule till they are in a case to move forward and so on. And I find no way that goes beyond that way of repeating both in spelling, reading, writing and cyphering, and several Gentlemen, vizt ministers and others, has commended it and some schoolmasters take to it and tho' I speak it I have met with no children of the standing or time of mine could come up with them on all accounts or hardly upon any; I also give them tasks (when able) to learn out of Books according to their ability, but one Girl exceeds all. She had a great many parts in the Bible by heart and had the whole Book of St. John and hardly would miss a word. I put them to spell twice a week and likewise to catechism and likewise I catechise every Saturday and often on Thursdays. Some times I set them to sing Psalms also other exercises I put them to. I also had some Quakers children on Long Island and some Presbyterians in New England. I asked some of the Quakers what exercise they would allow their children to learn besides spelling, reading and writing. Some gave me liberty to teach their children the Lord's prayer, the creed and the ten commandments. Those and some others got the Church Catechism by heart as well as the Church people's children. Some of the Parents when they understood it they sent for me and were much offended. However I asked them to hear the children rehearse it, all the Parents being in place which gave the above liberty with a design to take their children from my school. So the children were called. I began with my bold boy and the rest followed and after few words at first went as far as the Sacraments the which I knew they would hear nothing of that but as for the rest they said that they had never heard a better thing and told me to keep them to it; It was on Long Island. Several of them are grown up, and are firm in church, and some of their parents also. Some of the Presbyterians turned to the Church both Parents and children tho' they for the generality make use of the Assembly's Catechism. Sir, I have done according to my ability as much for the poor as any in these parts, also in setting forward towards the worship in the Church which I hope will prosper and flourish tho' I am but a weak limb and can do but little, and desiring the Lord that he may bless it."[28]

Mr. Jones's account is interesting not only for the explanation of method but for the insight it gives into the school program. Three other reports may be offered to indicate the nature of the latter. In 1715 Rowland Ellis, the Society's schoolmaster in Burlington, New Jersey, gave his program as follows: "After morning prayers each class reads a chapter or two in the Old or New Testament, then cypher, write, or read, and the small children spell, at 11 o'clock all but the Quakers go to Church, read & write till 4, then spell & go to prayers. On Tuesdays, Thursdays & Saturdays every week, and in the Church, every Sunday, he catechises these children that are of the Church."[29]

The two Huddlestons are the only schoolmasters in New York who have given a program of the day's work. "I teach," wrote William Huddleston, "in the morning reading and writing till 11—then the Bell rings them to prayers, where they daily appear to the great growth of the Church—In the afternoon they spell, read, write, & cypher from 1 to 5, when they read the Psalms for the day, & every one answers that can read—then they sing a staff or two of the Psalms they have just read—thus ends the day."[30] Three times a week he taught "the Catechism & on Sundays, Graces & prayers by heart." "On Sundays after prayers & sermon" the pupils returned to the school, where "they that could read," repeated "the texts & proofs of that days Sermons." The first class then answered "a Chapter or two out of Lewis' Explanation," and the rest repeated the catechism. Then, "after prayers & psalms sung," he dismissed them.[31] Besides adding a half hour to the working day, Thomas Huddleston carefully followed the method of his father. He said: "The needfull at present is to acquaint you with ye Condition of my school and ye Method and Success of my Teaching. I do teach them to read and write in ye forenoon from Eight till a half an hour past Eleven. And ye afternoon, I teach them to read write & cypher from one till five and so Conclude with

[28] Perry, Hist. Col., *op. cit.*, II, pp. 169–171.
[29] S. P. G. Journal, III., p. 156.
[30] Sept. 14, 1716, S. P. G. Letter-book, A, 12, p. 244.
[31] *Ibid.*

Singing of a staff or two of a Psalm. I alsoe teach them their Catechism three Times a week, their Graces and prayers after that. Those y^t^ are in ye first and Second Classes I cause them to answer me a Chapter or two in Dr. Lewis's Explanation of ye Church Catechism which I hope will be well pleasing to Almighty God & will be satisfaction to my Honourable Masters."[32]

The overpowering amount of religious instruction is to be noted. With most of the sects it was typical of the period. Constant and unwearied inculcation of the Scriptures was the one antidote for the menacing wiles of the evil one. Dutch liberality in Sabbath observance was especially horrifying to the very orthodox, and assiduous activity was prescribed to counteract it. Referring to this "wantonness" on the part of the Dutch, Chaplain Sharpe represented the Church of England attitude towards it. In doing so he gives us one possible reason for the extremely religious curriculum. Another reason was that it coincided with the desires of the Society, and was in correspondence with the curriculum of the charity schools of the S. P. C. K. The following is quoted from Chaplain Sharpe's proposals of 1713: "That above all they be taught to sanctify the Lord's day, which alas! is but very little regarded in all places of the Country. The laws of the land do restrain all serville labor on this day and so farr its' not transgress'd but then its' consum'd to worse purposes, vizt. Idleness and drinking, play and wantonness. The Dutch for the most part pretend to follow their great writer Cocceius and allow only that part of the day which is set apart for publick divine Service, when that is over its' usual to see the men walk on the Change the children and negroes playing in the streets and in the Country trap ball, bowling & the like: this I have often observed with great concern and believe it may be more easily prevented for the future by a religious education than remedyed now. If the minds of the Youth are tinctured with a religious concern for the honour of times places & persons set apart for the more immediate Service of God we may reasonably hope to see a visible reformation of manners. If the Youth that are now the main Actors in these disorders are taken off & reclaimed, what may we expect when they come to be Masters particularly heads of families and Magistrates in the land but

[32] Letter, undated, but received March 1725, *ibid.*, B, 1, p. 106.

that like zealous Joshua they will resolve and do. I and my house we will serve the Lord. To this end I now propose when they come from Church that they meet in the School and spend an hour or more. Let the Master read some Catechetical instructions as Hammond, Bray, Newsome, &c. Let them read in order a Chapter of the whole duty of Man some Chapters of the New Testament, and conclude with psalmody & prayer & so return to their houses with impressions of Holiness upon their hearts to sanctify the Evening in the several families to which they belong."[33]

The only text-books were those for reading. These were of two classes—the one class made up of books that were to be read for their content, and the other used largely as a stepping-stone to the art, having thereby much of the nature of our present technique books. But the content of the second class so far as there could be content, was, like the first class, nearly altogether religious and moral. The records, it must be admitted, are so inadequate regarding text-books, that only in a general way can they be indicated here.

On the whole, the scarcity of books was such that schoolmasters thankfully availed themselves of any they could procure. Beginners were usually given some kind of a practice book before going on to the content books. For these various texts were used, since there was no uniformity or regularity in the different schools. There is absolute evidence that horn-books, A B C books, primers, and spelling-books were used at different times and in different places. Because of this, it is a fair assumption that one or another kind of these texts was being used by every schoolmaster.

If we except the Indian hornbook, referred to in another chapter, Cleator is the only schoolmaster of the Society who definitely reports the use of the "Horne book."[34] Two schoolmasters used A B C books;[35] and Elias Neau, the catechist, used what was probably an adaptation of these, namely, the "A B C with Church Catechism."[36] Primers were studied

[33] Lambeth Archives, 841, fol. 18 f.

[34] 1714, S. P. G. Letter-book, A, 9, p. 225; A, 10, p. 169.

[35] Gildersleve in 1718, *ibid*, A, 13, p. 433; Journal, III, p. 299. Forster in 1718, Letter-book, A, 13, p. 434.

[36] *Ibid.*, A, 3, p. 174.

by the children in Rye[37] during the time of Cleator at least, and by the children of West Chester in the time of Forster.[38] In New York City they were, in all probability, constantly used, though mentioned in connection with the Huddlestons and Hildreth only.[39] These primers, we may conclude, combined features of the catechism with their usual characteristics. In two instances we have a basis for the belief. Forster states that "Children read & spell in Primmers *with* the Ch. catechism when to be got;"[40] and Cleator speaks of "Catechisms *or* Ch. of England primers."[41] Moreover, there appears to be a close relation between the primers and the "Catechisms broke into Small questions" sent to Forster at West Chester,[42] as well as the "Catechisms broke into short sentences" sent to Gildersleeve at Hempstead.[43] Such books were very likely adaptations, with primer additions, of "The Church Catechism broke into short Questions" which the S. P. C. K. schools were using.

The earliest mention of spelling books was in 1712.[44] In 1733 Davies at Southampton requested and was allowed a set of "Tho: Dyche's Spelling books."[45] This was doubtless the same as "A Guide to the English Tongue, in Two Parts," by Thos. Dyche, an edition of which was published by Hugh Ganies, New York, in 1753.[46] Spelling books were also dispatched to Auchmuty at New York and to Charlton on Staten Island.[47] Hildreth was allowed "Fisher's Spelling books" in 1767;[48] and about 1770 Colin McLeland at Johnstown had most of his pupils "in their Spelling books."[49] Whether Dyche's and Fisher's texts differed in any significant way from the Dilworth spelling book is uncertain. Possibly they were somewhat more strictly

---

[37] Indicated by Cleator 1709; 1714, 1717, *ibid.*, A, 5, p. 10; A, 9, p. 225; A, 10 p. 169; Journal, III, p. 6.

[38] *Circum*, 1717, S. P. G. Journal, III, p. 401.

[39] By Wm. Huddleston in 1715, 1716 and 1722, S. P. G. Journal, III, p. 113; Letter-book, A, 11, p. 356; A, 16, p. 261. By Thos. Huddleston in 1725 and 1729, S. P. G. Journal, V, p. 86; Letter-book, B, 1, p. 106; B, 1, p. 61. By Hildreth in 1767, S. P. G. Journal, XVII, p. 231.

[40] *Ibid.*, III., p. 401. Italics not in original.

[41] *Ibid.*, III., p. 289. Italics not in original.

[42] 1718 S. P. G. Letter-book, A, 13, p. 434.

[43] 1718, *ibid.*, A, 13, 433; Journal, III, p. 299.

[44] Requested by Cleator, S. P. G. Letter-book, A, 8, p. 114.

[45] S. P. G. Journal, VI, p. 124; Letter-book, B, 1, p. 9.

[46] See Ford, Journal of Hugh Gaines, Printer, I, p. 88; Evans, American Bibliography, 1639-1820, No. 6995.

[47] S. P. G. Journal, XII, p. 104; XIII, p. 137; XV, p. 4.

[48] *Ibid.*, XVII, p. 231.

[49] S. P. G. Letter-book, B, 3, p. 342.

orthodox and modeled upon texts adopted by the S. P. C. K. The Dilworth text, on the other hand, had such general circulation and use, and was so well adapted to Church schools that it is questionable whether it was not in use in the S. P. G. schools even more than those texts of which we have specific mention.

As soon as the pupils could read sufficiently well, they were advanced to the various religious texts by means of which they were to be grounded in a knowledge of the Scriptures and in the tenets of the Church. For this reading the following books served as texts: The Church Catechism, *Lewis's* Exposition of the Church Catechism, The Psalter, The Common Prayer Book, The Testament, The Bible. The order in which these were read depended on their availability. Where choice could be made, the order seems to have been catechism or psalter, or both, followed by Lewis's Exposition thereof,[50] while the remaining books were used interchangeably. Special emphasis was laid on the learning of the Church catechism by heart as soon as possible, that children might thereby become early candidates for Communion. The psalter and prayer book were given much attention also because of their place in the Church service. Testaments presumably furnished all of the historical pabulum of the curriculum, save the Bible itself. The latter was apparently used less extensively in the schools than other books. Many tracts were put in the hands of pupils but evidence is lacking to show that they were used as texts. The design of the Society was to distribute its tracts so as to have them carried into the homes for family reading.

The range of books listed for the charity schools in England was wider and doubtless the supply of each kind was more adequate. While this is true, it can also be said that the S. P. C. K. schools furnished the model from which the sister Society adapted the text-books for the colonial schools.

Most of the books came from England and were largely the result of the Society's generosity. With a great amount of direct evidence there is the further presumption that grants of books were more frequent than present records show. But some books were supplied in the province itself, in all probability, though there is no direct proof of this beyond the citation here-

[50] S. P. G. Journal, VIII, p. 186; XV., p. 260; Letter-book, B, 3, p. 167.

tofore made of the benefactions of Trinity Vestry. There *is* presumptive evidence in the fact that some of the text-books were being imported and edited by New York printers.[51]

Through the courtesy of Mr. George A. Plimpton of New York City, who generously allowed the writer to examine his remarkable collection of early text-books, a description of some texts similar to those used in the Society's schools can be included here. The first is a copy of the thirty-first edition of *John Lewis's* Exposition of the Catechism, printed at London in 1769 for the S. P. C. K. The full title of this little 16 mo. book is, "The Church Catechism Explained by Way of Question and Answer and confirmed by Scripture Proofs: divided into Five Parts and Twelve Sections; wherein is given a brief and plain Account of I. The Christian Covenant II. The Christian Faith III. The Christian Obedience IV. The Christian Prayer V. The Christian Sacraments." The contents of its ninety-eight pages are as follows, all of the sections given being arranged in the form of question and answer:

Dedicatory Epistle to members of the S. P. C. K. .... 2 pages
Preface .... 4 "
Introduction from Dr. Comber .... 2 "
Part I. The Christian Covenant .... 13 "
  Sec. 1. Of the Benefits of Baptism; Or, the Mercies afforded on God's Part.
  Sec. 2. Of the Vow of Baptism; or the conditions required on our Part.
Part II. The Christian Faith .... 25 "
  Sec. 3. Of the Creed; particularly what we are to believe concerning God the Father.
  Sec. 4. Of God the Son; particularly his Names Offices and Relations.
  Sec. 5. Of Christ's Humiliation.
  Sec. 6. Of Christ's Exaltation.
  Sec. 7. Of God the Holy Ghost, and the remaining articles of the Creed.
Part III. The Christian Obedience .... 22 "
  Sec. 8. Of the Ten Commandments; particularly of our Duty towards God, contained in the four first commandments.
  Sec. 9. Of our Duty towards our Neighbor; contained in the six last commandments.
Part IV. The Christian Prayer .... 9 "
  Sec. 10. Of the Lord's Prayer.

---

[51] The writer has found the following references to the importing and printing of books which were similar to those used in the Society schools: (1) William Bradford, 1733 advertizes imported books, New York *Gazette*, Nov. 26, 1733, and later issues; prints books 1740, Trinity Vestry Minutes, I, p. 215. (2) Hugh Gaines 1745 advertizes imported books, New York *Weekly Post-Boy*, Oct. 7, 1745; prints books 1753, 1755, 1761, Evans, American Bibliography, *op. cit.*, No. 6995, No. 7408, No. 8839. (3) Parker and Weyman at Beaver St., advertize imported books 1755, New York *Weekly Post-Boy*, Jan. 13, 1755 and later issues; print books 1753, 1754, 1761, Evans, *op. cit.*, No. 7039, No. 7183, No. 8893.

The second is an octavo text "Composed for the Use of English-Schools, and humbly offered to the Masters of the Charity-Schools—By their Loving Brother, T. C." It was printed by J. Downing at London in 1712. Following is the table of contents:

This book bore the title of "The Anatomy of Orthography: or a Practical Introduction to the Art of *Spelling and Reading* English, adapted to mean Capacities." The last text is one that probably was modeled after the A B C books sent out by the Society. This text, in the form of a pamphlet is entitled, "The A B C with the Church of England Catechism to which is annexed, Prayers used in the Academy of the Protestant Episcopal Church in Philadelphia; also A Hymn on the Nativity of our Saviour, and another for Easter Day." It was printed at Philadelphia in 1785 its contents being:

CONCLUSION

The support of schools in the province of New York by the Society for the Propagation of the Gospel in Foreign Parts forms but one chapter in its vast program of colonial evangelization. Through the encouragement of schoolmasters and missionaries, its field of labor during the eighteenth century covered nearly all of the original thirteen colonies, and was extended to the islands of the West Indies on the south, as well as to the north-eastern provinces of modern Canada. The chief motive of the Society was clearly the extension of Christianity to the virgin soil of America and keeping it alive among the Europeans pioneering in the transatlantic empire. Not only was Christianity to be fostered, but that particular form of it which was typified by the doctrine and worship of the Church of England. The seventeenth century had seen the position of the established Church most seriously assailed. It had also seen the growth of a religious independence and indifference which, to the orthodox, were the most alarming symptoms of the age. In America, too, the century had ended with the colonial Church in grave neglect. The need of systematically organized activity in behalf of the established Church, both at home and abroad, had been convincingly impressed on clergy and laity by the opening of the eighteenth century. Out of the awakened Church consciousness there developed three general aims, (1) the revivifying of the churches already founded by supplying them with more adequately trained ministers; (2) the planting of churches in places where there had never been any, or where they had fallen into decay; (3) the training of children in the tenets and worship of the church through the direct agency of schools. Appeals for the support of these designs were responded to with more than usual liberality.

Methods and procedure along the above lines were left to the leaders of the Church to work out. As the first chapter of this study has pointed out, the most prominent leader was Rev. Thomas Bray. The agencies organized by him and his co-workers and adopted by the Church were the two great societies, the S. P. C. K. and the S. P. G.

The support of schools in the Plantations was carried on by the S. P. G. with devoted interest. Where cases of retrenchment are to be found they are easily explainable as the result of the Society's funds, or the lack of co-operation and appreciation on the part of the colonists. With such cases in mind, there can still be no doubt that the patronage of schools in America by this Soiecty formed the foremost philanthropic movement in education during the colonial period.

In the colony of New York, the Society from 1710 to 1776 continuously supported between five and ten elementary schools. The number of pupils who received instruction in them was, as we have seen, seldom less than twenty and reached as high as eighty-six; while the usual enrolment was approximately forty. The variability in the personnel of the schoolmasters proved, at times, most unfortunate, but the story of inefficient and negligent teachers during the period is common to all sects and to all the colonies.[1] On the other hand it is doubtful if any settlement in the Plantations could boast of more worthy schoolmasters than the records of the Huddlestons and Joseph Hildreth have shown them to be.

The correspondence of the secretaries and other officers of the Society clearly indicate the design to have the colonial schools patterned after the schools of the S. P. C. K. in England. The leaders, however, possessed enough practicality to realize that such an ideal could be reached in part only. The charity school in New York City was, perhaps, comparable to the best type of the S. P. C. K. schools. As for the others, they cannot be considered as having much resemblance. Yet, bearing in mind the unusual obstacles that were involved, the movement *does* represent a most praiseworthy attempt to adapt the system of English charity-schools to the needs of the province. We have seen that support usually involved assurances from schoolmasters that a specified number should be taught gratis. The policy, at any rate, was a guarantee of free tuition, to some extent, in

[1] See Meriwether, Colonial Curriculum, p. 37.

all the schools. The Society's bounty was usually enough to cover the tuition of ten or eleven pupils at current rates of instructing. It is a fact, however, that the non-paying scholars were usually in proportion of one-fourth to one-half of the enrolment; while no fees were paid in Trinity School with the exception of about two years in the time of Thomas Huddleston. The use of the term "free school" in the colonial period needs more explicit interpretation.[2] If it may mean "free tuition," the S. P. G. schools were the most deserving in New York Colony to be so classified.

As to a public school system the case is somewhat different. There can be no question regarding the attitude of the Society itself. The great desire in London was so to engage public opinion in the colony that self-support of the schools would, after a few years, be assumed by the inhabitants. This, it was hoped, would give the Society an opportunity to render assistance to the newer settlements. But the time failed to come when the aim could be adopted as a working policy. Poverty and educational indifference were factors which the Society had to contend with. This was certainly true in the case of *many* of the English colonists. As to the more favored among them, who had the power and inclination to educate their children, either the special tutor or the private school were the favored agencies—a view to which they had been well schooled by generations of tradition. With particular reference to the eighteenth century, it is evident that the Society's encouragement of schools furnished the nearest approach to a public school system that was to be found among the English colonists in New York. Notwithstanding the interruptions which have been pointed out, they seem to have been the most regularly maintained of any. They were not reserved for the sole benefit of the children of Church adherents, but admitted pupils generally. And they were provided with a system of inspection which may be looked upon as semi-public in character. Whether the Society's schools gave encouragement to the public school system, ultimately inaugurated by the State, is questionable. But when the State did enter upon an educational policy, it could well have profited by the stimulus of the century and more of achievement of at least one of the Society's foundations—Trinity School.

[2] Meriwether, *op. cit.*, p. 36.

BIBLIOGRAPHY

Source Material

1. Abstracts of the Proceedings of the S. P. G., being annual reports of the Society. Fairly complete copies are in the New York Public Library and the New York Historical Society Library.
2. American Bibliography, 1639–1820. Chas. Evans, *editor*. 4 vols., Chicago, 1903–6.
3. Andrews, C. M. and Davenport, F. G. Guide to the Manuscript Materials for the History of the United States to 1783, in the British Museum, in Minor London Archives, and in the Libraries of Oxford and Cambridge. Washington, 1908.
4. Baxter Manuscripts, in Dr. Williams's Library, Gordon Square, London.
5. Bray Manuscripts, Sion College Library, Victoria Embankment, London.
6. Brokerby,———. Some Proposals toward propagating the Gospel in our American Plantations. In a bundle of S. P. G. papers in the N. Y. H. S. Library.
7. Calendar of Sir William Johnson's Manuscripts. Richard E. Day, *compiler*. Albany, 1909.
8. Charity-School Reports, being accounts of the S. P. C. K. Charity Schools. Sion College Library.
9. Collections of Papers, being rules and regulations printed by the S. P. G. Among bundles of S. P. G. papers in the N. Y. H. S. Library.
10. Colonial Laws of New York from 1664 to the Revolution. 5 vols. Albany, 1894.
11. Documentary History of New York. E. B. O'Callaghan, *editor*. 4 vols. Albany, 1850–51.
12. Documents relative to the Colonial History of the State of New York. E. B. O'Callaghan and B. Fernow, *editors*. 15 vols. Albany, 1853–1887.
13. Ecclesiastical records of the State of New York. 6 vols. Albany, 1901–06.
14. Files of New York colonial newspapers, as cited: New York *Gazette*, 1733, 1750–52, 1753–73; New York *Mercury*, 1753–1768; New York *Weekly Post-Boy*, 1746–1749.
15. Fothergill, Gerald. A List of Emigrant Ministers to America. London, 1904.
16. Hawks Transcripts of manuscripts in various archives of England. *Collected* by Rev. F. L. Hawks, 1835. Church Mission House, New York City. See especially 2 vols. of New York documents and 1 vol. designated, "General Conference."
17. Keith, George and others. Journal of Travels on the Continent of North America, London, 1706. Among S. P. G. papers in N. Y. H. S. Library.
18. Manuscript records of the Bray Associates. Minute-books and correspondence. Archives of the Associates, Tufton St., Westminster, London.
19. Manuscript records of the British Museum. Additional Mss. as cited; Sloane Mss. as cited. British Museum, London.

20. Manuscript records, Archives of Lambeth Palace, London.
21. Manuscript records, unbound, Archives of Fulham Palace, Fulham, London.
22. Manuscript records of the S. P. C. K. Minute-books. Archives of the Society, Northumberland Ave., Charing Cross, London.
23. Manuscript records of the S. P. G. (1) Journals of Proceedings, vols. 1–24; (2) Letter-books, series A (copies of originals), vols. 1–26; Letter-books, series B (originals), vols. 1–25. Archives of the S. P. G., Tufton St., Westminster, London.
24. Minutes of the Common Council of the City of New York, 1675–1776. Herbert L. Osgood and others, *editors*. New York, 1905.
25. Minutes of the Vestry of Christ's Church, Rye, 1710–1794.
26. Minutes of the Vestry of Trinity Church, New York, to 1790.
27. New York Historical Society collections. Publication fund series. 38 vols. (to date). New York, 1868–1906. Volumes for 1870, 1896 used.
28. Perry, William Stevens, D.D. Historical collections relating to the American Colonial Church. 4 vols. Hartford, 1870–78.
29. Pratt, D. J. Annals of public education in the State of New York. Albany, 1872.

Secondary Material

30. Allen, W. O. B. and McClure, Edmond. Two Hundred Years: The History of the Society for Promoting Christian Knowledge, 1698–1898. London, 1898.
31. Baird, Charles W. History of Rye, Westchester county, New York, 1660–1870. New York, 1871.
32. Berrian, William, D. D. An Historical Sketch of Trinity Church. New York, 1847.
33. Bolton, Robert. History of the Protestant Episcopal Church in the County of Westchester, 1693–1853. New York, 1855.
34. Classified Digest of the Records of the S. P. G., 1701–1892. 5th edition. London, 1895.
35. Clews, Elsie. Educational Legislation and Administration of the Colonial Governments. New York, 1899.
36. Disosway, Gabriel P. The Earliest Churches of New York and its Vicinity. New York, 1868.
37. Dix, Rev. Morgan. History of the Parish of Trinity Church in the City of New York. 4 vols. New York, 1898.
38. Ford, P. L. Journal of Hugh Gaines, Printer. 2 vols. New York, 1902.
39. Grant, Mrs. A. M. Memoirs of an American Lady. New York, 1846.
40. Hooper, Joseph. A History of Saint Peter's Church in the City of Albany. Albany, 1900.
41. Humphreys, David. An Historical Account of the S. P. G. London, 1730.
42. Moore, W. H. History of St. George's Church, Hempstead, Long Island. New York, 1881.
43. Onderdonk, Henry, Jr. Antiquities of the Parish Church, Jamaica. Jamaica, 1880.
44. Pascoe, C. F. Two Hundred Years of the S. P. G. An Historical Account of the Society for the Propagation of the Gospel in Foreign Parts, 1701–1900. London, 1901.
45. Perry, William Stevens, D.D. The History of the American Episcopal Church, 1587–1883. 2 vols. Boston, 1885.
46. Smith, Hon. Wm. History of the late Province of New York from its Discovery to 1762. New York, 1829.
47. Valentine, D. F. History of the City of New York. New York, 1853.
48. Weber, Samuel Edwin. The Charity-School Movement in Colonial Pennsylvania. Philadelphia, 1905.